Artificial Intelligence
in Geography

Artificial Intelligence in Geography

Stan Openshaw
University of Leeds, UK

and

Christine Openshaw
University of Sheffield, UK

JOHN WILEY & SONS
Chichester · New York · Weinheim · Brisbane · Singapore · Toronto

Other Wiley Editorial Offices

John Wiley & Sons, Inc., 605 Third Avenue,
New York, NY 10158-0012, USA

VCH Verlagsgesellschaft mbH, Pappellalee 3,
D-69469 Weinheim, Germany

Jacaranda Wiley Ltd, 33 Park Road, Milton,
Queensland 4064, Australia

John Wiley & Sons (Canada) Ltd, 22 Worcester Road,
Rexdale, Ontario M9W 1L1, Canada

John Wiley & Sons (Asia) Pte Ltd, 2 Clementi Loop #02-01,
Jim Xing Distripark, Singapore 129809

Library of Congress Cataloging-in-Publication Data

Openshaw, Stan.
  Artificial intelligence in geography / Stan Openshaw and Christine Openshaw.
    p. cm.
  Includes bibliographical references (p.   –   ) and index.
  ISBN 0-471-96991-5 (cloth: acid-free paper)
  1. Geography—Data processing. 2. Artificial intelligence.
    I. Openshaw, Christine. II. Title.
  G70.2.064   1997
  910'.285—dc21   96-45100
                                                                           CIP

British Library Cataloguing in Publication Data

A catalogue record for this book is available from the British Library

ISBN 0-471-969915

Typeset in 10/12pt Times from the author's disks by Vision Typesetting, Manchester

Printed and bound by Antony Rowe Ltd, Eastbourne

For

Miranda, Rachel, Amy and Jasmine

Contents

Foreword

Work on this book started when I moved from Newcastle University to Leeds University in the autumn of 1992. To my horror none of the courses I used to teach on quantitative geography and GIS at Newcastle University were applicable. They were either being done by others or involved courses that experience suggested were almost impossible to teach, such as old-fashioned statistical methods to geographers who knew no maths and were persuaded (by others) that anything vaguely scientific in human geography must by definition be both fundamentally unsound and too hard! So the solution was to try and do something completely different that would in the long term subvert the current wisdom and provide a platform for geographical careers in research and outside. I cannot now remember why I thought that an introduction to artificial intelligence was such a good idea other than it seemed to be extremely widely applicable throughout geography; see Openshaw (1992). I think it was because of an interest in neural networks and an even longer-standing interest in genetic algorithms had made me susceptible to the AI virus. The various AI themes all seemed to interlink and the closer you examined the area the more and more coherent and geographically relevant it became (Openshaw, 1994a, b). Suddenly there was a blinding light leading to a strong imperative to consider the wholesale adoption of the AI paradigm as a core geographic skill. Almost everywhere you looked in geography *with your AI specs on*, you find both immediate applications and one or more compelling reasons for wanting to adopt an alternative approach that promises greater flexibility, fewer assumptions that matter, and an bility to jump over the existing constraints that had initially slowed down and then stopped dead the quantitative revolution in geography a decade or more ago. AI is such a good idea. It also helps promote the basic concept of computational approaches to doing all kinds of geography. In an era of terraflop computing machines this is clearly a future essential idea. On reflection, of course, I suddenly realised that I had been doing what would today be classified as AI-type work for about 20 years. The problem was that my default definition of AI was wrong. Seemingly it always appeared to be something much cleverer than what I was actually doing. My default definition was wrong!

The principal difficulty is writing a book on a subject for which virtually all the literature is expressed in technical and non-geographical jargon belonging to other disciplines. It is not inherently difficult, it is just that the innate simplicity of AI has been lost and is heavily disguised in what is largely incomprehensible technobabble. Maybe this gives it an aura of respectability. Maybe it is a subconscious attempt to keep disciplines like geography out by preserving the great secret of AI that it is a wonderfully simple and straightforward technology! Well, this smoke screen worked and to some extent it continues to work! Yet there is *now* a vast literature about applicable AI-based methods and ideas that are very geographically appropriate. It is just that the geographers who should have been noting this were distracted by other far-reaching developments in their discipline (Openshaw, 1993). GIS is one aspect that has served as a major distraction. The quest for statistical competence is another, whilst those that are mathematically literate tend to be resistant to AI approaches that favour what is essentially almost the exact opposite of their traditional approaches and value systems; instead of process modelling based on physics and science there is a black box. So those geographers best equipped to understand these tremendous developments in AI were, and still are, largely looking elsewhere. This is both sad and a major opportunity (for us!) especially as there is now not the slightest shadow of any doubt that AI is the future technology that will underpin most of geography in the broadest sense. Many geographers *today* may well not like such a claim; but wait 10 to 20 years before judging whether it was in fact so extravagant a statement.

Meanwhile there are many practicable AI tools around. Let us start to use them. This book will hopefully help. I am very indebted to my co-author (and wife Christine Openshaw) who apart from the usual functions of a co-author and researcher, took on the additional and almost impossible tasks of (a) correcting my Geordie English that survived a classical education and (b) ensuring that the contents are intelligible to non-experts and the non-technically minded. Her view was that if she could understand it (she is not a geographer but a computer technician in a planning department) then how could a geographer fail to do so. Readers are invited to test this conjecture for themselves.

I am also grateful for three years' worth of geography undergraduates and master's students at Leeds who were brave enough to attend the lecture course on which this book is based. It is interesting that the undergraduates tend to favour this course more than the postgraduates in GIS do! I tell them in the first lecture that the course objective is simply to introduce open-minded geographers with little computing background and no great knowledge of either statistics or mathematics, to some of the actual and potential applications of AI in geography. This is not a book about AI *per se* but about AI in geography. I am a geographer and I am proud of it. No assumptions are made about any abilities to do matrix algebra or to integrate and differentiate functions. AI is not a mathematically intense subject. It is not intensely statistical. It is not hard from a computer science perspective. It is partly a tool kit and partly a way of thinking about life, the world, the universe and geography. My course is a *gamble* (I tell them) but only a small one. The gamble is justified because of (a) the general future importance of AI in geography (and society), (b) its research significance as a paradigm for doing geography, and (c) because it is so easy! All I can say is usually the lectures had a high attendance rate by an audience that seemed to manage two-hour sessions of spellbound attention. I hope the book manages to capture some of this. It will (like my course) not produce general purpose experts in AI but hopefully geographers sufficiently enthused about this or that aspect of AI as to go away and develop real practical skills. Geographers do not have to develop new AI technologies (that is far too hard), but instead develop an understanding of what it can offer, discover which bits are most relevant and then how to use it. This is not a task beyond any geographer.

STAN OPENSHAW
May 1996

REFERENCES

Openshaw, S., 1992, "Some suggestions concerning the development of artificial intelligence tools for spatial modelling and analysis in GIS", *Annals of Regional Science*, **26**, 35–51.

Openshaw, S., 1993, "Over twenty years of data handling and computing in environment and planning", *Environment and Planning A*, Anniversary Issue, 69–78.

Openshaw, S., 1994a, "Artificial intelligence and geography", *AISB Quarterly*, **90**, 18–21.

Openshaw, S., 1994b, "Computational human geography: exploring the geocyberspace", *Leeds Review*, **37**, 201–220.

Acknowledgements

The authors wish to thank Maureen, for her careful typing of several difficult chapters, and Alison, Lois and David of the Graphics Unit in the School of Geography at Leeds University for the diagrams. Thanks to Ian, Tom, Ollie, Tim, Simon, Gary, Bob, Makis and Linda for their support and to all the students at Leeds University (MA in GIS 3BA) who attended the course from which the book was developed. There is Crown Copyright on the maps based on 1991 census editions. Thanks are also due to ESRC/JIS for buying the 1991 census data. The supercomputing effect support by EPSRC Grant GR/K43933 for the Human Systems Modelling Consortium at Leeds University is also gratefully acknowledged.

CHAPTER 1

Artificial Intelligence and Geography

This chapter provides a gentle non-technical introduction to some of the factors favouring the development of AI. It explains some of the reasons why AI is important to geography and it offers various definitions and explanations of what AI is all about. AI is not naturally hard or difficult. It is neither massively statistical nor mathematically complex; nor is it riddled with incomprehensible computer science. It can be, but the view here is that it must not be presented in a complex manner if geographers are to be introduced to it. Indeed one of the most attractive features of AI is its pervasive and inherent simplicity. This might come as a surprise, *but* it is abundantly clear that the best and most useful parts of AI are in fact based on very simple principles. In essence AI is the task of building intelligence and smart behaviours into computer systems and computer-based analysis toolkits that are currently dumb. AI is now widely used in applications that range from stock markets to sweet manufacture, from washing machines to car braking systems; so why not also apply it to geography?

1.1 AN EMERGING CRISIS IN A WORLD FULL OF DUMB COMPUTER SYSTEMS AND NON-SMART ANALYSIS AND MODELLING TOOLS

Computers are now widely, routinely, and very successfully used to automate many of the straightforward, deterministic and unthinking tasks that were once performed by humans. Many of these applications involved unbelievable amounts of human drudgery; for example, computing wages or manipulating paper file-based information systems. Nearly all current computer applications are therefore little more than an extension of the same basic principles that were the basis for the first Industrial Revolution: namely the use of machines to replace workers in performing low-level and highly repetitive tasks. Most of the manual tasks that have been computerised in the last 40 years were highly deterministic and could therefore be specified as a fixed sequence of instructions that replicated and automated the relatively straightforward clerical and arithmetic activities of humans. Such programs do not have to think, they merely have to do what they have been told to do; in the same way as the human systems they replaced were supposed to behave. However, the new computer systems work 24 hours a day, they do not strike, they do not require rest breaks, and they happily function as automatons, a kind of software and hardware slave that is highly efficient, totally obedient, relatively error free, flexible and increasingly cheap to build and operate.

The world is now run by these types of computer systems and they manage most aspects of our daily existence; for example, covering everything from bills, appointments, reservations, purchasing and financial transactions. They have no local intelligence capability other than that which was built into the programs at a distance in both space and time by the programmers and systems designers. For example, if you wish to divide the value of a variable denoted by X_6 by another variable called X_7 then it might well be prudent to first check that X_7 is not zero, else you will end up dividing a number by zero! Computers, in common with other calculators, do not like dividing numbers by zero and may yield either an unacceptable result (e.g. infinity) or else fail altogether. Now checking that the value of X_7 is not zero before dividing by it might seem to be an intelligent act but this form of intelligence is minimal, static, fixed, and was put there by the programmer. The program (or computer) did not know this was a clever thing to do! On the scale of machine intelligence quotients, this would rate a score of almost but not quite zero since a little bit of domain-specific knowledge was actually used! Likewise, any other fixed algorithms (or sets of instructions designed to solve specific problems by executing a fixed or predefined sequence of steps, no matter how clever) do not really constitute machine intelligence of any great consequence. For example, the statement instructing a computer to take the value of a particular variable and then set it to something else is not really an instance of machine intelligence, although it may well possess some of the attributes of an intelligent act; for example, if it were a conditionally dependent action.

Likewise, a database query, such as find all areas which have more than 20% unemployment and are within 2 km of a motorway, might well be a highly insightful query that is made possible and quick by some very "clever" or "neat" or "smart" database software, but again the intelligence did not come from the machine but from the human operator who decided it was the best question to ask in the first place. Similarly, obtaining good estimates of unknown parameters in a regression model or obtaining an optimal statistical discriminant function that distinguishes between this or that category of objects is not really AI. The intelligence built into these systems is no more than an extension and projection of the programmer's mind and intelligence into a form (i.e. algorithms) that others can use. Maybe this constitutes a form of machine intelligence; it certainly captures and represents some aspects of human skills and intelligence. However, it is not autonomous intelligence and it is perhaps little more than the computer equivalent of a iron tool. A hammer is not normally thought of as possessing any innate intelligence although originally it might well have been a very useful and highly intelligent creation. Like the hammer, much of the computer and software systems that exist today are not intelligent; they are driven via step-by-step algorithms designed to solve a fixed and tightly specified problem with no real or explicit opportunity for any autonomous machine intelligence of any form to be applied or revealed.

The basic problem would appear to be that the computing technologies which are able to automate and computerise human clerical activities cannot so easily be applied to tasks which do not have a predefined or deterministic solution sequence, or for which the problem is not well or explicitly defined. Yet this type of difficult task is increasingly common at many different levels and scales of activity. For example, you can use a statistical technique to test an explicitly formulated a priori hypothesis but you cannot easily use the same statistical method to help you to define, or even define for you, which hypothesis you should be testing. If you do not know or have no hypothesis to test then the best hypothesis-testing technology in the world is useless. Instead new hypothesis-generating and scientific discovery tools are required. You might wish that, somehow, all the available data are magically analysed to yield the best 10 hypotheses that you can then test. But how is this requirement to be met, especially if you do not know what to look for, and how is the computer going to find it? Clearly new technology is needed which is clever enough to meet these particular needs. The current lack of these tools is a critical deficiency, particularly evident in a geographical context. In a world rapidly being saturated and swamped by data which are being produced at an ever-increasing rate, there are virtually no analysis tools that are able to cope with such data riches in a flexible way. If we do not know what to look for then it is becoming increasingly hard to find it in the cyberspaces and geocyberspaces of the present and the near future. Our capacity to capture, store, and manage information about the modern world now far exceeds our ability to do much with it. Instead we store, we archive, and we increasingly construct data warehouses because we know that in the IT era information is the key resource and raw material necessary for the survival of many commercial organisations and for the efficient functioning of much of public administration. Sadly, nearly all of the available methods for its analysis, modelling and processing to extract value date from an earlier period of history when data were scarce and the analyst had to rely on his or her intuitive skills aided by intimate knowledge of what little information was available to formulate analysis tasks. Increasingly, this is not possible any more! In the data-rich world of the 1990s, much more intelligent computer analysis systems are desperately needed which can cope with the analyst simply not knowing what is going on or what hypothesis to test, or even what to expect or what not to expect, and where to find it!

Why should we have to assume that humans are so omniscient! Currently it seems that the best that we can do with much of the data riches is to collect, store and archive. Occasionally it may be mapped but usually we do not know how to analyse it in any reasonable manner. This failure is critical. It affects all levels of society; it damages the economic viability of the firm, and constrains the ability of the state to detect crime or monitor diseases, or to make good, full, and safe use of the available geoinformation for the benefit of us all. Openshaw (1994a) calls this "spatial analysis crime". This is defined as the neglect, for any reason, of the analysis of that spatial information for which there is a good or undeniable public imperative for analysis once the data exist in a suitable form. Increasingly the data exist, but what is missing are any even slightly intelligent means of analysis. The geographical information systems (GIS) revolution of the mid 1980s was characterised by major innovations in the collection, storage, manipulation, and management of geographical information. Yet its very success has caused a major crisis in that our abilities to do anything useful with much of the data it has fostered that go beyond the immediate applications that created the data, because most of the available analysis and modelling tools still largely correspond to a pre-GIS era. Here too there is a growing and increasingly urgent need for a major new revolution in the provision of smart tools able to make good and optimal *use* of the geographic information that now exists. In some ways the new need is for another GIS revolution, this time concerned with making good use of the information and not just aiding its collection and management.

Artificial intelligence is probably the principal hope for where these tools might either be found or inspired. Without a major input of new technology, it seems that it is virtually impossible to advance our knowledge and understanding of many geographical phenomena because we are unable to generate new discoveries from data or spot major patterns and relationships that are currently invisible, because whilst present in the data they are not in the mind of the investigator. The logical next step, and probably the principal hope for the future in many information-saturated disciplines such as geography, is the gradual development and increasing use of intelligent machines; software and hardware systems that provide a degree of smart automation of all the critical analysis and modelling functions. At a more general level, these systems will be required to build on and exploit the information-rich environments that computer automation has created. The reasons are not just economics or the undoubted convenience of locally intelligent consumer products, but the need for ever more powerful artificially intelligent tools and computer systems designed to help society cope with the ever more complex managerial task of survival.

The problem at present is that much of this potentially useful technology is in its infancy and still does not exist in anything like a final form or is not widely applied outside of research environments where it is largely a matter of academic curiosity. Additionally, those disciplines that in the longer term are most likely to be the principal beneficiaries are currently showing virtually no awareness of what AI can do for them. The slowly unfolding New Industrial Revolution is not just about a further transformation of the economics of production, or the creation of new consumer products relevant to global markets, it also involves the increased availability and embedding of autonomous smart systems in more and more aspects of everyday life. Make no mistake, these developments are important; however, the potential impact goes far beyond the smart washing machine because the same type of smart technology will be developed much further and will grow to affect most of the professional-, skill- and knowledge-based functions of society. As Schildt (1987: ix) puts it, albeit somewhat prematurely, "Few if any of the events that have occurred or will occur in the last quarter of this century will have as profound or lasting an effect upon human life as the creation of intelligent machines. The introduction of smart, autonomous computers and robots will cause a fundamental restructuring of society." This process is now well under way even if the current rate of progress appears so slow that little seems to have changed. This is merely the lull before the inevitable storm. It should be noted that most of the basic technologies already exist in one form or another. The scene is now set for rapid innovation once the circumstances either demand it or encourage it. The principal barriers were once those of feasibility, later they were cost obstacles, but now it is mainly that of a limited awareness. As human geographers and social scientists, do we merely watch and study this process as it emerges, commenting and writing theoretical critiques on the impacts on this or that group in society; or do we start to use the technology to improve the science in our social science so that we may more actively utilise the new technological developments in a much more active and far less passive manner?

The AI revolution is now well under way, and has been ever since the 1980s. So do not be misled by the current rarity of smart systems, and the current lack of demonstrated power and applicability. AI is relevant not just to the geography of the future, but it is very applicable to the geography of now! Indeed, it is true that the ability of computers to see an object and recognise it, or to hear, or to spot a map pattern or a spatial relationship in a database without being told precisely where and when to look and what to look for, does not yet approach the abilities of a newly born baby or even an insect. But this situation could change at virtually any moment and, in particular contexts, it is already no longer so accurate an observation as it once was. Unseen and unknown by those who either do not look, or do not know where to look or what to look for, or are not involved, major progress is being made at an ever-increasing rate on a very broad front. **AI is simply an attempt to endow a computer with some of the intellectual capabilities of intelligent life forms but without necessarily having to imitate exactly the information-processing steps that are used by human beings and other biological systems to attain varying degrees of intelligence, because replicating the natural processes is still too difficult to contemplate at present**. Nevertheless, there are already sufficient tools that work well enough to suggest that major progress can be made almost whenever we wish, although most geographers have yet to realise it and those that do suffer all the traditional problems that face pioneers during the early stages of any major new revolution that characteristically seeks to totally subvert and then replace the established status quo.

1.2. ARTIFICIAL INTELLIGENCE IS IMPORTANT TO GEOGRAPHY

So why should geographers take AI seriously? Firstly, the importance of AI both now and in the future is increasingly being recognised in many different subjects and there is absolutely no good or sound reason to believe that geography is going to escape. Secondly, it is clear, and the book seeks to demonstrate this fact, that AI is potentially highly relevant to many areas of human and physical geography. It would appear to provide a new widely applicable paradigm for doing and thinking about geography, although by its very nature it is not ever likely to become the basis for a new geography. There is nothing explicitly geographical about AI; from a geographical perspective it is totally alien technology. **AI is merely a toolkit and a way of thinking; it is not an end in itself in a geographical context.** However, it does provide the basis for a major new paradigm for doing geography and also, more generally, for the social sciences. It promises a new and highly flexible approach to many previous impossible and difficult intellectual and practical problems. Particularly attractive is the fact that it provides a means of bridging the gap between the soft and the hard sciences. In an AI context information need not just be numeric but encompasses the totality of different information types. Smart systems can use both quantitative and qualitative information and knowledge without being restricted to simple numeric representations and formats; see Openshaw (1996).

AI is also very, very exciting! Experience suggests that many of us have a high level of natural curiosity about it. History suggests that many of the ideas and concepts are highly infectious; perhaps their very attractiveness all too often results in an over-exaggeration of their importance with excessive hype about their capabilities. This is understandable, if only because of the need for the AI adopters to overcome deeply ingrained suspicions and prejudices held by non-adopters; but it is also dangerous and does AI no great service. Nevertheless, there is little doubt that at least some of us, perhaps the majority, find that the idea of intelligent machines helping humans to solve their problems is very appealing. There is no good reason why geographers should be any different.

Indeed the words "artificial intelligence" are all around us. It is increasingly being used, perhaps mistakenly, in the workplace environment and on all manner of consumer products. For example, the "AI Edit" key on an upmarket hi-fi stereo system, a clever car engine management system, or the AI controls on some auto focusing cameras. It may not be the "right sort" of AI. It may not even justifiably count as AI; but it is there and it is clever and smart compared with what was there before; maybe that is all that matters. Intelligence has always been a matter of degree.

Geographers cannot isolate themselves from what is happening in the world about them. Zadeh (1993) observes that the early 1990s have witnessed a significant increase in the rate of growth of MIQ (machine intelligence quotient) of consumer products and industrial systems. This has mainly been due to the commercial use of soft computing technologies in developing more intelligent systems that can be embedded in consumer microelectronics. By contrast in geography there is very little evidence of any applications of AI whatsoever, let alone any increase over the last three years. There are as yet no geographical equivalents to the "AI Edit" button of the hi-fi system or the clever auto focusing of the modern camera or the "I feel" fuzzy logic controller of an air-conditioning system. Even some washing machines now contain fuzzy logic. The question is really, why is this technology not also being used in geography? Are the problems that geographers face really any harder than those faced by the engineer who seeks to build an intelligent air-conditioning controller that takes into account personal preferences and other soft or qualitative information? The answer is probably "no"; indeed, the main problems in geography are a lack of awareness of what is now becoming possible and probably also artificially induced but philosophically inspired barriers that deem as a matter of principle that anything scientific is bound to be inherently unsound. It is perhaps very ironic that most real sciences consider AI to be a non-science, almost a black art! Yet in principle the same technology that permits the "I feel" fuzzy logic of the intelligent air-conditioning system could almost certainly be used to build computer models of equivalent soft and qualitative human systems.

AI offers a computer-based and computational technology that transcends what mathematical modellers and statistical geographers have ever been able to do. It side-steps their problems by operating in a very different world that views almost every problem as in principle being soluble by intelligent computation. As computers become faster and it is discovered how to build more intelligence into the analysis and modelling systems relevant to geography, so it is inevitable that AI or AI-inspired or AI-based technologies will dominate here also. Maybe the importance of the AI label or logo is greatest when the novelty level is highest. With time it will be taken for granted that all systems are intelligent and people will find it hard to believe that this was once the exception rather than the rule (Openshaw, 1995).

There are also other good reasons for arguing that AI is, or should be, attractive to geography. It is important because it provides a basic toolkit of technology that is of wide applicability to much of geography, with particular relevance to those soft areas previously left untouched by the quantitative, mathematical modelling, computer, and GIS revolutions. However, the argument here is not just that there is now a new set of possibly useful computer algorithms and methods that geographers may find useful, but that the concepts and principles that lay behind AI are also of fundamental importance to the way in which geographers conceive of doing whatever is their brand of geography. As a result when the AI revolution in geography happens it will involve much more than merely importing yet another set of new computer tools limited to selected areas of quantitative geography and the world of GIS, but it will be a part of a fundamental transformation of the ways by which geographers do and think about their species of geography. Viewed from this perspective the AI revolution in geography needs to be put alongside the spatial data explosion of the late 1980s and the emerging new era of parallel supercomputing in the 1990s. Openshaw (1994b, c) combines these developments to argue for the emergence of a new style of geography that is highly computational in nature. AI plays an extremely important part in this view of computational geography in that it provides the platform for (a) attempting to overcome many of the hard problems that have defeated previous generations of quantitative and mathematical geographers, (b) updating the geoprocessing, spatial analysis, and modelling technologies that currently exist, (c) a means of extending computer based analysis into the soft areas of human geography that are currently without science and are increasingly regarded as being outside of science, and (d) more generally to create the philosophical and methodological basis for a new twenty-first-century version of geography that will be needed to exploit the new opportunities in the emerging geocyberspace in an IT-rich and IT-dominated world (Openshaw, 1994b).

There are many other reasons why AI is important to geography. The major ones are summarised in Table 1.1. It can also be observed that historically geography and geographers have always been extremely entrepreneurial and have traditionally been quick to adopt new technologies and jump on emerging bandwagons early. It is a source of some concern that this has not yet happened with AI, which is not a new technology, and even the great upsurge in neurocomputing interests since the late 1980s has not as yet had (in 1995) much visible impact on geography although things look set to change (Hewitson and

Table 1.1   Some reasons why AI is important to geography

- AI exists, it works, and it is being used by other disciplines so why not in geography?
- Many geographical problems have proven hard to handle using more conventional technologies but are of a type that may be expected to greatly benefit from AI
- AI is fashionable and geographers have never been slow to exploit new developments
- There are benefits to be gained from being an early adopter of new relevant, particularly, applied technologies
- A basic AI toolkit exists and is readily available in the form of books, software and knowledge; so most of the hard work has been done by others, elsewhere
- Computer hardware is now big enough and fast enough to cope with many geographical problems
- There is a set of problems readily available that are immediately suitable for AI applications and it is likely that AI will inspire major new areas of research in geography
- The emergence of soft computing technologies is of considerable potential importance to many areas of human geography
- AI is a major source of inspiration from which new geography relevant ideas might be gained
- AI puts the historic overemphasis on philosophical aspects in geography into perspective: put your AI spectacles on and geography suddenly looks very different
- AI probably needs a highly susceptible discipline such as geography to demonstrate its wider usefulness and utility in new areas of contemporary and commercial relevancy; and mutuality could ease its introduction into geography
- AI is exciting

Crane, 1994). The concern now is that without investing in AI geography may not survive as a vibrant discipline. All new, potentially revolutionary technology provides a number of opportunities and threats. It might be relevant to observe that there has already been a lot of investment in AI; there is still a lot of money to be made out of AI; whole new areas of AI-inspired research are likely in the near future, and there is always a competitive advantage in pioneering new technologies early. Indeed AI enthusiasts from other disciplinary backgrounds may well increasingly view geography as a rich source of applications relevant to the world today. Unless the geographical profession takes care, they could find large areas of traditional geographical interest being taken over.

Other excuses concern the fact that AI can be great fun. Most of the hard work has been done by others. Much of the technology is readily and freely available; for example, from various sites on the internet. Indeed, the principles are not unique to geography and this is undoubtedly useful in terms of the job market. AI should help stimulate the fertile imagination, it is a source of much potential excitement and it is of considerable current relevancy, thereby enhancing many a curriculum vitae.

1.3 WHY ARTIFICIAL INTELLIGENCE IS SO IMPORTANT TO HUMAN GEOGRAPHY

Maybe largely technocratic arguments are themselves still not sufficient motivation for many human geographers who may well see themselves as operating on a different epistemological plane than that populated by most quantitative geographers. It is useful then to consider why they too should be interested in AI. Indeed, it might be argued that these soft human geographers with an often amazing degree of ignorance of, and prejudice against, virtually anything scientific that is related to GIS, quantitative geography, and AI, are the greatest single obstacle to the introduction of AI into some very important areas of geography (Pickles et al, 1995). It is apparent that geography presents many hard-to-solve problems when viewed from a normal science perspective and this hardness has fostered a very different, non-scientific approach, together with supporting philosophies and associated pseudo-theoretical frameworks. Indeed historic difficulties of operationalising a useful and meaningful human geographical science is perhaps the principal reason for the seemingly widespread disenchantment with science in some areas of human geography and may even explain the considerable emphasis currently put in human geography (in common with many other social sciences) on other (by which is meant non-scientific) methodologies with a particular preference at present for soft and qualitative descriptive approaches dedicated to describing and sometimes even managing to understand the unique. From a science point of view, it should be appreciated that much of this work in contemporary geography is little more than sophisticated journalism. Some have called it, perhaps unkindly, the Catherine Cookson approach to doing geography (Openshaw, 1991, 1992). To others it looks more like sociology or cultural anthropology than any resemblance to anything that people might recognise as being the legitimate and traditional concern of geography. However, whilst telling plausible fairy tales may well be useful in understanding how complex spatial human systems operated at one place at one point in time, it should be appreciated that they contribute little that is scientific and virtually nothing that is capable of useful generalisation either as theory or hypothesis or testable model. There is an increasingly powerful argument that this is simply not good enough any more. All too frequently, modern human geography amounts to little more than the partial description of what is unique. It is declared to be geographical because the study happened to be located at a particular place. There is no doubt that some of this soft understanding is useful knowledge and it is known that many other sciences also experienced a similar observational phase at some time during their history. However, maybe it is time that human geography moved on and that, now the tools exist, much more attention needs to be given to converting soft knowledge and description into something more in accord with a basic scientific format that is relevant to contemporary real-world concerns and capable of useful application.

Viewed from a broader perspective, it might even be considered to be a disgrace that very much more is not being actively done to model the key human systems of the world and that there are still virtually no useful models anywhere of any of these key human systems. Openshaw (1995) argues that human systems modelling (HSM) should now rank alongside the other important grand challenge areas recognised in the hard sciences, such as physics, chemistry, biology, and engineering. It is not unreasonable to expect geographers to be taking a lead role here and that AI will provide at least some of the critical techniques able to convert and utilise much of the soft knowledge that human geographers have developed by offering a means of embedding it in the computer modelling and decision support systems of the future. This challenge is simultaneously a matter of major concern for society as well of unbelievable importance for the social sciences and human geography. Much of the data is about people and their day-to-day behaviour. It is not acceptable to argue that for this or that seemingly good social theoretic reason it is best to look the other way. If the social sciences do not pick up the challenge of starting to model human systems using the full range of available research methods and information-processing technologies then other disciples will. As Openshaw (1995) puts it, there a is need for a major new grand challenge in science that is concerned with human systems. This is at least as important as understanding the human DNA or many of the problems in theoretical physics. In the past the social sciences and human geographers have escaped the need to do this; there were no data and the analysis and modelling technologies were inadequate. Neither of these restrictions still holds. A combination of AI with high-performance computing provides the basis for a 20–50-year grand challenge research programme dedicated to understanding human systems.

The excuse that logical positivism is philosophically flawed is no longer relevant. It is also interesting to note that this complaint only seems to have most affected those that were either historically unable to do science or became disillusioned (long ago) with the problems of being scientific in a difficult human geographic context. No one is arguing for a rebirth of a narrowly focused logical positivism or for a pedantic normal science but for a return to the general principles of science. Geographers, human geographers in particular, are now at the front line in the "war" to save their discipline. If human geography is to survive as a distinctive discipline within social science then it is about time that geographers started to reassert their geographical origins and started reminding others of the importance of space and the fundamental necessity to understand human behaviour in spatial contexts. The world needs good science about human systems. These systems have a strong spatial dimension and it is the job of geographers to provide it. To achieve this goal, AI has a very important role to play as geographers start to rethink how they can both become more scientific, make good use of the totality of knowledge they have built up about how human systems operate and behave, make what they do more widely acceptable within science as a whole, and begin to exploit some of the new technologies (of which AI is the principal one) that now exist and which may assist in these tasks.

At a time when most of the developed world's population is urban it is unacceptable that nearly all the models of urban and regional systems are little different from those developed 30 years ago when data were scarce and computers were very slow. This gross neglect is increasingly hard to justify when the data and computing technologies needed to build good models of human systems exist but are not being applied. The technology needs application rather than development. Currently, it is seemingly easier to model global climatic circulation systems or study the atmosphere of Mars or follow the behaviour of endangered marine mammals as they travel the world's oceans, than it is to model any of the human systems at virtually any level. Of course it is important to be able to construct descriptive tales about the effects of capitalist company X on town Y or describe how IT may create a new global Third World, but not if it never leads to any improvements in scientific knowledge or it is impossible to do any good alpha-rated science on it. Over the years several of the social sciences have successfully created a pseudo-scientific world of their own. The justification for this separate social non-science world rests heavily on being able to demonstrate that more scientific approaches cannot work in this artificially separate world. However, today the validity of this assumption is now in doubt. The challenge for the AI community is to demonstrate that they can contribute to the social sciences and break into this soft world of inward-looking pseudo (social) science and bring it back into the realms of real science. The challenge for geographers is to apply and evaluate the new technologies that are increasingly being used in the world outside geography and make good use of them in their world of geography. It is simply no longer tolerable that we cannot reasonably model, describe in a replicatable and rigorous fashion, or predict, or forecast virtually any of the key spatio-human systems in the world today.

So it is argued that the historical justification for much of the current style of human geography has been eroded if not totally removed by developments in IT and AI. Indeed it is rapidly becoming possible to tackle the problems in geography that previously could not be solved and begin to evolve a new style of geographical science more appropriate for doing geography in the twenty-first century. This new geography is not a rebirth of quantitative geography. There is really little in AI that is quantitative geography in the traditional sense. A concern for statistics and mathematics is replaced by a focus on computation as the power behind AI that will allow it to tackle many of the problems of geography. The challenge for the 1990s is to start to exploit the soft knowledge and understanding that has been built up over the last 20 years by becoming more scientific and embedding this knowledge in computer systems via AI. AI provides many of the tools for doing it and together with major developments in high performance supercomputing, it fosters the belief that maybe, just maybe, it might even be possible!

1.4 SO WHAT DO GEOGRAPHERS NEED TO KNOW ABOUT ARTIFICIAL INTELLIGENCE?

It is useful to start with an assumption that is reflected throughout the contents and style of this book. AI is not hard to grasp or inherently difficult although the language and concepts might at first appear a little strange! It is almost as if there has been a deliberate conspiracy by those disciplines involved to fabricate an AI technospeak, with several different dialects, in order to stop the non-AI world discovering how wonderfully straightforward and simple the concepts underlying AI really are. It does not require any in-depth mathematical or statistical knowledge. Indeed, in some cases it offers a generic substitute technology for many existing statistical methods and mathematical modelling techniques. It can even be viewed as a kind of one-stop universal problem-solving toolkit. There is also as yet little deep theory of AI to worry about and it is largely philosophy-free. Furthermore, there is no reason why you cannot use AI without necessarily having first to understand it all. Many of the learning curves are short, but be prepared—it is also a highly empirical and applied technology. This makes it both useful and extremely relevant. However, the empirical emphasis is very important because it is left to the user to demonstrate that when and where it matters, the technology actually works. AI is all about solving problems more efficiently and perhaps more effortlessly than ever before but its novelty is such that whenever you use it you will need to prove it works, and ideally that it performs much better than any alternative that might exist to compete with it. However, such has been the quiet success of AI the onus of proof is changing. Once this was a purely a matter of proving via conventional benchmarks that there was a benefit from using AI in those applications where conventional benchmarks existed. The AI advocate was on the defensive in a critical and hostile world. Now it is possible to become more proactive and declare that if you continue to persist with conventional technology then you only do so if you can demonstrate that the AI alternatives yield no worthwhile benefit.

The tremendous breadth and depth of AI can cause some problems for beginners. Clearly it is also always useful to know something about the origins, something of the different fields within AI, the potential and limitations and directions of the subject, but there is no need to know it all before trying to apply any of it. It is possible to pick and choose from a menu of applicable tools. As ever, it is important to seek to eventually become experts in those specialist bits of AI that have most to contribute to geography, with the need to acquire a great deal of knowledge about some highly focused parts of the technology judged most relevant to particular geographical applications. However, it is also exceedingly important to note that there is no prerequisite to become experts in AI at the expense of being experts in geography. There are so many sad examples of geographers becoming so engrossed in a new subject that they quickly forget most, if not all, of their geography or even why they embraced the area in the first place. For example, how many of the geographers who sought to become statisticians or others who turned to social theory or anthropology or ethnology or other areas of philosophy and political science have ever come back with improved, geographically relevant, understandings? As a geographer, your interest in AI should be purely to serve your geographical concerns. **This is very important**. If you become a general expert in AI and forget all about your geography, then you will almost certainly fail to do anything useful in a geographical context with your AI skills. It really is necessary, therefore, to keep a strong geographic focus on AI with regard to what tools might be considered useful and the nature of the problems of such geographical interest that require attention. Beware of merely going on a hunt for suitable problems that would seem suitable for a particularly fashionable AI technique. A problem-solving orientation is also useful because it provides a means of being selective and focused. This should save time; it should make it easier to reach research frontiers; and it should allow a concentration on those real applications that matter most. Remember too that once you, the reader, embrace AI you really do need to succeed; else your failure may serve to put others off and that would be a pity!

AI is a tremendously exciting, highly seductive, and massively appealing technology but it is essential to keep reminding ourselves of the underlying geographic focus, of geographic applications and the need to justify its use in a geographical context. The objective is to explore AI in geography and not become engulfed in the AI whirlpool. Be warned—this is not so easily avoided! The whirlpool is extremely appealing and probably much easier to fall into, rather than practise really useful AI in geography. (Openshaw, 1994d).

5. WHAT IS ARTIFICIAL INTELLIGENCE?

This is where the confusion can start. It would seem that AI workers tends to have their own pet definitions relevant to their context and subject interests. There is also often an implied historical dimension to it, with different definitions reflecting the prevailing AI fashions at the time they were made. So be careful. Many definitions of AI strongly depend on your point of view and most overemphasise comparisons with human intelligence.

There is no really adequate single definition because the subject spans such a broad area. Nevertheless, here is a selection of definitions by some of the leading authors. Some focus on the intelligence achieved by the results; others emphasise the nature by which intelligence might be obtained:

> AI is the science of making machines do things that would require intelligence if done by men (Minsky, 1968: v).

> AI is the ability of machines to do things that people would say require intelligence (Jackson, 1985: 1).

The problem here is that it is all too easy for previously unknown discoveries to be declared self-evident once they are known. A very useful trick of belittlement! For example, once upon a time one of the authors found a previously unknown cancer cluster by the use of a slightly smart method that required no prior hypothesis about where to look for cancer clusters (see Chapter 3). A real discovery? You might well think so, but some of the *post hoc* criticism at that time was along the following lines: "Well it was so obvious that a even a blind person with a white stick would have spotted it!" Of course, until the particular location had been identified no one had previously thought to look there. Now is that not being intelligent? If it had been found by a human being, it would have been regarded as a highly intelligent act; but because it was discovered by an automated machine-based analysis procedure, it is dismissed as being inconsequential. It is not difficult to imagine many other examples in statistical geography where automated machine-based solutions might be regarded as both simultaneously very useful and self-evident by different sets of end-users. For example, in modelling a nonlinear relationship a neural network might well deliver a much better result than the geographer might have managed with a widely available conventional statistical package. Now suppose the neural network attains a similar level of performance as that achieved by a world famous statistical expert. Does this indicate that the neural net should be abandoned because one human expert in the context of a single application was able to perform at a similar level to a novice statistician who had recently discovered how to run a neural network program on his PC? What does this demonstration prove? Or, given the scarcity of real human statistical experts able to perform at this level, maybe the comparison is wholly inappropriate. It also underplays the virtues of neural network technologies that can easily handle situations where there are no conventional statistical alternatives and no existing human experts. Maybe the implications are that it would be more sensible to teach the neural network approach to all first-year geographers as a substitute for statistical methods that are orders of magnitude poorer because they are linear and too simple for the real world of geography! Different pressure groups and vested interests tend to hold very different and often highly polarised views. The more that AI offers an alternative viable technology to conventional methods, so the greater the squeals of protest from those who are about to be replaced or who think they could be.

Other definitions of AI focus on understanding the nature of intelligence as a process that can be understood and then built into machines For instance:

> AI is the study of the computations that make it possible to perceive, reason and act (Winston, 1992: 5).

> The key notion is intelligent problem solving and the key to intelligent problem solving, as opposed to a brute-force approach, is to apply the same kind of techniques that humans use (Forsyth and Naylor, 1985: 1).

> The object of research into AI is to enable a computer to perform the remarkable functions that are carried out by human intelligence (Shirai and Tsujii, 1982: vii).

> AI is a very general investigation of the nature of intelligence and the principles and mechanisms required for understanding or replicating it (Sloman, 1991: xx).

Some of this tends to become very pompous and often reflects an interest in a particular type of AI, for example knowledge-based systems. Others take a more pragmatic view and argue that problem solving is the main objective and there is no need to understand or define intelligence or understand exactly how it is achieved by biological systems in order to mimic and use it. An engineering perspective would emphasise the importance of seeking to copy and imitate the processes that appear most useful. Maybe from a practical or applied point of view, it is more important, but much less satisfying, to know it can be achieved—rather like a clever trick that works. Some of the areas of AI concerned with the creation of fast and efficient search heuristics (see Chapter 3) might well reflect this clever tricks view. Indeed not all of AI is biologically inspired by observation of human and biological systems and there is a wealth of clever algorithmic methods that some would regard as intelligent, albeit of a limited sort. For example, finding the shortest path through a network in a highly efficient rather than via a totally brute-force approach is really quite a smart thing to do. It is clearly an intelligent solution to a problem that might otherwise not be soluble via total enumeration. However, the intelligence here comes from the programmer or mathematician and is not generated by the machine. Nevertheless, such methods are clearly part of AI but with a relatively low level of machine intelligence.

Forsyth and Naylor (1985, preface) write:

> Artificial Intelligence (AI for short) has always been the "department of clever tricks" within computer science. It is concerned with leading-edge problems which are hard for computers even if—like vision—they are easy for people. Some AI problems, like playing chess well, are difficult both for people and computers.

Smith (1984: 147) explains AI in a similar way:

> Artificial Intelligence (AI) may be regarded as an attempt to understand the
> processes of perception and reasoning that underlie successful problem-solving and
> to incorporate the results of this research in effective computer programs. At
> present, AI is largely a collection of sophisticated programming techniques.

In general, these various definitions reflect two broad strands of thought about
AI. The first involves attempting to understand how human intelligence operates,
to identify the principal mechanisms and processes, so that it might be possible to
replicate some of the functionality in computing machines. The second seeks
merely to develop systems able to mimic what human beings do without
necessarily claiming to understand the underlying processes in any great detail.
Ultimately the two approaches will probably converge, but initially and right
now, it is much easier to adopt the second strategy. Indeed there is some evidence
that already sufficient is known to inspire some very interesting and practically
useful AI technologies. However, the objective in many instances cannot merely
be to replicate aspects of human thinking behaviour. The real goal has to be the
development of problem- or application-specific machines that can be made to
act intelligently, sensibly, and if required with tremendous creativity in areas
where they may far outstrip the abilities of human beings, otherwise, what is the
point?

From a theoretical perspective, the ability to create machines that can replicate
human reasoning and intelligence might well be a major scientific achievement,
whenever it is possible to do so. However, it is unlikely that the world can wait for
that breakthrough to occur nor will it necessarily be sufficient to provide the
types of benefits that AI is expected to deliver right now. In a geographic context,
the holy grail is probably the creation of systems of amplified intelligence, systems
that can outperform humans by many orders of magnitude in those special tasks
to which they are applied.

Perhaps a more reasonable definition is that AI is the art, rather than the
science, of trying to make machines think for themselves; rather like the smart
toaster that is sometimes able to trigger a smoke alarm when the toast is done
although it might have been better if it just popped out shortly before the black
smoke became visible! A machine able to decide for itself when the toast is
sufficiently brown to eat, a decision that humans are sometimes quite good at, is
seeking to imitate human intelligence by understanding the underlying decision
making processes and culinary preferences of the user. The latter approach might
be regarded as an engineering solution based on a somewhat simpler heuristic but
one that will at least never burn the toast even if the degree of browning might
never be optimal. **AI then is an attempt to mimic the cognitive and symbolic skills
of humans using digital computers in the context of particular applications. This is
not so much a matter of seeking to replicate skills that are already possessed by
humans but of attempting to improve and amplify our intelligence in those**

applications where it is deficient and can benefit from it most. Moreover, there is also no restriction of having to refer to humans. The development of smart systems can involve non-human attributes. For example, systems that self-organise under their own control might be regarded as being exceptionally intelligent; but totally alien in that there are no direct human comparisons that can be made other than to argue that life itself is like some kind of self-organising process and this feature can be observed in many natural and biological systems. Likewise, the incorporation of feedback loops into systems that previously did not possess any might be regarded as an exceptionally clever thing to do; for instance, it would allow an otherwise dumb system to respond to change in its environment. Is such a system not showing signs of being intelligent? There is a danger in becoming too narrowly focused in what is and what is not considered to be evidence of machine and/or software intelligence. A broader interpretation puts more emphasis on self-determination and self-initiated actions; indeed any system that can respond to the unexpected by itself and without being formally instructed to do so, might be regarded as displaying evidence of being intelligent in the right sort of way.

Of course, such general definitions of AI are interesting but not necessarily all that helpful to geographers. The basic underlying notion is that of intelligent problem solving, which is of course why some people study, and try to mimic, key aspects of human intelligence and build them into computer systems. The hope is that by understanding human intelligence, how the brain works, and how certain biological systems attain intelligent behaviour, it may be possible to simulate similar kinds of behaviour on computers and thus be in a position to solve problems better than previously, as well as extending the range of problems that can be tackled. **This desire somehow to replicate or emulate or simulate the key characteristics of biological intelligence on computing machines to solve practical problems is what AI is all about.** However, these AI systems are highly specific. They are not concerned with the creation of general purpose artificial intelligences but create instead domain-dependent and very narrowly focused subsystems.

This narrowness of focus clearly alarms some people. Hasemer and Domingue (1989: 5) write:

> It is quite a frightening thought that AI seems to be well on course for the creation of the mechanical equivalent of a victim of cerebral palsy: it is intelligence well up to adult human standards but enclosed in a world of its own, its senses dim or completely absent, unable to communicate with ordinary people, unable to move without help, and unable because of these limitations to understand more than a tiny fragment of the world around it. We shall probably treat such machines as our ancestors treated their human slaves, putting them to work on mundane tasks 24 hours a day until they become obsolete and we let them die.

It is almost an emotionally sad experience to contemplate machine murder! If we are clever enough to create artificial life in our computer systems, is it really murder when they are killed by the program terminating? A later chapter deals with this aspect. Yet this type of intelligent machine is probably exactly what we want and maybe is also the best that might be hoped for in many practical situations. The principal difference between ourselves and Hasemer and Dominuel mainly concerns the nature of the tasks considered suitable and also the level of performance that is to be attained before such machines might be considered to be geographically useful. Geographers are not interested in simple mundane automatons but have much higher expectations about the nature of the functions that might be achieved.

It is also important to be aware of the black–white response that AI often engenders in people. Chabris (1987: 15) writes:

> ...many people possess an almost religious faith in artificial intelligence... others violently resist the notion that a machine can be made to think like a human being.

There is considerable scope here to develop and play on these fears. Perhaps the hope is that they provide a means of outlawing the technology, or constitute grounds for an ethical or moral or religious or whatever justification for preventing the further development and use of AI technologies. At best these fears belong to the world of sci-fi, at worst they are being exaggerated, hijacked, and articulated by vested interests (or cliques of threatened or concerned researchers) mainly for mischievous reasons. As always in IT, it is not the technology that has the potential for evil but the user.

The previous discussion emphasises that there are three broad approaches to AI:

1. Top-down—where you select instances of intelligent behaviour and try to design machines able to replicate it;
2. Bottom-up—the study of biological mechanisms that underlie human intelligence and that characteristic of other living systems in the hope that it will permit machines to become more intelligent and adaptive;
3. Pragmatic—the design of systems that can perform useful functions regardless of how they achieve this goal.

In addition, it is possible to identify different types of intelligence. **Transferred intelligence** is really an extension of the programmer's skills, e.g. heuristic search methods. Clever technology, but is cleverness the same as intelligence? **Result intelligence** occurs when the results are novel, surprising, useful or smart in any (or some) ways. For example, an intelligent GIS uses models to go beyond the map, enabling it to discover cluster patterns. Another example could be of the "what if" or "I did not know that" type, better known as smart autonomous systems. The machine is now largely autonomous within a fixed domain. You no longer tell it what to do or even how to it, just tell it what you want. The machine learns or discovers how to do it itself. In some ways the smart autonomous system combines the previous two forms of intelligence. These distinctions will become much clearer in later chapters.

In general, you do not have to be terrified or awe-struck by AI and some of its pretentiousness. To quote Forsyth and Naylor (1985: preface):

> Now you have spent a tidy sum of money on a home computer, why not do something clever with it?

AI is really nothing more than the development of a certain type of computational technique, that is operationalised via a computer program that causes it to behave in a certain way that can be regarded as possessing intelligent behaviour. As Hasemer and Domingue (1989: 3) put it:

> AI is essentially the study of a certain class of computational technique. Via a computer program an AI technique is applied to a computer and causes it to behave in a certain way. When the resulting behaviour would be described as "intelligent" were a human being to behave in the same way, AI counts it as a success.

Note that there is no need to define intelligence or to build brain-like machines in order to mimic it, since for most of us intending users, exactly how this artificial intelligent behaviour is manufactured is much less important than its achievement. But it is important to be aware of the limitations. Stripped of all its pomp, self-righteousness and pretensions, AI is little more than a collection of computer techniques expressed in this or that programming language which no matter how clever and sophisticated they may appear ultimately ends up as a stream of machine instructions that are today little different from those of 40 years ago, and the whole lot is usually implemented on conventional computer hardware. So what is there to worry about?

Hillis (1985: 1) explains it like this: "Perhaps one day, perhaps soon, it will become possible to build a machine that is able to perform the functions of a human mind, a thinking machine." However, the construction of a full blown AI is not yet within our grasp and may not be for another 50–100 years or so. Hillis uses Picasso's 1905 *The Watering Place* to illustrate this point. The human being, even a five-year-old child, can almost effortlessly summarise the painting in a single sentence such as: "It's a group of people and horses." Yet it would take the fastest supercomputer many days, maybe years, of compute time to come up with something similar, assuming we are clever enough to program it to answer that question. Hillis (1985) argued that massively parallel computer hardware might help, as indeed it would. However, in some ways the real problem is how to program the computer to answer the question in the first place; never mind how long it might take. Indeed, it is very interesting that this programming task would either be regarded as almost impossible, possible but extremely difficult, or very easy, depending on which AI path you choose to stroll down. But even if you could program a machine to answer the question, would that be intelligent behaviour or merely pattern recognition? Some of us would say "Wow, yes" while others would say "Well, no, not really'! Yet AI is only really a means whereby we seek to be more intelligent in our problem solving either by becoming smarter or cleverer as to how we do it or just by being able to do it and overcome problems that were previously impossible to solve. Maybe the latter is what machine intelligence is all about. **The aim is to become clever or gain knowledge or make discoveries by becoming more computationally oriented, by trading machine speed for intelligence.** According to this view, AI is a means by which intelligence can be gained by computation. Moreover, as our computers become rapidly faster and bigger in memory, then this ability to compute our way towards machine intelligence becomes ever more appealing. Yet already in some areas, machine speeds are more than sufficient to sustain and create intelligent systems.

To many the ability to solve important but previously impossible problems by any route is worth while. If it is AI based, or AI related, or machine based, or mimics some biological system in some highly intelligent and clever way, who cares? Are semantics so important when there is a massive new problem solving toolkit ready for us to use?

1.6 CAN MACHINES THINK?

A final question is whether or not machines can think. How would we know it, if they did? Or is it quite irrelevant to AI to geography and the social sciences?

AI raises some very profound philosophical questions about the nature of intelligence and of humankind. The aim of AI is to develop computing machines that have characteristics normally associated with human intelligence. The problem is that most of us still do not know how we think and there is no unambiguous definition of what intelligence means and thus no clear cut benchmark for assessing machine intelligence. Maybe the problem is that there is an expectation that intelligent machines are intelligent in ways reminiscent of human beings. This immediately causes some difficulties because for some it more or less denies the possibility that a program can be intelligent if it does not perform the task in the same way that a person would. Remove this restriction and the concept of intelligent programs and machine intelligence may well be much easier to cope with and become far more comfortable to live with. **The definition of an intelligent program is simply some software that acts intelligently but without having to solve the problem in the same way a human would.** In fact it might be best to remove all references to human beings altogether, since this implies a fundamental restriction on the performance of intelligent machines that will sooner or later in the future be regarded as somewhat unnecessary and crippling.

Clearly, this question "Can machines think?" is a very sensitive subject that raises many concerns; for example, "Is there thought without experience?" and "Is there intelligence without life?" "I" think or "she" thinks causes us no problems, but if we replace "I" or "she" by "machine" or a PC, the effect can be very disconcerting. Whilst a well-trained dog is considered smart if it fetches a newspaper from the letter box or a baby is regarded as being intelligent when it successfully places two blocks of the same colour on top of each other, the same tasks when performed by a robot are not considered at all smart! The robot is merely considered to be running a program that was designed to manipulate blocks and as a result is not actually thinking about the task but simply doing what it was programmed to do. It would appear that the dog and child chose to do their tasks, as distinct from doing something else, but that the robot had no choice in the matter because it had been programmed to do it. But is the dog or the human child that different? Surely they too have been programmed (i.e. trained or encouraged) to perform the required task and the robot, via a simple conditional branch, might have decided not to do the function that was demanded of it. The real difference here might well involve the level of intelligence being displayed rather than question its existence. Clearly, all software has some degree of intelligence built into it.

Currently the only test of whether a machine can think is Turing's test of machine intelligence (Turing, 1950). It is not a set of rigid criteria but nevertheless it is an unambiguous test of whether machines can think. Turing reasoned that most human beings accept that most other human beings are intelligent and, therefore, if a person cannot determine whether he or she is dealing with another human or a machine, then we must accept that such a machine is intelligent. In his test, the operator holds a two-way conversation with another entity, via a keyboard, and attempts to get the other party to reveal whether it is a machine or another human being behaving very awkwardly. This experiment has still to be performed seriously and also no machine as yet displays sufficient general intelligence to perform well on it in any non-trivialised way . However, it should be added that it is still not known whether the attainment of general AI is within the bounds of computational ability, and if it was attained, whether it would be of any great use in geography. It is useful to recall that our interest is in creating superintelligence in a problem-solving applied domain, not just ordinary, general intelligence *per se*. It is interesting to note that Turing (1950) also wrote that his question is really too meaningless to be worthy of discussion because he thought that by the late 1990s the use of words and general educated opinion will have changed so much that we will be able to speak of machines thinking without expecting to be contradicted. Turing was highly optimistic about the prospects of this supercomputer. He declared, "I believe that in about fifty years' time it will be plausible to programme computers ... to make them play the imitation game so well that an average interrogator will not have more than 70 per cent chance of making the right identification after five minutes of questioning" (Turing, 1950: 19; Feigenbaum and Feldman, 1963). Mickie and Johnston (1985) went further and argued that this question is also highly distracting. "It is a mistake to take up too much time asking, 'Can computers think?' 'Can they be really creative?' For all practical purposes they can. The best course for us is to leave the philosophers in their dark room and get on with using the creative computer to the full" (quoted by Firebaugh, 1988: 15).

It is at this point that some confusion can set in, because some AI researchers focus on using AI to investigate human intelligence *per se*. Others wish to design more intelligent machines, perhaps based on the human as a helpful model for simulating intelligence in a machine in a problem-solving context. As geographers, we are only really interested, like many potential end-users of AI, in developing clever problem-solving technologies. It is useful that Winston (1992: 8) writes:

> Note that wanting to make computers be intelligent is not the same as wanting to make computers simulate intelligence.

Again, it is the former that geographers are interested in. The prime objective is to try and solve real-world problems, which is essentially an engineering goal, rather than learn more about intelligence *per se*. However, maybe the two approaches are not so mutually exclusive as they appear to be in that knowing more about intelligence will undoubtedly assist in solving problems. Perhaps also the most relevant definition and measure of machine intelligence applicable to many geographical contexts, is to assess whether machines can solve important problems at least as well, but ideally much better, than any geographer can. Ideally, this technology should extend to handle all manner of problems and tasks that are currently either beyond what human beings can presently do or experience great difficulties in performing.

1.7 ARTIFICIAL INTELLIGENCE IS WIDELY VIEWED AS BEING FUTURE ESSENTIAL

Regardless of its many forms and different definitions, AI is important for one further highly compelling reason. It is widely regarded as being future essential and ultimately unavoidable. Sooner or later AI-based technologies will be commonplace everywhere. It is not a matter of *if*, only *when*. There are clearly benefits in being an early adopter but not so early as to be too far out on a limb. Picking the right moment to adopt AI is clearly difficult but for many disciplines that moment is either now or has already passed.

Firebaugh (1989: xix) writes:

> It is the author's firm conviction that technological and institutional forces are rapidly converging to create an environment in which many of the past promises of AI can be realised.

Brain and Brain (1984: vii), what a good name for an AI person, express it in the following way:

> AI is undoubtedly an increasingly important area in computer development which will have profound effects on all our lives in the next few decades.

Michie (1988: xxiii) writes:

The growth in recent years of AI has been without historical precedent, as also the diversity of impacts on human activities. These developments call for a new generation of professional people trained to think in fresh ways... We cannot yet fully make out the shape of the coming Knowledge Revolution. But we know that it will be unlike anything seen on earth before.

Winston (1992: 6) claims:

The long term applications stagger the imagination ... the near-term applications involve new opportunities.

Yes, indeed. There is a major gap between what we do in geography and what we could do if we invested in AI. The fact is that many people are taking the possibility of AI very seriously. Also, progress is now occurring on several fronts simultaneously. As Aleksander and Burnett (1987: 9) put it:

... those who look forward to the advent of intelligent machinery with enthusiasm have tended to over-estimate the chances of success, while those who view the prospect with foreboding have tended to under-estimate the benefits that success might bring.

Whilst many of these prognoses about the future of AI have grossly over-estimated the speed of the AI revolution, there can be little doubt that it is coming and that it is already well under way. Historians of 100 years hence will regard the unbelievably crude and clumsy AI technologies of the late twentieth and early twenty-first centuries with utter disbelief and amazement, rather like how today we view many of the tremendous scientific advances of the nineteenth century. The fact that there was a debate about not using it will stagger their imaginations even further.

1.8 WHAT DOES ARTIFICIAL INTELLIGENCE CONSIST OF?

The definitions and thus content of AI mainly reflect its origins with fragments from four principal disciplines: psychology, biology, philosophy, and computer science, with added strands from linguistics, mathematics, logic, and engineering. It is heavily jargonised, with each contributing discipline presenting AI using different language and quite often different technospeak. Geographers will have problems with them all. However, this technical jargon tends to disguise the outstanding fact that AI is in essence a fairly simple technology. Stripped of the complicating languages that tend to be used in so many texts to obscure the facts and mystify the uninitiated, many of the concepts are very simple; indeed, anything based on copying nature at work tends to be beautifully simple.

A number of major themes within AI can be identified as being of potential geographical interest. They include:

- language—computational linguistics and natural language processing
- heuristic search in the context of game planning and general algorithms
- knowledge representation and use in automated reasoning and expert systems
- fuzzy logic and systems modelling
- pattern recognition
- robotics and artificial life
- computer vision
- machine learning
- neurocomputing
- evolutionary programming

Many of these topics and themes are the subject of subsequent chapters. Others are ignored although they may well be relevant to geography; it is just that the linkages and contributions are currently less evident.

1.9 ARTIFICIAL INTELLIGENCE IS A FUTURE ESSENTIAL TOOLKIT FOR GEOGRAPHY

It is probably not too much of a simplification to summarise the key areas of AI that are of geographical interest. However, it is likely that most of the broad subject areas within AI have some geographical relevancy. For example, the analysis of place-names, forenames and surnames has long been a traditional geographical activity. One cannot help feel that some of the AI work on natural language is very relevant here, as also is speech recognition research.

Smith (1984) suggests the following benefits may be provided by AI:

1. AI techniques associated with the cognitive approach offer the possibility of developing very detailed models of spatial decision-making in which the individual's representation of the world is considered a major determinant.
2. Improved spatial data retrieval and analysis by the development of knowledge-based GIS.
3. AI techniques promise to make the modelling of complex geographical systems more manageable, because of the use of more general symbolic representations arguing that various logical languages provide the basis for constructing such models.
4. The application of cognitive approaches of AI modelling decision-making behaviour leading to what he terms as a truly experimental science of behaviour based on the simulation of individual behaviour in environments inaccessible to scientific observation.
5. The adoption of an engineering approach to geographic problem solving. Expert systems can be used both to model a phenomenon and provide decision aids useful for solving problems with a geographical dimension. He argues that this "may permit applied geography to achieve a status that was previously deemed impossible by inadequate methodologies applied to

complex problems" (Smith, 1984: 156).
6. The solution of problems that were previously impossible or difficult to solve.
7. An extension of the narrowly focused statistical, analytical, and numerical techniques used by geographers to the much broader realm of symbolic processing.
8. If AI techniques are properly applied they should allow researchers to spend more time on creative thinking and less on technical drudgery.

We would agree with all these suggestions but note that in the 10 years since they were written nothing much has happened or changed. However, speculations in these general ways are both interesting and useful, if only so that others may make similar comments of ourselves in a further 10 years' time. Our suggestions as to what geographers might well expect AI to contribute to them are in Table 1.2. It is very easy to become over-enthusiastic and geographers need to be aware that not everything that AI appears to offer or promise can be realised in a practical geographical setting immediately or with minimal effort. There is still much basic research needed at the AI–geography frontier. On the other hand, it is probably not too much of an overstatement to declare that, in common with many other disciplines, AI is a future essential technology for geography. The problem at present is its slow take-off within the geographical discipline. There are many reasons for this which are summarised in Table 1.3. However, few of these problems are anything other than a delaying mechanism. It is unthinkable that the AI revolution will not happen soon in geography or, indeed, that it is not already well on its way. It is also unthinkable that the greater use and uptake of AI tools and principles can fail to enrich the subject in many fundamental ways. Smith (1984: 157) writes: "It is quite probable, in fact, that AI techniques may lead geographical research and applications into a position of much greater prominence than they currently enjoy." AI provides the basis for new ways of doing old geography, new solutions to old problems that could not previously be solved, new solutions to new problems, and in essence the basis for the further evolution of the subject. Those that continually and excessively dispute its worth (probably

Table 1.2   Major geographical expectations from AI

- Better and new models of human spatial systems
- Better and new spatial analysis methods
- New approaches to old problems
- An ability to solve previously insoluble problems
- Greater flexibility
- A chance to become more geographically realistic
- An opportunity to join in the AI excitement
- A basis for starting to use the masses of spatial information created by the GIS revolution
- A means of extending the range of computing in geography into the softer areas
- A platform for becoming much more scientific in how geography is performed

Table 1.3   Some problems with AI in geography

- A general low level or total lack of awareness of AI
- A tendency to remember only the past failures of AI
- A lack of demonstrated examples and flagship projects showing off the benefits and strengths of AI in a geographic or social science context
- Most of the AI literature relates to non-geographic applications
- Absence of any research initiatives in this area
- Some deeply ingrained prejudices in that current research training tends to focus on the conventional world of statistics and carries with it a deep scepticism of AI
- Philosophical barriers to thinking creatively about being smarter in the way geography could in the future be performed

---

because they do not understand anything about AI) and fail to learn the new technologies will surely discover that sometime, probably quite early in the twenty-first century, they themselves to be obsolete and their skills probably replaced by smart systems. It is not the end of geography but rather the beginning of a new era in which smart machines work as extensions to the geographers traditional skills and imagination in tacking both old and new problems to far higher standards of achievement than ever was possible before.

1.10 QUESTIONS AND ANSWERS

Q   What does the term "machine intelligence" mean? Does it denote an intelligent machine?

A   Usually these days it is the software that is programmed to be intelligent and because software runs on a computing machine, the term "machine intelligence" is sometimes used. Machine intelligence refers to both hardware and software systems. The situation is a little confused because software can sometimes be given a hardware implementation. Also, in the early days of AI, some of the experiments involved the development of mechanical or electromechanical machines (with gears, pulleys, clutches, etc.) that attempted to behave in intelligent ways, so maybe the term machine intelligence originated in these early mechanical marvels.

Q   I have flicked through a few "introductory" books to AI in my local bookshop and find them almost impossible to understand. Do I need to be a skilled computer scientist or a mathematician or a statistical expert before I will be able to understand AI?

A   No. Usually the basic underlying principles are very simple, it is just the manner in which they are presented that makes them appear difficult. The apparent degree of difficulty tends to increase once texts start to refer to either computer implementation in a particular favourite language that you may well have never come across before, such as Prolog or Lisp; or if the text is targeted at a particular discipline which determines both the technical jargon, the notation, the examples, and the language used. Since this is most unlikely to be geography, no wonder you can have problems. *We do too!*

Q   In AI where precisely does the intelligence come from?

A   No computer is naturally intelligent. Without software systems most will not do anything useful whatsoever. The intelligence comes from the systems that are run on a computer. It has to be programmed in. However, this does not necessarily mean that the behaviour of the resulting system is totally deterministic, fixed, and forever destined to be totally and completely dumb. The aim of AI is to design and develop computer systems (usually now software) that behave in ways considered to be intelligent in those areas in which they operate. The level or degree of intelligence may be no "great deal" but then the same can be said about many humans! So if software or computing machines start doing vaguely intelligent things or start showing signs of intelligence in applications that previously had none, it is only because they were programmed to act like that. Moreover, at the same time you should be aware that computers can be programmed to program themselves so that the resulting behaviour, and results, might be a total surprise to the developer of the original system. Indeed, it might well be argued that the development of autonomously intelligent systems that are machine, rather than man-made, may be the best hope of attaining high levels of machine intelligence in many areas of AI. Nevertheless, the original program would still have to be an invention by a man or a woman.

Q   Smith (1984: 156) writing in the *Professional Geographer* states that "A first requirement involves the knowledge of at least one AI programming language." So do geographers need to start their AI research training by learning Prolog or Lisp?

A   No. Prolog is only really useful to one area of AI associated with knowledge representation and reasoning. Fortran or C are not the best languages to use in that context; you could but the programming tasks could become more difficult. On the other hand, no one would sensibly want to program a neural net or a genetic algorithm in Prolog but, of course, you probably could. Lisp is another well-established AI favourite computing language. It has some nice properties but then so too do Assembler and BASIC. It is largely a matter of selecting "horses for courses" and few AI folk claim to operate on more than a few different courses. It is also quite clear that you can use AI technology without having to program it yourself. There are many different packages that allow you access to many of the tools. In the 10 years since Smith (1984) wrote his pioneering paper, the world has changed almost completely. AI is, today, much easier for geographers and others to get into. It is no longer the almost exclusive preserve of the expert computer scientist, or whatever.

Q   What is the greatest danger in seeking to develop AI applications in geography?

A   Developing systems that, far from being intelligent, are in fact actually stupid! AI is an intensely empirical subject. If it works you use it, or more prudently you test it against minimum performance benchmarks. Only if it passes the tests do you use it, and begin to believe in it. Smart systems can easily become stupid when faced with the unexpected; really smart systems will continually monitor their own performances and dynamically switch to whatever technology looks like working the best, or even tell you that they are no longer working as well as they should. Intelligence is, therefore, partly a function of how a technique or system operates in a particular context and partly a function of embedding it in a smart systems framework that constantly checks its own performance.

Q   The AI revolution has the potential to replace many older dumb methods. This has potentially serious long-term implications for skill-based subjects such as statistics. Should I switch completely to AI-inspired methods?

A   No. It is important to test the emerging new technologies by confronting them with the older methods they seek to replace. Furthermore, some of the conventional statistical analysis skills are still extremely relevant; for example, as a means of investigating the levels of uncertainty inherent in the outputs from AI tools. What AI does do, is to offer some hope of lifting some or many of the barriers and constraints that have restricted the performance of more conventional technologies. The wise person would seek to work with AI not attempt to destroy it, although many think or hope (wrongly) that it will soon disappear. It is, of course, not AI that will disappear, but its critics!

    If the question concerns whether or not certain AI methods, such as neural networks, should be taught to geographers as a practical means of modelling geographical systems, then the answer has to be yes on the grounds that: (1) it is easier, (2) has widely applicable generic technology, and (3) offers some real prospect of good performance.

Q   Are some areas of geography more suitable for AI than others?

A   No, not really. It is true that quantitative geographers and those interested in GIS may well find the technology more naturally appealing than a social theorist or a geosociologist might. This is only because they are more likely to be computer oriented. However, the potential of AI embraces all areas of geography; indeed it may well be that the greatest short-term benefits may be most readily gained in the soft, non-quantitative and computer-free areas of geography that have so far largely escaped the computer. Some AI tools significantly extend the domain of computation as a practical basis for doing geography. This is very important and the hysterical shrieks of the soft geographers when confronted with this suggestion should in no way be allowed to distract from the evident potential opportunities that a more sober reflection would undoubtedly reveal.

Q   Computation appears to be the power behind AI, is that so?

A   Yes. In AI we often try to gain intelligence via computation. However, number crunching is seldom sufficient by itself since it is only by the incorporation of knowledge of one kind or another that adds significant amounts of extra intelligence.

Q   AI is hyped-up technology whose potential and performance have been so greatly exaggerated that its failure to actually deliver anything has, somehow, been ignored. Do you agree?

A   Yes and no! Of course AI cannot and does not seek to replace overnight a lifetime of hard earned understanding of some horribly complex geographical phenomenon. It is also, just like everything else the geographers have ever used, likely to be overvalued and misused by at least *some* of its practitioners. These problems are not unique to AI. The potential, however it may appear to be exaggerated, is nevertheless real and moreover is within reach. It is not a question of *if* but *when*. As for failing to deliver anything useful, that is a matter for debate. It is also a matter of scale, and of significance. Maybe we should let future historians judge what the AI revolution achieved, but then of course the historians may well be prejudiced in favour of their fellow machines!

Q   Where does the intelligence in AI really come from? What different types are there?

A   There are at least three types:

1. Results-based intelligence. This might best be seen in the exclamation "Hi. I didn't know that. That's interesting, isn't it? Wow", etc.;
2. Machine intelligence in which the intelligence results from the behaviour of a machine running more or less under its own control;
3. Algorithmic intelligence, a technique or computer procedure suddenly works better and more efficiently as a result of being programmed to be intelligent. For example, adaptive methods that self-optimise; a clever spatial search method, such as a quadtree.

Ultimately it is likely to be the second type of intelligence, perhaps because of the third type, that promises most for the future. Meanwhile, the short-term evaluation of AI will depend initially on the first type.

Q   Will there ever be a general purpose intelligent supergeography machine?

A   Probably one day but not for a long while. Right now attention is probably best focused on getting started on particular tasks such as improved models of spatial systems, space-time forecasting of important spatial data, better exploratory data analysis tools, etc. The short-term aim is more likely to be restricted to adding smart spatial analysis buttons to GIS; for example, click here to find evidence of localised clustering or click here and a spatial model is built for you.

Q   I have heard much about the internet; is it possible to teach oneself AI via exploring the World Wide Web (WWW) and network subject lists?

A   Yes. There is a vast amount of text, software, and information available to you. Explore it and who knows what you may find, or where it exists. The WWW is changing extremely rapidly. However, you will probably need to be strongly focused on what it is you want. So some preliminary knowledge, gained from reading a book like this, might provide an extremely useful starter.

Q   OK, I am convinced but what sort of questions on AI could you possible ask geographers and what sort of course structure would you develop?

A   One way of answering the question is briefly to describe the introduction to the use of AI in geography module that has been run in the School of Geography at Leeds since 1993. See Appendix 1.

APPENDIX 1 STRUCTURE OF THE INTRODUCTION TO THE AI COURSE IN THE SCHOOL OF GEOGRAPHY, UNIVERSITY OF LEEDS

The most difficult task is persuading either third-year undergraduates or postgraduates that the subject is not hard, that it does not require vast amounts of computer expertise and a high level of statistical knowledge. Most geographers in most departments of geography merely want to attain good grades for a modest amount of effort. By the time they reach a state in their courses where AI is on offer, many probably have painful memories of compulsory statistical practicals, of being bombarded with partly understood statistical theory, and of struggling with statistical packages that whilst easy to use usually have fairly long learning curves. When faced with subsequent course choices that appear easy, non-complex, and descriptive (e.g. Peasant life in the Southern Andes or Women in Barbados, or the Music of K.D. Lang), you will not get many volunteers for a course on AI. It is true, AI does hold a strong fascination **but** it also has the illusion of being hard! Also, many courses on the philosophy of geography often have the effect of persuading students that anything to do with the computer and quantitative geography is fatally flawed, probably evil, and no longer relevant. You need to counter these views by more balanced arguments perhaps along the lines that AI is good for your CV, it is not hard, it is exciting, it is innovative, and it is relevant to geography. Posters, pictures, seminars, etc. of AI being used all help. With time, these acceptance problems will diminish.

The course outline used at Leeds reflects 11 weeks of 2-hour lectures with associated computer demonstrations and assessed work. It is designed to fascinate, to excite, to give many geographical examples, and generally to retain student interest. It works, if only because most students do extremely well (marks wise) although this may well reflect the self-selection process. As AI becomes more visible in earlier years then interest might be expected to snowball, particularly in physical geography where the students are still expected to perform mathematical modelling and therefore will find many areas of AI both relevant and fairly easy (compared with what they have already experienced).

The structure reflects one persons view of those areas of AI most likely to be of interest to geographers. It also reflects the contents of this book which originated as a course text for this module.

Objectives of module

On completion of the module students will be able to demonstrate:
  (i) an understanding of the current and potential uses of AI in geographical study;
 (ii) an understanding of the technologies of AI;
(iii) skills in the use of software related to the principal areas of AI;
(iv) an understanding of the conceptual and methodological issues inherent in the production of computational geographical knowledge.

Outline syllabus

1–2 Introduction to AI in geography
  3 Heuristic search and exploratory geography

4 Expert systems and intelligent knowledge-based geographical systems
5 Neurocomputing principles
6 Supervised neural modelling
7 Unsupervised neural nets
8 Genetic algorithms
9 Artificial life with spatial analysis applications
10 Fuzzy logic modelling
11 Computational geography and computational intelligence

Form of teaching

Lectures 12 × 2 hours and includes computer demonstrations, computer-aided learning, and short projects.

Examples of past examination questions

1. *Either* Discuss the various definitions of artificial intelligence. Which one do you prefer?
   Or "AI is not having much impact on geography as yet." Why?
2. Describe the search methods used in the geographical analysis machine. How might they be improved?
3. What is neurocomputing and why is it attracting so much interest?
4. *Either* What is the genetic algorithm? Describe and comment on two geographical applications.
   Or What is artificial life? Some consider this to be extremely useful in geographical analysis. Why?
5. What is a smart system? How would you go about building one?
6. *Either* What is meant by brute-force search? Illustrate your answer by reference to geographical cxamples.
   Or "It is possible to become smarter by becoming cruder in approach"? Discuss.
7. "Expert systems promised much but delivered little." What are expert systems? Discuss this assessment of their usefulness in geographical contexts.

REFERENCES

Aleksander, I., Burnett, R., 1987, *Thinking Machines: the search for artificial intelligence*. Oxford University Press, Oxford.

Brain, K., Brain, S., 1984, *Artificial Intelligence on the Spectrum Computer: make your micro think*. Sunshine Books, London.

Feigenbaum, E.A., Feldman, J., 1963, *Computers and Thought*. McGraw-Hill, New York.

Firebaugh, M.W., 1988, *Artificial Intelligence: a knowledge based approach*. PWS Kent, Boston.

Forsyth, R., Naylor, C., 1985, *The Hitch-Hiker's Guide to Artificial Intelligence*. Chapman and Hall, London.

Hasemer, T., Domingue, J., 1989, *Common LISP Programming for Artificial Intelligence*. Addison-Wesley, Reading, Mass.

Hewitson, B.C., Crane, R.G., 1994, *Neural Nets: applications in geography*. Kluwer Academic Publishers, Dordrecht.

Hillis, W D., 1985, *The Connection Machine*. MIT Press, Cambridge, Mass.

Jackson, P.C., 1985, *Introduction to Artificial Intelligence*. Dover Publications, New York.

Kosko, B., 1994, *Fuzzy Thinking*. Harper Collins, London.

Michie, D., 1988, "Foreword", in M.W. Firebaugh, *Artificial Intelligence*. PWS Kent, Boston, Mass., p. xxii–xxiv.

Mickie, D. and Johnston, R., 1985, *The Creative Computer*. Penguin Books, London.

Minsky, M. (ed.), 1968, *Semantic Information Processing*. MIT Press, Cambridge, Mass.

Openshaw, S., 1991, "A view on the GIS crisis in geography or using GIS to put Humpty-Dumpty back together again", *Environment and Planning A*, **23**, 621–628.

Openshaw, S., 1992, "Further thoughts on geography and GIS: a reply", *Environment and Planning A*, **24**, 463–466.

Openshaw, S., 1994a, "GIS crime and spatial analysis", *Proceedings of GIS and Public Policy Conference*, Ulster Business School, Ulster, pp. 22–35.

Openshaw, S., 1994b, "Computational human geography: exploring the geocyberspace", *Leeds Review*, **37**, 201–220.

Openshaw, S., 1994c, "Computational human geography: towards a research agenda", *Environment and Planning A*, **26**, 499–505.

Openshaw, S., 1994d, "Artificial intelligence and geography", *AISB Quarterly*, **90**, 18–21.

Openshaw, S., 1995, "Human systems modelling as a new grand challenge area in science", *Environment and Planning A*, **27**, 159–164.

Openshaw, S., 1996, "Parallel supercomputing applications in GIS", in *Proceedings of Joint European Conference and Exhibition on Geographical Information*. IOS Press, Amsterdam, pp. 661–670.

Pickles, J. (ed.), 1995, *Ground Truth*. Guildford Press, London.

Schildt, H., 1987, *Artificial Intelligence Using C*. McGraw-Hill, Berkeley.

Shirai, Y., Tsujii, J., 1982, *Artificial Intelligence: concepts, techniques and applications*. Wiley, New York.

Sloman, A., 1991, "A personal view of artificial intelligence", in M. Sharples, D. Hogg, C. Hutchison, S. Torrance, D. Young (eds), *Computers and Thought*. MIT Press, Cambridge, Mass., pp. ix–xxix.

Smith, T. R., 1984, Artificial intelligence and its applicability to geographical problem solving, *Professional Geographer*, **12**, 147–158.

Turing, A.M., 1950, "Computing machinery and intelligence", *Mind*, LIX, no. 236, reprinted in D.R. Hofstadter and D.C. Dennett, 1981, *The Mind's I*. Bantam Books, New York, pp. 53–68.

Winston, P.H., 1992, *Artificial Intelligence*. Addison-Wesley, Reading, Mass.

Zadeh, L.A., 1993, "The role of fuzzy logic and soft computing in the conception and design of intelligent systems", in E.P. Klement and W. Slany (eds), *Fuzzy Logic and Artificial Intelligence*. Springer-Verlag, Berlin, p. 1.

CHAPTER 2

A Brief History of Artificial Intelligence

This chapter provides a short introduction to the history of AI. It is always useful to see where new developments such as AI come from. An understanding of history puts the development of AI into context. This may help geographers avoid repeating some of the mistakes made by others in the AI area and also help identify where the major opportunities for AI applications in geography lie. Moreover, this historical perspective may help you avoid adopting an unduly narrow perspective of what AI is and what it does. At different points in history different flavours of AI were fashionable. Advocates tended to view AI only in terms of their flavour of AI. For example, there is the strange notion that AI is expert systems and nothing else; a view that was quite fashionable in the 1980s. So be careful, different AI textbooks often tend to view AI as being a different subset of tools and ideas. Geographers would do well to adopt the broadest possible definition and see AI as covering an extremely wide range of different, diverse, and often totally unrelated techniques. However, underlying this diversity is a common dream, that of developing smart and adaptive computer-based technologies that might be useful in various applied contexts. There is clearly more than one way of achieving this goal and the history of AI bears ample testimony to a rich diversity of ideas and technologies that are relevant.

2.1 HISTORICAL OVERVIEW

For convenience, let us ignore the first 2000 years with its legend of Pygmalion, talking heads, and Frankenstein-like monsters (Corduck, 1979). The history of AI is both colourful and turbulent. Many of the key developments have not been smooth. Typically each innovation has been characterised by surges of enthusiasm followed by waves of recrimination as few of the developments in the short term have lived up to their early expectations or even fulfilled most of what was once promised. However, AI is now much more mature and viable tools do exist. The extravagances of past claims are now moderated by an ever-increasing track record of successes. Make no mistake, AI works; the hard part is discovering how best to make it work for you!

A highly simplified, historical summary is given in Table 2.1. A number of

Table 2.1   A simplified historical summary of AI developments

Decade	Major focus/development
Pre 1930	Sci-fi writing and mechanical swans
1930s, 1940s	Theoretical speculation
1950s	Primitive neural networks
1960s	Heuristic search
1970s	Expert systems
1980s	Neurocomputing, genetic algorithms, and artificial life
1990s	Genetic programming, fuzzy logic, and hybrid intelligent systems

periods of AI fashions can be identified. It is important to note, however, that the periods overlap and do not form a simple linear sequence of decade-specific developments. Nor has all the knowledge been lost as one wave of fashion swept away the preceding one. In each era different people tended to be involved. The advocates of previous outmoded fashions often still continued their researches. In many ways the AI enthusiast of the mid 1990s and beyond would do well not to specialise in any single one of these areas but in several of the more promising ones. The latest developments in intelligent computer systems are emphasising the importance of mixtures of techniques and hybrid technologies. Fortunately, geographers and social scientists are mainly active and potential users of AI rather than developers. We do not have to know how to create new AI tools or attempt to reach the current frontiers of AI research. Our challenge is different and not nearly as difficult. We merely have to discover how best to apply and exploit those tools that already exist and seemingly work so well in many other areas of application. It is true that this involves understanding the technology well enough to spot the opportunities for applying it and for avoiding misuse. However, and this is the key to believing that AI technologies are well within the reach of the average geographer, the depth of understanding needed to develop viable AI-based applications is much more easily acquired and is much less technically complex than that needed to develop completely new AI tools from first principles.

2.2 THE EARLY YEARS, 1930s AND 1940s

Speculations as to the possibility of a mechanical intelligence have been made by many people; for instance, Turing (1936) in his theory of computable numbers; Von Neumann in 1948 with the first modern computer; and Wiener (1948) defining cybernetics as an entire field of control and communication theory whether in machine or in the animal. The idea of putting together hardware and control programs to create new thinking entities, artificially intelligent machines that could potentially rival human beings, was and still is extremely attractive. Many extremely interesting theoretical ideas were presented and discussed. However, experimental research did not start until electronic digital computers became generally available in the 1950s. Turing argued that one day machines might be able to think, as human intelligence must be a computable process and that the brain functions as a type of computer. This line of thinking reasons that since it is the program that provides the computer with intelligence, so we need to model and understand intelligence in order to program machines to be intelligent. This was or maybe still is a key belief in some areas of AI. So an early objective in AI was to develop machines able to display general intelligence. However, Turing also argued that maybe it was easier to teach a machine to do something specific rather than attempt to program into it human being levels of intelligence. Indeed it is interesting that nearly all the recent successes of AI have occurred when attention has been focused on mimicking intelligent behaviour in narrowly focused and highly specific areas of application. The early visions of the general purpose artificially intelligent machine is still a dream and its practical realisation is still probably 50–100 years away. This is not what AI is currently about; or at least that is not what we would want from it in a geographical context. Fortunately, there is no need to wait. There is much that already exists and is ready to use; so lets get on with it!

2.3 THE FIRST NEURAL NETS ERA: 1950–70

McCulloch and Pitts (1943) describe an artificial neural net modelled loosely on the supposed workings of the human brain. They worked on the frog's visual system. The basic assumption was that the brain was a very effective problem solver so they endeavoured to simulate a brain. Hardly revolutionary, but nevertheless emulating the supposed functioning of the brain has proved to be a major source of inspiration. Indeed it is very noticeable that much of AI can claim to be biologically inspired. However, it was not just the brain that has been a source of inspiration but many other aspects of biological systems, particularly the mechanisms whereby species evolve and adapt to their environments, although these developments came much later.

McCulloch and Pitts might be regarded as stirring up many different scientific imaginations at a time when the technology needed to build synthetic neurocomputers simply did not exist. However, this has never stopped the real pioneers. For example, Edmund and Minsky built an electromechanical learning machine in the early 1950s that sought to simulate rudimentary brain-like behaviour using clutches and pulleys! Do not laugh; remember the Babbage mechanical computer of the mid nineteenth century was the forerunner by over a century of the modern computer. What can be done with cogs and wheels and pulleys can also be done with electronic hardware and software. The ideas are often far more important (initially) than the technology used to operationalise them. So this electromechanical learning machine was clearly well advanced for its era. Equally futuristic was Rosenblatt's (1958). The PERCEPTRON was an electronic brain that could be taught to recognise simple patterns. It was a self-organising automaton based on a very crude model of the retina in the human eye.

Nevertheless, the PERCEPTRON engendered considerable enthusiasm. It was widely thought that a richly interconnected system of artificial neurons could start by knowing nothing, be trained, and end with the capacity of being able to do almost anything. Unfortunately, the fact that the human brain contains about 10 billion neurons, not a mere 16 or so, was completely overlooked and that even with today's hardware, it is still not possible to model all aspects of even an ant's nervous system adequately. Back in the 1950s, the primitive valve-based analogue circuitry and primitive digital computers were much too slow, the available software tools were far too rudimentary, and even the Fortran compiler had just been invented! It was a period of massive false optimism completely unsupported by empirical reality or anything resembling or recognisable as modern computing technology. The fact that the technology actually worked to some limited extent was quite astounding! It was also a period of fundamental questions. For instance, can a computer be programmed to program itself? Questions that can only now in fact be answered.

Nevertheless some very important legacies date from this period. Indeed the term "AI" was seemingly first used in 1955 and is attributed to McCarthy. Several computing terms also reflect this early period; for example, the term "electronic brain" is sometimes used instead of "computer"; and the term computer "memory" is still widely used for "storage". However, this first neural nets era ended more or less abruptly in 1969 after it was proven in a seemingly rigorous manner that the perceptron was useless as a practical tool because it was unable to solve an extremely simple problem (Minsky and Papert, 1969). The impression was given that this meant that neural networks would never be able to do anything really significant; a wholly erroneous and perhaps mischievous view that reflected a desire to change the direction of AI towards expert systems. It was not until major developments in microprocessors that the neural network paradigm was revived in the mid 1980s. In the more advanced computing environments the problems of the 1950s neural networks were speedily and easily overcome and the criticisms refuted. However, back in the 1960s the failure of the perceptron caused much general disillusionment with AI because of the high expectations that it had created. In fact it very nearly killed off the entire area; indeed, a UK government's Lighthill Report (1973) recommended phasing out the AI research programme in 1973. In the USA the situation was not quite so bad. The USA has always been more supportive of AI and indeed their researchers are seemingly better at performing "off the wall" research than Europeans. Maybe there is a West Coast factor here! More significant to its future, there was also a major military imperative in the USA that supported much AI research activity at that time, albeit often disguised as something else. The now discredited words such as neural networks were not often used and terms such as associative computer memories were substituted instead!

2.4 HEURISTIC SEARCH IN THE 1960s AND 1970s

As computer hardware improved from the late 1950s onwards so an enthusiasm developed for what might be broadly termed heuristic search methods. During the 1960s there was a popular belief that computers with the general intelligence levels of humans could soon be developed via the creation of systems capable of playing chess or solving mathematical puzzles (Minsky, 1961). Human intelligence was thought to involve symbolic manipulation as found in searching and comparing; tasks that computers could also perform. Problem solving (and thus, intelligence) was regarded as equivalent to a search through a space of possible solutions guided by some heuristic rules. This is still a highly relevant idea that underpins many machine-based attempts at scientific discovery and database exploration, for instance data mining. However, in the 1960s it was soon realised that this objective of building general purpose intelligence via heuristic search methods was far harder than was originally anticipated. Again, there was considerable misplaced optimism! Nevertheless some progress was made. Many of the heuristic search methods that were devised were problem independent and reasonably "intelligent". Ernst and Newell's (1969) general problem solver (GPS) could solve puzzles with well-defined rules, but it could not solve any real-world problems. For example, "Has this person got the flu or measles?" This apparent inability to be real-world useful led to another change of emphasis.

From a geographical perspective this heuristic search era is more interesting for the search algorithms that it produced (and continues to produce or stimulate) than for its attempts to create GPS-type systems or master-level chess-playing software. Many problems in geography can be viewed as search problems so in principle at least some of the AI technology from this period is relevant.

2.5 KNOWLEDGE-BASED SYSTEMS, 1960–1980s

By the mid 1970s the early hopes that AI would soon provide the world with general purpose thinking machines had more or less totally evaporated. As a result, there was a return to the more basic problem of modelling human reasoning and of the representation of knowledge. However, pessimism changed to optimism when it was realised that many commercially important applications are sufficiently constrained micro worlds to be amenable to rules-based reasoning relevant to task-specific rather than general purpose intelligence. Computers could become more intelligent by building knowledge bases to complement databases. The result was two decades of expert systems work.

Expert systems represent a very different approach to modelling or attempting to replicate the processes of human intelligence. Human experts seem to use a large number of rules of thumb, based on knowledge and experience that are relevant to a specific function. Expert systems were developed to operationalise this model of intelligence and it was soon realised that computers could actually display intelligent behaviour if the domain in which they worked was sufficiently restricted. This is also the first phase in the commercialisation of AI.

In the early 1980s these so-called intelligent knowledge-based systems (IKBS) became extremely fashionable. There were a number of examples that more or less worked. The best known include: DENDRAL (1967) which interprets mass spectrograms; MYCIN (1974)—a medical diagnosis system; and PROSPECTOR (1978)—a geological prospecting system. These systems, often developed by postgraduate students, encoded knowledge as production rules to which simple reasoning procedures were applied. These rules represent the knowledge of experts! They work inasmuch as they can emulate human experts in situations which are rules based and for which the rules can be accurately and unambiguously defined. Please note that knowledge in the form of these rules is the key ingredient but it is very hard to capture. Many experts have no clear rule sets they use, and if they have, they find it hard to download them to the knowledge engineer. Expert systems are an extremely attractive and seductive technology that was (and probably still is) fundamentally flawed. It was attractive because the idea of packaging *experts* in computer form is so appealing. They also offer the user the opportunity to act like an expert without being one or even having to understand much that is going on in the domain of interest. As a result it attracted considerable funding in the 1980s but it too was grossly oversold. At that time it was often described as the technology that would take over from humans, that would absorb the expertise of many blue- and white-collar workers, run offices and workshops, and pave the way for a new knowledge-based revolution in society. It seemed the answer to skill shortages, and it appeared to be a good way of saving lifelong skills and experiences. However, as prototype system after prototype system so amply demonstrated, the appeal of the idea nearly always far outstripped what the technology could actually deliver in the form of finished systems that were useful in solving actual real-world problems in operational environments. Nevertheless, expert systems do exist and continue to flourish albeit in a restrained way. The technology is fundamentally flawed because ultimately much more is expected from AI than at best the replication of some of the skills of human experts. In the social sciences the real problem is not the absence of experts but the lack of superintelligent experts able to outperform the current best experts on many of the hard problems that need to be handled and solved. In many ways the real need is for superintelligent rather merely humanly intelligent expert systems.

A major contributing factor in the apparent success of expert systems and which engendered considerable enthusiasm for IKBS was fear of Japan's Fifth-Generation Computing Initiative. It was argued that computers designed for the IT era needed to be able to process and handle knowledge; not just data or numbers but soft information. The Japanese objective was to define and develop a new type of computer system for the 1990s with a view to dominating world computer markets. Work started in 1982 and it was widely seen as a major competitive industrial and economic threat. It stimulated a major burst of new research funding for this type of AI. In the UK, the Alvey Report (1982) identified four areas of research: software engineering, VLSI (very large-scale integration), IKBS, and MMI (man–machine interface). The European response ESPRIT (European Strategic Programme for Research in Information Technology) quickly followed. However, as before in AI, pessimism soon set in and there emerged major doubts about whether IKBS was a successful technology. These doubts coincided with a revival of neural computing as a viable tool. As a result in the late 1980s and in the 1990s the definition of IKBS has been broadened to encompass neurocomputing and any other forms of machine learning and thus avoids being linked only with expert systems. So IKBS in the broadest sense is not tied to any one form of AI and it continues to flourish. In the guise of fuzzy logic modelling the rule-of-thumb-based notions of expert systems have made a comeback but in a totally different form. Similarly, the use of genetic algorithms and other machine-based learning procedures have resulted in new types of self-optimising and self-training IKBS. There is at last some hope of superintelligent IKBS (SIKBS) emerging at least in the context of specific applications.

2.6 NEURAL NETS 2: 1986 ONWARDS

These doubts about expert system based IKBS coincided with a revival in fortunes of machine learning in general and neural nets in particular. The previous perceptron problems were solved by the mid 1980s. In the USA, the Department of Defense identified neural computing as a high priority strategic technology, probably for missile guidance systems. In addition there has been a new burst of interest and enthusiasm in many countries since the mid 1980s. This was driven partly by hardware developments (in particular the universal availability of powerful but cheap PCs), partly by the many examples of practical and commercial usefulness, and partly by a realisation that neurocomputing was a significant advance that has many practical applications in many different areas. A demonstration of a neural network (NETtalk) being trained to speak convinced many of its potential power. Neurocomputing is very important also because it extends the scope of computing into many soft areas that were previously regarded as being outside the domain of conventional computer modelling and analysis. Its innate abilities to handle noisy (or uncertain) data as well as chaotic nonlinear relationships are also extremely important. Both these features make neurocomputing of considerable attraction to geographers. Indeed, without doubt, neurocomputing is now widely seen as being that bit of AI which is now most immediately relevant to geography. There are many potential applications and there is even a basis here for a whole new geographical modelling and analysis revolution.

2.7 EVOLUTIONARY PROGRAMMING AND ARTIFICIAL LIFE

It is important to realise that neurocomputing is not the totality of AI that is relevant to geography. Neither is it necessarily the most useful! There are other areas of machine learning that are highly significant and potentially very important. There is now considerable interest and enthusiasm for genetic algorithms, artificial life, and evolutionary computing. Since the mid 1970s it has been known that intelligent behaviour in machines can be created by artificially simulating the biological process of natural selection (Holland, 1975). This analogy can be used directly to solve complex optimisation problems as well as to build artificial life forms that exist as autonomous agents dedicated to solving problems. However, what is more important to geography is that these powerful tools can be readily used to develop new approaches to many existing geographical problems, for example in developing better locational optimisation procedures or as the basis for creating better performing models of urban systems or as the search mechanisms in exploratory spatial data analysis systems. This, and not neurocomputing, is probably where the greatest potential for AI in geography now lies. It provides a means of creating autonomous smart systems that can be designed to tackle many problems via a bottom-up route.

2.8 FUZZY LOGIC AND HYBRID INTELLIGENT SYSTEMS

Finally the 1990s are also a time where a technology invented a quarter of a century earlier is suddenly the most widely used of all AI methods. Fuzzy logic control systems are appearing in more and more consumer and industrial products. Fuzzy logic also provides an alternative paradigm for doing science that is particularly appropriate for areas of human geography and the social sciences where the normal science paradigm has always proved difficult to implement and inadequate; see Openshaw (1996) for a review. Furthermore, in common with neural networks, this is a nonlinear modelling technology. It is widely used in industry but as yet there are hardly any geographical applications of it. Fuzzy logic provides yet another framework for redoing, rethinking and re-expressing most of the conventional modelling and statistical applications of geography. Finally, when fuzzy logic is combined with neural networks and/or genetic algorithms, there is a basis for a whole new generation of advanced intelligent hybrid systems. The principal features of these new systems are nonlinearity, adaptiveness and an ability to combine what knowledge exists with machine-based methods to develop any new knowledge which is needed but is missing.

Clearly, there is a mass of AI riches all around us. In many ways we are spoilt for choice and there is no need to be too selective or too prescriptive. It is much too soon for that. The history of AI, like that of geography, is dominated by fashions that change at fairly frequent intervals. Each new fashion has left behind a toolkit that, rather than being discarded when it goes out of fashion, can be used to tackle appropriate geographical problems. Geographers do not need to keep up with the AI fashion world but merely identify the mature and stable bits that work, that look as if they might be useful, and leave others to investigate the many good ideas that are still only good ideas rather than the basis for applicable technology. Geographers could, if they wished, seek to innovate and add to the riches of the AI world; however, they might be much better employed by seeking to use AI to the greatest possible effects within the world of geography with which they are most familiar.

2.9 INTO AN AI-RICH AND INCREASINGLY AI-DEPENDENT FUTURE

A US Office of Technology Assessment (1986) report declared that by the middle of the twenty-first century there would be few fundamental barriers for machine intelligence left and thus over the long term, intelligent machines would meet or surpass humans in most cognitive skills. Such forecasts have been made before and have so far always been proven to be wrong, but maybe this view needs to be taken more seriously since the idea of "thinking machines" is simultaneously both fascinating and repulsive. Yet it is still only a matter of time before they become commonplace. Some believe that the most profound contribution to society that results from attempts to build thinking machines is a greater appreciation of human intelligence particularly the uniqueness and power of the human mind. However, AI will eventually succeed and extend the scope and domain of our thinking machines not as substitutes for ourselves, but as intelligent aids able to greatly expand the power of our own capabilities and intelligences.

Chorafas (1989: 248, 249) adds the comments:

> Without AI enrichment, the incredible shrinking computer chip remains unconscious and impotent, in spite of its internal processing capabilities. Learning machines are the new frontiers in AI.

and

> By the year 2000, there will be available a machine of nearly human complexity: the android brain.

Who is to say now that this will not happen sometime in the next century even if 2000 is perhaps a little too early? However, building a machine that is as complex and intricate as the human brain does not mean that it will possess any of the features of the human brain. Building smaller and faster computer chips and then packaging them in a massively parallel form would without doubt be extremely useful as the basis for extremely high performance computers, but without the algorithms, the AI tools to run on them, and the understanding of intelligence needed to create real artificial intelligences, what use will that be? Only when we can start building real general purpose intelligence systems will the benefits of smaller and faster computer hardware become a critical component. At present we are seemingly much further along the computer hardware route than the intelligence route. Is it really likely that if we could build a neural network with a neuronal density equivalent to that found in mammalian life forms we will have created an intelligent machine? We doubt it. Perhaps the most profound contribution to society resulting from attempts to build thinking machines will be a greater appreciation of the brilliance and complexity of the human mind itself. Maybe it is easy to agree with Sharples et al (1989: 316) when they write:

> When we do achieve the first great successes in artificial intelligence, when we can regard an automaton as a trusted friend and mentor, when we can entrust a machine to enrich our culture through song, dance and literature, then we will have learned vastly more about our own strengths and limitations.

Maybe as geographers it is best to overlook the more pompous human intelligence perspectives of AI, forget the emotional aspects, and concentrate on using AI methods to improve the geography that can be done in our lifetime. We have more than enough to do by just achieving that much! Indeed, as Aleksander and Burnett (1987: 202) note:

> What we should be looking forward to is not the day when machines start to treat us as pets, but a time when they will have become sufficiently intelligent to make it worthwhile for potential users to give them house room.

For geographers that time is the present!

An important driving factor now in the continued development of AI is increasing computer speeds. AI is essentially an attempt to compute our way out of our problems using smart and adaptive methods that nevertheless in part owe their level of smartness to the computer power available to them. Faster, cheaper, interconnected, and widely distributed computers are everywhere, and these developments are continuing at a rapid pace. Indeed, more dramatic jumps in machine speeds are predicted for the next few years. Much of AI is still computer-speed dependent, as it seeks to compute its way towards higher levels of machine intelligence. It is interesting to note then that the remaining barriers are about to be removed but that at present very little high performance compute time is being devoted to AI applications. Table 2.2 outlines some of these changes as the computer world undergoes a major technological transformation brought about by the emergence of various generations of parallel supercomputing.

It is likely that we shall have to rely on AI more and more to handle our

Table 2.2   Increasing machine speeds by date

Year	Speed (megaflops)
1980	60
1992	1 200
1994	36 000
1996	150 000
1998?	2 500 000

Note: a megaflop = 1 million floating point operations per second. A 486 PC can probably manage about 1 megaflop.

problems and the critical factor is the availability of proven methods that work. The question is not *if* but *when*. It seems that most short-term successful applications of AI are likely to be small in scale but broad in range (Sharples et al, 1989). Most plausible geographical applications fit in well with their multiple different but highly focused, separate, application themes.

Finally, it is probably also worth noting that the future of AI is not totally in the hands of the AI researchers but is also related to underlying global developments in economic and political decentralisation, the degree of thirst for computer-provided knowledge, the need for new and more powerful technological fixes to the world's ever-worsening problems, or conversely a rejection of the information society.

2.10 WHAT MIGHT GEOGRAPHERS EXPECT FROM AI?

It needs to be recognised that AI is prone to hype. Its advocates are full of enthusiasm and excitement and this can readily lead to exaggerated claims about performance and benefits. Maybe the potential will always outstrip practical reality but at the same time what is now possible in practice is quite astonishing and is more than sufficient to justify major geographical investments in the technology. Currently, there is an increasing concern that geographers have simply failed to notice the ongoing developments in AI that are relevant to their discipline.

Artificial intelligence consists of a set of tools with which we can try to build intelligent systems in our areas of interest. The key geographical questions are as follows:

1. What is it that we can now do much better using AI than traditional methods?
2. What hitherto unsolved problems can now be solved by using AI?
3. How do we rethink what we do as geographers to exploit AI?
4. What new approaches to geographical study does AI make possible that had not previously been considered?
5. How do we go about exploiting and exploring the potential of AI for geography and geographers?

These questions are not just relevant to the quantitative specialisms and GIS but encompass *all* of geography.

Some of the major geographical expectations from AI probably include:

1. more creative exploratory analysis of GIS and mappable databases with new insights and new knowledge
2. new theory about geographic systems created by machine
3. better fitting process models
4. new approaches to building geographical models of spatial systems; and even
5. a new perspective of geography itself

AI fosters the emergence of a new style of computational geography. The basic idea is to use large-scale computing to handle fundamental problems of geographical description and analysis. Computationally intensive approaches are well established in theoretical physics, chemistry, biology; so why not geography as well? GIS provides a data rich environment in which to operate and also provides an important applied context. AI offers the tools that could be used to create new paradigms, new ways forward, new horizons, and the basis for a new beginning. If we put all the ingredients together—GIS databases, massively parallel computer resources, and AI tools, is this not the beginning of a new geography? (Openshaw, 1994a). Alternatively, does it mark the beginnings of a new superdiscipline that is IT based and encompasses the domain of both geography and the social sciences?

To recap, AI might be simply defined as being any computational method that either uses knowledge in the broadest sense or algorithms or computational power to add a degree of AI or smartness of a non-deterministic sort to applications and problem solving that previously lacked it. This is seen as encompassing both complete toolkits (viz. expert systems software and neurocomputing packages) as well as the algorithms and principles that are employed in these and other attempts at machine intelligence. The aim is to become smarter by using either computational or algorithmic or knowledge-based techniques to tackle the problems of geography. This technology is of considerable potential importance to geography for a number of reasons that have already been discussed.

2.11 PRINCIPAL GEOGRAPHICAL APPLICATIONS OF ARTIFICIAL INTELLIGENCE

Openshaw (1992, 1994b) provides a broad overview of existing and potential AI applications relevant to geography. This provides a useful starting point for describing the types of applications where AI is thought likely to have most to offer; see also Table 2.3. These generic applications can be divided into four broad types:

1. Existing uses of AI technologies
2. Those computer applications in which AI readily provides a plug-in complement or alternative to existing quantitative and mathematical modelling methods;
3. Potential applications of AI methods that have been shown to provide useful tools in comparable situations in other disciplines; and
4. Highly speculative applications of a new kind not previously seen but which seem to offer sufficient potential benefits in the future to justify the costs and risks involved.

There are a number of existing examples of AI being used in geography. In both GIS and remote sensing spatial information systems it is not unusual for expert

Table 2.3   Major AI themes of geographical interest

- Heuristic search: location optimisation and spatial analysis, zone design
- Expert systems: interface design and package usage
- Neurocomputing: modelling spatial systems and as an assumption-free substitute for conventional statistical methods that typically do not work well on spatial data
- Evolutionary algorithms and programming: smart search, spatial analysis, locational optimisation, and model design
- Artificial life: new ways of exploring high-dimensional and multimetric geographic databases for patterns and processes of interest
- Robotic vision: handling of spatial objects to identify recurrent patterns as theories and concepts
- Fuzzy logic: to aid the modelling of soft systems and for new approaches to incorporating knowledge in analysis and modelling geographical systems
- Machine learning: to data mine some of the spatial data swamp that is rapidly engulfing geography and many other disciplines

---

systems to be used; or more commonly being suggested as of possible future value. In fact the traditional view of AI in geography is that of expert systems or rules-based knowledge engineering designed to automate either highly skilled tasks in cartography (such as map generalisation and name placement on maps) and planning (rules for selecting good locations in complex situations); see Chapter 4. The problem is that most of these tools do not exist in anything approaching a fully operational form as distinct from design specifications. The designs often look very good but they are seldom developed into live, working, and useful systems. The reasons of course relate to the open-ended nature of many of the applications and the difficulty in establishing relevant expert knowledge. In any case who really wants an AI system that can at best perform no better than the human expert? The problem in many areas of geography is not the shortage of experts but that there are no human experts good enough. The promise of AI has to be in developing intelligent systems capable of superhuman levels of performance; either by solving previously insoluble problems or outperforming systems previously dependent solely on human skills and knowledge.

The type 2 applications are much more useful from a practical point of view. It is now apparent that developments in neurocomputing, particularly in feed-forward back propagation networks (see Chapters 5 and 6), can provide a cost-effective and high performance replacement for much of the mathematical and statistical models that geographers have developed over the last 30 years. Most of the urban and regional systems (see Wilson, 1970, 1974; Batty, 1976; Wilson and Bennett, 1985 and many others) date from a time when computers were about 10^8 times slower than a 1995 workstation and spatial data were rare, with only small data sets being available offering very poor levels of spatial resolution and representation (Openshaw, 1995a). Most if not all of these models were developed as data free theoretical speculations using what would today be considered to be fairly primitive mathematical modelling methods in a largely data scarce environment. They could hardly be tested and their applied use relied more on faith than on empirical fact. By contrast, the 1990s are a time of massive data riches and in many ways the challenge is not just to feed vast amounts of spatial data into old models but also to use the data riches to create new model representations. Neurocomputing provides precisely this opportunity. Maybe the "old" models are still the best that are available, but maybe also neural net equivalents will soon provide far superior levels of performance and representation. Certainly, the small number of empirical comparisons that have so far been performed suggest that in applications where there are relevant data, and comparisons are possible, the new methods will almost certainly always triumph; see, for example, Openshaw (1993) and Fischer and Gopal (1993). However, such empirical demonstrations mark the beginning, not the end, of a new era in modelling urban and regional systems. The easy phase is over and the challenge is now the development of replacement modelling systems that not only perform well but which also contribute to the development of theoretical understanding.

Neurocomputing and fuzzy logic modelling provide the basis for revitalising many areas of urban and regional modelling by providing a superior means of modelling highly complex and chaotic spatial systems in a more efficient, flexible, and realistic fashion; this greatly simplifies the modeller's task and allows more time to be spent thinking about the geography of the problem and less about the complexity of the mathematics. Suddenly, it is becoming possible to take a giant step forward in areas which have been static for almost a quarter of a century, via a computational strategy that exploits both the increasingly available masses of data and increasingly fast computer hardware. (Openshaw, 1994a).

However, it is important that neurocomputing is kept in perspective and used for those problems that need it rather than those than can readily be solved via far simpler means. The problem is that neural net models are both high performers and potentially brittle. The black box nature of the technology renders it impervious to any simple interpretation; users need faith, backed up by some good validation results. The danger is that the neural net enthusiasm virus replaces common sense. One way of restoring sanity is always to seek to confront neural net models with more conventional alternatives and then use computational statistics and cross-model validation techniques to identify the best and "safest" performers. One easy way of achieving this goal of intelligent modelling is by creating modelling machines that routinely examine a range of alternative models and then select the best in the context of a particular data application and given specific user preferences about how performance is to be measured. The marketing machines of Openshaw (1994c, d) are of this type and offer another route towards building intelligent systems. One of these systems, the so-called intelligent geodemographic machine, evaluates its performance against various benchmarks and will detect when it is no longer safe to use. This fully automated system is designed to be locally optimal in the context of a specific application on particular data; it comes with the limited guarantee that it will be hard if not impossible to readily obtain better results.

It is also apparent that many statistical techniques can be replicated by neural networks; see Smith (1993). That is no great deal. The really important point is that there are many statistical modelling applications that can be performed by neural networks for which there is either no conventional statistical alternative or none that works as well; for example, nonlinear regression of complicated relationships, regression of qualitative data relationships, nonlinear spatial regression with spatial dependencies, regression with two or more dependent variables. Once applications move, as they should do, into modelling the dynamic behaviour of complex geographical systems there is probably no alternative to neurocomputing. Similarly, an unsupervised Kohonen neural net might well produce results equivalent to a more conventional classifier, but once the problems of classifying spatial data are included (i.e. geographically varying levels of data reliability, small number problems and place specific variable measurement noise) then there is no longer any conventional statistical alternative that is nearly as flexible in what it can do; see Openshaw (1994e) and Openshaw and Wymer (1995).

Furthermore, is it sensible to classify data ignoring in the process all the knowledge that exists about what results might be expected? Is it intelligent using a smart method to model data and yet not be able to include any of the knowledge that we have built up over the years? Many quantitative geographers simply relate better results to the use of better algorithms; in reality better results also require that good use is made of the knowledge that exists about what results to expect. Currently, in census classification research, none of the 50 years of accumulated knowledge on the nature of residential areas in cities is used. Maybe AI will eventually provide a means of incorporating it.

The third category of applications involve the use of AI algorithms and technologies as problem-solving tools. There is a wide range of algorithms developed largely or partly by the AI community which offer useful tools for problems within geography. Examples would include the following:

(a) Simulated annealing and tabu search optimisation methods that are resistant to multiple local optima to develop better spatial optimisation models. The zone design system of Openshaw and Rao (1995) uses a simulated annealing algorithm and tabu search to provide an efficient way of aggregating N small zones into M large zones to optimise some nonlinear function subject to restrictions imposed on the topology of the results. This is described further in Chapter 3.

(b) There are a number of heuristic search methods that can be used as an alternative to brute-force approaches that are potentially relevant to various optimisation and analysis problems in geography; see Chapter 3. For example, a brute-force search is used in the geographical analysis machine and the geographical correlates exploration machine of Openshaw et al

(1987, 1990). These methods seek to explore spatial data for localised pattern by looking everywhere in situations where the researcher had no a priori knowledge of where or when to look or even what to look for. As geographical databases increase in size and complexity so there is a major need for new types of spatial analysis technology able to explore data for patterns and relationships without being hindered either by lack of human knowledge or conversely by too much incorrect human knowledge.

(c) Genetic algorithms (GA) and genetic programming (GP) techniques promise to open up a vast Pandora's box of new approaches to many geographical problems; see Chapter 7. Currently the number of applications are few but there is likely to be a vast explosion of interest soon. One early example is the model breeding machine of Openshaw (1988) and more recently Turton et al (1996). They used GA and GP to explore the universe of possible mathematical models that can be generated from the available model pieces in the search for models that provide good (and potentially general useful) fits to multiple spatial data sets. If it works well, this offers a new approach to building a wide range of human systems models by an entirely different route. The problem at present might be the six to seven weeks of supercomputer time it would take to breed one set of models. Birkin et al (1995) report another application of GA to search for maximum profit retail sites. Clearly, there is considerable geographical potential for this very flexible technology.

(d) Another example is the use of artificial life to create autonomous spatial database-exploring creatures that are free to roam around databases for anything vaguely unusual; see Chapter 8. The unusualness that is being sought here is measured by statistical methods; a unique combination of the old and the new; see Openshaw (1995b, 1995c; Openshaw and Perrée, 1995, 1996). There are a vast number of spatial databases that exist but have yet to be exposed to any in-depth analysis.

(e) There are also many applications for machine learning methods to discover from data good rules that define relationships or discriminate between different areas. Database mining is in its infancy but in data-swamped subjects such as geography it is of fundamental future significance.

(f) There are many applications for fuzzy logic; see Chapter 9. The ability to become imprecise and to build useful computer systems based on soft knowledge is probably where right now the greatest instant gains may be made in many social sciences, once the power and benefits of the technology are more widely appreciated (Openshaw, 1996). It is a pity that many of the opportunities of being able to simulate the remarkable human ability of attaining imprecisely defined goals in a highly fuzzy situation is beyond the current knowledge base of most of the geographers and social scientists who would find it most useful. Those that still mumble about logical positivism and such things could do much worse than read Kosko (1994). Ideally, they also need to read and understand Yager et al (1987) and Zadeh (1993); sadly, that might well prove impossible. In some areas of geography, the AI revolution will have to come from outside, not within.

(g) Finally, there is a growing enthusiasm for hybrid systems based on a mixture of different approaches; for example, a spatial classification system that incorporates an unsupervised neural network based classifier with knowledge about potentially misclassified cases so that the system can be asked to reconsider them.

2.12 CONCLUSIONS

It might be argued that whilst the final category of highly speculative type 4 applications are potentially the most exciting from a research perspective and are where the greatest future gains may well lie. The other three categories are more advanced and the benefits can be obtained now with minimal risk and much effort. The promise here involves the large-scale and systematic exploitation of AI to re-engineer how geographers have done geography for the last 50 years or so. There are a number of exciting possibilities if only we would look for them. In fact virtually everywhere the educated AI eye looks in geography there will be applications for AI. For example, Openshaw (1994f) suggests that robotic vision techniques could be used to search for spatial concepts expressed as two- and three-dimensional patterns. He notes that the old geographers were able to identify idealised visual models of complex reality, expressing these models as theories and descriptions. Modern geographers have never had the technology able to do anything remotely as complex and most statistical methods operate by removing the spatial dimension completely. The cost is that the large-scale application of robotic vision techniques to search for commonly recurrent spatial objects, invariant to the distortions caused by scale, rotation, etc., will probably require teraflop hardware speeds; but there is no reason why the research cannot start now. That is just one application. Can you think of any others of interest in your area of geography?

It is likely that with a fairly modest investment of effort most geographers will be able to successfully apply many of the methods described in this book with only a very small risk of failure. Most of these applications will have a high prospect of being successful and there is a vast research agenda just lying there waiting for a start to be made. It would seem that almost wherever we care to look there are multiple actual, instant and potential applications for using AI in geography. Geographers would be most foolish not to try and exploit these new methods. In 100 years' time doubtlessly geographical historians will look back to the late twentieth century and wonder why the AI revolution was so long in coming.

2.13 QUESTIONS AND ANSWERS

Q   What is the easiest way of getting started in AI?
A   Use the internet and the WWW search engine. Type in some keywords and off
    you go.
Q   Why is AI so fascinating?

A   Probably because humanity feels lonely and wants there to be other
     intelligent systems on the planet which may act as advisors (and perhaps one
     day as friends). So if these intelligences are not naturally provided why not
     create them? Others might prefer a simpler explanation. With all the problems
     we have in the world today we need more intelligent technologies to help us
     cope.

Q   Why do some people refer to some of the different species of AI as if they are
     not really AI at all?

A   You should know this answer. It reflects the historical evolution of AI. For
     example, some AI researchers only regard expert systems as AI, especially if
     they are expert at building expert systems. Some regard artificial life as
     theoretical biology! Well maybe it is, *but* it is also the source of considerable
     inspiration in the development of artificially intelligent machines. Do not be
     blinkered. Go for the broadest possible interpretation. AI technologies have
     something in common, namely the attempt to create intelligent and smart
     computer systems. It really does not matter how this is achieved, it is all AI by
     intent.

Q   Could smart machines take over the world economy?

A   Yes. It is already happening to a small degree with neural networks being
     used to run share-dealing systems and other AI technologies being used to
     detect fraud and manage foreign money exchange rates. The degree of
     penetration depends on a number of factors: the availability of AI tools that
     work better than other systems, on cost, on need, and on political controls.

Q   Could smart systems run our day-to-day lives?

A   Yes they already do and the extent of their activities will continue to increase.
     Air-conditioning systems, lifts, car electronics, washing machines, burglar
     alarms, cameras, TVs, video, etc. all contain some forms of AI.

Q   Could smart machines take over our world and colonise it at our expense?

A   Yes they could in theory; see Chapter 8 on artificial life. The idea of self-
     replicating machines is not new and is theoretically possible. Machine-based
     dry life that shares the principal features of wet (biological) life can be built.
     Whether they will ever colonise planets at our expense depends on techno-
     logical advances that have not yet been thought of, on a willingness (or
     clumsiness) by ourselves (really our children's children) to allow it to
     happen, or a catastrophe of unimaginable magnitude that make our survival
     dependent on it, or a mad dictator wishing to take over the world via it! It is all
     possible but probably not very likely. Meanwhile, lets make the most of what
     we have rather than criticise it for what it might, perhaps, one day be able to
     do.

Q   Are the risks of machine intelligence worth while?

A   Yes. AI is an intrinsically safe technology, compared with others we already
     have such as genetic engineering or nuclear weapons. AI like GIS is merely a
     toolkit and a way of thinking about problems. It is 99% a power of good; the
     remaining 1% that could be bad does not yet exist! There are some grounds
     for social concern, for example if medical decisions are made by machines.
     How can intelligent computer systems be built with human attributes such as
     compassion and affection? Well one day they will; we more or less know how
     in general it can be done! In many ways the real intelligent machine revolution

still lies in the future, maybe the key precursor development will be broad-band domestic communication networks! Meanwhile, lets use it in geography. Lets redo those bits of geography that matter most but have been hindered by the restrictions of the pre-AI technologies that we have had to use. Lets investigate those new applications where suddenly computer-based approaches using smart tools is a real possibility. Lets just do it and not worry about it. It is there to be used!

Q   Why do we need machine intelligence?

A   That is obvious. We constantly need to find better solutions to old problems, solutions to previously impossible problems, and solutions to problems that previously did not exist. The world we live in, this is true also of the internal micro-worlds of specific disciplines, is constantly becoming more complex. There is a high degree of dynamism. In many ways each year that passes increases the need for more intelligent technologies merely so that the status quo may be preserved.

Q   What does AI really mean for geography?

A   There will not be a dramatic revolution that starts at time A and finishes at time B. AI is not like that. Instead the number and range of the available tools applicable to geography will steadily increase. The number of beneficial applications will grow. The demonstrations of benefit will win over those who care to look and are not unthinking followers of narrowly blinkered paradigms. The harder the problems that geographers invent the stronger the attraction of AI. Undergraduate students may be relieved to know that the advent of superintelligent AI toolkits might allow them to spend more time doing real geography rather than learning about the tools they would use if there was any time left after the training process to do any geography.

REFERENCES

Aleksander, I., Burnett, P., 1987, *Thinking Machines: the search for artificial intelligence.* Oxford University Press, Oxford.

Alvey, J., 1982, A programme for advanced information technology. Report of the Alvey Committee. Department of Industry. HMSO, London.

Batty, M., 1976, *Urban Modelling.* Cambridge University Press, Cambridge.

Birkin, M., Clark, M., George, F., 1995, "The use of parallel computers to solve nonlinear spatial optimisation problems", *Environment and Planning A*, **27**, 1049–1068.

Ernst, G., Newell, A., 1969, *GPS: a case study in generality and problem solving.* Academic Press, New York.

Fischer, M.M., Gopal, S., 1993, "Neurocomputing—a new paradigm for geographic information processing", *Environment and Planning A*, **25**, 757–760.

Holland, J.H., 1975, *Adaptation in Natural and Artificial Systems.* University of Michigan Press. (Second edition MIT Press, 1992.)

Kosko, B., 1994, *Fuzzy Thinking.* Harper Collins, London.

Lighthill, J., 1973, "Artificial Intelligence: a general survey", *Artificial Intelligence*, SRC, London.

McCorduck, P., 1979, *Machines Who Think.* Freeman, San Francisco.

McCulloch, W.S., Pitts, W.H., 1943, "A logical calculus of the ideas imminent in nervous activity", *Bulletin Mathematical Biophysics*, **5**, 115–133.

Minsky, M., Papert, S., 1969, *Perceptions: an introduction to computational geometry*. MIT Press, Cambridge, Mass.

Office of Technology Assessment, US Congress, 1986, "Artificial Intelligence; a background paper", US Government Printing Office, Washington DC.

Openshaw, S.,1988, "Building an automated modelling system to explore a universe of spatial interaction models", *Geographical Analysis*, **20**, 31–46.

Openshaw, S., 1989, "Making geodemographics more sophisticated", *Journal of the Market Research Society*, **31**, 111–131.

Openshaw, S., Cross, A., Charlton, M. 1990, "Building a prototype geographical correlates exploration machine", *International Journal of GIS*, **3**, 297–312.

Openshaw, S., 1992, "Some suggestions concerning the development of artificial intelligence tools for spatial modelling and analysis in GIS", *Annals of Regional Science*, **26**, 35–51.

Openshaw, S., 1993, "Modelling spatial interaction using a neural net", in M.M. Fischer and P. Nijkamp (eds), *GIS, Spatial Modelling and Policy*. Springer-Verlag, Berlin, pp. 147–164.

Openshaw, S., 1994a, "Computational human geography: exploring the geocyberspace", *Leeds Review* **37**, 201–220.

Openshaw, S., 1994b, "Artificial intelligence and geography", *AISB Quarterly*, **90**, 18–21.

Openshaw, S., 1994c, "Developing smart and intelligent target marketing systems: Part 1", *Journal of Targeting, Measurement and Analysis for Marketing*, **2**, 289–301.

Openshaw, S., 1994d, "Developing smart and intelligent marketing systems: Part II", *Journal of Targeting, Measurement and Analysis for Marketing*, **3**, 31–38.

Openshaw, S., 1994e, "Neuroclassification of spatial data", in B.C. Hewitson, R.G. Crane (eds), *Neural Nets: applications in Geography*. Kluwer Academic Publishers, Boston, pp. 53–70.

Openshaw, S., 1994f, "A concepts-rich approach to spatial analysis, theory generation, and scientific discovery in GIS using massively parallel computing", in M.F. Worboys (ed.), *Innovations in GIS*. Taylor and Francis, London, pp. 123–138.

Openshaw, S., 1995a, "Human systems modelling as a new grand challenge area in science", *Environment and Planning A*, **27**, 159–164.

Openshaw, S., 1995b, "Developing automated and smart spatial pattern exploration tools for geographical information systems applications", *The Statistician*, **44**, 3–16.

Openshaw, S., 1995c, "Developing intelligent and user friendly spatial analysis tools for data rich GIS environments", *Proceedings of Joint Conference and Exhibition on Geographical Information*, The Hague, Vol. 2, pp. 417–425.

Openshaw, S., 1996, "Fuzzy logic as a new approach to scientific geography", *Environment and Planning* **28**, 761–768.

Openshaw, S., Blake, M., Wymer, C., 1995, "Using neurocomputing methods to classify Britain's residential areas", in P. Fisher (ed.), *Innovations in GIS2*. Taylor and Francis, London, pp. 97–112.

Openshaw, S., Charlton, M., Wymer, C., Craft, A.,1987, "A Mark I Geographical Analysis Machine for the automated analysis of point data sets", *International Journal of Geographical Information Systems*, **1**, 335–358.

Openshaw, S., Craft, A.W., 1991, Using Geographical Analysis Machines to search for evidence of cluster and clustering in childhood leukaemia and non-Hodgkin lymphomas in Britain", in G. Draper (ed.), *The Geographical Epidemiology of Childhood Leukaemia and non-Hodgkin Lymphomas in Great Britain 1966–83*. Studies in Medical and Population Subjects No. 53. OPCS, London, HMSO. 109–122.

Openshaw, S., Perrée, T., 1995, "Intelligent spatial analysis of point data", *Proceedings of 50th Session of the International Statistical Institute*. Beijing, China, pp. 797–815.

Openshaw, S., Perrée, T., 1996, "User centered intelligent spatial analysis of point pattern data", in D. Parker (ed.) *Innovations in GIS 3*, Taylor and Francis, London, 119–134.

Openshaw, S., Rao, L., 1995, "Algorithms for re-engineering 1991 census geography", *Environment and Planning A*, **27**, 425–446.

Openshaw, S., Wymer, C., 1991, "A neural net classifier system for handling census data", in F. Murtagh (ed.), *Neural Networks for Statistical and Economic Data*. Munotec, Dublin, pp. 73–86.

Openshaw, S., Wymer, C., 1995, "Classifying and regionalising census data", in S. Openshaw (ed.) Census Users' Handbook. GeoInformation International, Cambridge, pp. 353–361.

Rosenblatt, F., 1958, "The Perceptron: a probabilistic model for information storage and organisation in the brain", *Psychological Review*, **65**, 386–408.

Sharples, M., Hogg, D., Hutchison, C. Torrance S., Young, D., 1989, *Computers and Thought*. MIT Press, Cambridge, Mass.

Smith, M., 1993, *Neural networks for statistical modelling*. Van Nostrand Reinhold, New York.

Turing, A.M., 1936, "On computable numbers", in *Proceedings of the London Mathematical Society*, **42**, 230–265.

Turton, I., Openshaw, S., Diplock, G., 1996, "Some geographical applications of genetic programming on the Cray T31D supercomputer", in C. Jesshope and A. Shafarenko (ed.) *UK Parallel '96*. Springer, Berlin, pp. 135–150.

US Office of Technology Assessment, 1987, ...

Von Neumann, J., 1958, *The Computer and the Brain*. Yale University Press, New Haven.

Wilson, A.G., 1970, *Entropy in Urban and Regional Modelling*. Pion, London.

Wilson, A.G., 1974, *Urban and Regional Models in Geography and Planning*. Wiley, London.

Wilson, A.G., Bennett, R.J., 1985, *Mathematical Methods in Human Geography and Planning*. Wiley, Chichester.

Wiener, N., 1948, *Cybernetics*. Wiley, New York.

Yager, R.R., Ovchinnikov, S., Tong, R.M., Nguyen, H.T., 1987, *Fuzzy Sets and Applications: selected papers by L.A. Zadeh*. Wiley, New York.

Zadeh, L.A., 1993, "The role of fuzzy logic and soft computing in the conception and design of intelligent systems", in E.P. Klement and W. Slany (eds), *Fuzzy Logic and Artificial Intelligence*. Springer-Verlag, Berlin, p. 1.

CHAPTER 3

Heuristic Search in Geography

Heuristic search tools are of considerable geographical significance. Whilst not especially intelligent in an artificial sense they are nevertheless of practical value. They also possess a fascination all of their own. There is something intriguing about iterative procedures that creep (or run) towards a solution to a problem that may otherwise not be soluble. Who cares whether these algorithmic and computational procedures are massively smart; it is their problem-solving capabilities or results that we are after and this is far more important than how they look when viewed from this or that AI perspective.

3.1 PLAYING GAMES

Nearly all AI books have sections on heuristic search yet for many geographers it will appear, at first sight, to be one of the least relevant areas of AI and also the one least likely to contain much explicit evidence of machine intelligence. So how did heuristic search ever appear on the AI agenda? Well, the answer is both simple and historic. Problem solving is a fundamental aim in AI and the ability of a human being or a machine to solve problems is a common means of assessing their intelligence. If a problem cannot be solved by deterministic means either because it is too hard or has no explicit analytical solution that is proven to be correct or because there are too many potential solutions to make total enumeration feasible, then maybe it can be solved by either trial and error or some other clever or smart means of programming the computer to search for a solution. Hence the long standing importance of heuristic search methods as a means of intelligent problem solving. It follows then that problem-solving machines may be regarded as intelligent mainly because of their ability to search for solutions to problems that otherwise would not be solvable. This definition of intelligence and also of how intelligence might be gained does much to explain the AI community's interest in playing games such as chess and with more exotic puzzles such as the Towers of Hanoi. It may also explain the geographer's initial reluctance to believe that there is much or anything of any great relevance here because of an apparent lack of analogous problems to these types of puzzles in geography to which the methods can be applied.

So game playing and puzzle solving is very attractive to AI researchers mainly because they appear to believe, or once believed, that activities such as chess require a high level of intelligence and if therefore, machines could compete in this area, then they will have taken a major step forward in establishing their claim to being intelligent. This is obviously an oversimplistic fallacy! Nevertheless game playing has other attractions to the AI community, in particular many games can be easily represented and it is far more a purely intellectual and thus academic challenge than many real-world problems. Maybe this appeals to the non-applied scholar who views the pursuit of knowledge as being more significant than application and/or commercial exploitation (today this might be regarded with some sympathy as being a quaintly old-fashioned view). The contribution that AI can make is essentially to demonstrate how clever the researchers themselves are by providing smart, or some other kind of knowledge, based heuristics for playing games and solving puzzles.

This preoccupation with academic games and puzzles should not be too distracting. Some of the puzzles and games involve very large search problems; for example the 15-Tile Puzzle has 20 trillion possible board combinations (16! or 16 factorial or if you prefer it can be written much more verbosely as

$$16 \times 15 \times 14 \times 13 \times 12 \times 11 \times 10 \times 9 \times 8 \times 7 \times 6 \times 5 \times 4 \times 3 \times 2 \times 1$$

which is a very large number); the travelling salesman problem has 10^n (i.e. 10 to the power of n) routes, where n is the number of cities; even checkers has 10^{40} (i.e. 10 to the power of 40 or 10 followed by 40 zeros) end games, chess has 10^{120} games and Go an unbelievable 10^{761} games. These are unimaginably large numbers; much greater than the total number of atoms in the universe!) So maybe methods that can function well with handling these games might also be able to handle other types of heuristic search problems, or at least inform them. Only "smart" or intelligent search methods are likely to be able to make much or any impact on these types of problems. In some ways the search spaces in geographical problems are even larger; for example, a spatial optimisation problem can involve identifying the best site for 100 facilities given 3000 possible locations, a problem for which there are 3000!/100! solutions; expressed in English this is equivalent to 3000 factorial divided by 100 factorial, a number that is so large it cannot be readily written out. So it is conceivable that at least some of the vast amount of intellectual investment expended here might just be really useful in a geographical context. Indeed, one of these traditional puzzles, the travelling salesman problem, has always had some geographical interest. A very common problem in retail distribution, fault repairs, delivery of post and other journey-planning applications in transport GIS involves optimal route planning and the travelling salesman problem (and the special case of the Chinese postman problem) are clearly relevant.

A heuristic can be defined as a method or trick or rule of thumb that solves or assists in solving a problem but is not guaranteed to do so. Heuristic search is the application of these methods to problems involving some kind of search in the broadest sense. This is very relevant because most discoveries of both a scientific and a geographical kind have occurred as the result of some kind of search process. If this can be automated and performed by machines then, in principle, at least there is a basis here for a machine based approach to scientific discovery and knowledge creation relevant to a broad spectrum of applications and users. By comparison, "search" in a geographical context has characteristically involved some kind of spatial or locational analysis; for instance, the discovery of new countries in the fifteenth to seventeenth centuries, the discovery of more localised geographical knowledge via exploration of the interior of continents in the eighteenth and nineteenth centuries or a search for optimal locations for retail facilities in the twentieth century. In all three cases there are considerable unknowns, high levels of risk and uncertainty. The AI perspective is useful because it emphasises the importance of other types of search that are also very relevant to modern geography that may involve much more complex and higher-dimensional spaces than two- or three-dimensional maps of the earth's surface. When extended to encompass information flows, this has been called "searching the geocyberspace" in which the search and discovery activities of twenty-first-century geography will increasingly be focused (Openshaw, 1994). The new research frontiers are no longer in the three dimensional real world of the earth's surface but also in the multiple domains and dimensions of the databases created by IT; a projection of the IT cyberspace on to the map. This exploration task is also a search problem, comparable to the search for the New World in the sixteenth century. Explorers of the traditional geographic sort used manual search mechanisms, viz. hearsay, rumours, folklore and common sense. Heuristic search might be regarded as a more abstract and machine based equivalent more suited to the immense geocyberspaces of the twenty-first century. The attraction for geographers is that the same or similar kinds of heuristic search technologies that create chess and other game-playing systems might also have something useful to offer in solving geographical problems. Or so it once seemed when one of the authors first investigated heuristic search, a quarter of a century ago! It turned out then to be a mirage but useful nevertheless although, as we will see, more so because of the general principles rather than due to the detailed technology on offer.

3.1.1 Spatial search

There is a long-standing geographical literature involving the application of combinatorial optimisation and search methods that the AI world would consider to be heuristic search; see for example, Gould (1966), Scott (1971) and Massam (1980). In fact there are two broad types of spatial search problem relevant to geography. One kind involves finding best locations or exploring geographical data spaces for evidence of spatial patterns and relationships. Another kind involves the study of the behaviour of people in searching for shops or new houses or employment. It is really the first type of search that heuristic search methods may be able to assist and inform although AI technology is relevant to both. Table 3.1 summarises the results of a Gould (1966) and Massam (1980) review of spatial search activities. Heuristic search methods would certainly be regarded as relevant to all these long-standing geographical search problems.

Heuristic search might be regarded, therefore, as a class of computer-based methods able to find the approximate answer to hard problems that cannot otherwise be given exact solutions, usually because there is a large, sometimes extremely large, number of possible solutions that may have to be examined. Raggett and Bains (1992) provide a useful example. Suppose you have a bunch of keys and have forgotten which one opens your front door. Most people will try each key at random, they then become frustrated, and quickly lose track of which keys they have tried and end up repeatedly trying the same key without realising it, until more or less by chance they stumble across the correct one. Only a few (mostly female) will try one key after another in a systematic way, rejecting the wrong keys until the correct one is found. So it is with heuristic search. It is important to carefully think through the problem, how to represent it, and then how to solve it in an efficient manner.

A heuristic search procedure is essentially a set of rules, or an algorithm of some form, which will produce solutions to a problem but without necessarily finding the best possible solution or even knowing how good (or bad) the best solution really is. This type of search procedure is often used to cover a wide range of different methods ranging from simple trial and error to highly elaborate, knowledge based, intelligent search procedures. These methods are of AI interest because of the practical importance that search tools have to the development of intelligent systems and also because without the creation of intelligent search methods, many large or complex search problems (as well as various puzzles and games) would be impossible to solve.

In searching for solutions, humans use knowledge, rules of thumb, intuition, guesses and other forms of risk taking, and experience to assist this process by finding short-cuts, even if they often get it wrong! So why not attempt to mimic and then optimise this type of human intelligent search behaviour in software that runs on a machine? There are many different spatial analysis and modelling

Table 3.1   Summary of Gould's review of spatial search

Gould's search process	Search problem	Search space
Space search and strategy	Pursuit and evasion	Two-dimensional
Searching for oil and ores	Spatial hit or miss sampling	Three-dimensional
Searching mathematical surfaces	Heuristic search	Three or more dimensions
Search behaviour of animals	Path finding	Two- or three-dimensional

Source: adapted from Massam (1980) and Gould (1966).

problems in geography that might be solved by searching and thus exploring solution spaces for either any solution or the best possible result. Indeed, at a more general level, scientific discovery might well be regarded as a search process that operates in a more abstract space. Geographical examples of searching would include looking for something that is spatially concentrated, for example mineral deposits. There are many possibilities, for example the five-colour map problem; solving an equation that has no simple solution; selecting the best K from M variables to use in a regression model; finding the optimal value of a function when there are a large number of unknown parameters to estimate; discovering patterns and relationships in spatial data; determining optimal locations for facilities; finding the optimal route between 100 cities; developing good performing models, and creating new theories and knowledge by searching or exploring abstract information spaces.

There are some common features to this general class of search problem. In particular three aspects usually occur:

1. There is an objective function which is to be optimised so that a goal or purpose is met to the best possible extent.
2. There is a small or large or almost infinite universe of possible solutions that need to be considered and explored, either fully or partially, explicitly or implicitly, whilst searching for the best possible result.
3. There needs to be some means of moving around the theoretical solution search space in order to find the best possible desired result.

There are many problems that can be expressed in this way and general purpose methods that can perform efficient heuristic searches are clearly of some interest to many different application areas.

3.2 HEURISTIC SEARCH METHODS OF THE TRADITIONAL ARTIFICIAL INTELLIGENCE KIND

Not surprisingly, given the previous discussion, a number of heuristic search methods have been developed. Often "brute-force" or exhaustive searches of all possible solutions are infeasible; because of the amount of computer time needed since in many complex search problems there is a combinatorial explosion in the number of possible solutions that need to be investigated. For example, suppose you have three cities which you want to visit. Your objective is to minimise the total distance travelled and to avoid visiting the same city twice; this is the so-called travelling salesman problem. One way of discovering the best route is to examine all possible paths between the three cities and make a note of the shortest route. At first sight this appears to be a trivial problem that can be worked out by hand with a piece of string. However simple it may appear when few cities are involved the number of possible routes undergoes a combinatorial explosion as the number of cities increases. Nor does it go away even when you make a whole set of simplifying assumptions such as the cities are fully interconnected, they can be reached without passing through each other, the shortest distances between any two cities is equal to the direct link, and the distances are symmetric. In general there are $(n - 1)!/2$ different solutions. If n is small this is not a problem; e.g. if n is 10 then there are 1 814 400 possible solutions to be searched. However, if n is increased to 20 then there are now about 1.2×10^{18} solutions (Larson and Odoni, 1981); so many solutions that computer time becomes a problem. You could switch to a highly parallel supercomputer, but this is still not fast enough: and if you really wanted to solve real-world problems with 50 or 200 cities then you need a very different search heuristic other than total enumeration. In practice it is often not feasible to identify the global best solution by simply searching or examining all the alternative solutions, so you will need either a computational short-cut that will yield the same result as an exhaustive or global search would and can be proven to do so, or some other kind of heuristic method devised, that may never identify the global best result but will probably find what it is hoped is still a very good result. Of course this lacks the assurances of optimality but it might be good enough without being the global best and it might also be the best possible result that can be achieved.

Many of the heuristic short-cuts that the AI researchers developed involve methods that search graphs. The problem of interest is given a tree representation. This allows the search space to be readily visualised (as a graph or tree) and also permits use to be made of various techniques borrowed from graph theory. However, the use of graph-theoretic methods tends to mean that the approach become difficult for the non-expert mathematician, whilst the tree nature of the problem representation is also hard for some (like the authors) to cope with, particularly when they persist in using inappropriate languages such as FORTRAN! Fortunately, the review of these particular graph theoretic methods can be very brief because, in general, few of them have any great geographic relevancy or the power to handle most of the search problems in geography. It is more useful to see what lessons can be gained than to develop any deep expertise in methods that may not be all that useful.

Suppose you want to find the shortest path from city A to city F; see Figure 3.1. First change the problem space to yield a tree representation. You can do this by tracing all possible paths from a given node that does not create a loop. The aim here is to start at city A and end at city F. Note that in Figure 3.2 there are four possible paths from A that end at F. In a more realistic problem the total number of paths in a tree explodes exponentially, making the derivation of fast search methods very important.

There are two broad classes of search method; blind procedures and those that are heuristically informed and thus more locally intelligent and hence computationally efficient. The task then is simply to search the tree in Figure 3.2 to find the shortest path between cities A and F whilst doing the least amount of searching.

The blind search methods explore the tree in a systematic manner but hopefully without having to explore all the branches. For example, in Figure 3.2,

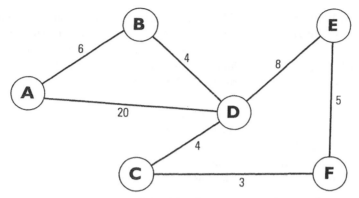

Figure 3.1   Map of six cities linked by a load network

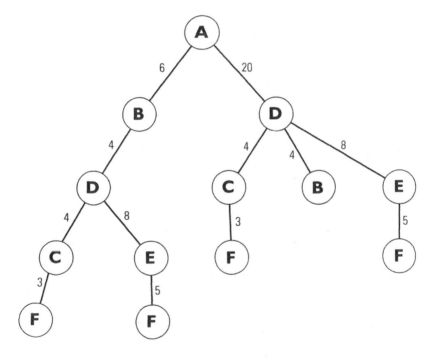

Figure 3.2   Tree representation of Figure 3.1

the left-hand branch (A–B–D–C–F) has a cumulative distance of 17. The next branch (A–B–D–E–F) has a distance of 23, so once we get to node E, the cumulative distance of 18 already exceeds the previous best, so we can abandon that branch at E and save some computational effort. Likewise the third branch A–D–C–F and indeed all other A–D branches can be ignored because the A–D distance of 20 exceeds the previous best of 17 and can, therefore, never be optimal.

This is clearly common sense. However, restrictions of this nature are problem specific. In a completely blind search you would merely use the tree representation as a convenient means of generating all possible solutions without missing any out. Clearly, the way in which trees are searched can have a major effect on the amount of computation performed. **Depth first search** blindly goes down each branch, then back up again when no further downward movement is possible. **Breadth first search** goes down the tree in a progressive manner. This can require both a vast amount of time and large amounts of memory with large problems, as all the nodes at each level have to be stored. Slightly better is **beam search** which also spreads through the tree layer by layer but only the best nodes are considered. Another variant is **best first search** which expands the best partial path.

Heuristically informed methods can be dramatically more successful particularly on synthetic problems! An attempt is made to change the order of the search so that the most promising ones are considered first and, hopefully, large areas of the tree can be left unexplored. **Hill climbing** is a class of methods that attempt to do this; for example, when seeking to reach the summit of a mountain going up gradient (hill climbing) is clearly better than going down. This principle is the basis for many heuristic search algorithms although it is clearly application dependent. So in Figure 3.2 node B is clearly a better start than node D and therefore the subtree associated with B is explored first. Heuristic search procedures are not necessarily optimal because they are not exhaustive. However, as the sizes of search tree explode, then they are clearly very useful in many real-world contexts. Related search methods that are useful in searching graphs or tree representations are: branch and bound, sometimes called A^* search, dynamic programming, alpha-beta pruning and minimax. Branch and bound methods are particularly appealing because for suitably formulated problems they yield optimal results, but in a geographical context it is often hard to develop suitable problem formulations and even when you do, the computing times may still be unacceptably large.

With the exception of network problems in GIS, most search problems in geography are not easily or usefully given a graph representation nor, if they can be represented in this way, capable of being solved using any of the classical tree search methods. So maybe it is possible to simply note that these tools exist, check that your problem has no easy or available graph-theoretic solution, and then consider a different approach. Another issue is the difficulty of parallelising, in a sufficiently coarsely grained manner, many of the tree search methods. In some ways the algorithms are highly tuned but essentially serial, and their very algorithmic cleverness, for instance recursive tree decomposition, makes it difficult to make efficient use of parallel supercomputing hardware with large numbers of processors.

3.3 SOME ILLUSTRATIONS OF HEURISTIC SEARCH

There is a great danger at this point of losing sight of the nature of the problems for which heuristic search is useful and of becoming so mesmerised by graph-theoretic approaches or pompous AI search technologies as to fail to realise how different heuristics might perform on different classes of problem. Consider a very simple example of no great complexity as a reminder of what heuristic search is all about. Suppose you have a set of N numbers, e.g. 100 000 of them. Now suppose for some reason that is difficult to understand you have a set of 1000 random numbers which you wish to find in this list of 100 000. You are an impatient type of person and thus want to perform this search as quickly as possible. How would you do it?

The simplest heuristic search is sequential. You go through the 100 000 numbers searching for a match on each one of your 1000 randomly selected target numbers. This might be regarded as a brute-force blind search. You will end up performing 100 000 times 1000 comparisons (100 million), which is quite a lot although modern workstations are very fast. You can do slightly better by sorting the target numbers so that it is possible to reduce the total number of comparisons by a half. Another possibility is a random search; that is, you randomly sample the list of 100 000 numbers until you find each of your 1000 target numbers or get near to it; or maybe you merely get totally fed up waiting! Another method is a binary search; which is a simple standard method of searching a list of sorted numbers (Bentley, 1986). Another heuristic is a focused random search. This simple method starts off with a small random search over a wide range of possible values, but increasingly it becomes focused around the current best solution, see Conley (1981). The search is still random but the range of search is progressively reduced. The question is: which of these heuristic search methods works best? This is now a matter of empirical experimentation in a situation where the correct result is known.

The results are shown in Table 3.2 for different list sizes (N). The computing times are for a Sunsparc 10/41 workstation. Note how inefficient the sequential search is compared with the binary search. The number of expected comparisons for the sequential search is $(N + 1)/2$ compared with $\log_2 N$ for the binary search. The random search heuristic is even worse and it takes a very long time to solve this number-matching problem but the point is that it does nevertheless work. It is just very inefficient for this problem for which there happens to be a much better alternative. However, suppose there was no alternative then, despite the computational cost, it would still work; see Appendix 1 for a general description of a random search heuristic. In the present application it is clearly a silly technique to apply when a binary search is so much better. By comparison, the focused random search is astonishingly good and it may even start to outperform the binary search on larger problems since the computing times are not directly dependent on the size of N but could be designed to be a constant independent of N. A basic description of this method is in Appendix 2.

Table 3.2   Performance of different number-searching heuristics

Heuristic algorithm	1000 target numbers	10 000 target numbers	100 000 target numbers	10 million target numbers
Sequential search, time taken	0.1	1.3	13.3	1 336
Random search, time taken	1.5	18.2	249.2	30 156
Binary search, time taken	<0.01	<0.01	<0.01	1.8
Focused random search, time taken	0.5	1.0	1.5	4.9

Note: time is seconds on a Sunsparc 10/41 workstation.

Imagine now a more complex problem for which there is no binary search possibility, as is quite common; for example, in problems not concerned with finding values in a sorted list which is after all a somewhat specialised and non-geographical activity. In many more complex problems the geographer may well find that there is no alternative to either total enumeration or a random search heuristic of some form. Once problem sizes preclude the former, then a focused random search is possibly all that is left; for example, the Monte Carlo search method used to solve a particular type of 0–1 nonlinear programming problem in plan generation (Openshaw and Whitehead, 1985). On these types of problem various other "smart" random search methods exist and perform search in an intelligent way: Appendices 3 and 4 describe two general types of intelligent random search methods, that of simulated annealing and tabu search. Finally, another very useful search method is the genetic algorithm described in Chapter 7.

3.4 HEURISTIC SEARCH TO OPTIMISE A FUNCTION

So it is emphasised that heuristic search is no longer purely or was ever mainly a tree-based graph-theoretic process, despite the attractions and elegance of graph theory. You need to be aware that in general more knowledge and/or different problem representations can lead to better solutions without having to identify any trees to search! Furthermore, it has also been emphasised that many problems of geographical interest can be treated as search problems, although traditionally many have not been viewed in this way. For example, the optimisation of a function is a search problem, the search is for good or optimal parameter values (i.e. solutions). Model design is another type of search problem, in which the search is for good model specifications (i.e. equations). In general most search problems in geography involve the optimisation of a function that represents the task in hand. A very basic example is the assignment of values to the unknown parameters in a mathematical or statistical model so as to maximise the models fit to data by minimising the errors; the so-called calibration or parameter estimation problem. Standard continuous space, real number optimisation problems can often be readily solved either by analytical means or by using conventional mathematical optimisation methods, particularly if the functions are linear. Only rarely will it be necessary to use heuristic search or trial and error search methods. However, as geographers become more ambitious in their computer applications or focus on more complex problems they may readily reach and be constrained by the limits imposed on what they can do using conventional methods. Once upon a time there was nothing that could be done; today AI technologies offer a way forward.

Consider a simple computer model that has one unknown parameter (x) and the aim is to find the best value (for x) that minimises some function $f(x)$ (e.g. the goodness of fit of a model for which x is a parameter). Figure 3.3 shows an example generated by plotting the value of the function for a number of different values for x (e.g. if $x = -5$ then function is 20.1, if $x = -4.9$ then function is 18.61, etc.). This might be regarded as equivalent to a blind sequential search. The best value can be identified by eye from the graph, i.e. try squinting at Figure 3.3 and identify the bottom of the curve. If the model is linear in x or nonlinear but well behaved then one or other standard optimisation method can be used instead. These methods start with a guessed value for x and then compute the gradient of the function with respect to x in order to discover how to move "downhill" in the landscape that the function represents. This is used to suggest another trial value for x, and the procedure is repeated until a "flat" area is reached. Now is that not smart! Well perhaps it is not too daft. If the function is linear in x it might be possible to obtain the optimal result even more easily, by solving some simultaneous equations, rather than searching (this is used in statistical packages to estimate linear regression parameters rather than minimise the sum of squares of the errors). However, only the simplest of optimisation problems can be handled in this manner. The world tends to be much more complex, highly nonlinear, and in general far messier than the fairly straightforward problems that linear and standard mathematical optimisation methods can readily cope with. Once your functions become nonlinear (which is good because

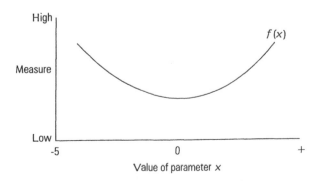

Figure 3.3   Searching for a good parameter value

this makes them more realistic) they tend to become much more complex, perhaps discontinuous, and generally much less well behaved (this is bad because it often means that conventional methods will probably no longer work, optimality can no longer be proven, and it can cause all manner of numerical instability problems).

Figure 3.4 gives some simple examples of functions that cannot, with any confi-

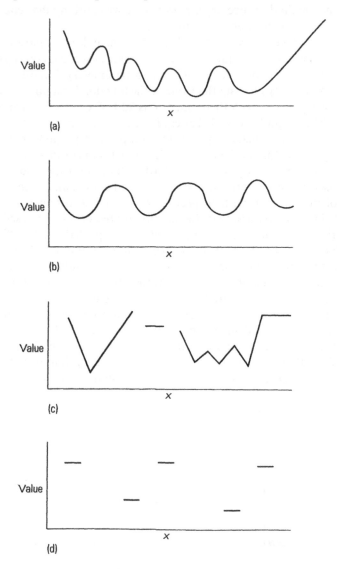

Figure 3.4 Functions that are hard to handle: (a) non-convex function; (b) multiple optima; (c) a discontinuous function; (d) integer x

dence, be solved using conventional nonlinear optimisation techniques. In Figure 3.4(a) different starting values for x will result in different final results, because most methods move downhill and stop at the bottom and they have no means of going uphill and down into the next valley! They do not know and have no way of knowing that there is another valley. In Figure 3.4(b) there are multiple different solutions and once again the standard methods could find any of them but without knowing that others exist and without having any means of finding out except by trial and error and this may not work. In Figures 3.4(c) and (d) there are other problems due to discontinuities in the functions. However, viewed as a heuristic search problem then various possible solutions methods exist; for example, some Monte Carlo based global optimisation methods look for the best of many different local solutions generated by considering many different starting values for x; see the simulated annealing, tabu search and genetic algorithm sections. Of course most geographically interesting optimisation problems involve not one x but many, and the function landscapes can no longer be so easily mapped or visualised in a graphic form. If the function has only one or two parameters then it is easy to spot these problems by graphing the function via a spreadsheet as in Figure 3.5. However, many multi-parameter functions cannot be so readily visualised and thus there is no way of knowing what sort of valley–hill and discontinuity arrangements exist in the more complex higher-dimensional spaces. The problems immediately become harder once it is impossible to "see" what they look like. In many ways the user is blinded by the dimensional complexity of the problem and may be quite unaware of the difficulties that non-convexity and other discontinuities may be creating. Some of these discontinuities may reflect the nature of the function; others may result from problems with the mathematical subroutine library, the form of floating point arithmetic being used, and how it handles arithmetic exceptions (e.g. those caused by trying to store numbers that are either too large or too small to be accurately handled). The simple exponential function can cause all manner of difficulties if the arguments become either too big or too small. Most optimisation routines have no way of handling these problems other than by stopping or by becoming stuck at the wrong location. The user may not even be aware that this is happening.

Diplock and Openshaw (1996) provide a good illustration of some of these problems. Figure 3.5 shows a plot of the performance of a simple origin constrained spatial interaction model with a exponential deterrence function

$$T_{ij} = O_i D_j A_i \exp(\beta \, C_{ij})$$
$$A_i = 1/\sum_j D_j \exp(\beta \, C_{ij})$$

where T_{ij} is the number of trips from origin i to origin j, O_i is the number of trips starting out in zone i, D_j is the number of trips ending in zone j, C_{ij} is the cost or distance between i and j and β is a parameter that has to be estimated.

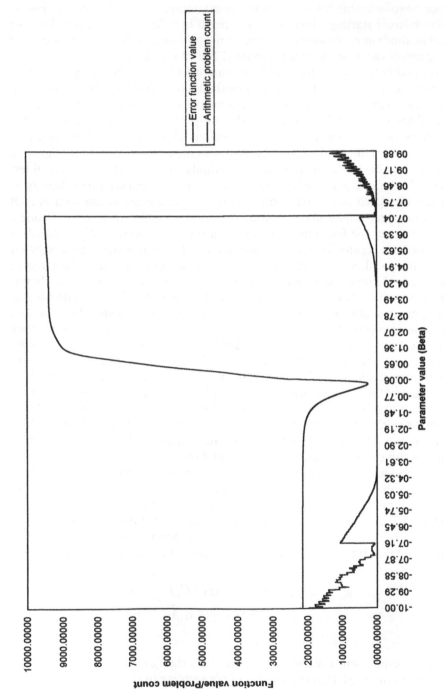

Figure 3.5   Error function behaviour of a production-constrained spatial interaction model

Conventionally, β would be estimated to maximise the fit of the model to observed data using a nonlinear optimisation technique. Alternatively, as in Figure 3.5, a large number of different values for β (from -10 to $+10$) can be plotted. The optimal result can then be defined as that β value which produces the smallest error. However, the exponential function can easily cause arithmetic exceptions; e.g. exp (88.8) will produce a single precision underflow (i.e. a number that is not quite zero but too small to be accurately stored in a workstation that uses IEEE arithmetic), or exp (-87.4) will produce a single precision overflow (i.e. a number set to infinity because it is larger than the machine can store which is $3.402 \times 10^{+38}$). Worse can follow in that arithmetic on zero or values of infinity can also cause results which are undefined; in IEEE terms this is termed a NaN (not a number). Figure 3.5 shows a small convex stable region in the range of β between -1 and $+1$; to the left underflows cause problems, to the right it is initially overflows followed by NaNs at which point the function appears to plunge to zero error. A NaN is neither greater than, or less than zero! In Figure 3.5 the "smallest" value of the function is in the NaN region to the right of the graph. This is, of course, not the right answer but it could so easily happen depending on the complexity of the function being optimised. Once you move to nonlinear optimisation problems then it is also important to switch to more powerful heuristic search methods; in particular you should read the chapter on genetic algorithms. This problem is potentially extremely serious and can impact on all statistical models in geography that use exponential functions, for example log-linear modelling. The problems become more complex when the number of unknown parameters increases. In Figure 3.6 Diplock and Openshaw (1996) present a view of the goodness-of-fit function of a multi-parameter competing destination spatial interaction model. Note that the regions of stability are now separated by areas of numerical instability. Conventional optimisers cannot be guaranteed to work well (or at all) in these circumstances.

Just for a change let us now consider a different type of optimisation model. Suppose the purpose is to maximise the value of a profit function (p) subject to constraints by assigning optimal values to two variables x and y. The task here is to find values of x and y that maximise p:

$$p = 28\,000y - 270x$$

subject to a constraint

$$x + y = 1000$$

This is very easy to solve even without a computer and after a few seconds thought you will deduce that setting to y to 1000 and x to zero is best. If the problem had been more complex and there was a sufficient number of equality constraints then you may have also been able to identify the optimal result easily. You could also have used software packages to perform the same task if there is

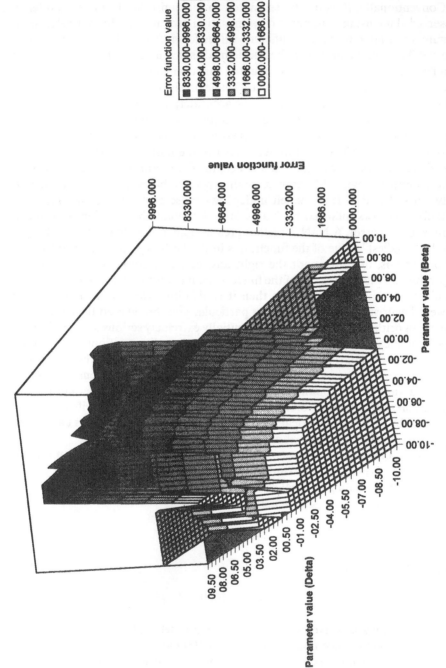

Figure 3.6   Multi-parameter fitness landscape of a competing destination spatial interaction model

no simple analytical solution. If the x and y are real numbers it is a linear programming (LP) problem. If they are integers it is an integer linear programming (ILP) problem. However, now consider a much more complex nonlinear function:

$$p = [350x_1 + 400x_2 + 700x_3] \times [\{x_1 + x_2 + x_3\} / x_3 + x_3{}^2]$$

subject to

$$x_1 + x_2 + x_3 = 40$$
$$10x_1 + 15x_2 + 30x_3 \leqslant 700$$

x_1, x_2, x_3 are integers: $x_1 \geqslant 5$, $x_2 \geqslant 5$ and $x_3 \geqslant 5$.

This function is nonlinear simply because it is no longer additive but contains multiplication and divides. As a result it is now impossible to solve using any standard mathematical optimisation procedure, despite there being only three parameters. It is a nonlinear, non-convex, integer optimisation problem. It cannot be differentiated because of the integer parameters. Yet viewed as a search problem this function can be easily solved on a PC, in only a few seconds!

How do you do that you wonder? Well you start by noting that x_1, x_2, and x_3 are integers with ranges of 5–30. So why not enumerate all 17 576 possible values of these integer variables. Of these only 158 pass the constraints and you simply select the best which is $x_1 = 19$, $x_2 = 8$, $x_3 = 13$. Simple and moreover optimality is completely guaranteed! It can also be easily parallelised. But, is this a good example of machine intelligence or is it a better illustration of an intelligent user spotting an opportunity? Certainly it is a useful trick that can be quite widely applied; see for example Conley (1980); but it is of limited applicability. Few of the nonlinear optimisation problems of geography will be suitable for solution by total enumeration because the spatial nature of locational problems usually results in vast search universes.

A very different problem arises when there are 42 trillion (or more) possible values for the parameters, or maybe several hundred parameters to estimate. Clearly the same exhaustive strategy cannot be used. Instead you would have to use a non-enumerative heuristic search method of some form. A focused random search might now be a useful way of proceeding. In a parallel supercomputing environment you could farm out the function evaluations to different processors and attain high degrees of speed-up. Another possibility would be to use a genetic algorithm. Yet another would be to adopt Conleys (1981) idea of generating many different random parameter values that satisfied the constraints and then keep the best result. Another possibility would be to convert the constraints into a function that measured the degree of constraint violation, multiply this by a large constant and add it to the objective function. The resulting objective function plus penalty function could then be optimised either all at once or via a sequence of steps that gradually increase the weighting given to the constraint violation term. You gain in terms of computational tractability but you lose any assurance of optimality. All you can hope for now is an approximately optimal solution that is good enough for your purpose. This is partly a matter of faith, partly a matter of being confident in the method being used, partly a matter of attaining performance targets in terms of problem relevant benchmarks, and partly confidence that a better result cannot easily be gained. Some numerical experimentation can be a useful aid to your overall degree of confidence in the quality of the solution. As a general rule do not readily accept anything that is heuristically generated on face value without some further empirical testing and numerical exploration. Maybe also it is a matter of good luck. However, methods that rely on serendipity and good luck are usually incapable of replication and are hence not an attractive technology. So be careful. Replication is an important feature of science.

If attaining a better result or obtaining a solution to a previously impossible problem via computational means is a measure of machine intelligence, then heuristic search methods can deliver it, although the intelligence being witnessed here is mainly that of the programmer working with a very powerful computer. On the other hand, the outcome itself might be considered to be extremely intelligent. As computers become faster, so many more problems in geography become amenable to computational solutions via the application of search methods of one form or another using high performance computer hardware; maybe this is all that matters and who really cares how intelligent the solution method really is? Yet it is also the case that genuinely machine smart heuristic search methods are sometimes possible; see the chapters on genetic algorithms and artificial life. Quite often the secret in applying heuristic search is to recognise that a problem of interest can be viewed as having **two** stages. **Stage one** involves the realisation that it might be solved via some kind of search probably initially of a purely brute-force nature, because it is often easier to consider the problem in this way and because it really does not matter initially how crude or smart this search may be. The trick is to identify the search problem without worrying too much too soon about how to solve it in an optimal manner. **Stage two** occurs later when the search process is upgraded by the use of smarter methods that may be quicker or more elegant or thought likely to yield results of superior quality. However, you only indulge in this optimisation phase if it is really relevant to the importance of the application being performed as it could easily absorb the next six months of your life. AI-based tools have the potential to inject a high degree of machine-based intelligence into solution procedures that are themselves almost completely dumb but quite often you need to start with a dumb search method.

3.5 SOME APPLICATIONS OF BLIND SEARCH IN GEOGRAPHY

To recap, blind or brute-force search involves complete enumeration of all solutions considered relevant. It has the following general characteristics:

- It is a comprehensive exploration of the search space.
- It is globally optimal, since it has investigated all the possible solutions.
- It is not always feasible if there are too many solutions to examine.
- It can be wasteful of computing resources but only if there are more efficient alternatives.
- It is dumb, being completely uninformed by any knowledge of the problem.

However, if a problem is important enough to require a solution, if it is suitable for a brute-force approach, and if the available computer power is sufficient to allow it to be performed, then do it! Who cares if it is inelegant or requires six days or six weeks on a PC or workstation. Elegance can always be added subsequently and sometimes at an immense cost in your time and effort. As supercomputers become faster and faster, many more problems of a geographical nature become soluble via brute-force search. The parallel supercomputing era stimulates the prospects of using the new hardware not just to make old problems run faster but to apply the computer power to new and very different applications. It is probably here where the opportunities are greatest to take a giant step forward by becoming more computationally extensive in a highly parallel way. It is this realisation that underpins a new geocomputational paradigm for doing geography in the twenty-first century that is available now (on simple problems). Let us look at some more geographical examples.

3.5.1 Case study 1: finding nuclear power station sites

Nuclear power siting involves (in part) trying to identify locations that meet population siting criteria; see Openshaw (1986) for a review. This is clearly a spatial search problem in a GIS domain. Traditionally it was done by manual means, viz. an engineer exploring on foot previously identified "likely" locations in a small number of predefined regions of interest, usually coastal and near existing national grid power lines. The definition of a potentially interesting location reflects population distribution in relation to demographic siting criteria, accessibility to demand centres, geological factors, landownership and other engineering requirements. Traditionally, the case made to support a specific site has been that there is a general shortage of suitable sites and, therefore, it has to be here (wherever here happens to be located). In a heavily populated country like Britain it has been assumed that few sites will actually meet the siting criteria. A geographically interesting question is, therefore, where are all the potentially suitable sites from a demographic point of view? A heuristic search to answer this question is described in Openshaw (1982). It involves the following blind search process.

Step 1   Cover the UK by a fine mesh of 1 km grid squares; for this purpose the UK could be regarded as being contained in a rectangle of 1219 km (north–south) by 650 km (east–west) based on Ordnance Survey grid referencing.

Step 2 Obtain small area population data reported either by the 1971 census for 150 000 1 km grid squares or in the 1981 census for 130 000 enumeration districts and 150 000 in 1991. For each of these small areas there is a 100 m, resolution point reference.

Step 3 At each 1 km grid intersection apply a set of population siting criteria; see Table 3.3 to see whether that location meets the siting criteria.

Step 4 Identify all the locations that meet the demographic criteria and draw a map or generate statistics.

If a 1 km mesh grid search is used, then there are 792 350 (1219 times 650) possible grid squares to be examined, each of which involves the spatial retrieval of census population data for six distance bands and a comparison made against the population limits, in Table 3.3. The results are shown in Figure 3.7. Note that the resolution of the results partly reflects the size of the search mesh and also the spatial representation of the small area census data. A 500 m mesh size would have increased computer run times by a factor of 4; a 100 m mesh by a factor of 100. However, the locational error inherent in small irregularly shaped census areas grid referenced by a single point to an accuracy of 100 m suggests that a 1 km mesh size is probably about right. There are dangers in pushing geographic information too far! The results in Table 3.4 show what happens when different siting criteria are used. The surprising result here is that the demographic siting criteria are not as restrictive as they were historically assumed to be and that there are many potential sites from which a choice could be made.

The question is whether or not this counts as knowledge creation. Furthermore, where is the intelligence in this process? There are four possible answers:

1. New knowledge or surprise in the resulting map visualisation, along the lines of "I never knew that before."
2. The discovery of the interactions between siting criteria and small area data is valuable and useful in understanding the locational process being studied.

Table 3.3   Some radial and sector population limits for the relaxed demographic siting criteria for nuclear power sites in the UK

Distance band (miles)	Assuming uniform maximum populations in all distance bands	
	Maximum population limit in any 30° sector	Maximum population in distance band
0–1	1944	4750
1–1.5	4205	9822
1.5–2	5810	13382
2–3	16718	36800
5–10	251908	494000
10–20	1004348	1849333

Figure 3.7   Population feasible nuclear power locations

Table 3.4   Percentage of sites that fail to satisfy various siting criteria

Siting criteria	All UK	Coastal squares
Early remote criteria	38	38
Later remote criteria	25	33
Relaxed criteria 1	17	17
Relaxed criteria 2	12	13

Source: Openshaw (1986).

3. There is now a broader appreciation of the problem of siting a nuclear power plant, for example, there are many more sites than the nuclear industry once claimed.
4. It was only possible by the development of fast, clever, spatial data retrieval methods that made the analysis feasible on the available hardware of the early 1980s.

It is argued that here the intelligence comes from the insights provided by the results and the ability to solve the spatial search problem. The latter, if done crudely, would have involved 200 000 million distance calculations. Instead, by using an efficient algorithm for the spatial data retrieval, it can now be done in a few hours on a workstation or on a PC. An extension of this approach would be to plug in a reactor accident casualty prediction model so that the sites could be ranked by numbers of casualties that a reference accident might cause. Openshaw (1986) describes how to achieve this; see Figure 3.8. Figure 3.8(a) shows the location of the best (i.e. smallest casualty) 5000 locations. Figures 3.8(b)–(e) report

Figure 3.8   (a) Best 5000 minimum reactor casualty; (b) best 10 000; (c) best 20 000; (d) best 50 000; (e) best 100 000. All based on 1 km squares

the best 10 000, 20 000, 50 000, and 100 000 locations respectively. Map presentations of this type can be used to inform the political and public debate about the location of unpopular facilities by putting the problem into a broader and more realistic context. That is clearly a smart development!

3.5.2 Case study 2: an optimal nuclear bombing strategy

Another variation of the same basic map search process is seen in Openshaw and Steadman (1982) who try to demonstrate the potentially very serious consequences of a nuclear war on Britains population by devising an optimal nuclear bombing strategy. The optimal bombing problem involves defining an optimal set of targets that would cause maximum casualties for a hypothetical attack involving a series of 1 megaton airburst nuclear bombs, using casualty rules that predict deaths from blast effects as a function of distance. The basic algorithm is as follows:

Step 1   Define casualty rules.
Step 2   Perform a 1 km grid mesh search for maximum casualty location.
Step 3   Reduce population data to remove dead people.
Step 4   Repeat steps 2 and 3 for K bombs.

In case you share the author's morbid interest in such matters, the casualty rules are as follows: create four concentric rings around ground zero (with radii of 3.96, 6.42, 10.65 and 16.75 km), compute population within each distance ring, and apply blast deaths probabilities of 1.0, 0.52, 0.05 and 0.0 respectively. Seriously injured probabilities are 0.0, 0.4, 0.45 and 0.25. If you are seriously injured twice you are assumed to die. This information is based on Office Technology Assessment (1980), Gladstone and Dolan (1977), Openshaw et al (1983) and Openshaw and Steadman (1983), to which those with an interest in this depressing subject are referred.

The results are shown in Table 3.5; see also Figure 3.9. This might be regarded as a particularly eccentric type of spatial optimisation problem. Its use here is really to challenge the reader to think about how to improve the search process rather than ponder the effects of nuclear weapons or to investigate nuclear power station siting strategies. So how might the heuristic search process be improved or speeded up and how could the search be made more intelligent?

3.5.3 Making spatial searching more intelligent

The spatial search process used in both case studies is quite comprehensive, it is geographically systematic but totally dumb! In the applications briefly described here it simply did not matter because the emphasis was on the novelty of the results and the work was unlikely ever to be repeated. The cleverest part was the fast spatial data retrieval based on a two-dimensional collision-free hash look-up

Table 3.5 Cumulative nuclear war casualties

Number of bombs used	Number of people killed (millions)	Cumulative dead people (millions)
1	2.73	2.7
2	1.18	3.9
3	1.17	5.0
4	1.08	6.1
5	1.03	7.2
10	0.67	11.3
20	0.42	16.4
30	0.33	20.1
40	0.28	23.1
50	0.23	25.7
97	0.12	33.7

Source: Openshaw and Steadman (1982).

Figure 3.9   Optimal casualty nuclear bomb targets

that made the brute-force search feasible at a time when computer hardware was not powerful enough to handle the computational load; see Openshaw (1982) for details. A good heuristic algorithm allows you to do today what would otherwise require the next generation of superfast high performance computer. So it is an important AI question as how to improve the computational efficiency of the search process, not the spatial data retrieval, so that the results might be obtained far more speedily and without any need to make subjective assumptions about the size of grid to use. The best methods would be grid size invariant. It is noted that there is no obvious way of using tree search methods as the problem cannot readily or naturally be represented in that form. However, the search can be made instantly more intelligent by using knowledge to exclude stupid, silly and impossible locations. In the UK, nuclear power plant need either a coastal or large lake or big river location. This knowledge can be used to greatly reduce and restrict the search process. For instance, there is no point in examining locations in the middle of the North Sea! Yet of the 792 350 one kilometre mesh intersections examined less than one-third are on land. If it is possible to incorporate this knowledge then in principle the search problem size is reduced by a factor of 20; see the coastal search results in Table 3.4. Likewise other GIS-based overlays for urban areas, areas of outstanding natural beauty, lakes, steep hills, etc. could also be used to restrict the areas searched. In all these examples the incorporation of domain- or application-relevant knowledge should greatly speed up the search and yet have no impact on the quality of the results. In fact knowledge of other types of exclusion area would further reduce the search by another factor of 10. The attractions here of incorporating knowledge is not just that of computational efficiency but it gives the entire analysis a much higher degree of credibility and appeal. Brute-force methods that waste most of the computing time evaluating totally stupid and impossible locations engender no warm or feel good factor about the technology. However, back in the early 1980s when this research was first performed the necessary GIS overlays simply did not exist.

There are also other ways of making the map search process appear more intelligent. In particular the use of a uniform sized mesh could be replaced by a variable mesh size that either reflects local population density or by a search strategy that took into account other results generated for nearby locations during the search; for example to avoid sites near to infeasible sites whilst feasible sites might be explored in finer spatial detail to find the edges of the feasible regions.

In general GIS has the potential to make virtually any map based search process more intelligent by the incorporation of external knowledge and thus become more efficient simply by using common sense to restrict the areas of search, although GIS itself is not innately intelligent. However, there are limits to how far this process can help and there is a danger of losing the benefits of comprehensiveness and lack of spatial bias if the exclusions are based more on hypothesis than non-controversial fact. Further performance improvements require the search process itself to become more adaptive and intelligent in its operation. Consider the nuclear bombing example. Clearly the search for targets could be restricted to regions around the most promising locations, for example urban areas or near urban areas. Given a digital map representation of these regions this could be easily added. The search algorithm may also be improved further. One way would be to devise a search heuristic that could operate as follows; compute populations for urban areas, rank them by size, search around the few largest ones and then having established the maximum casualties so far use this to reject all other urban areas with a smaller population size. This process can be repeated as many times as required, although its efficiency will tend to diminish as the populations of the urban areas are reduced. Maybe an even better method might be to search the country using a widely spaced or coarse meshed two-dimensional grid to determine good locations for a finer search. A local search at a finer grid size would then look for better results. The grid size could also be made locally adaptive, becoming bigger in areas of poor results (compared with the current best) and finer in areas where better solutions are being found.

Another possibility is to seek to represent the problem in a different form. Many search problems can be made simpler (or harder) by changing the nature of the problem representation. The population distribution of the UK can be viewed as a density surface and a three-dimensional map surface searcher developed that will explore the edges (for the nuclear power plant problem) or the peaks (for the nuclear bombing problem) for good locations. The potential improvement in performance is probably much greater than that achieved by imposing knowledge from a GIS although this too could be imposed on top of the surfaces to effectively cut out the infeasible areas by resetting the surfaces to the poorest possible value.

Given the importance of map searching in geography further research is needed into how best to solve this generic type of search problem. There are many interesting possibilities and the two case studies examined here could be used as test beds for developing spatial search heuristics relevant to a much broader class of spatial search problems. A final observation is that one of the benefits of a brute-force total enumeration spatial search is that it is easily adapted to handle much more complex evaluation criteria. The power station siting example involved the question of meeting population constraints and the nuclear war case study used a simple casualty model. It is not difficult to use much more complex functions, to apply multiple objective functions and goal programming formulations to the total list of feasible or generated solutions. Global optimality is more or less guaranteed (subject to grid size resolution issues) because no potential solutions have been ignored and, in the process, the hardest part of any nonlinear optimisation task avoided! The principal restrictions are, of course, a problem that can be handled via a brute-force approach and computer hardware fast enough to make its solution by total enumeration feasible.

3.5.4 Map searching as a parallel process

It is noted that a key feature of many geographic map search problems is a high degree of parallelism in the search process. This implicit parallelism is extremely useful particularly in view of the increasing availability of highly parallel computing hardware. Parallel computers work best on computational tasks that can be segmented into a large number of independent activities capable of being executed concurrently so that many processors can be working on the same problem. Conventional computers have a single CPU and perform operations in a serial manner so that the main factor limiting the speed of the application is mainly the speed of the processor. Parallel hardware in theory, and sometimes also in practice, permits a speed up of up to m times, where m is the number of processors. A Cray T3D parallel supercomputer with 512 processors permits a suitable written parallel program based on an algorithm that is scalable to be run up to 512 times the speed taken on a single processor. A critical aspect concerns the degree of granularity of the parallel tasks. If it is too fine or involves too little computation then it may be hard to obtain good levels of performance on parallel computers. At its simplest, a most desirable state is a computational process that involves a large number of computationally intense but independent tasks each of which can be farmed out to a separate CPU with either little or no interaction between them until after they have finished. As chip processor speeds increase so the amount of computational power available is likely to increase by two or three orders of magnitude during the late 1990s. Those computing intensive applications that employ scalable, parallel, algorithms will clearly benefit most. Several areas of AI already have suitable techniques for distributed parallel supercomputing and it is here where the impact of further computer speed increases will be most readily felt, especially where the quality of the results and the applicability of the methods are currently computer time restricted.

Map search is an excellent example of a geographical processing problem that is well suited to parallel computing. Such a problem might even be regarded as being embarrassingly parallel by comparison with many other problems where it is much harder to tease out the parallel activities. The two case studies are examples of parallel search problems, indeed as are many systematic searches over a two-dimensions map space. A particularly attractive common feature to note is the complete independence of the evaluations at different map locations. The only concern might be whether the amount of computation being performed at each grid intersection is sufficient to offset the overheads of communicating the results. There are various solutions to these problems, for example batching up the search tasks so that each processor is given a list of several sites to look at.

The nice thing for geographers is that map search is a parallel process. Suppose you want to search a two-dimensional map space for something, then the following generic algorithm could be used:

Step 1   Define a grid size.
Step 2   Cover study region with a grid.
Step 3   Evaluate a function/model/set of rules at each grid intersection and save the results.
Step 4   Make a list of best results and display them.

Note that **step 3** can be performed in parallel, that is the outcome of evaluating one location is independent of all others. What this means is that in effect you can be incredibly dumb and stupid in spatial search heuristics provided you do so in a highly parallel fashion! This has an interesting side-effect in that quite often clever heuristics such as binary search are optimal only in a serial processing environment because they are not explicitly parallelisable (except at a very fine level) and that crude methods become more computationally attractive because of their simplistic parallel nature. The emerging era of parallel supercomputing may well discourage the use of clever heuristics that have no parallel equivalent. Of course granularity of the tasks is very important. Binary search is only inefficient in a parallel programming sense if a single binary search is to be distributed over 512 processors. If, however, it is only one part of a more complex process of computation, then each of the 512 processors can do their own binary searches. So granularity or the scale at which the concurrency exists is very important. Fortunately with many geographical applications this is not a problem.

3.6 MORE SOPHISTICATED EXAMPLES OF HEURISTIC SEARCH

3.6.1 Case study 3: spatial network optimisation

Birkin et al (1995) present an example of a heuristic search problem involving the optimisation of a network of car showrooms. The problem of finding optimal locations for facilities has a long history in geography. Recently it has become important as retail chains, restaurants, health and financial service organisations have sought to optimise their regional and national networks. A common problem is how to find an optimal allocation of M outlets to N possible locations so that some measure of overall network performance is optimised; for example: total profits, total sales turnover, maximum accessibility and various measures of client convenience and utility.

Birkin et al (1995) describe one such problem as

$$\text{maximise } Z = f\left(\sum_j D_j^1\right)$$

where D_j^1 is the number of cars of type 1 sold at location j. D_j^1 is given by an origin constrained spatial interaction model used to represent customer behaviour:

$$D_j^1 = \sum_i O_i Q_j^1 \exp(-\beta c_{ij}) A_i$$

$$A_i = 1 / \sum_{k=1}^{T} \sum_{j=1}^{n} Q_j^k \exp(-\beta c_{ij})$$

where Q_j^k is the number of dealers at location j selling car type k, O_i the total number of cars purchased by people living in origin zone i and C_{ij} the cost of travel from i to j. In this problem the aim is to maximise Z by finding an optimal set of M zero–one values for the Q_j^1; note that all other Q_j^k $k > 1$ values for Q_j are assumed to be fixed and represent the distribution of competitors.

A realistic national network optimisation problem of this type may well involve 2755 origin zones, 822 possible sites and a desire to locate 60 outlets simultaneously. There are in this example

$$^{822}C_{60} = \frac{822!}{60!}$$

possible different solutions to the problem. Clearly an exhaustive search strategy is out of the question. Birkin et al (1995) outline various solution procedures ranging from their idealised representation planning (IRP) algorithm to a genetic algorithm. Another way of solving this problem is to use a Monte Carlo search heuristic. Other possibilities are versions of the algorithms described in the Appendices, particularly simulated annealing and tabu search. Note that in this instance a new random solution can be easily generated from a previous best solution. Simply switch for a randomly selected D_j^1, some of the 1 values to 0 and some previous 0 values to 1. This creates a single move list that provides the basis for the Monte Carlo optimisation methods described in Appendix 4. You could of course develop multiple (rather than pairwise) moves if you wished, and there are many different selection and swapping heuristics that you could investigate. A key user requirement in all heuristic search applications is a willingness to experiment. In fact a version of the Monte Carlo heuristic described in Appendix 4 outperformed a genetic algorithm based network optimisation procedure by a factor of over two times (Turton and Openshaw, 1996). So the latest technology (i.e. genetic algorithms) need not always outperform older heuristics.

3.6.2 Case study 4: zone design

Another long-established example of heuristic search is that of zone design. The optimal partitioning of space for a variety of purposes and reasons has long been of interest; for example, electoral redistricting, location-allocation, new definitions of local authorities, identification of fire cover regions, and the design of telecommunication networks to provide good geographic coverage. The increasing availability of statistical data for small areas for which digital boundary information is available creates the possibility of user-defined flexible geographical reporting frameworks for more and more statistical information. For example, in the UK the availability of digital boundaries for the 1991 census enumeration districts permits users to define their own zoning systems. This is a source of both considerable problems, for instance the modifiable areal unit problem (Openshaw, 1984) whereby the same data aggregate to different zones produces different results, and also of considerable potential, for instance users can now design the zoning systems they wish to use rather than be forced to use whatever others have provided for them. Additionally, it is becoming clear that zone design is a fast emerging specialism within the area of spatial data management. The re-engineering of spatial zones can help standardise data representation issues, it can help preserve confidentiality by minimising dis-closure risks and it can offer new insights into the nature of geographical patterns; see for example Openshaw and Rao (1995).

The zone design problem is a special type of combinatorial optimisation problem in which the set of unknown parameters is the zoning system. Openshaw (1977a, b, 1978a, b) defines the problem as

$$\text{optimise } F(Z)$$

where $F(Z)$ is some user-defined function of the M zone data created by the spatial aggregation operator Z when applied to a set of N small zones. The problem is complicated because there are constraints on Z; for example each of the N small zones can be assigned to only one of the M bigger zones in Z, each zone must be allocated and all the small zones assigned to the same big zone must be internally connected. Additionally, the user may impose various problem-specific equality and inequality constraints on the problem; these may be either zone specific or refer to the global properties of the data generated by Z.

Clearly this problem lies well outside the domain covered by conventional optimisation methods. Openshaw and Rao (1995) outline three different heuristic search methods that they used; a mild version of Monte Carlo search, tabu search and simulated annealing. They sought to re-engineer the almost 3000 census enumeration districts in 1991, in Merseyside into regions of equal population size. Table 3.6 shows the average error between the target population and the actual size of each region. Note how it becomes harder to achieve this task as the number of regions increases. Note also the superior performance of the simulated annealing heuristic and the slightly less good and sometimes erratic performance of the tabu search based algorithm. On simple problems the Monte Carlo methods works well enough but more complex zone design functions often need a simulated annealing solution. This can take over 100 times longer; see for example, the large increase in computing times in Table 3.7. A parallel version is described in Openshaw and Schmidt (1996) and this may well be the answer to large-scale zone design applications particularly as the computing time problems become worse as additional constraints are introduced into the zone design process.

Another example is the attempt by Openshaw and Alvanides (1996) to reaggregate the census enumeration districts in Leeds–Bradford to create areas of equal economically active population. This allows them to map unemployment using areas about the same size as wards but with the confounding effects of variation in size of denominator being removed. Figure 3.10(a) shows a map of

Table 3.6   Results for equal population size zonations

Number of regions required	Algorithm*		
	Monte Carlo	Tabu	SA
10	1.5	1.2	1.5
20	7.6	11.9	3.2
30	7.7	4.2	5.3
40	13.4	6.3	7.1
50	16.3	11.3	7.3
75	14.1	13.1	7.8
100	22.3	14.9	9.2
150	25.3	32.2	1.0
200	34.3	53.4	8.8

*The Monte Carlo result is the best from starting with 10 different random zonings. The tabu and SA (simulated annealing) results are unaffected by the choice of initial random zoning systems.

Table 3.7   Computing times (seconds) for equal population results in Table 3.6

Number of regions required	Algorithm		
	Monte Carlo	Tabu	SA
10	730	5169	19 575
20	1 182	3306	9763
30	1 671	2915	10 679
40	1 880	12 828	10 156
50	1 861	3877	9903
75	2 010	5684	10 493
100	2 053	5169	12 579
150	2 434	12 876	13 877
200	2 229	7875	131 766

Note: Computing times are for Sun-Supersparc 10 model 40 workstation.

percentage unemployment for 63 census wards in the Leeds–Bradford region of England. The variable population size of the wards may well distort the visual imagery. In Figure 3.10(b) the 2315 census enumeration districts are reaggregated into 63 regions of approximately equal economically active population size. Figure 3.10(c) shows the same data but this time partitioned into 63 regions of equal accessibility to unemployed. These maps were generated by an Arc/Info GIS based zone design system (ZDES) that uses the three different zone design heuristics discussed here; see the WWW page for Leeds School of Geography, UK. Maybe this ZDES system is a good place for those interested in AI to start with.

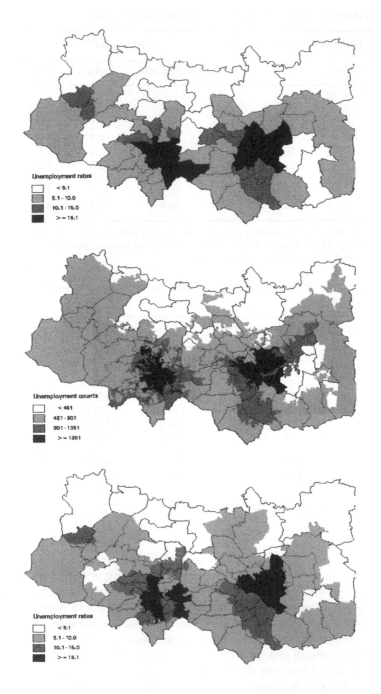

Figure 3.10 (a) Unemployment by 63 wards; (b) unemployment by 63 zones with equal economically active population; (c) unemployment by 63 zones with accessibility on economically active population.

The basic algorithms used in ZDES are described in the Appendices; however, interested users would be well advised to develop variants that experimentation by trial and error suggests will work well with their problems and on their data. This is a highly empirical application area. You need a combination of luck, perseverance and skill if the best results are to be gained. It is, however, also a completely fascinating subject. There is just something so wonderfully thrilling about iterative algorithms that gradually converge on a good result. Once bitten by the iterative heuristic algorithm bug it is very hard to escape!

3.7 EXPLORATORY SPATIAL ANALYSIS AS A MAP SEARCH PROCESS

3.7.1 Case study 5: the geographical analysis machine

A key observation from a geographical perspective is that there is now a major opportunity for making many geographical analysis and modelling tasks smarter by becoming cruder and more computationally intensive in approach especially if it is also highly parallel. The automation and large-scale application of fairly simple analysis procedures can be used to gain intelligence and create new knowledge by searching for interesting results. The increasing data riches of the post-GIS revolution world emphasise the importance of exploratory spatial data analysis (Rhind et al, 1988). Traditionally, spatial analysis was hypothesis driven (i.e. mainly confirmatory in nature) and operated under conditions of limited data and a few expert users working on a very small number of usually academic problems. Increasingly the availability of spatial information has far outstripped both the skills of the users and the supply of a priori hypotheses. Much of the data are in new application areas and contexts for which there is little or no prior theoretical knowledge, let alone many or any precisely formulated a priori hypotheses to test. The needs of the end-users have also changed. They are now much less research orientated and more likely to be applied. Additionally there are few spatial analysis methods that can actually cope with the new needs. These needs may be simply characterised as a need to know **what, when** and **where** to look for interesting results in a spatially referenced database. It is no longer sufficient to expect the end-users to do all the work. Drawing maps of data and then expecting the user somehow to spot the patterns or discover new relationships in databases containing masses of mappable data is neither acceptable nor sufficiently powerful. Add to this data overload the importance of spotting local patterns rather than global ones, the need for results that are study region invariant, and some assurance that if something important exists it will not have been missed, then it is not difficult to understand why new AI-based tools are needed; see Openshaw (1991, 1994). For example, if you are interested in the clustering of diseases then it hardly makes much sense in many contexts to pretend you know in advance precisely where to look, that you know in advance the scale and nature of the clustering, and you know in advance precisely what to look for. Sometimes you might be able to meet this requirement but most of the time you will not. AI might well be expected to offer some help for what is a fundamental geographical analysis task. What you really need is some kind of intelligent query system (IQS) that once given a vaguely defined idea of what you are looking for, will then go away, do a vast amount of exploratory analysis of the spatial database and then suggest to you a small number of queries that will identify data records that seem to constitute potentially interesting patterns. Why should the user have to do all the hard work? That is what AI is for! The question now is how to convert this desire for an IQS into a heuristic search problem that can be solved.

One possible solution is described in Openshaw (1987, 1990), and Openshaw et al (1987, 1988, 1989). They developed a geographical analysis machine (GAM). The objective was to identify localised patterns (i.e. clustering) in spatial data without knowing in advance where to look. It might be regarded as a first-generation intelligent spatial database explorer, no doubt the first of many, yet it was based on a very simple principle. If you do not know where to look for spatial clustering in a database then look everywhere. Because the machine is doing the looking prior human knowledge is now irrelevant, removing the risks of *post hoc* hypothesis testing. Moreover all locations are treated equally so there is no spatial bias in the search process. It can handle scale and data uncertainty by empirical means. It assumes that the patterns of interest consist of localised clustering but requires no detailed knowledge of either scale or frequency of these patterns. It uses a brute-force or blind search method to make up for ignorance of not knowing where to look or what to look for by looking everywhere.

The GAM Mark 1 circa 1987–88 was based on the following method:

Step 1   Define a study region.
Step 2   Cover the region with a grid mesh.
Step 3   Set circle size, at j kilometres.
Step 4   Systematically examine all circles located on grid intersections of a lattice arbitrarily defined as 0.8 radius of j kilometres so that the circles overlap by about 80%.
Step 5   For each circle retrieve a population at risk count (i.e. children) and incidence data (i.e. cancers).
Step 6   Compute the probability of an excess cancer rate under a Poisson assumption.
Step 7   Display "interesting" circles on the map, viz. these with a small probability of being a chance event.
Step 8   Repeat for all circle locations defined by the grid mesh.
Step 9   Repeat steps 4–8 for range of circle radius (i.e. 1, 2, 4, 8, 16 km) considered to be of potential interest.

The results are shown in Figure 3.11 (for a disease that clusters) and Figure 3.12 (for a disease that does not). Note the very different map patterns that have been

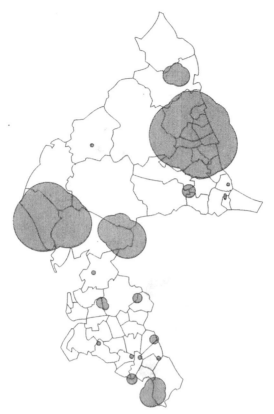

Figure 3.11

created. Any intelligence comes from visualising the results. Interpretation is entirely descriptive and it relies on human eyeballing of the map patterns. It leaves unanswered questions such as: how do you know if the apparent patterns of significant circles are random? What causes the patterns? Is it due to data errors or abnormalities or real-world phenomena or chance? GAM is purely a descriptive spatial analysis procedure in that it provides clues about location of pattern, its scale, and form of pattern but it is not definitive; it cannot be. Indeed this restriction reflects the endemic fundamental limits of all geographical analysis in that it is suggestive of possible causation but it is not by itself proof of anything.

GAM also causes many problems. The concept in 1987 of an "analysis machine" was a highly emotive issue that was hard for some people to accept; maybe it still is. An "analysis machine" implies an automation of statistical analysis skills and this may appear as a threat to those who possess such rare skills. It is also important to avoid undue excitement when reporting the results of such analysis machines as the results could be spurious, for example created by multiple testing. There is still a need for validation no matter what method is used. The results are essentially descriptive, focusing on patterns rather than

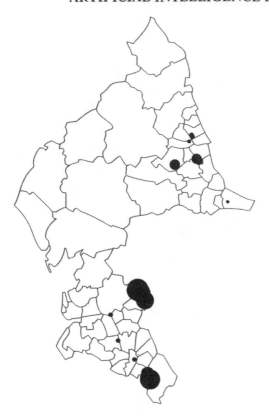

Figure 3.12   No indications of disease clustering

process, and there could well be various scale, aggregation and ecological inferencing problems. However, the original results of GAM were more or less corroborated, although subsequently described as being obvious! There is now little doubt that GAM was a major advance and that there are many different heuristic searches that could be developed to handle this problem; see for example Besag and Newell (1991), Openshaw and Craft (1991) and Openshaw and Perrée (1996).

But is GAM intelligent? The GAM search process is systematic and optimal in that it will not miss much, but interpretation does depend on the user. GAM did discover the putative "Gateshead cancer cluster" and this may well be one of the few real achievements of spatial epidemiology since Snows work on cholera in the nineteenth century. So it may be claimed that GAM did provide useful insights about the database being investigated and maybe even about cancer. Subsequent versions of GAM are more intelligent. The latest GAM/K version has cluster recognition rules built into it; see Openshaw and Craft (1991). The latest version uses a search driven by a genetic algorithm adopting some ideas from artificial life (see Chapters 7 and 8). So why are GAM-like spatial analysis methods not being more widely used? The answer is relevant to AI in that it reflects a number of general factors, including it is not in any of the proprietary GISs. It was never generally available. It may still be regarded as a controversial technology particularly by those establishment experts who remain firmly wedded to more traditional statistical methods. Furthermore, it is readily criticised on the grounds that validation is not easy, it is computationally intensive with the original work needing a Cray YMP supercomputer, and finally, it is difficult to know what to do about the results!

Viewed from an AI perspective GAM is a very fragile technology. The search is exhaustive, so if you reduce cell size to increase the number of locations being examined or to handle higher resolution spatial data then the computing times may become unbearable even though it is naturally parallel. Unlike many of the previous examples of heuristic search it is much less evident how to use GIS and knowledge to reduce the number of locations being examined. It is, of course, possible to avoid empty regions but that is all. Any further restrictions, for example to areas near nuclear installations, would damage the comprehensiveness of the search and constitute hypothesis testing rather than map exploration. When you do not know where to look, then you really do need to look everywhere! However, with GAM this can easily cause major computational problems. The early GAM needed vector supercomputers such as the Cray XMP and the Cray 2 to cope with the computational task (Openshaw et al, 1989). It would run even better on a parallel supercomputer because of the implicitly parallel search process. However, even a very fast parallel machine would be unable to handle either much larger problems or finer resolution data, or disaggregation of the problem by time period and disease type. The problem here concerns the search process that whilst highly parallel in nature may still be extremely computationally intensive. The original GAM evaluated several million circles; disaggregation by time and disease category could easily increase this number by a few orders of magnitude. Likewise, if the statistical evaluation component is made more robust, for example by using resampling methods to correct for multiple testing, then computing times could easily be increased by another factor of 1000 or even 10 000 times. Very soon no computer would be remotely fast enough to cope. However, GAM can be greatly speeded up by changing the nature of the search process, particularly by switching to a more intelligent albeit non-comprehensive search mechanism; see Chapter 8 on artificial life for details.

3.7.2 Case study 6: the geographical correlates exploration machine

The GAM search paradigm has been developed further to search for spatial relationships in a GIS database. Increasingly GIS data exist in the form of map coverages; each map layer or coverage represents a particular type of information, for example a geology map containing regions of solid rock types, a vegetation map. GIS gives the user an opportunity to perform fairly complex spatial queries, such as compute the cancer rate within 1 km of a major road, on a particular rock type, within 200 m of an overhead power line. However, what GIS does not do is to have any mechanisms able to suggest the questions or spatial queries (e.g. what combinations of map overlay) that are likely to yield interesting results. The user is supposed to know this, i.e. have a hypothesis ready to test. But what happens if there are no relevant hypotheses to test and the end-user is unable to invent any? Indeed this is a very common situation in many areas of geography given the post-GIS world-wide data explosions that have occurred. Again in a GIS context there is a great and growing need for an intelligent query system (IQS) that can explore the millions of possible spatial queries that could be issued to identify either those patterns or relationships of interest and identify those that may be worth further investigation.

Openshaw et al (1990) describe one way of trying to build an IQS based on heuristic search. This geographical correlate exploration machine (GCEM) is an attempt to generate and search a universe of all possible permutations of map coverages to identify those that interact with the point data of interest, creating evidence of localised spatial associations. Unlike the GAM, the spatial patterns here reflect the overlay of multiple map coverages and not merely circles of different sizes. GCEM might be considered as being similar in principle to a stepwise regression model but with map overlays as the predictor variables. If M is the number of coverages then there are 2^{M-1} possible permutations of map overlay. Each sequence of map overlays creates a map with many smaller polygons on it and the task is to identify locationally unique polygons that yield unusual results. In a cancer data context, an unusual concentration here may indicate a potential relationship of some kind between the coverages that created the search polygon and the data being analysed. These areas can be examined further subsequently using conventional GIS technology.

The GCEM algorithm is another type of exploratory spatial analysis system that involves the following steps:

Step 1   Define a set of M coverages and tag the data points with polygon labels and codes.
Step 2   Generate a permutation of the M coverages with K overlays in it.
Step 3   Compute Poisson probabilities for observed cancer counts for each of the overlaid polygons: it uses a virtual overlay simulator that is much faster than any GIS, see Openshaw et al (1990) for details.
Step 4   Flag any polygons that appear associated with an unusual disease incidence.
Step 5   Return to Step 2 and complete the search of all the possible permutations containing K from M coverages.
Step 6   Report those spatial queries that produced the most interesting results.

GCEM was run using the coverages shown in Table 3.8. The results shown in Table 3.9 are obtained. The smallest probability level was produced for areas

Table 3.8 Coverage/predictor variables used

Coverage description	Type	Scale of source map
1 Motorway buffer 1 km	Polygon	1:625000
2 Primary road buffer 0.75 km	Polygon	1:625000
3 Main road buffer 0.5 km	Polygon	1:625000
4 Other road buffer 0.25 km	Polygon	1:625000
5 Hazard buffer 1 km	Polygon	1:50000
6 Geology	Polygon	1:50000
7 Overhead power line buffer 0.5 km	Polygon	1:50000
8 Gasworks buffer 1 km	Polygon	1:50000
9 Waste incinerator buffer 1 km	Polygon	1:50000
10 Chemical works buffer 1 km	Polygon	1:50000
11 Large substation 1 km buffer	Polygon	1:50000

Notes: Geology coverage has five categories: 6.1 Limestone, 6.2 Alluvium, 6.3 Cornbrash, 6.4 Coal measures, 6.5. No geology. All the remainder are either in or out of a buffer zone of specified width.

Table 3.9 GCEM results

Poisson probability	Number of cancers	Number of children	Details of coverages in association
0.000116	8	2008	− 1 − 2 3 6.2 7 − 9 − 10
			− 1 − 2
			− 1 − 2
0.000194	9	2754	− 1 − 2 − 4 6.2 7 − 9 − 10
			− 1 − 2 − 4 7 − 9 − 10
			− 1 − 2 − 4 7 − 10
0.000199	8	2176	− 1 3 − 4 6.2 7 − 9 − 10
			− 1 3 − 4 7 − 9 − 10
			− 2 3 − 4 7 − 10
0.000219	8	2207	− 1 − 2 3 − 4 7 − 9
0.000296	8	2310	− 1 − 2 3 − 4 6.2 7
			− 1 − 2 3 − 4 7
0.000297	9	2922	− 2 − 4 6.2 7 − 9 − 10
			− 2 − 4 7 − 10
			− 2 − 4 7 − 9 − 10
0.000320	9	2953	− 1 − 2 − 4 7 − 9
0.000330	8	2349	− 1 − 2 − 3 6.2 7 − 9 − 10
			− 1 − 2 3 7 − 9 − 10
0.000355	8	2375	− 2 3 − 4 7 − 9
			− 2 3 − 4 6.2 − 9
0.000378	7	1821	− 1 − 2 3 − 4 7 − 8 − 9 − 10
			− 1 3 − 4 7 − 8 − 9 − 10
			− 2 3 − 4 − 7 − 8 − 10
0.000456	8	2469	− 1 − 2 3 7 − 10
0.000467	8	2478	− 2 3 − 4 6.2 7
			2 3 − 4 7

Notes: the minus sign in front of a coverage denotes outside the polygons of that coverage.

within 0.5 km of a main road, on alluvium, and within 0.5 km of an overhead power line. The question now is what precisely does this mean. The answer is made difficult because the map coverages are clearly surrogates for other data that are not directly represented in the GIS database; for example, it could be socio-economic information or certain types of pollution. However, this difficulty of interpretation is not a fault of GCEM as distinct from a problem in geographic analysis that is not new; for instance, distance has long been a general purpose surrogate for many different missing variables. This is yet another illustration of a major geographic fact of life.

A more specific problem with GCEM is that once the size of M exceeds about 15, then there are too many map overlay permutations to search and GCEM suffers from a combinatorial explosion. Rewriting GCEM for a parallel super-computer helps to delay the effects of the combinatorial explosion, since steps 2–5 can be performed concurrently. Ultimately, however, the data will win and once M exceeds about 25 computer times will probably become unacceptably large. However, this might well be more than enough to perform some very useful analysis, because even in a highly exploratory search there is seldom a requirement to use all the available data in a wholly unthinking manner. AI will never replace a bit of human common sense and a little thought! It is much better to combine both. Also it is important to "feel your way" and learn about the data by breaking the problem down into smaller pieces gradually, and carefully working your way up to the big one! Finally, try and think laterally. There must be several other ways of performing GCEM-type searches. Can you think of any?

3.8 CONCLUSIONS

Searching under control of heuristics is clearly a very useful and widely applicable tool in both AI and geography. It is claimed here that many exploratory analysis/model/knowledge discovery problems in geography can be handled via brute-force or intelligent searches. The new era of highly parallel computing machines and fast workstations and PCs introduces new possibilities that are increasingly relevant here. Moreover, as GAM and GCEM demonstrate, the use of automated yet simple analysis and modelling procedures applied to large databases via supercomputing can yield seemingly extremely interesting geo-graphical results. Both GAM and GCEM originally required the fastest available supercomputers, yet barely six years later they can be run on a PC. Both are based on very simple ideas but, if required, their brute-force searches can be replaced by more intelligent search procedures. If it is not necessary in order to perform a new experimental application, then you may well be advised to postpone further developments. New approaches based on bottom-up (rather than top-down heuristics) can produce far more efficient search procedures and particular attention is drawn to genetic algorithms and artificial life (see Chapters 7 and 8). If you are interested in novel algorithms with vast potential then a closer study of tabu search might well be extremely beneficial.

Often it is not hard to improve search mechanisms when you know what you want to do. As ever deciding what to do is the hardest part in seeking to exploit AI in geography, particularly in new areas where there is no guidance from previous work and most applications are completely new, but this can also be the source of considerable excitement.

Heuristic search suggests that there are also a number of different approaches to machine intelligence. One might be referred to as transferred intelligence; maybe this is really an extension of the programmer's skills, e.g. neat heuristic search methods. It may well be clever technology, but is cleverness the same as intelligence? Another is what was called result intelligence. Here it is the results that are novel or surprising or useful or smart in some ways: for example, the so-called intelligent GIS systems that use models to go beyond the map (Birkin et al, 1996) but maybe this is not really what is meant by AI but a timely reminder that you can be intelligent in other ways. Another example is the cancer cluster detection problem and the identification of potentially suitable nuclear power sites. They present possibly surprising or new results of the generic "I did not know that" type. A third form of intelligence would be that created by the activities of what might grandiosely be termed smart autonomous systems. Such a machine is now largely autonomous within a fixed domain. You no longer tell it what to do or even how to do it, just what you want. The machine learns or discovers how to do it the best way, by itself. In some ways this combines the previous two forms of intelligence. Maybe this is the sort of geographical AI that we need most.

Nevertheless heuristic search is a very important means of solving or attempting to solve a broad range of geographical problems. It might not appear to be particularly AI-ish but the results may well be. However, please do not get over-enthusiastic about the magic words "AI". They may in practice not mean much, and certainly there is no reason to fear or be humbled by them; on the other hand if you have managed to create a new technique or produced some new and interestingly novel results based on AI, then why not make the most of the AI logo!

3.8.1 Some questions for you to ponder

- Can you identify some geographical analysis and modelling problems that involve a search process of some kind?
- How would you attempt to make GAM or GCEM more intelligent?
- In a heuristic search context what would be **your** definition of intelligence?
- Is being able to solve a problem, either more efficiently or at all, being intelligent or merely clever?
- What is intelligence in a geographical context? Is it being able to run to the nearest pub when you are dying for a pint?

3.9 QUESTIONS AND ANSWERS

Q   What is a heuristic search?

A   A software procedure designed to provide a solution usually to a problem that either could not be solved as well, or as efficiently, or at all, by any other means. This can range from the seemingly mundane (e.g. sorting a very long list of numbers) to the possibly irrelevant but highly interesting (e.g. chess-playing machines) to the geographically relevant (e.g. location optimisation and exploratory spatial data analysis).

Q   Is heuristic search the best route for introducing AI into geography?

A   Probably not. There are much more relevant technologies that can be used as plug-ins for existing conventional techniques. It is much easier to make a quick impact via that route. Heuristic search applications are important but are much more specialised and it seems that the applications most likely to make best use of them still need to be developed. Still, history will no doubt prove us wrong and we hope it does!

Q   What is an algorithm?

A   A step-by-step description of how to solve a particular problem usually (but not always) presented in a form that can be programmed for a computer. An example might be how to use this book!

Step 1   Read introduction to see whether it is worth reading the rest.

Step 2   If step 1 outcome is favourable then study contents page more carefully.

Step 3   Identify the most useful or interesting AI technology and skim contents of relevant chapters.

Step 4   Either repeat step 3, or give up and go to the pub to recover, or read conclusions to discover whether AI has any future in geography.

Step 5   If fascinated then start reading contents more seriously, if not fascinated then have a read of the discussions at the end of each chapter, starting with Chapter 1. If interest level remains low then go back to the pub to recover, else go to step 1 and try again.

Step 6   If totally horrified and you are starting to hate anything to do with AI then start looking for quotes that can be used later to damn the authors and deconstruct their work, else if you are already an AI expert then dismiss authors as being ignorant geographers (or whatever) and try to write a better introduction book yourself.

Step 7   If totally bored by contents, then don't go into AI; maybe growing rose trees might be better for you.

Step 8   If it is too easy then reflect on the fact that the book is designed to be a non-technical introduction for fairly simple-minded geographers (and other of similar ilk) who want a gentle introduction to AI but without much of the technical complexity and jargon.

Step 9   If it is too lacking in GIS relevancy then maybe your definition of GIS is too parochial, AI is a toolkit and some of these methods are very relevant to GIS.

Step 10   Else enjoy it and recommend it to all your friends to buy!

Algorithms usually have 10 or fewer steps in them and offer a high-level description rather then detailed pseudo-code. They can therefore be highly frustrating if you subsequently wished to program them without understanding all the finer details, not all of which are given. For example, the reader could attempt to convert this algorithm into an expert system (see next chapter) but then what use would that be?

Q   Where is the search component in exploratory spatial data analysis?

A   If you are interested in the analysis of disease clustering and you do not know, in advance, precisely *where* on the map to look, then you will need to search the map. Search is a means of making up for the lack of knowledge. Quite simply, if we do not know anything then maybe we can some of what we are looking for by searching for it.

Q   OK, but where is the search in model building?

A   Well, that is an easy one. The task of specifying a mathematical model involves identifying one (or more) equations from a set of alternative possible equations. Ideally you use theory to guide this process or some mathematical model builder which is assumption dependent, but what happens if you have no good theory to guide you? How do you "find" a model? One traditional solution for simple linear statistical models is stepwise regression, i.e. select best K from M predictors either by trying all 2^M permutations or by using a less extensive stepwise search (as employed in current statistical packages). The former guarantees that the optimal result is found, but the latter is much faster. If we return to mathematical model building of a nonlinear sort then again there needs to be an exploration of the universe of alternative models, a search for the "best" (however defined) result. Heuristics (of any sort) that can guide this process will be of tremendous value when we discover how best to develop them.

Q   What is location optimisation?

A   Many problems in geography involve finding the best location for something; examples include steelworks, shopping centres, fire stations and hospitals. Usually there is a wide choice of alternatives and often attempts are made to determine the best or optimal location in relation to various "objective" functions such as transportation costs, accessibility and retail sales. An algorithmic method or heuristic that attempts to find the best location either by evaluating all or some of the alternatives is commonly used. If there are too many locations for complete enumeration of all the alternatives then a search heuristic would be used to do the best it can but it may not produce globally optimal results.

Q   Are non-optimal answers acceptable?

A   A characteristic feature of many heuristic methods is the lack of proof of optimality. Whether this is a problem depends on the context. If a problem that previously could not be given any solution can now be solved, even in an approximate manner, then that may well count as an improvement. Equally, even if you use a method that is considered to yield "the optimal result" how in fact do you know that it really has done so in practice? For example, the optimal value of a function usually depends on various assumptions, for example that it is continuously differentiable and convex. Are these realistic assumptions? What happens if the problem turns out to have multiple different optima or multiple local optima that you find depending on where you start to search?

Q   Is heuristic search really separate from other areas of AI that could also be applied to search problems?

A   There is no need to become territorially minded. If a genetic algorithm can be used as a heuristic search method then use it. In general as AI develops and matures the best methods will be those that contain their own forms of natural in-built intelligence. The role of the software designer will change to that of designing systems that can behave intelligently under their own control rather than be purely algorithmic in a highly deterministic way that is dependent on the knowledge and skills of the programmer.

Q   I still don't understand what heuristic search means.

A   Well, it is simply a means of solving problems (or puzzles) by searching for a solution. Imagine a maze and then remember how you would try and trace a path using a pencil as you wandered around looking (or searching) for the way out (the solution). Now consider developing a computer procedure that attempts to solve the same problem but hopefully more efficiently than you can.

Q   What has graph theory to do with it?

A   This is merely **one** means of describing (or representing) the problem in a general form which can be worked on in the search for a solution. There are often many different ways of doing this. If you find graphs confusing then do it some other way.

Q   Why are some graph-theoretic algorithms inherently unsuitable for parallel supercomputing?

A   Note that there is no claim that they cannot be ported on to parallel hardware, only that there is a reasonable chance they may not be able to make efficient use of the hardware if the parallelism is too finely grained in relation to processor speed. Parallel supercomputers work best on problems with "large" areas of computation that can be performed concurrently by many (not just a few) fast processors. In practice this will increasingly favour simple methods. In a database context this means simple data cubes rather than hierarchical data structures such as quadtrees. So unless you can use a graph-theoretic approach to segment the search domain into a reasonably large number of components that involve a reasonably large amount of computation that can be performed concurrently, then perhaps not much progress may be made.

Q   Are any of these graph-theoretic algorithms likely to be of any use in geography?

A   Maybe yes, maybe no. They exist. If you have suitable problems why not use them? What you don't do is go on the hunt for problems that match what they can do just so that you can use them.

Q   OK, but is finding the shortest path between two points on a network a good example of AI?

A   It is probably not AI but it is a good illustration of how you can use a heuristic search procedure to quickly find (in this case) the optimal solution to a problem that would take much more computer time if done crudely by total enumeration.

Q   Fine, but isn't it pushing things a little too far to declare that a binary search is intelligent?

A   No one would claim that the binary search heuristic is artificially intelligent. Certainly the search is highly efficient and is thus a neat or smart, even intelligent, way of searching an ordered list, but the intelligence is clearly external to the algorithm. It reflects the genius of the human mind who was clever enough to develop a fast search heuristic that only really dumb people would not want to use. The method itself is adaptive to the search process but is not otherwise intelligent. Its claim to fame rests entirely on its computational efficiency.

Q   How does a nonlinear optimisation procedure work?

A   Imagine a one-dimensional graph of a function plotted against an unknown variable. It attempts to find the lowest point of the curve. If there are two unknown parameters to look for then again the optimal values define the deepest hollow. Likewise in higher dimensional spaces, although we have no idea of what a hollow looks like in a 27-dimensional space; but there will be something equivalent that defines the minimum of the function's landscape! The various algorithms attempt to search this function landscape efficiently to find the lowest point (if minimising) or the highest point (if maximising). This task is easiest in one dimension and becomes progressively (and often rapidly) harder as the number of parameters (and dimensions) increase. One key assumption made by conventional nonlinear optimisers is that the functions are continuous smooth curves with only a single optimal location that can be reached from any starting position. In practice this may not happen and you may not even know that this is so! Hence there is often some benefit in using less efficient but more robust global search heuristics that trade off computer time for assurances about the quality of the solution. As computers become faster and computationally intensive routines more affordable so this becomes a sensible strategy to adopt.

Q   How did you model nuclear weapon effects?

A   A highly oversimplified approach was used here. First, only deaths were considered, not seriously injured. Second, only blast effects are included on the grounds that these effects are probably most predictable of all nuclear weapon effects. Third, all weapons were of the same size (one megaton of TNT equivalent) and were detonated in the air at a height designed to minimise fall-out and maximise blast effects. To assume that all weapons are of this size is clearly extremely artificial and quite unrealistic. However, please remember that this was designed to be illustrative not definitive; readers interested in a more detailed study of nuclear weapon effects should read Open shaw et al (1983).

Q   What is the Chinese postman problem?

A   A good question. The challenge is to determine the optimal route for a postman who is delivering letters to homes on both sides of several streets. It is a variant of the travelling salesman problem. Presumably by minimising the postmans walk distance it might be possible to improve his or her productivity, reduce staffing levels, and thereby provide yet another example of GIS being used as an instrument of social evil and unemployment!

Q   What is a hill climbing heuristic?

A   This is an algorithm that tries to solve a problem by evaluating a number of local moves and then selecting the best. You then move a little and then repeat the process until no further improving move can be made. There is an analogy here with the walker trying to find his or her way up a hill making only upward moves, whilst being unable to see the summit. At any location, the gradient can be measured and steepest direction of ascent identified. Imagine moving up a bit and then re-evaluating the gradient. This is analogous to how a nonlinear optimisation procedure works. The procedure can easily stop at a flat bit (e.g. a col) short of the summit. Note that hill climbing could equally well be hill descending; the same principles apply; and the term "steepest descent" used instead of hill climbing. In AI (and optimisation work) the "hill" is a function of some kind. Hill climbing methods can easily become stuck due to unevenness in the landscape being searched, especially in higher dimensional spaces. Simulated annealing is one way of avoiding suboptimal results. As the number of dimensions in the landscape increases so you need to change to more sophisticated technology, probably genetic algorithms to be on the safe side.

Q   Monte Carlo search methods use random numbers to define the search. How can you ensure that the same procedure run twice will generate exactly the same search?

A   Of course normally you would not expect to do so unless the problem was extremely well defined. However, it is reasonable to expect similar or even sometimes identical results. If for testing purposes you wish to generate exactly the same sequence of random numbers then why not merely start each run with the same random number seed; usually a time or process identification number will be used.

Q   Are random numbers random enough?

A   There is a vast literature on the randomness of different random number generators. In a search context do not worry about it. If a method does not work do not blame the random number generator! The worst problems usually occur when you want parallel random numbers that are different or if you generate so many random numbers so quickly that the sequence starts to repeat but even then it should not affect you.

Q   In Appendix 1 there is a Monte Carlo optimisation algorithm. How is this intelligent? It looks totally dumb!

A   Ah well, it is of limited intelligence other than a freedom from assumptions. It is a non-parametric method. It does not matter how complex or multi-modal the function being optimised looks like. It may, by chance, stumble across a good result. Any slight claim to be intelligent relates to this flexibility and freedom from restrictive assumptions. On the other hand, its claim to be dumb is much more clearly specified. It is extremely dumb. It has no way of knowing when or even if it has found a good result. Moreover, it runs for as long or as short a period of time as you tell it to! So at best it is a neat method, at worst it is totally dumb and wasteful of computer time. In practice it usually functions well as a pragmatic method.

Q   In Appendix 2 there is a focused Monte Carlo search. How is that more intelligent?

A   Being intelligent is not always a practical benefit. Here the method is more likely to focus on and then zoom into the optimal region. It is slightly adaptive and thus perhaps a little more justified in its claim to be "neater". In practice it often works well and can solve problems hitherto insoluble, so maybe it is smarter technology.

Q   What is special about simulated annealing?

A   The basic idea is extremely simple and appealing. The blacksmith has traditionally slowly cooled a lump of metal whilst bashing it into shape with a hammer. Simulated annealing is an attempt using a computer to mimic the metallurgical process of annealing, whereby metals are heated to a little below their melting point and then cooled slowly; this gives time for their atoms to arrange themselves into a perfect lattice. In AI it would be applied to a function optimisation problem. Instead of the function optimiser only making downhill moves, with a simulated annealing approach it can also move uphill. When the "temperature" is high, the function is highly fluid or melted and the optimiser can go up and down quite steep gradients. Slowly the "temperature" is lowered and the proportion of uphill moves is slowly reduced, ending up with a purely downhill move strategy. The hope is that this allows the optimiser to explore a much wider part of the function landscape before starting its local search for the optimal result. In practice it can mean run times increase by a factor of 100 (or more) but, equally, if the function is not globally convex and well behaved it is a highly effective means of finding optimal or good results that are independent of the starting values. One of the problems is that this is essentially a serial rather than a parallel process and as a result it is hard to parallelise although it can be done (see Openshaw and Schmidt, 1996).

Q   Why is the geographical analysis machine called a "machine" when it is only a piece of software?

A   The original search process was so computational intensive that when it was first invented (circa 1986) it really needed a dedicated mainframe computer to run it. Some of the early runs took the equivalent of two days of continued running on a large mainframe dedicated to the task. The computer was in effect performing only one function, it had become a *de facto* geographical analysis *machine*. Now of course with the dramatic increase in chip speeds and massive improvements in performance, you could actually have dedicated geographical analysis machines (of some kind or the other) running 24 hours a day, 365 days a year, perpetually on the hunt for patterns that matter in data that are important enough to warrant it.

Q   The classic GAM used no such intelligent search process, but performed a systematic or brute-force search. How can this possibly justify the adjective "intelligent".

A   Well, the inventors never did claim it was intelligent. Any claims relate not to the search process but to the significance attributed to any pattern discoveries it makes. It has the potential to generate results that by being discovered justify the accolade of intelligent. Ultimately this is highly subjective. GAM can be given a more intelligent search engine or have knowledge built into it and then it might be considered as doubly intelligent! How this might be achieved is partly a matter for the reader to ponder over but it is also partly covered in a subsequent chapter on genetic algorithms and artificial life.

Q If I am using an AI spatial data explorer of some kind why should I have to do anything other than click on the RUN button?

A There are dangers in expecting too much from AI. The aim is to try and establish an intelligent partnership between a person and machine, with each doing what they are best at. A little careful thought about the selection of variables might be extremely helpful provided this selection is neither too stringent nor too enthusiastically applied nor too crippling on the analysis. Vagueness rather than prescription should be the order of the day.

Q Finally, is heuristic search the area of AI most likely to produce geographically interesting results, or should I focus on a different AI technology?

A Maybe yes, maybe no. It really all depends on the nature of your interests. AI is a very broadly defined area that is grossly under utilised in a geographic context. With a little luck and some perseverance you could probably make a major impact in any area of AI you care to choose right now!

APPENDIX 1 A SIMPLE MONTE CARLO SEARCH PROCEDURE

The idea is very simple. You evaluate thousands or millions (or more) randomly generated solutions to a search problem and keep the best one. For example, if you are estimating parameters in a model then define reasonable upper and lower values for the parameters and generate random values between these limits. If you investigate aggregation effects then generate random zoning systems, perhaps using the algorithm of Openshaw (1977c), and then keep the best. It is crude but can be surprisingly effective. Moreover, it can be readily parallelised; simply run each trial (or batch of trials) on a separate processor.

A basic purely Monte Carlo search algorithm is as follows:

Step 1 Generate an initial random starting solution to a problem.
Step 2 Evaluate some function that measures performance and make this the current best result.
Step 3 Generate another random solution (or make one or more random changes to a current solution) to generate a new solution.
Step 4 Evaluate the function measuring performance.
Step 5 Keep this solution if better than previous best.
Step 6 Repeat steps 3–5 N times, where N might be a very large number depending on how much computer time you can afford.

The principal problem is that the quality of the results depends on the number of randomly generated solutions that were investigated, on your ability to distribute these random solutions intelligently (i.e. in the region where the optimal solution might be expected to occur), on the nature of the problem, and also on the extent to which external knowledge can be used to constrain the search. The benefits are principally:
1. Simplicity.
2. Effectiveness as it often works reasonably well on problems that cannot be solved by any other means.
3. It is easily parallelised since on a parallel computer each of the N repeats of steps 3 and 4 can be executed concurrently.
4. It is much quicker and pragmatic than a "search all" technique that might take the computer 32 trillion years to complete (cf. the computer in the *Hitch Hiker's Guide to the Galaxy!*).

5. Another advantage is its flexibility, in particular its ability to handle integer parameters and mixed integer and real problems.

The hardest part is in step 3 where you have to use an application-specific random solution generator. There are various ways of doing this and the zoning design example might help demonstrate this aspect.

It is particularly important that the random solutions being evaluated provide good coverage of the solution space. One strategy is to start with a solution and change it a little (making a small random change to somewhere in the neighbourhood of the current solution). Another is to generate a vast population of random results. The principal difficulty is that a good result may never emerge especially if there are large numbers of parameters. Also it is a great way to waste computer time. It should be the algorithm of last resort as there are usually much better ways of searching; see in particular the Chapter on genetic algorithms.

As a footnote, Stan remembers grappling with a nonlinear parameter optimisation problem that involved producing FORTRAN code for the first and second partial derivatives of a spatial interaction model. Six months flashed by before the necessary FORTRAN program had been produced and tested. Yet even the crudest of Monte Carlo optimisers knocked up in 10 minutes flat would have yielded the same parameter values to about three or four decimal places. It might have taken a day of computer time (on a primitive IBM 360/30 computer with 64 kbytes of memory) but even that would have been considerably more efficient than two person-years of effort albeit not nearly as elegant a result!

APPENDIX 2   A SIMPLE MONTE CARLO FOCUSED SEARCH HEURISTIC FOR NUMERICAL OPTIMISATION

In a numerical optimisation context the simple Monte Carlo algorithm of Appendix 1 can be improved by focusing the search in a slow but progressive manner around the current best result. Conley (1981) outlines an extremely simple but often highly effective way of doing this. His algorithm may be stated as follows:

Step 1   Generate an initial random starting solution to a problem and specify upper and lower values for each parameter (these may be quite large).
Step 2   Evaluate some function that measures performance and make this the current best result.
Step 3   Generate a random set of parameter values centred on the current best solution and within the specified upper and lower ranges.
Step 4   Evaluate the function-measuring performance.
Step 5   Keep this solution if better than previous best.
Step 6   Repeat Steps 3–5 N/M times, where N might be a very large number depending on how much computer time you can afford and M is about 20 to 50.
Step 7   Exponentially reduce the ranges (viz. divide by 2).
Step 8   Repeat previous steps 3–7 M times.

This method centres the random search in an ever-narrowing range around the current best solution, so that it will tend to funnel into the right answer. There is an underlying assumption, however, that the optimal solution is not isolated and hence far away from other randomly accessible parts of the search space. If you are happy with this assumption then this is an extremely simple solution to many large-scale nonlinear optimisation problems that may not be soluble by any other means. However, it is suitable only for conventional types of optimisation; you could not use it for some complex problems such as zone design because of the difficulty of focusing the results around a particular random zoning system in a useful way.

APPENDIX 3   A SIMPLE MONTE CARLO FOCUSED SEARCH HEURISTIC SUITABLE FOR ZONE DESIGN

Some search problems are so heavily constrained that the random search process needs to be altered in order to yield feasible results. The algorithm in Appendix 1 can be easily modified to do this. Step 3 can be replaced by a sample of possible feasible moves in the neighbourhood of the current best solution. One way of doing this is as follows:

:
:
Step 3   Using the current best solution as the starting point generate a list of K feasible random changes to the current solution.
Step 4   Either evaluate all K and select the best or randomly select one from the list and evaluate it.
Step 5   Replace the current best if there is an improvement.
Step 6   Repeat steps 3–5 a large number of times or until no further improving moves can be made.

The hardest part is identifying a feasible movers list. In a zone design context the AZP algorithm of Openshaw (1977a) merely selects a region at random and then tests all the zones in bordering regions that are contiguous to it and which could be moved out of their current region without destroying its internal connectiveness.

APPENDIX 4   A SIMULATED ANNEALING SEARCH PROCEDURE

One of the problems with the more focused type of Monte Carlo optimisation is that it can get stuck in local suboptima, since a move is only made when a better solution is found. This precludes any temporary poorer moves on the way to a better end result. One solution is to restart the search several times from different random starting positions (e.g. a different random number seed generates a different search) and choose the best. Alternatively, switch to a superior optimisation technology. Simulated annealing is one such method; see Aarts and Korst (1989). Simulated annealing is also sometimes called the Metropolis (or H-bomb) technique (after Metropolis et al, 1953). It is widely used as a global optimisation method suitable for problems with multiple suboptima (Kirkpatrick et al, 1983). It offers a robust Monte Carlo optimisation for problems that need it (Openshaw and Rao, 1995).

A basic hill climbing heuristic can easily be converted to a simulated annealing approach as follows:

Step 1   Define an annealing start temperature t and an initial solution x.
Step 2   Randomly generate a new set of values (q) in the neighbourhood of x and measure the difference in function values ($d = f(q) - f(x)$).
Step 3   If the solution q is an improvement then set x to q, remembering to keep the global best result in a safe place.
Step 4   If there is no improvement then still set x to q if $N(0, 1.0)$ is less than $\exp(-d/t)$ where $N(0, 1.0)$ is a uniformly distributed random number in the range 0.0–1.0.
Step 5   Repeat Steps 2–4 until a minimum number of moves occur or until some time

limit is exceeded.

Step 6   Reduce the temperature *t*; usually an exponential cooling schedule is used, so set a new value of *t* as 0.95 times its previous value.

Step 7   Repeat steps 2–6 usually for about 100 temperature changes or until several temperature changes occur without any improving moves being made.

The acceptance decision allows uphill (i.e. poorer than current best) moves with a probability that decreases with temperature. The hardest part is determining a sufficiently slow annealing sequence relevant to the problem in hand so that there is a good chance that the optimal result is found. Also the initial temperature is critical and this has to be set to a realistic value, which is also problem specific and may have to be determined by trial and error. Finally, this method will often consume at least 100 times more compute time than a simpler hill climber. It is also extremely serial in nature and therefore hard to parallelise although it can be done (see Openshaw and Schmidt, 1996). On the other hand, it often produces the best results.

APPENDIX 5   A TABU SEARCH PROCEDURE

Another solution to the problem of getting stuck is the tabu search method developed by Glover (1977, 1986). This started life as an integer programming method that is now regarded as being suitable for a much broader class of combinatorial and optimisation problems (Bland and Dawson, 1991; Glover and Laguna, 1992). It also tends to be faster than simulated annealing although perhaps not quite as good. The basic concept is very simple to describe and implement. You start by taking a basic Monte Carlo or other hill climbing local optimiser and having made a successful move you tabu it (i.e. prevent the reverse move being made) for a fixed length of time (defined as a number of iterations or search attempts). It uses memory to prohibit reverse moves and thus forces the search into domains that it might not otherwise examine. In practice tabu search is extremely aggressive but its performance is dependent on careful tuning and customisation of the algorithm to suit the problem of interest. There are many possible variations and the idea is very easily implemented. One of the most useful variations is to include an aspirational criterion that allows the tabu constraint to be overruled if no good solution is found within the allowed moves but there is a better solution in the list of tabued moves; see also Glover et al (1993). An example involving a zone design application is given in Openshaw and Rao (1995).

REFERENCES

Aarts, E., Korst, T., 1989, *Simulated Annealing and Boltzmann Machines*. John Wiley, Chichester, Sussex.

Bentley, J., 1986, *Programming Pearls*. Addison-Wesley, Reading, Mass.

Besag, J., Newell, J., 1991, "The detection of clusters in rare diseases", *Journal of the Royal Statistical Society*, Series A **154**, 143–155.

Birkin, M., Clarke, G., Clarke, M., Wilson, A., 1996, *Intelligent GIS*. GeoInformation International, Cambridge.

Birkin, M., Clarke, M., George, F., 1995, "The use of parallel computers to solve nonlinear spatial optimisation problems: an application to network planning", *Environmental and Planning A*, **27**, 1049–1068.

Bland, J.A., Dawson, G.P., 1991, "Tabu search and design optimisation", *Computer-Aided Design*, **23** 195–201.

Conley, W., 1980, *Computer Optimisation Techniques*. Petrocelli, New York.

Conley, W., 1981, *Optimisation: a simplified approach*. Petrocelli, New York.

Diplock, G., Openshaw, S., 1996, "Using simple genetic algorithms to calibrate spatial interaction models", *Geographical Analysis*, **28**, 262–279.

Glanstone, S., Dolan, P., 1977, *The Effects of Nuclear Weapons*. US Printing Office, Washington, DC.

Glover, F., 1977, "Heuristics for integer programming using surrogate constraints", *Decision Science*, **8**, 156–166.

Glover, F., 1986, "Future paths for integer programming and links to artificial intelligence", *Computers and Operations Research*, **13**, 533–549.

Glover, F., Laguna, M., 1992, "Tabu search", in C.R. Reeves (ed.), *Modern Heuristic Techniques for Combinatorial Problems*. Basil Blackwell, Oxford, pp. 70–150.

Glover, F., Taillard, E., deWerra, D., 1993, "A user's guide to tabu search", *Annals of OR*, **41**, 3–28.

Gould, P.R., 1966, "Space searching procedures in geography and the social sciences", Working Paper 1, Social Science Research Institute, Hawaii University.

Kirkpatrick, S., Gelatt, C.D., Vecchi, M.P., 1983, "Optimisation by simulated annealing", *Science*, **220**, 671–680.

Larson, R.C., Odoni, A.R., 1981, *Urban Operations Research*. Prentice-Hall, New Jersey.

Massam, B.H., 1980, *Spatial Search*. Pergamon, Oxford.

Metropolis, N., Rosenbluth, A.W., Rosenbluth, M.N., Teller, A.H., Teller, E., 1953, "Equations for state calculations by fast computing machines", *Journal of Chemical Physics*, **21**, 1087–1092.

Office of Technology Assessment, 1980, *The Effects of Nuclear War*. Croom Helm, Boston.

Openshaw, S.,1977a, "Optimal zoning systems for spatial interaction models", *Environment and Planning A*, **9**, 169–184.

Openshaw, S., 1977b, "A geographical solution to scale and aggregation problems in region-building, partitioning, and spatial modelling", *Institute of British Geographers, Transactions*, New Series, **2**, 459–472.

Openshaw, S., 1977c, "Algorithm 3: a procedure to generate pseudo random aggregations of N zones into M zones, where M is less than N", *Environment and Planning A*, **9**, 1423–1428.

Openshaw, S., 1978a, "An empirical study of some zone design criteria", *Environment and Planning A*, **10**, 781–794.

Openshaw, S., 1978b, "An optimal zoning approach to the study of spatially aggregated data", in I. Masser and P. Brown (eds), *Spatial Representation and Spatial Interaction*, Martinus Nijhoff, Boston, pp. 95–113.

Openshaw, S., 1982, "The geography of reactor siting policies in the UK", *Transactions of the Institute of British Geographers*, New Series, **7**, 150–162.

Openshaw, S., 1984, *The Modifiable Areal Unit Problem*. CATMOG 38, Geo-Abstracts, Norwich.

Openshaw, S., 1986, *Nuclear Power; Siting and Safety*. Routledge, London.

Openshaw, S., 1987, "An automated geographical analysis system", *Environment and Planning A*, **19**, 431–436.

Openshaw, S., 1990, "Automating the search for cancer clusters: a review of problems, progress and opportunities", in R.W. Thomas (ed.). *Spatial Epidemiology*, Pion, London, pp. 48–78.

Openshaw, S.,1991, "A new approach to the detection and validation of cancer clusters: a review of opportunities, progress and problems", in F. Dunstan and J. Pickles (eds), *Statistics in Medicine*. Clarendon Press, Oxford, pp. 49–64.

Openshaw, S., 1994, "Computational human geography: exploring the geocyberspace!" *Leeds Review*, **37**, 201–220.

Openshaw, S., Alvanides, S., 1996, "Designing zoning systems for the representation of socio-economic data", Working Paper, School of Geography, University of Leeds.

Openshaw, S., Charlton, M., Craft, A., 1989a, "Searching for leukaemia clusters using a geographical analysis machine", *Paper and Proceedings of the Regional Science Association*, **64**.

Openshaw, S., Charlton, M., Craft, A., Birch, J.M., 1988, "An investigation of leukaemia clusters by use of a geographical analysis machine", *The Lancet*, 6 Feb., 272–273.

Openshaw, S., Charlton, M., Wymer, C., Craft, A., 1987, "A mark 1 Geographical Analysis Machine for the automated analysis of point data sets", *International Journal of GIS*, **1**, 335–358.

Openshaw, S., Craft, A., 1991, "Using Geographical Analysis Machines to search for evidence of clusters and clustering in childhood leukaemia and non-Hodgkin lymphomas in Britain", in G. Draper (ed.), *The Geographical Epidemiology of Childhood Leukaemia and Non-Hodgkin Lymphomas in Great Britain, 1966–83*. HMSO, London, pp. 109–122.

Openshaw, S., Cross, A., Charlton, M., 1990, "Building a prototype geographical correlates exploration machine", *International Journal of GIS*, **3**, 297–312.

Openshaw, S., Perrée, T., 1996, "User-centred intelligent spatial analysis of point data", in D. Parker (ed.), *Innovations in GIS 3*. Taylor and Francis, London, 119–134.

Openshaw, S., Rao, L., 1995, "Algorithms for re-engineering 1991 census geography", *Environment and Planning A*, **27**, 425–446.

Openshaw, S., Schmidt, J., 1996, "Parallel simulated annealing and genetic algorithms for re-engineering zoning systems", *International Journal of Geographical Systems* (forthcoming).

Openshaw, S., Steadman, P., 1982, "On the geography of a worst case nuclear attack on the population of Britain", *Political Geography Quarterly*, **1**, 263–278.

Openshaw, S., Steadman, P., 1983, "Predicting the consequences of a nuclear attack on Britain: models, results, and implications for public policy", *Environment and Planning C*, **1**, 205–228.

Openshaw, S., Steadman, P., Greene, O., 1983, *Doomsday: Britain after nuclear attack*. Blackwell, London.

Openshaw, S., Whitehead, P., 1985, "A Monte Carlo simulation approach to solving multi criteria optimisation problems related to plan-making, evaluation, and monitoring in local planning", *Environment and Planning B*, **12**, 321–334.

Openshaw, S., Wilkie, D., Binks, K., Wakefield, R., Gerrard, H.H., Crosdale, M.R., 1989b, "A method of detecting spatial clustering of disease", in W.A. Crosbie and J.H. Gittus (eds), *Medical Response to the Effects of Ionising Radiation*. Elsevier, London, pp. 295–308.

Raggett, J., Bains, W., 1992, *Artificial Intelligence from A to Z*. Chapman & Hall, London.

Rhind, D., Openshaw, W., Green, N., 1988, "The analysis of geographical data: data rich technology adequate", *Proceedings of IVth International Conference on Statistical and Scientific Database Management*, Springer-Verlag, Berlin, pp. 424–454.

Scott, A.J., 1971, *Combinational Programming, Spatial Analysis and Planning*. Methuen, London.

Turton, I., Openshaw, S., 1996, "Modelling and optimising flows using parallel spatial interaction models", in L. Bourge, P. Fraigniaud, A. Mignotte, Y. Roberts (ed.), *Euro-Par '96 Parallel Processing* vol. 2, *Lecture Notes in Computer Science*, 1124, Springer, Berlin, 270–275.

CHAPTER 4

Expert Systems and Intelligent Knowledge-based Systems

Expert systems are all about attempting to introduce human knowledge about problem solving into computer software. The general objective is to emulate the problem-solving capabilities of the human expert. The current USA and European market for expert systems is currently estimated as about £100 million in 1994. At first sight this is surprising because most people seem to think that expert systems had their 15 minutes' worth of glory over 20 years ago and that they have since expired. In fact the industry is alive and well but a little quiet. Their main role today is buried in automated help systems. However, the underlying concept of building knowledge into computer systems is far more enduring and generally applicable than a narrow focus on the traditional types of expert systems might suggest. In practice the traditional approaches tend not to work as well as was once expected, except under special circumstances. As a result the leading edge of the technology has moved on from a narrow initial definition of expert systems towards a more general intelligent knowledge-based systems approach where there are strong glimmerings of extremely useful systems being produced based on hybrid mixtures of neurocomputing, fuzzy systems and other forms of machine learning.

4.1 INTRODUCTION

In the 1950s, AI seemed to promise that computing machines with intelligence levels similar to humans would soon be built with their own electronic brains. However, it soon became apparent that this was a futuristic sci-fi dream and that any intelligence would have to be built into computing machines via other routes. One way of achieving this was thought to be by developing heuristic search tools that could compensate for the lack of knowledge and for a while, game playing and puzzle solving became fashionable intellectual activities. The hope was that the generalisation of the puzzle/game-solving technologies would provide a path to more general forms of AI. Sadly machines that could play chess were totally useless at doing anything else. Intelligence was not entirely a search process and a fundamentally different strategy of becoming artificially intelligent was needed. The essential difference between human intelligence and machine intelligence had been overlooked. Expert systems (ES) changed things by offering an approach to building intelligent computer systems that could replicate some of the abilities of humans and, very importantly, could actually make a contribution to solving or handling real-world applied problems that were neither games nor puzzles. Suddenly AI possessed a commercial value and looked set to become a corner-stone of subsequent IT developments, or so it seemed in the early 1980s. Naylor (1983: 3) captures some of this enthusiasm when he writes: "There are two major faults possessed by most existing expert systems and these two faults are: that you, personally, don't understand how they work, and that you, personally, haven't got one." These faults can, in extreme cases, be quite serious.

Expert systems are an attempt to build computer systems that seek to mimic and replicate the behaviour of the best human experts in a particular decision-making task (Schildt, 1987). Rather confusingly, ES is sometimes regarded as being synonymous with AI itself; however, this is grossly misleading and a potential source of confusion. As has been emphasised, AI is not a single tool discipline but a bundle of several different technologies that share a common goal, namely that of building intelligent computing machines. Certainly ES is a trendy and highly seductive technology but it is at best only a small part of what AI is all about. The very idea of being able to capture, encapsulate and then utilise human knowledge so as to build intelligent artificial systems is extremely attractive for at least three reasons: (1) it might be useful, (2) it is almost instantly achievable to some degree, and (3) it does seem to be needed both now and in the future. The idea of having access to ES able to behave in ways that might be considered intelligent and knowledgeable is extremely attractive. Moreover the very words "expert systems" can themselves engender an aura of mystique and respectability around computer technology that might otherwise be regarded as drab, mundane and uninteresting. The same considerations apply to geographical applications of ES as much as to any others. However, it is important to be realistic. Conventional ES is a fundamentally flawed technology, although it still offers some potential for useful application and, like heuristic search, the ideas that lie behind the technology may well be of greater value that the current achievements of the technology itself. Certainly, the tremendous enthusiasm for AI based on ES that started in the early 1980s has seldom resulted in either systems that justify many of the heady claims or systems that are in widespread use. As a result ES has not yet moved into the IT mainstream but maybe it still will. From a geographical perspective, there would appear to be many attempts at building ES particularly in certain areas of GIS, but seemingly far less than 1% of the prototype systems appear to survive into full systems that work. The great triumphal fanfare of initial hype, hope and excellence of theoretical design just does not seem to materialise into fully operational systems. Maybe it is more fun attempting to build these systems than finishing them! However, it is possible that this will change especially as the emphasis is shifted from overly simple ES of the traditional 1980s style to more sophisticated hybrid intelligent knowledge-based systems of the 1990s and beyond. This chapter reviews some of the past, discusses the problems and offers some thoughts for how geographers might be able to exploit some of the ideas emanating from this area of AI.

The overall objective in ES is to discover how to add a human knowledge component to computer systems that previously lacked it. This reflects the view of many AI workers who believe that intelligent systems can only be built if they contain both knowledge and have mechanisms for using it in a particular domain. Some, such as Sowa (1984: 22), go further than this and narrowly define AI as "the study of knowledge representations and their use in language, reasoning, learning and problem solving". Others, such as O'Leary (1994), consider that AI is the discipline of *building intelligence into computers* (our emphasis) by using decision and process rules extracted from human experts that best summarise such essential knowledge and express it in a form where it can be readily accessed and used. An ES is essentially no more than a computer program that contains expertise (i.e. knowledge) about something specific and important so that it can answer questions from the user relating to that expertise. It is important to note that ES are highly task specific and are not general purpose or universal experts in everything, but then neither are the humans they are seeking to mimic. Expert systems, or, if you prefer, intelligent knowledge-based systems (IKBS), attempt to solve problems by the application of expert knowledge expressed as fairly simple rules and thus seek to emulate an experts problem-solving behaviour (Fox, 1990).

4.2 DEFINITIONS OF EXPERT SYSTEMS

Expert systems are often considered exciting because they are generally regarded as being a useful and achievable form of AI. They were also the first historically significant developments in AI that have yielded commercially useful results. There are various definitions of an ES. Some of the best emphasise what ES attempts to do; for instance:

> An Expert System is an intelligent computer program that uses knowledge and inference procedures to solve problems that are difficult enough to require significant human expertise for their solutions (Feigenbaum, 1982: 5).

Or

> An Expert System is a knowledge based system that emulates expert thought to solve significant problems in a particular domain of expertise (Jackson, 1986: 17).

Likewise in a similar vein that they

> Apply expert knowledge to difficult real world problems (Waterman, 1986: 18).

A key feature is that they address problems normally thought to require human specialists for their solution; see Michaelsen et al (1985: 303). Other definitions emphasise how ES function. For instance, Raggett and Bains (1992: 77) describe an ES as "a program that embodies 'expertise' about something and which allows the user to ask the computer certain questions about that expertise". Or as Marshall (1990: 5) put it: "An Expert System is, from the point of view of its users, a computer program to be used in the same way as any other. But from the point of view of its designers and implementors, an Expert System is quite different from a conventional computer program. For one thing, it incorporates a knowledge base, containing the knowledge it needs, and it operates by manipulating that knowledge in some formal manner." The British Computer Society explain it as follows: "An Expert System is regarded as the embodiment within a computer of a knowledge based component, from an expert skill, in such a form that the system can offer intelligent advice or take an intelligent decision.... A desirable additional characteristic ... is the capability of the system, on demand, to justify its own line of reasoning... The style adopted to attain these characteristics is rule-based programming" (see Forsyth, 1984: 9–10).

A less modest definition is given by Firebaugh (1988: 335) who writes: "Expert Systems are a class of computer programs that can advise, analyse, categorise, communicate, consult, design, diagnose, explain, explore, forecast, form concepts, identify, interpret, justify, learn, manage, monitor, plan, present, retrieve, schedule, test and tutor. They address problems normally thought to require human specialists for their solution." Other definitions include such grandiose terms as automated advisors, computerised assistants and virtual consultants; for instance, Feigenbaum (1982: 5) writes that an ES "can be thought of as a model of the expertise of the best practitioners of the field".

Finally, it is interesting to note that from a GIS perspective ES are seemingly the principal or indeed only area of AI applications in GIS. The *Association of Geographic Information (AGI) Yearbook*'s only reference to artificial intelligence is an entry for IKBS defining it as: "An interactive computer system, using programming techniques of AI, designed for efficient problem solving and answering queries on the basis of knowledge acquired from experts" (1989: 171).

4.3 WHY ARE EXPERT SYSTEMS SO POTENTIALLY USEFUL?

Why on earth should we want computers to do the sort of things that people already do quite well? Why would we want a piece of software that was a geographical ES? There are various answers that can be given, including:

- The things people want to do are the things people already do.
- They can make scarce skills and expertise more readily, widely and cheaply available.
- A reduction in error is possible because an ES is very knowledgeable about the problem being addressed.
- They help in the preservation of critical expertise as a future resource beyond the life span of any human expert.

- They ease the management of complex situations by unravelling the maze of rules, for example, relating to immigration and laws, eligibility rules for additional social security payments, sentencing guidelines for magistrates, tax regulations.
- They offer consistency and fair treatment in complex decision-making by ensuring that the rules are consistently and objectively applied without emotion, prejudice or favour one way or the other.
- Speed and efficiency are increased because of automation.
- They can offer decisions based on the best available skills and a broad range of expert abilities unlikely to be possessed by any single person.
- They offer a degree of competitive advantage.
- They are a means of commodifying and packaging an intangible resource (i.e. expert knowledge) in a form that can be readily and widely distributed and sold.

If you could capture in software the "geographical intelligence" of the world's leading geographers then would that not be worth while attempting? What might the gains of knowledge be if a software version of David Harvey or Walter Christaller had been built and could then be interrogated many years later about aspects of their work and the thinking that lay behind it. Well it would be *if* it could be done. As we shall discover, ES are not yet able to perform this function, nor indeed are any other areas of AI. This capability still lies somewhere in the medium-term future. Expert systems are far too limited in their ability to represent knowledge to permit this type of development. Meanwhile, maybe the best we can do is to use multimedia to capture the essence of human experts at work.

The main attractions of ES are availability and convenience. Expert systems do not sleep or eat or have holidays, so unlike the human expert, they are constantly available. Human experts are often in short supply and training new ones is sometimes a lengthy process, whereas ES can be easily copied and thus used to make a scarce resource much more widely available. Expert systems do not die and take their knowledge and experience with them when they go. They always operate at peak performance levels, they do not get tired and will always generate optimal and consistent results, albeit within the limitations of their knowledge base. The lack of a personality ensures neutral and emotionally unimpaired advice at all times. There is also the not insignificant novelty factor that at last computer systems can be built that behave in a similar manner to human experts. No doubt, if required, such systems can be given a more human feel via voice synthesis, so whether or not the idea is a good one, the idea of building ES or IKBS is quite frankly here to stay. The only significant uncertainty concerns how to build them, not whether we need them or whether there is a market for them.

However, do not get too enthusiastic too quickly! No single ES program can do everything and the levels of expertise gained in practice may not be that great. Also it is clear that the term "expert system" is often grossly and widely abused, for example as an innocent or deliberate attempt to dress up this or that totally dumb method in an AI guise. This raises such fascinating questions such as "Is discriminant analysis an 'expert system' for the classification of data?" However, a major distinguishing feature is the capability that a true ES has in explaining or justifying its decision or reasoning process in a language the user can understand. It follows then that a statistical method is not really a true ES although they could be embedded in one! Moreover statistical methods are not explicitly based on human rules but statistical concepts. Another fundamental distinguishing feature of an ES is the incorporation of human knowledge in one form or another rather than purely as data and this more than any other feature distinguishes an ES or IKBS from other pretenders that are less well endowed from a knowledge content perspective.

4.4 WHAT IS AN INTELLIGENT KNOWLEDGE-BASED SYSTEM?

Intelligent knowledge-based systems are often thought of as being the same as an ES. However, today a broader view might well be better advised in that an IKBS can be regarded as any kind of computer system that attempts to behave in an intelligent manner by the explicit incorporation of human knowledge of some sort. However, this does not restrict the knowledge base to a traditional ES approach but would include more indirect forms of knowledge representation as found in neurocomputing and fuzzy systems.

Again the term IKBS is often misused. For example, is a spatial interaction model used in a decision support system an instance of an IKBS? It can be argued that its application is "intelligent" partly because it uses knowledge about the spatial interaction system of interest and because the model itself forms a means of adding intelligence to a GIS that is otherwise lacking; see for example, the excellent book by Birkin et al (1996). However, IKBS is much more than the incorporation of little bits of numeric or vague problem independent theoretical knowledge in a GIS application. The knowledge has to be much more generic and also to be used in a much more intimate way if the resulting system is to be properly termed an IKBS. So if one day a real IKBS spatial interaction model is actually built it would have to include explicit general rules about the trip behaviour that the model attempted to represent and also a whole body of expert knowledge about how to apply the model and interpret the results. These rules would probably also change the model's predictions in some way. For example, in an origin constrained model a new destination zone would usually attract trips from all origins so its impact would be diffused over the entire system. A simple IKBS rule might be one that constrained the impact to within a maximum distance. Other rules could be imposed on the models predictions to make the model more realistic by the incorporation of knowledge about trip behaviour that the modeller knows about but the mathematical model does not. Examples of such rules of thumb would be to impose any interviewing opportunity rule such that no trips go beyond a very large destination to a much smaller one in the same direction regardless of what the deterministic mathematical structure of the model might suggest. Once you start to create computer systems that combine expert rules of thumb and qualitative knowledge with a mathematical or statistical model that is able to monitor its own behaviour and adapt to sudden changes in circumstances without much or any human intervention, then the resulting hybrid probably justifies the title IKBS. In general IKBS is all about adding human expert based knowledge to computer systems so that they can behave in a more useful and intelligent way in a problem-solving context and there are various ways of doing this. In geography, such IKBS modellers are still some years away.

4.5 WHAT DOES A SIMPLE EXPERT SYSTEM CONSIST OF?

Expert Systems are not a new idea and the earliest examples date from the 1960s, for example MACSYMA (1968), DENDRAL (1969), PROSPECTOR (1978) and MYCIN (1976). MYCIN consists of 400 rules; see Michie (1979). The XCON system used to configure VAX computer systems contains 8000 rules whilst the BMT system designed to configure fire protection equipment in buildings has over 30 000 rules (Michie, 1990). Japan's Fifth-Generation Computing Initiative and various national responses gave a great stimulus to research in this area. Commercialisation has been another bonus with the gradual realisation that knowledge is information which is both a resource and a commodity that can be bought and sold on the IT market-place.

Expert systems are based on a different form of programming. Normal or conventional programming involves some processes that obtain numerical results by applying an algorithm to a database. The numerical result may subsequently be converted into a decision or action of some kind via a different, usually informal, process involving human experts. By contrast, ES involve applying a reasoning procedure (based on inference) to a database containing knowledge rather than numbers. The result is a decision about a problem to which the knowledge relates. There are some similarities but the differences are also very important and have required the development of specialist languages for easing the task of handling knowledge and inference, for example PROLOG. The power of an ES derives from a combination of the knowledge it contains and the formalisms and inference systems it uses to apply the knowledge base (Fox, 1991).

Another way of defining what an ES does, is as follows. In geography it is common practice to process lots of numbers using a statistical package to obtain one or two statistics that represent some sort of analysis created by the application of the selected method when applied to the input numbers. In an ES there are no numbers to input, just a series of questions and answers that generate other questions and answers leading to a result in the form of a decision (or conclusion) of some kind. In this way the conventional ES attempt to mimic the behaviour of a human expert. Schildt (1987) gives the following example. Suppose you have found an unknown fruit and you have the following dialogue with a fruit expert:

Expert: Is it black?
User: No.
Expert: Is it red?
User: Yes.
Expert: Does it grow on a tree?
User: No.
Expert: Does it grow on a bush?
User: No.
Expert: Does it grow on the ground?
User: No.
Expert: Does it grow on a cane?
User: Yes.
Expert: Does the cane have thorns?
User: Yes.
Expert: It is a raspberry!

The ES contains all the knowledge needed to sustain this dialogue and a means of inferring an outcome. The knowledge base underlying this dialogue can be represented as a series of IF–THEN rules of the following form: *if* fruit is *red* and it grows on a *cane* and has *thorns then* it is a *raspberry*. This can be developed further to handle a wider range of fruit and also uncertainties in the user's response. For example, suppose the user had simply found a red fruit and had no idea of what it might have grown on. Then the system might have asked further questions about the fruit itself, for example its shape, size and texture, to try to establish its name. The final outcome might even have been a list of possible results together with associated possibilities. Another way of thinking about an ES is as a kind of sophisticated computer-based flow chart designed to solve a problem with many different decision points.

The real question for the geographer might well be: "What sort of geographical problems may benefit from this type of technology?" closely followed by "Do geographers possess sufficient knowledge to build such systems?" What types of systems would be of sufficient benefit and value as to justify the development costs? Do geographers have any or many suitable constrained problems that need scarce expert knowledge for their resolution?

There are many potential instances where such systems might be useful commonly found in areas where a user is attempting to apply some fairly complex computer tool and has only received a minimal level of training. For example, in the application of a statistical regression procedure with rules such as:

>*if number of predictor variables exceeds* 10 *then reduce them*
>*if skewness of a variable exceeds* 3 *then try a transformation*

if the R squared statistic is less than 0.2 *then change the variables*
if the standard error of the parameter for variable 3 *is too large then remove it*
etc.

Likewise the use of certain computer packages such as Arc/Info could benefit tremendously from the provision of automated expert help systems as well as expert advice about certain GIS operations.

There are various criteria that will characterise a successful ES. Firstly, there needs to be a generic problem that is common enough to justify the cost of developing an ES for it. Secondly, the problem has to be hard enough to need an expert with rare or expensive skills to solve it. Thirdly, the problem has to be definable using available information with clearly definable explicit rules that operate in this area. Finally, a typical problem is also one in which consistency and longevity are both important features else it may not be worth the effort.

There are a number of other key distinguishing features of an ES. These include:

1. It is limited to a specific application for which its knowledge base is relevant.
2. Data uncertainty can be readily handled or at least taken into account.
3. It can explain its reasoning.
4. It keeps facts and inference separate.
5. It is typically rule-based.
6. It delivers advice (not numbers) as output.
7. Building one is hard because of the problems of knowledge acquisition.
8. It makes money or at least has some prospect of attracting commercial attention primarily because it provides a means of packaging and commodifying knowledge.

Expert systems are regarded by many as the most significant practical product to emerge from over 40 years of AI research. It was certainly the first tangible commercial product; but some would say that they have been grossly oversold and that they have always promised much more than they have ever succeeded in delivering. Nevertheless, the basic idea has certainly proved to be very attractive and it is likely to be extremely long-lived in one form or another.

4.6 BUILDING A SIMPLE EXPERT SYSTEM

A conventional ES consists of four basic components: a knowledge base, an inference engine, a knowledge acquisition module and an explanatory interface. Figure 4.1 provides a brief outline of how the basic components are related.

4.6.1 The knowledge base (rule base)

The knowledge base contains facts, assertions and rules. It is much more than a database because it is not numeric and it contains the means of filling in missing

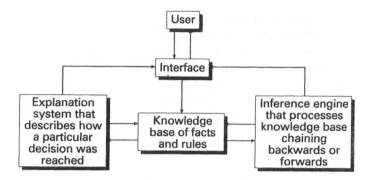

Figure 4.1   Components of an expert system

information, via inference. Knowledge is often represented as rules of thumb in the form of production rules; for example, IF (condition true) THEN (action). These rules can be used to store facts, e.g. if the light is red then stop, or to capture experience or rules of thumb that represent conventional wisdom, e.g. if the weather is hot then offer a cold drink. These rules are not usually embedded in software, although they could be, but are data for an inference engine of some form. There are various ways of representing knowledge. It is useful to remember that knowledge representation is the key to building an ES because it is knowledge stored in a symbolic form as data that is used to drive the decision making process. There are four different approaches to representing knowledge: production rules, inference networks, frames and logic-based systems. Most of these are too specialised to consider any further here.

If all this sounds hard and riddled with technical jargon, then maybe it is useful to realise that at its simplest an ES is little more than the computer equivalent of a flow chart. The "rules" are deterministic and totally defined, yet it is apparent they can be extremely useful in navigating complexity; for example, sentencing rules for magistrates whereby a very large volume of sentencing advice may be summarised as a large number of "IF-THEN-ELSE" rules. The rule base is a representation of all the knowledge relevant to a given situation. As such it can be extremely useful as a means of presentation, documentation and transference. Maybe people will feel happier to know that decisions are made on the basis of expert knowledge rather than whim or fancy. The creation of "IF-THEN-ELSE" rules may seem a trifle simple but the rules can be chained together so that one rule leads to another. Rules can be statements of fact or rules of thumb and have different levels of confidence attached to them.

4.6.2 The inference engine

The knowledge base stores "IF-THEN-ELSE" statements which allow conclusions to be made but only if there is some way of linking the user's response to questions, with the rules held in the knowledge base. The inference engine essentially determines what questions to ask the user and also which facts and rules to use in deciding on either the next question to ask or the answer to the problem. Clearly much depends on how well the inference engine interprets and processes the rules; else the system could end up swamping the user with many hundreds of unnecessary questions. There are three approaches to inferential reasoning that are commonly used: forward chaining involves reasoning from data to hypotheses; backward chaining attempts to find data to prove or disprove a hypothesis; and sideways chaining is a mixture of both.

Consider an example involving the following two rules:

$$\text{if } A \text{ then } B \quad \text{(Rule 1)}$$
$$\text{if } B \text{ then } C \quad \text{(Rule 2)}$$

Once A has been assigned a value (true in this case), the system concludes that the answer has to be C. In backward chaining the process is as follows:

$$\text{Find out about } C \quad \text{(Goal)}$$
$$\text{if } B \text{ then } C \quad \text{(Rule 2)}$$
$$\text{if } A \text{ then } B \quad \text{(Rule 1)}$$

therefore

$$\text{if } A \text{ then } C \quad \text{(Implicit rule)}$$

Now ask the question

$$\text{Is it true?} \quad \text{(Data)}$$

then the system can answer it.

Now you can query the system to ask it to explain why it made a particular decision. This sounds good but it is not all that interesting to be told that the decision was made because of rules 1, 49, 167, 259 and 3497! Nevertheless, some explanation is better than none at all, just do not get overly excited about it. In practice you would save yourself a lot of time and effort by using an ES shell system that greatly simplifies most aspects of building an ES. The really hard bit is creating the knowledge base and handling any uncertainty in it.

4.6.3 Handling uncertainty

There are various possibilities for handling uncertainty, none of which are easy: fuzzy logic, Bayesian logic, multi-value logic and certainty factors. The good news is that they all seem to work. At its simplest, conditional probability rules are applied. For example:

$$\text{if } E \text{ then } H \ (LS, LN)$$

where E is evidence for a hypothesis, H is a given hypothesis, LS is the degree of support for H if E is present, and LN is a measure of discredit if E is missing. Perhaps the really difficult part of handling uncertainty is knowing how much uncertainty there is in the knowledge base and then quantifying it. There are grave dangers when building in uncertainty handlers if the resulting levels of uncertainty are incorrect. The misplaced confidence displayed by the user may result in catastrophe as a user who is confident that his or her ignorance is being dealt with may behave quite differently if it remains a constant source of ongoing worry. The latter might well become too trusting of an ES that which may well be more imbecilic than a real expert!

4.6.4 Knowledge acquisition and knowledge engineering

Knowledge is a scarce and costly resource. Experience suggests that it is difficult to extract human expertise or elicit human knowledge and then encapsulate it in an ES form, for example as IF–THEN rules. Knowledge elicitation involves the grandiosely titled "knowledge engineer" interviewing experts to identify the underlying rules of thumb or expertise that they would use to solve the problem. This process is seldom easy unless the human system is well established and follows explicitly stated rules printed in books or manuals or laws. As a result knowledge acquisition is a major bottleneck in building ES. It is often hard to find or determine who is or is not the real expert. Additionally there may be conflicting opinions about a problem, or what you thought was a science turns out to be very much a black art full of mysticism of one form or another. As a result it is often difficult to extract all the necessary information from human experts. Then if that was not enough, testing and verification of the knowledge base present other problems. Accuracy is clearly important in any life-critical ES applications but how can you be certain there are no errors in the system?

4.6.5 Some ethical issues

There are various major moral and ethical questions in using ES. One key issue relates to responsibility. If an error is made, who is responsible? Is it the fault of the knowledge engineer or the human expert or the system software engineer who built the application or the vendor who designed the system shell or the computer hardware manufacturer on which the system was run? But equally, if an ES is not used, and avoidable human error occurs, is this not also a crime? Furthermore, there is the problem of end-user and consumer acceptance. Currently there are plans in the EU to try and prohibit automated decision-making computer systems that affect people. The EC Data Protection Directive (95/46/EC: article 15) states that "Member States shall grant the right to every person not to be subject to a decision which produces legal effects concerning him or significantly affects him and which is based solely on automated processing of data intended to evaluate certain personal aspects relating to him, such as his performance at work, creditworthiness, reliability, conduct, etc." Other questions concern whether or not end-users will accept expert advice given by machines and if such advice is given and used, should they be told about its origin? It seems that these and related concerns relegate ES to the role of advisor or an independent source of advice or information rather than as a primary decision maker and taker. On the other hand, in applications ranging from camera-focusing systems, user interfaces, smart help systems and other consumer control devices, ES are already widely and apparently happily used and accepted. The critical factor in influencing acceptability is seemingly the nature of the application and the visibility of the underlying technology.

4.7 GEOGRAPHIC EXAMPLES OF EXPERT SYSTEMS

Two key areas in GIS often targeted for ES are cartographic tasks such as name placement and map generalisation as well as spatial decision support functions. In a cartographic domain it has proved difficult to establish the rules that reflect the holistic and artistic nature of many of the principal manual map design processes. It has not been easy to formalise knowledge about design issues except in a trivial way.

Herbert et al (1992) and Joao et al (1993) describe a map generalisation machine that uses an ES to assist the user make sensible choices about the generalisation process, for example the choice of generalisation algorithm and related parameters. This assumes GIS users who are totally unfamiliar with map generalisation issues in which case the system might well be able to offer some useful advice. In theory this should work better than a standard generalisation method that runs with default parameters, but where is the proof? Maybe more should be expected with a comprehensive rule set covering the widest possible range of generalisation needs. However, even this might not be sufficient because a truly intelligent ES for map generalisation would also be able to determine whether the task in hand is impossible or if the advice given has failed to yield a useful result. Providing advice about parameter setting is really only a minimal step forward. A really useful intelligent ES would be able to experiment with different parameter settings and then evaluate whether or not the advice that was given is of any value. However, such a system goes beyond what ES have traditionally been regarded as offering.

It may be better simply to remove the human expert from the map design process altogether and develop genuinely automated generalisation software, perhaps along the lines of the Li and Openshaw (1992) natural principle of objective map generalisation. On the other hand, ES interfaces designed to simplify hard to use software packages are one area where useful systems can be derived. For example, many geographers would find an ES interface to the more complicated spatial statistical methods of considerable assistance. This is, of course, quite feasible because the problem is well defined and the rules of thumb employed by the statistical expert user should be readily acquirable.

Another example is Wadge et al (1993) who built an ES linked to the Arc/Info GIS to assist users in natural hazard assessment. It is an attempt to present information about natural hazards to planners and developers in an understandable way without having to consult many different subject specialists such as earth scientists for an interpretation of the available information. The idea is that the ES provides a basis for converting the information into practical planning advice. They test their system on landsliding in Cyprus and subsidence in Ripon. The concept of an information system designed for several distinct end user groups is not viewed as a breakdown of the traditional expert advice relationship as distinct from a basis for assimilating information into a more useful form. It is a pity that systems of this sort are still not available.

Expert systems work best in well-structured situations. There is woefully insufficient knowledge of many geographical problems and tasks to build meaningful, deep or even useful ES. For example, map design is an intuitive process not subject to formal logic, and mathematical modelling is an art rather than a science. Geographical knowledge bases are too weak for a knowledge engineering approach to be successful, except in a small number of highly constrained activities. Spatial decision support is one of these areas where good practice might be identified and coded as an ES.

Consider the following spatial data meta rules concerning land-use planning:

IF a land parcel is close to the airport THEN limit its height
IF a slope is less than 10° and the height is less than 1000 m and soil is good THEN land is suitable for arable farming

IF (x,y) belongs to zone 1 THEN rule A
IF (x,y) belongs to zone 2 THEN rule B
IF (x,y) belongs to zone 3 THEN rule C

Such simple-minded rules can be used to add considerable degrees of local intelligence to GIS applications related to site suitability that might be quite useful as a means of incorporating external knowledge, provided the rules are themselves deterministic. It might be imagined that this type of rule base could be extended to encompass all relevant situations, except human behaviour, and decision-making has seldom, if ever, been made in such a consistent and explicitly rule-based manner. Planning has never been practised as a rules-based process and the reasons for many historic decisions are seldom so formalistic as to be expressed as rules. Where rules do exist, there are often exceptions to them. Additionally, many meta rules can only be identified *post hoc*. Of course this is itself an interesting discovery but it does not bode well for rules-based planning systems.

One interesting way forward is to replace crisp or Boolean IF-THEN rules by fuzzy logic versions. Coughlan and Running (1996) describe examples where this approach can become much more useful when the rules are re-expressed in a fuzzy format. For instance, the previous land suitability rule can be reworded as if slope is **slight** and height is **not high** then arable suitability is **good**

where the fuzzy terms "slight", "not high", and "good" replace the previously precise values of zero to 10.0°, zero to 1000 m, and a probability of arable of 1.0; see also Chapter 9.

Another example of an ES is the formalisation of the hazard assessment process as a checklist of action steps, but even here there are limits to its utility. At the end of the day decisions have to be made. People may die if wrong decisions occur. The problem is that when the basis for the decision is obscure and informal, the risks of victims seeking litigation are small. Once there is an explicit basis for a decision, the attribution of blame and financial penalty aspects become much clearer; see Openshaw (1993). Maybe an ES able to assist the unskilled user to navigate through complex mapping (e.g. GIMMS) or GIS packages (e.g. Arc/Info) might be where the greatest practical benefits will occur. However, such applications, whilst useful, would hardly count as earth shattering or, perhaps, even constitute much of a commercial product.

Another application is much more useful. It is observed that ES work best with self-contained tasks. If they are regarded as a means of adding experiential knowledge to computer analysis processes that previously lacked any, then this whole area suddenly becomes much more useful to many areas of geography. For example, it is interesting to note that the 1991 version of the GAM (GAM/K) cluster detector (see Chapter 3) uses an "expert system" to detect clusters that matter (Openshaw and Craft, 1991). It applies the following rules to find spatially autocorrelated peaks of cancer excess in a three-dimensional surface generated by an exploratory map search procedure. The method is simply stated. A cancer cluster (or putative database anomaly if you are worried about the terminology causing fear in the media) exists if the following conditions are met:

Step 1   Find cell with maximum value.
Step 2   Flag as a possible cluster if the value decreases smoothly with distance for a minimum number of concentric distance bands.

This rules-based approach was developed from five years of experience in attempting to interpret the output from GAM. It is a simple feature detector that is quite generic since it is not parameterised in any way. It is this generality of the information base used by an ES that is another very distinctive feature.

4.8 AUTOMATIC RULE MAKING FROM EXAMPLES

Expert systems represent an attempt to become intelligent by defining and then using formal rules of logic relevant to a particular problem. The great difficulty is that problem solving is seldom a purely logical process based on the application of a set of simple rules. Another is that the rules are seldom known with much or any precision. Fortunately there are several other ways of representing knowledge, not all of which require the knowledge base to be based on "IF-THEN-ELSE" rules. Knowledge can also be stored as classified data or else converted into an artificial set of IF-THEN rules that appear to match a database. Intelligence arises from using a knowledge base of previously coded responses to assign values to new unknown responses. This paradigm for IKBS clearly leads to what is described as machine learning, data mining, and related approaches to creating systems that contain what might be broadly termed "expert knowledge" built up from the analysis of databases relevant to a particular problem. A neural network and fuzzy logic modellers are also able to provide a broadly similar approach.

4.8.1 Knowledge discovery systems

One of the earliest approaches to the creation of rules from data examples is that of Quinlan (1979). This may be regarded as a development of an even older exploratory data analysis technology known as AID (automatic interaction detector) which sought to predict the values of a dependent variable from a set of M categorical and continuous predictor variables. Successors to this technology are now widely used as trendy "data mining" tools. Openshaw (1989) describes some other variations of these methods which he termed database modeller (DBM) 1/2/3 depending on the nature of the variables. These systems produce predictive rules from examples held in a database. For example, in a large survey (or direct mail database) it is possible that the probability of responding is highest for the following selections:

> Aged 25–40 and in geodemographic clusters 1, 2, 3, 4 and with 2 cars and single then probability of response is 0.55
> Aged 45–60 and in geodemographic clusters 45, 46 and 49 with no cars living with wife but no children then probability of response is 0.001

The problem with this technology is the hierarchical nature by which the rules are generated, the difficulty many methods have in dealing with noisy data, and doubts about the predictive accuracy. These methods tend to be much better at describing a historical situation in terms of explaining what happened rather than being able to forecast or predict future situations and model what might happen. It is doubtful whether these are really "expert systems" as distinct from statistical modelling techniques. Nevertheless, some of these methods have been used to create ES; see Michie (1990). There are also many other ways of generating rules that appear to explain behaviour without first developing a hierarchical tree structure; for instance, you can use genetic algorithms and artificial life to create the modelling rules directly; see Chapters 7 and 8. Nevertheless, methods such as AID, CHAID and C4.5 continue to be used in commercial response modelling and database modelling applications; see Openshaw (1994a, b) for a review and Quinlan (1993).

The application of these and other data mining techniques to geography awaits a change of attitude (viz. a loosening of the very strong addiction to statistical methods) and an interest in the analysis of really large rather than fairly small databases. Too many geographers and quantitative social scientists still view the statistical analysis of data as a hypothesis driven activity and are still seemingly reluctant to indulge in more exploratory styles of analysis using automated and broadly based AI approaches. This is an ongoing cause of considerable concern because it implies a gross neglect of the data riches being created by developments in IT. Data mining is defined as the process of discovering and extracting new knowledge and useful information from databases using both AI and non-AI methods. Developments in IT have made it fairly easy to capture, store and manage vast volumes of information about many aspects of our daily existence. It is not just GIS databases that are involved in this data explosion. Data mining provides a means of getting at some of the potentially useful patterns and relationships hidden in the databases. Some if not many of these patterns **are** relevant to human geography yet many human geographers seems to be totally blind when it comes to using or exploring or even being aware of many of the new opportunities that now exist.

4.8.2 Memory-based reasoning (MBR)

Here, however, attention is focused on memory-based reasoning (MBR) as offering an alternative general purpose paradigm suitable for certain types of IKBS. This may also be termed a case-based reasoning process. The idea is simple enough. Humans often use analogical reasoning or experiential reasoning to learn and solve complex problems. They often remember what happened last time or features associated with a particularly successful outcome and then use this experiential knowledge to simplify and decide subsequent courses of action. This sometimes appears as guessing or acting on the basis of a hunch. There is no reason why this use of past experiences cannot be used to devise another type of ES. Knowledge is being used to make intelligent decisions.

Memory-based reasoning is attributed to Stanfill and Waltz (1986), Stanfill and Kahle (1986) and Creecy et al (1992); see also Aha et al (1991) and Atkeson (1986). It is based on the nearest neighbour classification approach in which a "record" is assigned to the most similar example case. It can be noted that many decision-making tasks involving data can be used to create a library of results; for example, given these variables as inputs then this is the "expert" decision that has been made. The variables could be virtually anything from free text, to categorical response to numeric modelling problems, or it could be a plain text to numeric code applications. The point here is that in many problems there is a finite (but maybe large) number of possible unique outcomes. Once a reasonably large sample of results has been obtained then it becomes feasible to apply an MBR approach to use the experience of "expert" decision-making that has been established and captured (in the database) to help deal with new situations that arise. The problem is that the power of such a system grows at a rate which is less than linear, whilst the computing times grow at a linear rate. The meaning of this statement will become clearer later. A basic MBR algorithm involves the following procedure:

Step 1   Build a reference database consisting of N data records with a known result or expert decision. The data can be text strings, numeric, etc. It does not matter. Likewise the expert result could be more text or a number or an observed value.

Step 2   Read a new record of a similar type as the database.

Step 3   Search the database for either an exact match or nearest match (or near match) using some measure of similarity between the target record and the records stored in the database.

Step 4   If the match level is acceptable then assign the record the appropriate response else add it to the reference database and either determine the correct response or else flag it as uncoded or else estimate the result in some way by perhaps by modifying the few nearest matches. Usually if no reasonably appropriate matching record can be found then a human created solution is needed. This is subsequently added to the database and it constitutes the learning component.

Step 5   Repeat steps 2–4 for all records.

Note that the three critical parts are: (1) the measure of similarity that is used in **step 3**; (2) the decision about whether the match level is acceptable; and (3) how to perform the search in **step 3** extremely efficiently via some clever heuristic. The similarity measure is straightforward but needs to be fairly carefully thought about. In principle it can take any form appropriate to the data but some will work much better than others. For example, if a distance measure based on numeric data is used it will work but you may wish to weight different variables differentially. Likewise comparing text strings can be done in a number of different ways; for instance n-grams or by soundex matching (viz. a means of matching incorrectly spelt words) but some will work better than others. The decision about match levels is again subjective and needs to be carefully tuned to the problem of interest.

The search process is naturally parallel; for example, if there are 20 000 records to be matched and 256 processors available then the task can be shared so that either each processor examines 1/256th of the database (held in local memory) or at any moment 256 different searches are being performed concurrently. Stanfill and Thau (1991) describe the application of this strategy on a massively parallel computer. Clearly MBR has considerable potential to provide the basis for fairly intelligent, experience based, adaptive computation that can readily exploit parallel computing environments. Indeed, given that these environments exist and are in search of commercial applications, and given that MBR is a relatively straightforward technology, this more than anything else may well propel MBR to the forefront of applied AI in the next few years.

Note that this method is very general and can be applied to an extremely wide range of problems. Note also that the expert knowledge that is built up is not deep knowledge in the sense that it is expressed as a set of IF-THEN-ELSE rules but is implicit and largely invisible. Neurocomputing is another way of tackling this type of the problem, although this method is much more direct. MBR is based on the premise that humans often use analogy-based reasoning that uses past experiences to handle complex problems. MBR is an attempt to do something similar using a computer. A neurocomputing approach may well be better if the data are noisy, distorted, contain a lot of variation, are ambiguous and too limited or otherwise deficient in quality and consistency for an MBR approach. For instance, neural networks have an ability to generalise to previously unseen new situations and this may well be extremely helpful. Chapter 6 describes an unsupervised neural network that has also been used to perform MBR functions.

A simple example would be a regression model. Suppose a sample of 1000 cases each with 10 variables measuring something is available, together with a response value. The task is to estimate a response for 1000 other cases. The MBR approach would involve finding the closest matching case in the library file of 1000 cases for each new case and then using as a prediction the related response value. Note that no statistical modelling takes place, rather the variables are used as a search key in a kind of nearest match or fuzzy retrieval process. Perhaps surprisingly many problems are inherently suitable for this approach if there is a suitable library data set available for it to use. It might seem neat to assume that a global response model can be defined with a handful of parameters, but it will never work well if the problem consists of M different functions or is complex in many different ways, for example the variables are non-numeric. An MBR approach is still applicable and is largely assumption free. Its weaknesses relate to the library database of experience, its quality and consistency, as well as the amount of computer time needed to perform the nearest matching process. Obviously 100 000 cases would be better than 1000 in a statistical problem, but if responses are required for 1 million unknown records then there would be a requirement for 100 000 million searches, and that is rather a lot!

Creecy et al (1992) describe a text-coding application. In the census (and many other surveys) there are a number of variables that are hard to code. Probably the worst is "occupation". A much easier but still difficult variable is "place-name". In both cases the traditional approach is to create a directory of occupations mapping a text description to an industry or occupation code; or in the case of place-names, a gazetteer giving a geographic reference. The US census has previously used an ES to help code occupations. Table 4.1 reports the results when compared with an MBR approach based on a 132 247 example database consisting of free text descriptions of occupations and a classification code. The MBR performed 20% better for occupation codes and 6% better for industry codes. This would have reduced total census workload by 25% and saved several million dollars. In the US 1990 census there were 28 million descriptions to be classified. It might be imagined that if the entire set of 28 million classified occupations was kept until the next census, then presumably most of the coding would be fully automatic.

Table 4.1 MBR versus an expert system

	% of industry codes classified automatically	% of occupation assigned automatically	Person-months of development time
Expert system	57	37	192
MBR	63	57	4

Source: Creecy et al (1992).

Handling free text searches requires that an efficient technique can be created to represent how similar any two strings of text are to each other. There are various ways of doing this whereby different words are weighted to reflect their value as a classification feature: Stanfill and Waltz (1986) and Creecy et al (1992) provide further details.

The MBR offers a number of benefits compared with classical ES:

- Potentially superior performance—being data-driven gives MBR an inherent advantage over systems that require the knowledge rules to be explicit identified.
- Ease of development.
- Flexibility, in that even experts cannot always identify the rules that will match specific responses, partly because rule building is still an art rather than a science.
- Performance can be improved by increasing the size of the library database and by updating it. For example, a medical diagnosis ES would have failed to diagnose Legionnaires' disease as indeed would the MBR approach. However, once there was a Legionnaires' disease case in the database, it would spot any subsequent ones. By comparison, the ES would probably need to be rebuilt.
- It can handle any form of record and any form of measurement system directly, unlike a neural net which would require the data to be recoded.
- MBR is scalable technology that can cope with open-ended problem solving and offers a generalised solution.
- Ease of updating and of handling dynamic data situations—MBR systems are easily updated and have low or no initial set-up costs. They are very easy to embed in dynamic database applications in which update frequency might be an important performance factor.
- It is straightforward to spot poor results since measures of uncertainty can be provided, whereas ES tend to hide the uncertainty.
- Results can be justified on the basis that the Kth requested possible cases are actually worse. The justification of an ES for a decision usually consists of a chain of rules, which may not always be that convincing or helpful to the end-user. An MBR offers the nearest (or even K nearest neighbours) as explanations and this tends to be more readily believable and understandable.
- The results are reasonably tolerant to noise in inputs and training data. There

is considerable inherent redundancy in MBR and this reduces the damage that noise could cause; see Stanfill and Waltz (1988).

- MBR allows exploitation of previously manual based and clerical exercises. These manual systems provide a basis for building an MBR and, therefore, are a necessary prerequisite. It also follows that MBR is a natural next step, building on previous experience and cruder systems. Like other machine-learning approaches it merely requires that the knowledge base is retained rather than "thrown away" after use.

The principal disadvantage is the need to trade computer speed and memory for knowledge engineering. It probably requires large parallel super computers to power it before its full potential can be realised. It is not parsimonious or, by any means, can it be considered to be a sophisticated approach. It is inherently crude; however, its crudeness is also its strength and as the computation costs become affordable then it provides a different and potentially extremely useful general paradigm for building IKBS. After all, a hallmark of an intelligent system is one that learns from experience and MBR certainly has this property.

4.9 OTHER TYPES OF INTELLIGENT KNOWLEDGE-BASED SYSTEMS

A final aspect concerns whether other types of IKBS can be developed that are not ES in the conventional sense. The failure of ES to fulfil their promise has resulted in various attempts to broaden the domain of IKBS. Certainly, instead of seeking to mimic expert decision-makers based on knowledge bases, it is also possible to develop less dumb and thus more intelligent systems, often just by thinking about the problem. A particularly easy way to develop smart systems is to introduce feedback loops and other devices that can make the behaviour adaptive and responsive to its inputs and performance. Another equally simple idea is to incorporate some "expert knowledge" into computer procedures that no matter how sophisticated the underlying statistical technology may appears are essentially dumb. There are many different ways of operationalising this simple idea.

Consider the following example. Suppose a large-scale census data classification exercise has been used to identify 50 or so residential neighbourhoods (see Openshaw and Wymer, 1995) for some examples. The classifiers that have been commonly used have their origins in the 1960s. Yet this is not the real cause of their dumbness, nor is the manner of their application a cause of real concern. No matter how good or how well they may have been applied, they are used in an uniquely dumb fashion. Let us examine why. Quite simply, the statistical methods are not knowledge based and make no use whatsoever of any existing knowledge about social patterns known to exist in the urban mosaic. Openshaw et al (1995) argue that spatial classifications of census data can be made almost instantly much more knowledgeable if they contain some elements of existing knowledge. They point out that to date all the census classifications produced in the world using multivariate statistical methods are suspect from a geographical perspective because they are based on a fundamentally incorrect implicit assumption, namely that there is no knowledge about the nature of social areas that exist in towns and cities other than what might be found in the data. Despite the importance of AI and data-mining technologies that seek to permit the data to speak for themselves, this is clearly a nonsensensical assumption! There is an extensive literature spread over at least half a century of descriptions and analyses in relation to the spatial social structure of many different towns and cities. Yet one of the authors of this book has spent over 20 years attempting to improve the quality of census classifications by purely algorithmic means. Each statistical classification begins with the incorrect assumption that absolutely nothing is known about the nature of the results. Imagine his embarrassment when it suddenly dawned on him that it would be possible to encode some existing spatial social area knowledge as rules that could be added to the census classification process as a means of improving the quality of the results. Even the simplest rules of basic spatial geography, such as nearby areas will probably be located in the same cluster, can be used to identify potentially misclassified cases and ask the classifier to reconsider them. Likewise, the social characteristics of rural areas will never be the same as found in city centres. So again why not build an ES layer into the census classification process to ensure that such suspect results are at the very least double checked for statistical consistency? It would not be difficult to encode several more basic social area rules and embed them into a hybrid spatial classifier that combined statistical criteria with geographical rules of common-ness. Figure 4.2 gives an illustration of how this might be achieved. However, this sort of embedded ES is clearly not what the traditionally defined systems were meant to do.

A similar state commonly occurs in remote sensing land cover classification. A field may be allocated to wheat even if it is known that it is too high for wheat to grow there. Existing knowledge is not being used at all. However, it is fairly easy to incorporate relevant knowledge when it exists. In the census classification example, there is a need to reduce global optimality in order to gain an improved local fit or to conform to some meta patterns that can be expressed as rules; for example, social gradients and neighbourhoods.

Another example concerns the need to develop computer systems of geographical phenomena that are adaptive, with feedback, rather than static. This subject is discussed further under machine learning. However, it is obvious that even a crude model that is allowed to update its parameters either in the light of experience or as new data come in, will be far better than one that once calibrated is kept fixed.

4.10 CONCLUSIONS

A conventional ES is a seductively attractive but often fundamentally flawed AI technology. It provides a means of duplicating human expertise in knowledge-

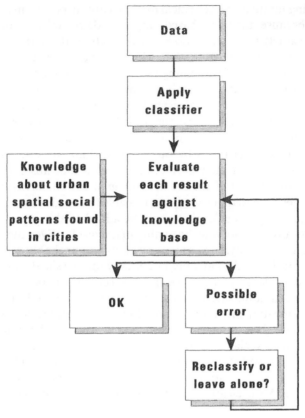

Figure 4.2

based application areas but this replication is in some senses highly imperfect and is expert only in the narrowest sense imaginable. It is a brittle technology that needs to be continually fed with new knowledge if it is to remain a viable ES. Moreover, it is not yet known how to build common sense into an ES or how to develop systems that can creatively respond to new situations or to adapt as circumstances change or how to improve their performance by experience or how to handle multi-sensory inputs and not just symbolic inputs. Some other forms of AI are much less reliant on human inputs and maybe it is these rather than the traditional ES that geographers should be focusing on. Furthermore, ES are not good at recognising when they fail, or if no answer exists, or if the problem lies outside their domain of expertise. ES are highly consistent but this can merely mean that they consistently and repeatedly provide the wrong answers. It may improve decision-making in some areas, for example in credit scoring assessment, but as yet there are only a few examples of outstanding success in non-critical decision-making, for example optimising computer configuration. However, few systems seem to work well without considerable effort and seemingly many never work at all. Many academic papers promise much, describe the theory and present untested prototypes, but then fail to deliver anything useful, particularly in the GIS domain. Expert systems can also take a long time to develop. If more than six months, is it worth while? Perhaps they are most useful in teaching applications or as interfaces to complex computer systems. The concept may also be fundamentally flawed, because they probably cannot outperform the human expert; maybe we need more than this from AI. Certainly in geography, the problem is not the lack of sufficient experts but in many problem areas there are no experts. The need is for a superintelligence not just a poor replication of existing experts. What happens if no expert knowledge exists or can be re-expressed in a suitable form? Maybe in many areas of geography the ES is simply an irrelevant notion either because (a) there are no real experts and or (b) their expert knowledge is fundamentally incapable of being expressed in a suitable form. In these circumstances other forms of IKBS are required.

Consider the geographical analysis machine of Chapter 3 that was used as a cluster hunter. It used no knowledge whilst performing its brute-force and totally dumb searches. However, it was considered hard to include any because there was no obvious basis for excluding many areas from the search other than in the most extreme circumstances. You cannot build an ES because at present knowledge about cancer clusters is too rudimentary. There is no knowledge base and as yet no real experts from which one could be developed. Moreover, ES lack the tools to create the knowledge needed to cope in these circumstances. Fortunately, other AI tools are of more use here. IKBS is viewed as going beyond a traditional ES of the classical type and encompasses a much broader range of knowledge-based AI. Most of this is dealt with in subsequent chapters (neural nets, machine learning and fuzzy logic). It is in this broader and wider interpretation of ES that much of the potential undoubtedly rests for the future, particularly in a geographic context.

Artificial intelligence is not a universally applicable magic technology. It involves a lot of hard work but it can also be useful. Faith is needed and also some luck in selecting the "right" applications in the first place. The cost of building IKBS is falling rapidly. New graphical user interfaces, animation and multimedia technologies are creating a need for matching levels of intelligent user interfaces. Users increasingly demand smart computer systems not dumb ones, systems that are adaptive and responsive to their revealed needs, and systems that make the task of using IT tools easier not harder. Rules-based systems have much to offer here. Likewise it should be appreciated that many end-users like the idea of ES helping them out. Maybe the idea is more important at present than the fairly crude (from a geographical perspective) ES technology that currently exists.

4.11 QUESTION AND ANSWERS

Q   Is a system expert because of its ability to solve problems at an expert level?
A   No, not necessarily. Non-ES based solutions can also perform as well or
    better. For example, linear programming is not an ES (in the traditional sense)
    but a mathematical optimisation procedure that will produce expert (in the

sense of being optimal) solutions to suitable problems. No human expert could do any better! So performance alone is not a sufficiently good criterion to define an ES.

Q   Is a rule-based system an ES?

A   Maybe. Many ES contain rules but programs can easily be written containing very silly rules. So the presence of rules in a software system is not itself sufficient to define an ES. Nor does the use of a particular programming language make the system an expert one.

Q   Why is an ES sometimes regarded as being brittle?

A   They tend to work only on narrowly defined problems. They will not work if there is no expertise relevant to a particular class of problems or if there are no expert(s) able to unload their expert knowledge into the system. If anything changes then the system can almost instantly become out of date and inefficient.

Q   Are ES the ultimate in AI?

A   No! They were/are an interesting development in the history of AI but time has proved the original ES concept to be too restrictive. Latterly more general ES developments incorporating various other forms of knowledge-based systems, often hybrids, may be much more powerful and useful. Also as knowledge bases are developed so it is also possible that the original notion of an ES as an expert advisor will be revived and become widely adopted in all manner of systems and consumer products.

Q   How expert is an ES?

A   It depends on the ability of the system builder to capture and adequately express the relevant knowledge base. It can thus vary from imbecilic to almost human being abilities but it will never go beyond human being levels of performance. It cannot, by definition! Some may well consider that this is insufficient.

Q   Is not the term "expert system" when applied to a set of IF statements a case of AI hype and exaggeration?

A   Yes to some extent. However, it is also important to understand the very real excitement at the discovery of how easy it was to go about building *some intelligence and knowledge* into a computer system at a time when AI was thought to involve building artificial versions of the human brain. ES was so much simpler and was as a result almost instantly attractive. Also the idea of being able to create and store knowledge about problem solving in a reusable and explicit form is a very significant one. Previously this knowledge might well have been written down (viz. in manuals, fault-finding charts, etc.) or been used in training courses, but now it can be put into an explicit computer format so that various logical operations can be applied to it. This should in theory improve the consistency and coverage of the knowledge base and also create a resource that can subsequently be used in other types of knowledge-based processing systems. Finally, ES is important because it permits the distribution, sharing and reuse of knowledge.

Q   OK, but in what ways are IF statements representations of human knowledge?

A   It is important to be somewhat narrowly focused here. Humans often seem to use some kind of IF rules sequence when problem solving; for example, if your car fails to start then (1) check battery, (2) if battery OK then check for loose wires, (3) if no loose wires then check for spark, (4) if spark then check for petrol, etc. An ES is little more than an attempt to capture all these "IF this then do that" rules that are relevant and then make them easily accessible to an end-user via a suitable interface. Looked at from this perspective then it is clear that an ES actually might just deliver something that is useful to the end-user that is intelligent in that it is expert knowledge based and seems to mimic the behaviour of the human expert when faced with a particular problem. The difficulty is of course that of defining all the rules that may or may not be relevant to a given problem situation. In the car example, in excess of 100 000 rules might easily be required to create an ES. Then, of course, there is the problem of attempting to build into the ES gut feeling and hunch making capabilities.

Q   So what problems in geography might benefit from ES?

A   There are many potential applications that involve the application of well-defined skills in constrained contexts which have rules. In principle any skill-based task that requires the application of knowledge and was originally performed by experts may benefit. For example, map reading or map drawing, or choice of map projection, or how to survey, use of a GIS, etc. ES could be built to provide expert help and assistance with all these skill-based activities in geography. Such systems could be used as a resource able to assist in doing geography, a means of expert advice, the basis for computer-aided instruction and for learning various geographical skills.

Q   Will ES ever replace human experts?

A   Yes, there is no reason why a mature, fully developed ES should not function well enough, one day, to replace human experts. However, it is important to see ES as a source of help and assistance, a means of gaining access to expert knowledge rather than necessarily being automated decision-making technology. No doubt ES will function as such at a low level in mission critical systems but there will be a natural and logical limit when they come to making decisions about humans. So whilst it might be acceptable to allow ES to make decisions about car-braking systems and air conditioners, it will probably be much less acceptable to many humans if it is known that decisions formerly made by responsible humans (under control of established management and organisational structures) were being delegated to machines. Humans never did control intricate car-braking electronics but they do control (i.e. administer, manage, decide) many other aspects that affect people's daily existence (perhaps to a much less significant extent but that is relevant). For example, an expert staff selection system that matched job applicants to jobs might well be regarded as quite intolerable despite the objectivity of the system compared with the established person-based selection processes with all the in-built racial, gender and other biases and hidden agendas. The point here is the world in which we live does not conform to the logic of simple science.

Q   Why are ES dumb?

A   They have no learning mechanism. The same set of inputs will elicit the same erroneous response. The only solution is to rebuild them.

Q   What is the so-called knowledge bottleneck?

A   It is not easy to create a set of rules relevant to a particular problem by
    "extracting" knowledge from the experts. Many experts have problems
    expressing the rules they use, especially in handling more complex tasks.
    Other rules are ill defined and fuzzy. This difficulty is euphemistically termed
    a "knowledge bottleneck". Maybe the real cause is not the difficulty of
    extraction or specification but the inappropriateness of the representation
    being used to describe the knowledge. There are various solutions; for
    example, memory-based reasoning and machine learning methods are
    possible responses that seek to handle the knowledge in an implicit, perhaps
    invisible, manner rather than explicitly.

Q   Can ES handle soft knowledge and theoretical concepts relevant to critical
    human geography?

A   Maybe not. Remember ES is a problem-solving or decision-making technol-
    ogy. It could (in theory) handle soft information but it would have to be
    expressed in terms relevant to a particular problem-solving task. It cannot
    really theorise or offer conceptual enlightenment except that which may
    result from the development of the rules base. If critical human geographic
    problems have relevant rules then yes, it could be useful. If the task is to
    define their rules then other machine learning methods might be more
    relevant.

Q   What other weaknesses does ES have?

A   There is a major potential, future litigational soft spot. Suppose a "wrong"
    expert decision is made. The basis for the wrongness can be identified in
    terms of rules stored in the knowledge base. Suppose one of the rules was
    incorrectly specified due to allegedly professional incompetence or system
    problems or software bugs. No doubt the legal profession would have a field
    day challenging the expert basis of the decision. Of course this is not new.
    They already do this but it is much harder because the evidence is often
    vague, controversial and intangible. ES changes this! Oh dear.

Q   Is IKBS really any different from ES?

A   Maybe. The view here is that IKBS represents a much broader and all-
    embracing concept. There are many different ways of seeking to build an
    intelligent knowledge-based system and ES is perhaps significant only
    because it was the first recognised development. IKBS is also a much
    better and accurate description of what AI might well be expected to
    deliver. Only if the various AI technologies can be assembled into compre-
    hensive hybrid systems that behave intelligently, do something useful,
    learn from their mistakes and use available knowledge, is much progress
    going to be made.

Q   Is memory-based reasoning any good?

A   Well, performance is application and data specific. Experiments indicate that
    it can perform extremely well in some applications when all others fail. There
    are also other ways of achieving the same function, for example via neural
    networks.

Q   Is matching records on one set of variables to determine a historic response
    really classed as an IKBS technology?

A   Well, yes. It is mimicking what humans do. It is using existing knowledge
    stored (or trapped) in a database, it has the capability of extending its

knowledge base by learning what to do about unmatched records and it is attempting to be systematic in its behaviour. Now isn't this some of the describable attributes for any IKBS?

Q   Do the various tree analysis methods (e.g. AID, CHAID etc.) generate IF rules for numeric data?

A   Well, their results can be expressed as such but they do not really create a knowledge base as distinct from offer a statistical analysis of a data set. This is not the same thing. Likewise discriminant analysis can categorise data into groups, but again the analysis is statistical and empirically specific rather than general using data-invariant knowledge that has a lasting rather than an extremely ephemeral value. Indeed this might be a useful way of distinguishing between a real ES in the classic AI sense and a hyped-up statistical pretender.

REFERENCES

Aha, D., Kibler, D., Albert, M., 1991, "Instance-based learning algorithms", *Machine Learning*, 6.

Association for Geographic Information, 1989, *AGI Yearbook*. Taylor and Francis, London.

Atkeson, C., 1986, *Roles of Knowledge in Motor Learning*. MIT AI Lab Technical Report 942, September.

Birkin, M., Clarke, M., Wilson, A., 1996, Intelligent GIS. GeoInformation International, Cambridge.

Creecy, R.H., Masand, B.M., Smith, S.J., Waltz, D.L., 1992, *Trading MIPS and Memory for Knowledge Engineering: automatic classification of census returns on a massively parallel supercomputer*. Thinking Machines Corporation Technical Report 192, Guildford, Surrey.

Coughlan, J., Running, S.W., 1996, "Biophysical aggregations of a forested landscape using an ecological diagnostic system", *Transactions in GIS*, 1, 25–39.

European Commission, 1995, "Directive 95/46/EC of the European Parliament and of the Council of 24 October 1995 on the protection of individuals with regard to the processing of personal data and on the free movement of such data", *Official Journal of the European Commission*, No L 281/31.

Feigenbaum, E.A., 1982, "Knowledge Engineering for the 1980s", Dept. of Computer Science, Stanford University, Stanford, California.

Firebaugh, M.W., 1988, *Artificial Intelligence: a knowledge based approach*. PWS Kent Publishing Co., Boston.

Forsyth, R., 1984, *Expert Systems: principles and case studies*. Chapman and Hall, London.

Fox, M,S., 1990, "Artificial intelligence and Expert Systems: myths, legends, and facts", *IEEE Expert*, 5, 8–22.

Fox, MS., 1991, *Introduction to AI and Expert Systems*. New Jersey, IEEE.

Herbert, G., Joao, E., Rhind, D.W., 1992, "Use of an artificial intelligence approach to increase user control of automatic line generalisation", *Proceedings of 3rd GIS Conference (EGIS'92)*, Munich, 23–26 March, pp. 554–563.

Jackson, P., 1986, Introduction to Expert Systems. Addison-Wesley, Workingham, UK.

Joao, E., Herbert, G., Rhind, D.W., Openshaw, S., Raper, J., 1993, "Towards a generalisation machine to minimise generalisation effects within a GIS", in P. Mather (ed.), *Geographical Information Handling—Research and Applications*. John Wiley & Sons, Chichester, pp. 63–78.

Li, Z., Openshaw, S., 1992, "Algorithms for automated line generalisation based on a natural principle of objective generalisation", *International Journal of GIS*, **6**, 373–389.

Marshall, G. 1990, *Advanced Students' Guide to Expert Systems*. Heinemann Newnes, Oxford.

Michaelson, R.H., Michie, D., Boulanger, A., 1985, "The technology of expert systems", *Byte*, **10**, 303.

Michie, D. (ed.), 1979, *Expert Systems in the Microelectronics Age*. Edinburgh University Press, Edinburgh.

Michie, D., 1990, "Machine executable skills from silent brains", in *Research and Development in Expert Systems VII*, Cambridge University Press, Cambridge.

Naylor, C., 1983, *Build your own Expert System*. Sigma Technical Press, Bristol.

Openshaw, S., 1989, "Making geodemographics more sophisticated", *Journal of the Market Research Society*, **31**, 111–131.

Openshaw, S., 1993, "GIS crime and GIS criminality", *Environment and Planning A*, **25**, 451–458.

Openshaw, S., 1994a, "Developing smart and intelligent target marketing systems: Part 1", *Journal of Targeting, Measurement and Analysis for Marketing*, **2**, 289–301.

Openshaw, S., 1994b, "Developing smart and intelligent marketing systems: Part II", *Journal of Targeting, Measurement and Analysis for Marketing*, **3**, 31–38.

Openshaw, S., Blake, M., Wymer, C., 1995, "Using neurocomputing methods to classify Britains residential areas", in P. Fisher (ed.), *Innovations in GIS2*. Taylor and Francis, London, pp. 97–112.

Openshaw, S., Craft, A.W., 1991, "Using Geographical Analysis Machines to search for evidence of cluster and clustering in childhood leukaemia and non-Hodgkin lymphomas in Britain", in G. Draper (ed.), *The Geographical Epidemiology of Childhood Leukaemia and non-Hodgkin Lymphomas in Great Britain, 1966–83*, Studies in Medial and Population Subjects No 53, OPCS. HMSO, London, pp. 109–122.

Openshaw, S., Wymer, C., 1995, "Classifying and regionalising census data", in S. Openshaw (ed.), *Census Users' Handbook*. Geoinformational International, Cambridge, pp. 353–361.

Quinlan, J.R., 1979, "Discovering rules by induction from large collections of examples", in D. Michie (ed.), *Expert Systems in the Microelectronic Age*, Edinburgh University Press, Edinburgh, pp. 168–201.

Quinlan, J.R., 1993, *C4.5: programs for machine learning*. Morgan Kaufmann, California.

Raggett, J., Bains, W., 1992, *Artificial Intelligence from A to Z*. Chapman & Hall, London.

Schildt, H., 1987, *Artificial Intelligence using C*. Osborne McGraw-Hill, Berkeley.

Sowa, J.F., 1984, *Conceptual Structures*. Addison-Wesley, Reading, Mass.

Stanfill, C., Kahle, B., 1986, "Parallel free-text search on the Connection Machine System", *Communications of ACM*, **29**, 1229–1239.

Stanfill, C., Thau, R., 1991, "Information retrieval on the Connection Machine 1 to 8192 Gigabytes", *Information Processing and Management*,

Stanfill, C., Waltz, D.L., 1986, "Towards Memory-Based Reasoning", *Communications of ACM*, **29**, 1213–1228.

Stanfill, C., Waltz, D.L., 1988, "The memory based reasoning paradigm", *Proceedings of Case-Based Reasoning Workshop*. Clearwater Beach, Florida, May, pp. 414–424.

Wadge, G., Wislocki, A., Pearson, E.J., 1993, "Mapping natural hazards with spatial modelling systems", in P. Mather (ed.), *Geographical Information Handling—Research and Applications*. John Wiley & Sons, Chichester, pp. 239–250.

Waterman, D.A., 1986, *A Guide to Expert Systems*. Addison-Wesley, Reading, Mass.

CHAPTER 5

Neurocomputing

Neurocomputing is a subject area within AI that all computer-minded or even all geographers should be interested in. It promises to revolutionise many of the computer analysis and modelling tasks performed in geography and to overturn many of the simplistic logical positivist criticisms that are often levelled at quantitative geography. It is also an extremely neglected area that has much potential that is geographically relevant. This chapter provides a simple non-technical introduction.

5.1 INTRODUCTION

We live in a world controlled by computers and increasingly more and more aspects of our daily existence at home and at work are dependent upon them. Computer systems dispense money, control critical systems ranging from car-braking systems to washing machines, they forecast weather, and manage many of our critical needs from water distribution to electricity and communication systems. These computer systems are becoming cheaper, more ubiquitous, more powerful and much more numerous. Yet as Chapter 1 emphasised, virtually all of them are totally dumb and probably 100% AI free! Carling (1992: 2) quotes John Denker of AT and T's Bell Labs who said that despite the speed and memory capabilities of modern high performance computers, the "achievements to date have the mental capacity of a slug". Carling adds it is a truly frightening prospect. "To imagine that our economic growth may be controlled by a machine with the potential of a slug, and one of lower than average intelligence at that."

Clearly raw machine speed does not directly equate with intelligence. It is not the speed of processing that matters but the way it is carried out. A modern computer with a fast CPU can perform thousands of millions of calculations per second, whilst our brain (which is a computer) only manages a few thousand. A million (or more) times slower. Yet the brain triumphs partly by the use of a massive amount of parallel processing; the one fast CPU of a supercomputer versus 10–250 billion slow CPUs in the brain operating in parallel in a highly co-ordinated way. However, it must also be doing something quite different and be using a very different paradigm for computing its way to intelligence.

Neural networks or neurocomputing (also called artificial neural networks, connectionism and parallel distributed computing) is one of the most exciting practical developments in AI and computing of the last decade (Dawn, 1994). It is of particular interest because it provides a basis for a dramatic extension of the capabilities of computing from high-speed arithmetic and data retrieval to address basic but more sophisticated information-processing needs, such as speech recognition, image understanding, robotics, common-sense knowledge processing and the construction of autonomous intelligent systems. Neural networks will provide some of the missing capabilities needed to convert the computer from being little more than a glorified calculating machine into a much more intelligent information-processing tool. The computer is still doing arithmetic but neural networks convert crude data-crunching activity into a more intelligent form of computing by seeking to simulate some of the processing functionality of the most complex of all biological systems, the brain.

Neural networks are also exciting from a geographical perspective because they have a tremendously wide range of potential geographical uses (Openshaw, 1993; Fischer and Gopal, 1993; Wang, 1994). They are also, by now, a well-proven and fairly mature technology. Indeed in many subjects outside of geography neural networks and fuzzy logic (see Chapter 9) systems have witnessed an explosive growth over the last five years mainly because of their ability to model complex nonlinear processes to arbitrary degrees of accuracy (Kosko, 1992), or as Nelson and Illingworth (1992: 24) put it: "Because the kinds of things neural nets can do address many of today's problems, a new industry is emerging. This is happening on several continents and involves a variety of disciplines." There are few risks associated with its use, but so far it has made virtually no measurable impact on the way geographers do much of their geography. Yet as Hewitson and Crane (1994: 1) note, the mere mention of neural nets evokes widely different responses ranging "from enthusiastic support through emphatic dislike, or simply blank looks of non-comprehension". This neglect is both surprising and worrying because it may well reflect a mix of at least some of the following: a deep-seated misunderstanding, an amazing lack of awareness (or ignorance) of developments in this area, a confusing nomenclature-ridden literature full of technical jargon that makes little sense to geographers, a bewildering broad spectrum of applications most of which appear to have no obvious geographic equivalent, an emphatic dislike of technology that seems to require a culture change with a switch from theory-based to data-based modelling, uncertainty as to the benefits, a complacency that any performance gained at the expense of understanding is not worthwhile, an aversion to new technology, a lack of interest in computer modelling as distinct from linguistic description of the unique, and a profound prejudice against anything that looks as if it lacks a well- established theoretical justification. Yet before long the neural computing floodgates will open and the neural networks revolution will happen in geography too. There can be no doubt about that; the only question is when (not if). Meanwhile, it would seem useful to try and improve general levels of basic understanding of how neural networks function, raise awareness of their potential and practical significance in geography, and prepare the way for the inevitable. In essence neural networks really are a tremendously useful and practical technology that can, more or less, instantly be applied with good effect in many areas of human and physical geography. They are both an alternative substitute for many of the models and tools we already have and a means of doing geography better. So what are neural networks and how do they work?

5.1.1 Solving problems that were previously impossible

Few of us have any difficulty in recognising an apple or being able to distinguish it from a pear. Somehow humans learned how to do this during childhood through a process of learning by example. There was no need to build an expert system or a rules database or a complex statistical pattern recognition search heuristic to perform this task. It just seemed to happen naturally, in fact people can classify fruit without ever seeing the particular examples before. Somehow we have the ability to generalise or to extract the "apple essence" of the apple and apply it to other unseen objects but this is not a faultless task, we do make mistakes but then we receive feedback and with experience we improve. Furthermore it seems we do the classification task effortlessly, almost without consciously thinking about it, and we can even do it if some of the fruit is missing or it has been squashed or gone mouldy (viz. the image is distorted and noisy). This "training" process or learning by example and experience is, perhaps, most explicit in a sports context, for example practising cricket. Neural networks are an attempt to mimic this ability of the brain to *learn* by example, to *generalise* from the specific to the abstract and to *handle noisy data.*

A most important aspect is that neural networks are not programmed in the conventional sense but they "sort of" programme themselves by learning a specific task from examples. In conventional computer programming, the programmer instructs the computer to solve a task using an explicitly and predefined algorithm, and the performance of the program is heavily dependent upon the skills of the programmer and is an extension of his or her intelligence in programming it. Conventional von Neumann computers are little more than massive programmable calculators. If you do not have an algorithm, you have nothing. If the algorithm does not work, the program fails and the code has to be changed by the programmer. There is no mechanism for the program to learn how to fix itself or to optimise its code itself from experience in running it. Every application tends to need its own program although, of course, methods for recycling codes are quite well developed. With a neural network there is still a computer program but the program contains no specific algorithms relevant to solving any particular problem. Instead the neural network program has to "learn" how to perform a particular task. This is fundamentally different technology. If you wish to model a relationship between variable A and three others, B, C and D, with a conventional approach you would specify a mathematical equation and then estimate any unknown parameters in it. You would write a one-off program to implement it either in a programming language or via a modelling package of some kind. If you use a wrong or inappropriate equation, it may not work too well or at all. With a neural network you teach or train the network software to predict variable A given values for B, C and D. You no longer have to write a one-off program since the neural network software is application independent, nor do you have to worry about using the wrong equation, because the neural network will have probably learned or discovered the best function to use by experience with your data. Neural networks are non-algorithmic and can solve problems for which there are no known algorithms. As such they are regarded by many as constituting a major new paradigm for programming computers to solve problems that are either hard or too difficult to solve via any other route.

However, merely replacing this or that conventional statistical or mathematical model by a neural network is not all that exciting nor worthwhile. For example, you could train a neural network to square root numbers or to perform arithmetic but that would be a real waste of the technology since there are better and far more efficient ways of handling these particular arithmetic problems. Instead, imagine now a problem that is hard or impossible to solve via a conventional route. For example, if variable A is categorical (e.g. has the values 1, 2, 4 and 5 that have no simple numeric meaning) then maybe existing statistical methods can still cope provided the imagined relationship is not too complex. Suppose now that the variables B, C and D are text representing an ASCII description of their values. Another example would be the task of coding a plain text string describing an occupation as a number representing a standard industrial classification code. These are no longer problems suitable for statistical modelling even if there is undoubtedly some sort of relationship, it is just too hard to envisage what it might be, or even how to represent it mathematically. However, the same neural network could be trained to handle them.

The ability of neural networks to be trained significantly extends the domain in which computer analysis and modelling can be applied. Suddenly, the soft and qualitative areas of geography become amenable to quantification and computer modelling. The social theoretic, radical, geographic and ethnological parts of cultural, sociological and political geography are now in the front line of a new computer-based quantitative revolution! No wonder so many people find neurocomputing so exciting. It brings with it a glimpse of an exciting future in which virtually anything can be modelled and studied if there is a suitable training database. Here, it might appear, is the ultimate technology, capable of doing all manner of previously impossible things relevant to geography (and many other subjects too). Maybe it is the beginning of the development of an ultimate one-stop shop technology that could replace many current statistical methods and mathematical modelling tools. If there is a need for dynamic models of chaotic nonlinear systems, then there is a basis here for building them. If there is a need to generalise and rescience many of the soft areas of social science then there is the basis for doing that too. If more flexible, less assumption-dependent and more spatial data-relevant geographical analysis and modelling tools are required, then it is here where many of the core tools exist just awaiting geographical exploitation.

An impressive range of neurocomputing technology exists, it is fairly well developed, and it can be simply taken as given and used. There is no prerequisite for a deep theoretical understanding of how precisely neural networks function and what they do. It is essentially, above all, an end-user-orientated technology designed to be used by practitioners who own the problems that neural networks can solve. However, whilst you can safely use neural networks as a black box, you do need to know something about how they work and how to use them, but you do not need to know all the theory. If your only view is of neurocomputing as a mysterious and magic black box that can do virtually anything, then *stop* at once. You are probably wasting your time. You need to know more than that if you wish to make safe and effective use of them. Beware also of the neural network virus. It is highly contagious and very infectious. Once bitten with the neural net bug, there is a danger that you might be misled into believing that neurocomputing is the only AI toolkit relevant to geography. Whilst it is certainly a powerful technology, there are in fact even more powerful AI tools discussed in later chapters! *So try and save some excitement and enthusiasm for later on and do not stop your explorations of the wonderful world of AI at the first seemingly miraculous technology you come across.*

5.2 SO WHAT IS A NEURAL NET?

Let us start by envisaging a neural network as a black box pattern recogniser that we can teach to discriminate between any other objects of interest. The first task in pattern recognition is to capture some information about the objects of interest. Imagine the objects of interest are village greens. Conzen (1947) in a pioneering study of the morphology of village greens in northern England developed a very detailed classification of their shapes, for example round, triangular, oblong, square, by eyeballing maps. None of the patterns are exact but the informal classifier (i.e. the expert geographer) was clever enough to handle the imperfections. The challenge here is to teach a neural net to distinguish between different types. Figure 5.1 provides a simplified representation of two distinctive types: triangular and elongated. A simple way of presenting this information to a computer is to raster the images. The simplest raster image would store the shapes as a pattern of 1s and 0s. You can obtain more precision by making the raster cell size smaller. Additionally, if you were doing this for real then you would have to consider different rotations and windowing in order to find where on a map a village green would be located.

This raster image produces a set of 100 variables each with the values of 1 or 0. The neural network is to have two outputs, one for each of the two village green shapes, and you could imagine these as light bulbs that "flash" on or off depending on whether it thinks the 100 variables of 0/1 represent an image of a triangular or an elongated village green. The black box is trained by presenting it with hundreds

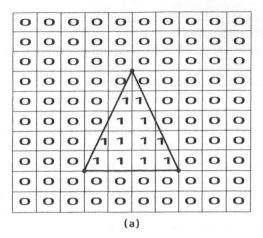

(a)

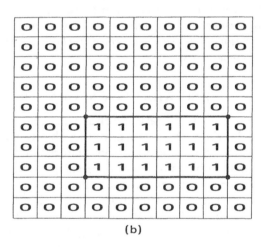

(b)

Figure 5.1   Raster representation of: (a) idealised triangular village green; (b) rectangular-shaped village green

and/or thousands of images of village greens for which the shape is known but which differ in various ways from the geometrical ideal shapes. If it gets the answer wrong, it gets the equivalent of an electronic kick. Gradually it will get most of its answers correct. It will learn to discriminate between the different types of village greens, or if you prefer, it will have learnt the mathematical function that maps the 100 inputs of 0–1 on to one of two outputs; see Figure 5.2.

However, it is possible that the black box may never be 100% correct. Some of the images may be very difficult to categorise easily either because of topographic site factors or due to the effects of over 1000 years of development pressures. In some cases the classification may be wrong. In others, the shapes are grossly distorted due to post-medieval changes in green morphology. It is also important to test the performance of the "trained" black box on a validation data set that it has not seen. The ability to generalise to new data is particularly important. The only real restriction is that the training data should be representative of the range of village greens thought likely to exist. Note that the black box will not only distinguish between different types of village green but it will give a probability against each. Moreover, it can be trained to handle noisy and uncertain data by feeding noisy and uncertain data to it during training; quite often the noise could be artificially generated by yourself (i.e. disrupt some of the raster images by randomly changing a certain percentage of 0s to 1s and vice versa).

So how does it work? If the black box employs neurocomputing methods then it will attempt to mimic the function of the human brain; hence the words artificial neural network. It is biologically inspired, as indeed is much of AI. The human brain is thought to contain 10^{11} neurons each receiving input from 5000–15 000 other neurons. By comparison most artificial neural networks are very much smaller. They are smaller even than the common housefly with 10^6 neurons and almost equal to the worm with 10^3 but even they will be much less connected. So most artificial neural networks are still sub-worm in their complexity. Furthermore let us be quite certain about one thing; pompous-sounding references to artificial neural networks mimicking brain functions are grossly misleading. Scientists simply do not know the precise details of how the brain functions, or even at present properly understand a single neuron. Neurocomputing is an engineering discipline that draws ideas and inspiration from studies of the brain but it is an extremely primitive technology by biological brain standards and the relationship with biology is at best very (very) tenuous. Despite the appalling poor quality of the artificial emulation, perhaps astonishingly, it is seemingly still good enough to tackle many practical problems. A key factor is the number of neurons and the number of interconnections that relate to a single problem, since it is the weights on the interconnections that store the patterns of interest and it is the weights and not the network or interconnections that are trained to represent whatever the network is to do. Maybe it is the complete focusing of attention on only one specific processing problem that compensates for the crudity of the artificial brain. Maybe also despite the poverty of the copy, emulation of the basic but grossly damaged and impaired neural processes is still sufficiently powerful to handle the problems it is expected to solve.

Inside the black box there is a set of neurons linked together to form a network; hence the term neural (derived from neuron) net or network. The neurons are biologically inspired and are very loosely modelled on what is thought to be some of the processes found in the human brain.

In this type of net each neuron is connected to every other preceding or following neuron; the lines represent this in Figure 5.3. Each line or connection has a weight attached to it. Training or learning involves changing these weights so as to minimise error in the outputs. For example, suppose the image of a

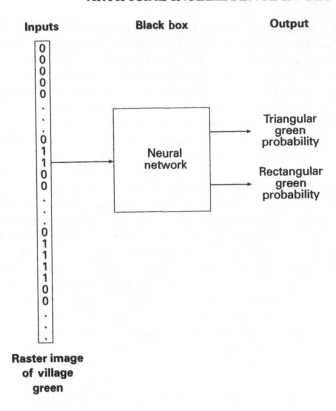

Figure 5.2   Simple neural network trained to recognise village green shapes

elongated village green is input and output neuron for a triangular green is selected. Then clearly this is wrong and the error is back-propagated (that is, sent backwards) through the network to adjust the weights to reduce the error next time the same or similar training data are input. It is noted that this simple type of network architecture will be referred to as a feed-forward multi-layer perception with 100 input neurons, 2 output neurons and 1 hidden layer that sits between the input and output neurons. Note how the inputs pass from one set of neurons in one layer to another. It is a parallel process as all neurons in any layer are operating in parallel. Hence why neurocomputing is sometimes confusingly called parallel distributed processing. The most fascinating aspect of the whole process is the fact that the neurons are simple summation devices and perform very simple processing. All the power and memory of a neural network come from the multiple layers and the adjustable connection weights, not from the processing sophistication of the neurons themselves. A biological brain with 250 billion neurons each with 10 000 to 15 000 weights clearly has an unbelievably large amount of storage and processing capability.

Figure 5.3 also gives a simple picture of an individual neuron. There are many

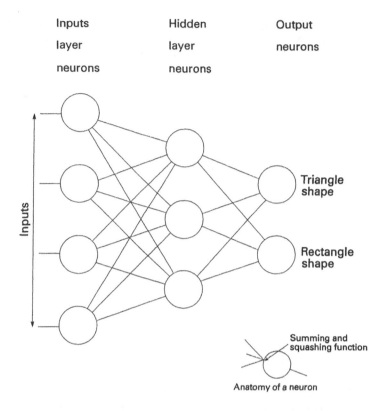

Figure 5.3   Innards of a simple neural network

inputs each with a weight attached to it but only one output. The output is the sum of the input values multiplied by the appropriate weight. However, in practice the output from the neuron would either be 0 or 1 (depending on whether the sum exceeded some threshold value specific to that neuron), or scaled between 0.0 and 1.0 according to a transfer function of some kind; more about this later. This neuronal processing is an attempt to copy what has been observed in biological systems.

So despite the misleading use of the term *neural*, artificial neural networks are only very loosely based on biology which is probably all to the good because we do not really understand how the brain works. Moreover, neural computing is about machines, not brains; biology serves only as an inspiration.

It would seem then the neural network used here is an information-processing system that is non-algorithmic, non-digital and parallel. It is not a conventional computer since it is not programmed, but trained. Moreover, like human beings, it develops a knowledge base by learning from experience. Brains do their computations in ways that do not depend on algorithms (Turing, 1939); so do neural nets. Therefore a key distinguishing feature of a neural network is its ability to learn from example. The following chapter explores different types of training which include supervised and unsupervised. The latter is particularly scary because the nets can also train themselves via self-organisation! These unsupervised nets are also extremely useful as can be seen in the next chapter.

5.3 A BRIEF LOOK AT THE HISTORY OF NEURAL NETS

5.3.1 The first neural networks: 1943–69

Perhaps surprisingly, neural networks are not a new development. The starting-point was an attempt to model the fundamental cell of the brain, the neuron. McCulloch and Pitts (1943) developed a simple model of the neuron that provided the basis for much subsequent research, including Figure 5.3. They showed that even simple types of neural networks could, in principle, compute any arithmetic or logical function. Their work was widely read and had great influence, for instance Wiener (1948) and von Neumann (1951) suggested research into brain-like computers. Another major development occurred in 1949 when Hebb postulated learning mechanisms based on animal experiments that could be used to train a net. Hebb (1949) inspired many other researchers and laid the foundations for neurocomputing. As a result many researchers examined issues in neurocomputing in the late 1940s and early 1950s. One remarkable development was the construction of the first neurocomputer (the Snark) by Minsky in 1951. It was a largely mechanical device. The first successful neurocomputer (the mark 1 Perception) was developed in 1957/58 by Rosenblatt; see Rosenblatt (1958). The Perception is of considerable interest because it was a trainable net that had a 400 pixels (20 by 20) image sensor. It might even have been able to classify Conzen's village greens. Rosenblatt is widely regarded as the founder of neurocomputing as it exists today. The ideas caught the imagination of many people. Moreover an important existence theorem developed at that time demonstrated that a neural network with three layers (one hidden) could in principle approximate any arbitrary continuous function (see Kolmogorov, 1957; Hecht-Nielsen, 1990; Cybenko, 1989), even though the proof is non-constructive and does not indicate how to achieve this result. Other learning machines with modifiable connections were developed in the early 1960s. The best known is the ADALINE (ADAptive LINEar combiner) which was developed by Widrow and Hoff (1960). Hoff later went on to invent the microprocessor. ADALINE was applied to a large number of "simple" problems and by the mid 1960s there were some commercial sales of what must have been the ultimate "swinging sixties" executive toy.

However, there were many problems. In particular there was little rigour in an area with a high degree of experimental emphasis. It seems that a large fraction of researchers were carried away by their own enthusiasm. For instance, predictions were made that artificial brains were only a few years away and other incredible statements (Hecht-Nielson, 1990: 16). Hype discredited the area and by the mid

1960s, researchers were running out of new ideas. It was also a time when computers were physically large, small in memory and very, very slow. A venomous campaign against neural networks started in the mid 1960s, culminating in Minsky and Paperts (1969) book. This book is generally regarded as causing the end of the first stage of interest in neural networks. It was based on a theoretical demonstration that there was a very simple pattern recognition task that single-layer neural networks were unable to accomplish. Minsky and Papert (1969) proved mathematically that a Perception could not implement the EXCLUSIVE OR (XOR) logical function. Nor could it handle many other predicate functions. This somewhat bizarre and trivial fact was used to argue that eventually all neural networks suffer from the same flaw as the Perception, giving the impression that neural network research had been proven to be a dead end. The underlying objective according to Hecht-Nielsen (1990: 16) was "to discredit neural network research and divert neural network research funding to the field of 'artificial intelligence'" in the form of expert systems. It worked but maybe the field had run out of ideas anyway and was far ahead of any industrial or commercial infrastructure that could use it. Even if the technology had worked flawlessly the potential applications were 10 or more years in the future.

There were several other causes of failure, including:

- unrealistic expectations and hype
- very slow and limited computer hardware
- a lack of multi-level training methods
- a lack of breadth in terms of the range of problems that could be handled
- the absence of a theoretical and mathematical understanding affected its scientific image and respectability
- a strong anti-lobby who wanted the money invested in AI research focused on expert systems
- the lack of commercial products, and with
- hindsight, it was just much too early!

Like the laser when it was first invented, the early neural networks were solutions that did not work well in search of problems that did not then exist.

5.3.2 The years of gloom and dormancy: 1969–82

After the critique by Minsky and Papert (1969), neurocomputing research went underground. The research continued under different headings, for example signal processing, pattern recognition, biological modelling and associative computer memories. Yet despite its lack of popularity there was an influx of new researchers (1966–69) who subsequently put the topic on a much firmer scientific footing by developing a sounder mathematical basis for it. Ironically, also much of the groundwork was prepared during this period, for a second revolution. New network architectures were also invented, particularly adaptive resonance theory; see Grossberg (1972); the cognitron (Fukushima, 1980); and the self-organising map (Kohonen, 1984). Also some practical pattern recognition machines emerged, in particular WISARD (Aleksander et al, 1984). Computer hardware was now developing very fast with the microprocessor revolution. The scene was set for a revival.

5.3.3 The new neural nets: 1982–86

The 1980s saw a revival in neural network research initially funded by the US Dept of Defense. Hopfield (1982, 1984) is credited with reviving interest in the analysis of fully connected nets, initially as a means of making advanced computer memories. Hinton et al (1984) developed a practical way of making Hopfield nets work. However, it was Rumelhart and McClelland's (1986) book on parallel distributed processing that perhaps did most to stimulate the rebirth of a new era of neurocomputing. The back-propagation learning algorithm developed by Rumelhart et al (1986) provided a practical means of training multi-layer neural networks and finally shattered the curse of the Perception! Equally important was the spectacular demonstration (NETtalk) of a neural network learning to speak (Sejnowski and Rosenberg, 1987) that did much to convince many previous sceptics of the potential of the new neural networks.

5.3.4 Take off: 1987–

A tremendous surge of interest in practical, applicable, neurocomputing soon followed. There has been an exponential growth in numbers of applications, in publications, in researchers, as the neurocomputing revolution spread from one field to another. There are also an increasing number of neural network based commercial products. The driving force was a commercial appreciation that the technology is useful and has some practical value. By comparison traditional expert systems were by now in slow stagnation, if not decline. The reason is mainly the difficulties of developing useful expert systems that could handle worthwhile problems. The knowledge base of expert systems is static and the systems have no automatic learning capability. Neural networks provide a viable paradigm for machine learning and once the implementation problems were overcome the technology has an amazingly wide range of potential applications. It is interesting that in geography and the social sciences the neurocomputing revolution has by the mid 1990s still not arrived, despite the efforts of some early pioneers to raise awareness (Openshaw and Wymer, 1991; Fischer and Gopal, 1993; Openshaw, 1993; Hewitson and Crane, 1994). The geographical reasons probably relate to the relatively small number of active quantitative geographers and the distracting effect that the GIS revolution has had on other areas of computer-based geography. In some ways it is also because the most fruitful applications for neurocomputing lie outside the themes normally associated with quantitative geography, and here as in other parts of the social sciences, there are major awareness and training issues that need to be addressed. The second neural network revolution will persist because: the increases in computing power make it affordable; the many software packages make it easy to apply and widely diffused; it offers improved performance and immense productivity advantages in that the methods are largely application independent; whilst greater theoretical understanding of the complexity of nonlinear systems emphasises the need for more powerful technology with which to model and analyse.

5.3.5 The promise of neurocomputing

It is abundantly clear that neural networks have the potential to learn many different tasks from image recognition to function representation, providing the basis almost for a universal toolbox. They can be trained to handle noisy and poor data, and are error tolerant. They can generalise to unseen situations and can be used as building blocks in more complex systems. Above all else, they really do work.

Aleksander (1988) identifies four promises. **Promise one** is that neurocomputing is computationally complete. Given an appropriate network architecture and appropriate training, then there are no computational tasks that cannot be performed. However, this does not mean that a network will necessarily be more efficient than a conventional computer or faster. For example, it would be a stupid way of performing arithmetic! On the other hand there are also tasks that nets can perform that conventional computers cannot and maybe it is in these previously computer impossible applications where the greatest potential lies.

Promise two concerns the network's functional use of experiential knowledge due to its learning abilities. Nets can perform functions beyond the capabilities of rule-based systems, for example pattern recognition, language processing and modelling functions. It significantly extends the domain of the computer into the softer application areas.

Promise three concerns performance. Networks can provide rapid solutions to problems that conventional computers take a long time over, for example the travelling salesman problem, even if there are speed limitations due to the simulation of parallel net processing on serial or even parallel machines. Some argue that neural net chips are the answer.

Promise four concerns the provision of insights into the computational characteristics of the brain. The hope is that better knowledge will, over the course of the next 50 or so years, lead to the improved neural network architectures of the future.

Haykin (1994) identifies a number of general benefits of neural networks, including:

- nonlinearity
- input–output mapping: network learns from examples to construct an input–output mapping for the problem at hand

- adaptivity: they can be structured to deal with non-stationary environments with real-time changes in weights
- they can provide information about the confidence associated with the results
- they readily handle contextual information
- fault tolerance
- universality and information processors: it is a generic technology that can be used to solve many different problems
- an underlying neurobiological inspiration suggests that as neurobiological understanding improves so too might our artificial neural networks

More importantly there is increasing evidence that the use of a neural network may make a significant difference in performance or a reduction in cost without compromising performance. They also offer solutions to problems that could not previously be solved and, more generally, provide a rich source of ideas and inspiration for developing non-traditional solutions to a whole host of hard problems. Maybe it is this latter aspect that should be the most appealing to a geographer.

5.4 A GEOGRAPHICAL APPRECIATION

The neurocomputing revolution is set to provide a radically different paradigm for performing many spatial modelling and analysis tasks in geography. Supervised neural network architectures of one form or another are those likely to have the most immediate and the greatest impact. There are a number of reasons for this belief:

1. They provide a replacement or substitute technology able to perform most of the functions of existing methods to an equivalent or higher level of performance.
2. They contain no critical assumptions about the nature of spatial data, instead those that matter can be learnt during training.
3. They require virtually no in-depth explicit prior knowledge of the processes or patterns being modelled.
4. They are largely free of mathematical and statistical complexity, and hence "easy" to use although "ease of use" is a subjective criterion
5. They offer considerable degrees of flexibility in the functions they perform.
6. They are well suited to processing noisy data and handling chaotic and nonlinear modelling tasks.
7. They will often outperform conventional methods on problems where there are more conventional solutions.
8. They can in principle handle areas of geography previously excluded from computer analysis and quantitative geography.
9. They provide a means of tackling applications that were previously thought of as being too hard to handle.

10. They offer a technology able to help geographers cope with the immensely spatial data-rich world that is emerging.
11. They function as universal approximators, a model-free modelling technology able to provide good computer models of many complex nonlinear systems.

So what of the possible problems? The following can be enumerated although not all need be globally applicable or are universally correct. Some are just a reflection of prejudice. Nevertheless it may help to "air" them. The usual list of criticisms include the following:

1. It is a black box technology.
2. It is a data-driven technology.
3. It is difficult or impossible to use or represent knowledge of the modelling task in building a neural network which implicitly assumes that everything has to be learnt from the data.
4. There are many different types of neural network to choose from.
5. Neural networks do little or nothing more than conventional statistical methods already do.
6. The technology is theoretically suspect (albeit spuriously attractive) because the analogy with the workings of the brain is so poor and there is no other well-founded scientific basis for it.
7. There are seemingly unresolved issues in application, for example length of training.
8. Some users become over-enthusiastic and resort to unverified hype and exaggeration.
9. It is a hard technology to learn or cope with due to large amounts of unfamiliar technical jargon borrowed from either electrical engineering, neurophysiology, or biology.
10. The level of understanding of the processes and patterns that the neural network found and is representing is poor or hard to extract.

Yet it is important not to appreciate the benefits that are on offer. In many ways neural networks offer the ultimate in general purpose modelling and analysis technology. They provide the basis for what might be termed a "one-stop shop" methodology that can deal with many, maybe nearly all, the modelling problems in geography, regardless of their specific details and the nature of the application. They certainly promise something akin to a universal methodology, a single set of software that can be applied to virtually any modelling task for which sufficient data exist and adequate amounts of computing resources are available. This claim is, of course, not unlikely to go unchallenged, especially by those skilled in the older conventional statistical and mathematical modelling technologies now under threat. It is important not to exaggerate the potential of a neurocomputing toolkit that is still relatively young and unproven in a geographical context.

It is important also to be realistic and seek to confront each neural network model or technique with benchmarks based on the best alternative technologies, where such methods exist (Openshaw, 1992). You do not immediately reject or throw away the alternatives, instead it is important in each and every application to demonstrate the actual benefits gained from neurocomputing methods. Whilst there is certainly need for caution, there is no need for pessimism. The demonstration that a statistical expert with two or three degrees and a few decades of experience is able to outperform a neural network on certain classes of problem where such a competition is possible, might seem to be convincing evidence that neural nets are unnecessary on the grounds that they do not do anything that existing statistical methods cannot do. However, such a view overlooks a number of fundamental aspects:

1. The neural network could be run by an undergraduate with no degrees and limited experience and may still come close to "beating" an expert which is quite remarkable.
2. The neural network is much cheaper, much more widely applicable and probably much quicker than the expert who is a scarce and expensive commodity.
3. In many applications neural networks can perform functions for which there is no equivalent conventional technology or provide far superior levels of model representation for where they already exist.
4. Neural networks can be used to emulate existing models either as a means of speeding up their computation or as a basis for numerical experimentation.
5. They can be embedded in existing conventional modelling systems as replacements for submodels that may not work too well; it need not be an-all-or-nothing technology.

However, it is also a highly empirical technology. The onus of proof does indeed rest on the user demonstrating that useful results have been obtained. Neurocomputing is also in many ways a brittle technology. It can work extremely well or be totally disastrous; whereas by comparison many conventional models are much more robust but mediocre and consistently poor performers that neither work brilliantly nor disastrously. A key requirement in using neural networks is, therefore, a demonstration that they work well enough in the context of the application to which they are applied. So whereas neural networks may appear to provide an almost magic universal technology of general applicability that seems to work and offer a replacement for all conventional methods, it is the responsibility of the user to demonstrate this on each and every application where it is used.

Despite the need for care and common sense, it is clear that a second computer revolution is under way with wide application in many areas of geography. Maybe it is ironic that this is happening at a time where, in many geography and social science departments, the full impact of the first computer revolution has either not been properly absorbed or, where it has, seems to be engendering an anti-computer backlash by those unfamiliar with what modern computer technology can actually do, as distinct from what it once did (20 years or more ago). So instead of geography departments teaching outmoded, old-fashioned, suspect classical statistical methods maybe it is time to teach our students about easy to use, more flexible, less assumption ridden, and generally far better neural network based modelling tools.

The claim that neural net models are probably the ultimate in black-box modelling clearly causes some attitudinal and philosophical problems for those who hold the view that every model has to have a soundly based theoretical rationale, that it has to be both understandable and also capable of being given a simple plain English description that tells a plausible story linking model parameters to the supposed processes they represent. For instance, there are many examples of regression model parameters being "explained" in this way in the geographical literature. The problem with a neural network based model is the difficulty in giving it any plain English representation of what it is actually doing or of describing the relationships it has found in the data. The question is, does this matter? Is it better to use possibly poorer models that can be "explained" or possibly much better empirical representations that cannot? People respond in different ways in different contexts. The academic researcher is probably extremely reluctant to abandon understanding for empiricism, giving up models based on what might be regarded as well-founded theory for models based purely on data. The other view is that there is a need for good performing models and if neural network based black boxes work well then why not use them. Is it really better to use a model that offers a poor representation of reality but can be readily explained than a much better performing model that is a black box? Sadly, many people prefer the former and are not even prepared to be flexible, which is one explanation of why local weather forecasts are often wrong when it matters most! The dumbest model of all is the process model that fails to represent adequately the process on which its legitimacy depends and this failure is either accepted (it is the best that we can do) or goes unnoticed.

Whether a model is explainable or not is also critically dependent on the skills of the model user. Many statistical models are inherently black boxes even to the experts, for example the Box–Jenkins ARIMA family of time series forecasting models. So the black box nature of the neural network model is not new or particularly different from models that geographers already use. Additionally, neural nets can be understood by either visualising some of their outputs (viz. three-dimensional plots of how the net's outputs change as two of possibly many input variables are changed) or by various other forms of numerical experiment designed to increase the users' understanding of what the net model does.

Geography statisticians sometimes complain that neural networks offer no means of quantifying the uncertainty in their outputs. Not only are there no confidence intervals but there are no estimates of standard errors either! That is certainly true but the deficiency is easily remedied. Once a neural network model

NEURAL

NETWORKS

WORK

Figure 5.4   Guess what?

is built, it can be "bootstrapped" to obtain confidence intervals on the outputs that reflect input data uncertainty. Be careful though, most spatial data are not samples so much of classical statistical inference (including standard errors) is inapplicable and irrelevant.

It is argued, therefore, that the benefits of seeking to apply neural net models to geographical problems probably far exceed the possible difficulties. Despite the need for some modest degree of caution, why not at least try to evaluate what neural computing has to offer? It is a most exciting technology because it removes many of the restrictions that hinder conventional methods when applied to spatial data and also greatly extends the scope of computer analysis into both the previous no-go scientific parts of soft science and also the hard, much neglected areas of spatial systems modelling. Finally, a most convincing reason for believing that neural networks are a useful technology is shown in Figure 5.4.

5.5 WHAT ARE THE POTENTIAL NEURAL NETWORK MODELLING APPLICATIONS IN GEOGRAPHY?

The view so far is that neural nets have the potential to cope with both traditional modelling tasks and also, as yet undefined, new problem areas described as being too soft for more conventional technologies. So what are the especially difficult characteristics of geographical modelling problems that would provide convincing arguments in favour of neural net modelling? The view is often expressed that spatial modelling and analysis present many hard problems and that to date progress has been made mainly by deliberately ignoring most of them. This

Table 5.1   Some of the special characteristics of
spatial data relevant to modelling

Scale and aggregation dependencies
Spatial dependencies
Space-time dependencies
Nonlinear relationships
Presence of discontinuities
Non-stationarities
Non-normal frequency distributions
Mixtures of measurement types
Surrogate data
Data outliers
Data of varying degrees of reliability
Many variables some of which are redundant
Non-numeric data

---

pragmatic approach underlay much of the quantitative and mathematical modelling revolutions of the 1960s and 1970s in geography; now thanks to the development of AI there is some prospect that it is becoming possible to do much better. A key challenge for the 1990s and beyond must be the discovery and development of analysis and modelling tools that can actually cope with the characteristics of geographical information and the needs of the geographical user. It is increasingly important to avoid making unreasonable assumptions about the nature of spatial data and to develop methods that can handle rather than ignore the problems (Openshaw and Fischer, 1996). Neural nets and high performance computers provide the tools for meeting this challenge. Whereas not all the problems can be solved right now, it is likely that at least some, maybe many, of the most important ones can.

Table 5.1 outlines some of the special characteristics of spatial data that neural net models need to attempt to handle. Some of these characteristics are endemic features of spatial data (e.g. spatial autocorrelation), others are features that are often present (e.g. less than ideal data). Geographical data have many potential sources of imperfection, they are seldom ideal, and probably never will be. The task is to do the best that can be achieved given that which exists rather than wait for the 100% or even 90% correct database that may well never happen (Openshaw, 1989). The ill-informed critic of quantitative geography is often concerned that the data are not right. They are, of course, quite correct but neural networks are very good at coping with wrong and poor data. The hope is expressed that neural net models that have been widely and seemingly extremely successfully applied in many other disciplines on problems that seem to be equivalent in degree of hardness (e.g. speech processing, dynamic control systems, signal processing) might also be successfully employed on the analysis and modelling problems of geography. It is not sensible not to try and herein lies the basis for the neurocomputing revolution in geography.

There are other hard problems in geography that also need to be addressed. So-called soft computing applications are very important in many areas where classical quantitative methods cannot be applied. For example, plain text processing to build models that link text, where both the predictors and the predicted variables in a model are non-numeric. Another example would be the prediction of ethnic origins from forenames and last names, the conversion of textual descriptions of occupations into a standard industrial classification code, modelling the content of speeches, and so on. All you need is a degree of imagination, neural network software, data, and a little bit of luck!

5.6 CONCLUSIONS

It is argued that neurocomputing provides the basis for a new approach to doing geography in general. The discussion has been in some depth because the criticisms that neural networks attract need to be countered. Similar criticisms can also be levelled at the genetic algorithm, evolutionary programming and fuzzy logic chapters of the book. That is why it is so important to try and explain why the subject is crucial and why there are so many potential geographical applications for it. There are major implications for quantitative analysis in general, spatial analysis, spatial modelling and spatial pattern recognition. It also extends the apparent applicability of computers to the soft areas of geography, for example spatial cognition and natural language processing, and opens up new areas of geographical analysis in previously hard areas, for example testing soft theory and qualitative modelling. By comparison, conventional quantitative methods in geography are fragile, highly assumption dependent, highly applica- tion specific, have strong assumptions built in, they require you to do all the hard work, they are often inappropriate, non-intelligent, and cannot handle noise and uncertainty that typically characterise spatial data. Quantitative geography of the conventional kind was never able to deal adequately with the complexity of many areas of geography. Switch to neural networks and the problems look very different.

There is some prospect that neurocomputing can provide the basis for a much more rigorous approach to many areas of geography. It is a highly flexible and adaptive technology that geographers can ignore at their peril. Also, unlike all other areas of AI, neurocomputing is largely an off-the-shelf technology. The basic tools exist and are widely diffused. All you have to do is to discover how to use them and you should be able to do that extremely rapidly by a number of different means: (1) buy an introductory text that also provides software; (2) surf the internet, downloading public domain neural network software from an increasing number of f.t.p. sites; and (3) study the examples and substitute their problems for yours. A lot is now known about neurocomputing so talk to some of the users and within a time frame ranging from a few hours to a few days you will be up and running as a neural networks beginner. Learn some more, read a few more books, try and understand what it is doing with data and applications with which you are familiar and before you know it, you will know enough to exploit the technology.

Finally, discovering how to use neural networks is an extremely future relevant skill. It is not a here today, gone tomorrow technology. On the contrary it is much more likely that their numbers, complexity, and sophistication will continue to expand rapidly. We conclude with the following quote from Haykin (1994: 41):

> Neural networks have certainly come a long way from the early days of McCulloch and Pitts. Indeed they have established themselves as an interdisciplinary subject with deep roots in the neurosciences, psychology, mathematics, the physical sciences, and engineering. Needless to say, they are here to stay, and will continue to grow in theory, design, and application.

5.7 QUESTIONS AND ANSWERS

Q   Neurocomputing is just too hard, I am only a non-quantitative geographer.
A   Rubbish. As long as you are not totally computer shy, you can rapidly teach yourself the basics.
Q   Neurocomputing is not for simple-minded geographers.
A   Rot. Being simple-minded is not the problem. A degree of enthusiasm and willingness to experiment are much more important, as is a *broad* appreciation of what neural networks can and cannot do.
Q   Neurocomputing requires a first degree in mathematics, a Ph.D. in computer science, and a Master in neurocognitive studies.
A   Double rot! It could do but if it really did need it then there would be only two users in the world. Just take a deep breath and get out there and experiment. Maybe you will soon become an expert. You can certainly teach yourself most of what you will need to know. Rest assured too that before long 11-year-olds will be using it to predict football scores! Are you really going to let the younger generations outsmart you?
Q   Which book do you suggest I read first to improve my knowledge of neural networks?
A   There are lots of introductions to neural computing so pick one or two that you can understand and which contain useful PC-based software. Some of our favourites were Hecht-Nielsen (1990), Carling (1992), Wasserman (1989), Beale and Jackson (1990) and Aleksander and Morton (1990). You are really spoilt for choice so that actually finding one to buy is rather like buying a new shirt or a pair of shoes! In fact the really difficult task is finding a more advanced book at an affordable price. Perhaps Wasserman (1993) might be a good intermediate choice.
Q   Are neural nets the ultimate AI technology likely to sweep all before them?
A   No!
Q   My neural net model is much better than its statistical alternative.
A   Prove it before gloating about it!
Q   My neural net model is biologically inspired and therefore better technology than this old model it has replaced. Haven't I done well?
A   No, you are being a trifle silly! The old model can also claim to have been the

product of a biological process, namely the brain of its creator. If you think you have a better model then prove it empirically rather than relying on ancestry or hyperbole.

Q   Are neural nets really electronic brains based on human brain like processes?

A   Not really. There is an analogy but it is exceptionally loose. The usual description is "biologically inspired" and at present this is the best one to use. Don't go overboard on the "brain" aspects at present; one day maybe but not yet. It is still early days.

Q   Exactly how biologically inspired is the neural net?

A   Inspired is the right word. The brain cannot possibly work as badly as our artificial creations do; else we would all be 100 years old before we had learnt how to walk if the brain used one of our standard "learning" methods. Our artificial brains emulate rather than replicate the workings of the biological brain, so it might be wise to play down the biological associations.

Q   If our artificial neural nets possess only a few hundred neurons is it ever likely to be able to do anything worth while when the brain has upwards of 100 billion neurons?

A   Yes, neuronal processing is extremely powerful. The brain has a few thousand permanently running tasks needed to keep us alive, managing limbs, the respiratory system, muscles; interpreting speech and vision and generating sounds, etc. all in real time. It is quite likely that only a small fraction of the brain is ever devoted to any single task; so maybe artificial neural nets dedicated to performing only a single function, not in a real-time environment, are adequate.

Q   In what ways are artificial neural nets artificial?

A   The real brain is a biological organism that uses a complex mix of electrical impulses and chemicals to transmit and receive information. Its basic components are very small; a neuron is typically less than 100 microns in width (or 1 millionth of a metre), it can be connected to upwards of 10 000–15 000 other neurons; and there are about 100 billion neurons forming a very compact three-dimensional network. Clearly anything that we try to do using software will be highly simplified, very artificial and extremely crude. Biological computers do not as yet even exist so all parts of our artificial neural nets are synthetic simulations of how we think (because we still don't really know) the real thing works.

Q   Which of the various words for neurocomputing do you prefer?

A   Neurocomputing seems best. Most of the rest sound pompous or mislead or are not sufficiently generic; for example, parallel distributed computing is confusing, connectionism says nothing, neural computing is better and neural networks is probably too specific. It is a matter of personal preference. Neural networks is perhaps the most widely used term.

Q   How close are we right now to building a real brain?

A   Not very near nor is it likely in the foreseeable future. As yet experts still do not fully comprehend the neural workings of either a slug or the simplest of insects. Our artificial software and hardware artificial brains are still far from being able to represent the connectivity of the brain, let alone emulate the numbers of neurons present even in the common housefly. Maybe over the next 50 or so years major strides will be taken; meanwhile lets stop getting swept away by the hype and mystique and get down to using the neurocomputing tools that now exist. Geographers are geographers and shouldn't aspire to become brain specialists! Who cares how they work or why, lets prove they do and then get on with the task of making good and safe use of them; that is more than enough.

Q Do neural nets bring a human level of intelligence to the problem to which they are applied?

A No. It is highly misleading and wrong to imply that they have or offer human levels of intelligence. They are essentially highly versatile pattern recognition technologies, they do not and cannot think. They have no consciousness, they are artefacts of the computer age. Useful, powerful, tools that can be usefully applied to a whole host of problems. However, they are also an immensely emotionally charged topic because they combine the mystique of the brain with the power of the computer and imply, wrongly, that the latter can now aspire to what the former does. The brain benefits also from the way in which it processes information. It is not just an arithmetic machine but performs much more sophisticated information-processing functions.

Q Biological modelling is the ultimate modelling technology?

A Some thought biological washing powder was powerful stuff until it brought them out in a rash! You need to prove such claims of superiority by careful, sober, comparative study, not assertion. Indeed the authors happen to think that genetically bred models might in the longer term be even better, but we cannot as yet prove it!

Q What will neurocomputing achieve?

A It is too early to say. They have certainly moved the traditional constraints on the applicability of the computer, they broaden the range of applications to which computers can be applied, they offer powerful alternatives to older methods and promise solutions to some previously unsolved problems, but that is probably all! They will not instantly make your PCs intelligent nor solve many of the world's problems, nor instantly make all conventional systems obsolete. They are a step forward but only a modest one and it is important neither to overstate their capabilities nor to underestimate their potential.

Q Are neural networks dangerous because they provide no theoretical understanding of the problem?

A Maybe that is true but in much of geography do we actually have any good levels of theoretical understanding about much or anything? Is not the ability to build better models through which numerical experimentation can greatly improve levels of understanding a useful way forward?

Q Are neural networks a miracle solution to all our hard problems?

A They are not the miracle solution to all modelling problems that some may claim but on a good day, with a little luck, and the right amount of experimentation they can often do very well on problems for which there are benchmark performances and seemingly brilliantly on other problems that previously could not be handled at all; although with the passage of time what initially seems to be brilliant may turn out to be mediocre as the capabilities of the technology expand and improve and user expectations grow.

Q Why this extended discussion of neural networks? What is so special about them?

A It is more what they represent rather than what they really are. They constitute a radically different way of thinking. One that recommends approaches that have long been taboo subjects. The whole idea of creating models from data is still alien to more traditionally minded geographers. To them the whole area smacks of naïve empiricism, of data crunching gone mad, of rampant blind analysis, of data mining, of dumb and mindless analysis performed by computer crazed troglodytes! But that is just one point of view. It is of course biased and, whilst understandable in a mild form, fundamentally wrong! AI challenges the conventional wisdom, it always has. However, AI also works. There are very strong grounds for genuinely believing that neural networks are extremely relevant to geography. Geographers need to accept that data-orientated analysis and modelling are quite acceptable. It is a valid, acceptable and increasingly useful way to proceed. Neural networks force us to confront the taboos and adjust to them. Thereafter the remaining chapters are hopefully more readily accepted.

Q Is there nothing in neural networks that statistical methods do not already do?

A Maybe this statement should be reversed. There is nothing in statistics that neural networks cannot do but there are many analysis and modelling applications for neural networks that have no conventional statistical solution. The other view is that, well, this debate is really pointless for three reasons:

1. Neural computing opens up new opportunities for statistical methods, viz. in hybrid systems.
2. The statistical aspects of neural computing need attention, viz. model validation, uncertainty estimation using computer-intensive statistical methods.
3. It is all statistical to some degree anyway.

When both hype and fears subside, neural computing will quickly become recognised as a set of potentially useful statistical tools that, rather than render statisticians instantly redundant will, as elsewhere, expand the range of opportunities available to them. Just because it is all a bit weak in terms of statistical theory need not make it bad or poor technology.

Q If neural networks are so wonderful where is the geographical evidence?

A It is coming! Have some faith! Be patient! Maybe you could become one of the missionaries?

Q Why has the neural network revolution taken so long to arrive in geography?

A This is covered in the chapter but maybe there is another reason. To exploit the power of neural networks you do not need to create or invent "new" applications; all you need do is to evolve the technologies we already use. Geographers, whilst highly enterprising, seem to have always found it easier to copy others than innovate. We live with a vast amount of borrowed and copied technologies, philosophies and concepts. Maybe, just maybe, we are finding it difficult to be sufficiently inventive and creative. Neural networks are also an explicitly applied problem-solving technology and this might well be another explanation for their relative neglect in more scholarly (i.e. non-applied) circles. They should appeal most to empiricists interested in quantitative analysis, modelling and GIS! Maybe this key set of researchers is too sparsely populated for there to be a quick response to the neural network revolution. However it will come. The neural net bug is already increasing the pool of the infected, and even as you read this, you too may now have been converted and your world of computer analysis and modelling will never ever be the same again. Ahhh! The neural net virus has claimed another victim.

REFERENCES

Aleksander, I., 1988, "The logic of connectionist systems", in I. Aleksander (ed.), *Neural Computing Architectures*. MIT Press, Cambridge, Mass.

Aleksander, I., Morton, H., 1990, *An Introduction to Neural Computing*. Chapman & Hall, London.

Aleksander, I., Thomas, W., Bowden, P., 1984, "WISARD: a radical new step forward in image recognition", *Sensor Review*, **4**, 120–124.

Beale, T., Jackson, T., 1990, *Neural Computing: an introduction*. Adam Hilger, Bristol.

Carling, A., 1992, *Introducing Neural Nets*. Sigma Press, Wilmslow.

Conzen, M.R.G., 1947, "Modern settlement", in *Scientific Survey of North East England*, British Association for the Advancement of Science, Newcastle upon Tyne.

Cybenko, G., 1989, "Approximation by superimposition of a sigmoidal function", *Mathematics of Control, Signals, and Systems*, **2**, 303–314.

Dawn, T., 1994, "Neural computing makes its mark in science", *Scientific Computing*, **3**, September.

Fischer, M.F., Gopal, S., 1993, "Neurocomputing—a new paradigm for geographic information processing", *Environment and Planning A*, **25**, 757–760.

Fukushima, K., 1980, "Neocognitron: a self-organising neural network model for a mechanism of pattern recognition unaffected by shifts in position", *Biological Cybernetics*, **36**, 193–202.

Grossberg, S., 1972, "Pattern learning by functional-differential neural networks with arbitrary path weights", in K. Schmitt (ed.), *Delay and Functional Differential Equations and their Applications*. Academic Press, New York, pp. 121–160.

Haykin, S., 1994, *Neural Networks*. MacMillan, New York.

Hebb, D.O., 1949, *The Organization of Behaviour*. Wiley, New York.

Hecht-Nielsen, R., 1990, *Neurocomputing*. Addison-Wesley, Reading, Mass.

Hewitson, B.C., Crane, R.G., 1994, *Neural Nets: applications in geography*. Kluwer Academic Publishers, Boston.

Hinton, G.E., Sejnowski, T.J., Ackley, D.H., 1984, "Boltzmann machines: constraint satisfaction networks that learns", Carnegie Mellon University Technical Report *CMU-CS-84-119*, Pittsburg.

Hopfield, J.J., 1982, "Neural networks and physical systems with emergent collective computatiional abilities", *Proceedings of National Academy of Science*, **79**, 2554–2558.

Hopfield, J.J., 1984, "Neurons with graded response have collective computational properties like those of two-state neurons", *Proceedings of the National Academy of Science*, **81**, 3088–3092.

Kohonen, T., 1984, *Self-Organisation and Associative Memory*. Springer-Verlag, Berlin.

Kolmogorov, A.N., 1957, "On the representation of continuous functions of many variables by superimposition of continuous functions of one variable and addition", (in Russian), *Dokl. Akad. Nauk. USSR*, **114**, 953–956.

Kosko, B., 1992, *Neural Networks and Fuzzy Systems: a dynamical systems approach to machine intelligence*. Prentice-Hall, Englewood Cliffs, New Jersey.

McCulloch, W.S., Pitts, W., 1943, "A logical calculus of the ideas immanent in nervous activity", *Bulletin of Mathematical Biophysics*, 5, 115–133.

Minsky, M., Papert, S., 1969, *Perceptions*. MIT Press, Cambridge, Mass.

Nelson, M.M., Illingworth, W.T., 1992, *A Practical Guide to Neural Nets*. Addison-Wesley, Reading, Mass.

Openshaw, S., 1989, "Making geodemographics more sophisticated", *Journal of the Market Research Society*, 31, 111–131.

Openshaw, S., 1992, "A review of the opportunities and problems in applying neurocomputing methods in marketing applications", *Journal of Targeting, Measurement and Analysis for Marketing*, 1, 170–186.

Openshaw, S., 1993, "Modelling spatial interaction using a neural net", in M.M. Fischer and P. Nijkamp (eds), *GIS: spatial modelling and policy evaluation*. Springer-Verlag, Berlin, pp. 147–164.

Openshaw, S., Fischer, M.F., 1996, "A framework for research on spatial analysis relevant to geo-statistical information systems in Europe", *Geographical Systems*, 2, 325–337.

Openshaw, S., Wymer, C., 1991, "A neural net classifier for handling census data", in F. Murtagh (ed.), *Neural Networks for Statistical and Economic Data*. Munotech, Dublin.

Openshaw, S., Wymer, C., Craft, A., 1991, "Using neural nets to solve some hard analysis problems in GIS", *Proceedings of EGIS'91*, Vol. 2. EGIS Foundation, Utrecht, pp. 797–807.

Rosenblatt, F., 1958, "The Perception: a probabilistic model for information storage and organisation in the brain", *Psychological Review*, 65, 386–407.

Rumelhart D.E., Hinton, G.E., Williams, R.J., 1986, "Learning internal representation by error propagation", in D.E. Rumelhart, J.L. McClelland (eds), *Parallel Distributed Processing: explorations in the microstructure of cognition*, Vol. 1. MIT Press, Cambridge, Mass.

Rumelhart, D.E., McClelland, J.L. (eds), 1986, *Parallel Distributed Processing: explorations in the microstructure of cognition*, Vol. 1. MIT Press, Cambridge, Mass.

Sejnowski, T.J., Rosenberg, C.R., 1987, "Parallel networks that learn to pronounce English text", *Complex Systems*, 1, 145–168.

Von Neumann, J., 1951, "The general and logical theory of automata", in L.A. Jefferies (ed.), *Cerebral Mechanisms in Behaviour*. John Wiley, New York, pp. 1–41.

Wang, F., 1994, "The use of artificial neural networks in a geographical information system for agricultural land-suitability assessment"; *Environment and Planning A*, 26, 265–284.

Wasserman, P.D., 1989, *Neural Computing*. Van Nostrand Reinhold, New York.

Wasserman, P.D., 1993, *Advanced Methods in Neural Computing*. Van Nostrand Reinhold, New York.

Widrow, B., Hoff, M.E., 1960, "Adaptive switching circuits", 1960 IRE WESCON Convention Record, 96–104.

Wiener, N., 1948, *Cybernetics*. John Wiley, New York.

CHAPTER 6

Applying Artificial Neural Networks

Artificial neural networks are a practical, widely applicable and extremely useful technology. There are numerous potential applications of neural networks in geography and there is a tremendous opportunity here to improve the performance of many geographical models and analysis procedures. Neural networks also significantly extend the domain of computing into areas previously considered too hard or exempt from mathematical modelling and statistical analysis.

6.1 INTRODUCTION

After Chapter 5 maybe you are feeling a little intimidated by the concept of a "neural network". Maybe the word "neural" puts you off! Well do not be! It is really simple technology once you get beyond the technical language, hype and jargon. It is all very straightforward. Indeed it suffers from the following advantages: (1) there is no complex statistical framework to confuse the uninitiated, (2) there are no really hard equations that only Ph.D. mathematicians can understand, and (3) the simplicity of the whole edifice is not disguised by being encoded in C + +, it could be, but BASIC or FORTRAN is just as good! Indeed the authors' first encounter with a neural network was a BASIC program given away in *Computer Shopper* (a magazine full of PC adverts) in 1990 (James, 1990). Prior to that, neural networks seemed to be a magical but totally mysterious technology, with the secrets hidden away in non-understandable jargon and impenetrable complexity that was more than enough to put off even the most ardent quantitative geographer. The tremendous beauty of a computer code is that ultimately the most complex of mathematics is reduced to a string of + , − , * and / operations. You can teach yourself mathematics like this provided the computer code is not too long and is simply written in non-object orientated form! With neural networks this is not a problem. "Oh" you declare, "that is how it works." "Bloomin" heck, that is not too difficult after all!" This remark also applies to most of AI. The greater the complexity of the technology then the less useful the result is likely to be. With AI nearly all of it is extremely non-complex, although at first sight it appears the exact opposite, that is, extremely hard. The reality is, of course, quite different but the secret is best kept so you can amaze your friends and associates by posing as an AI or neural networks expert. However, in case your bluff is called then maybe you will really need to know how to build a neural network application and, thus, something about how it all works. Fortunately, getting started is not hard, but becoming an expert is more difficult and time consuming but nevertheless extremely worthwhile. After GIS, practical knowledge and skills in neural networks probably make you more job-market attractive than anything else you might contemplate within the field of geography.

There are various ways forward; statistical packages such as SPSS and SAS provide neural network options so you could use these general purpose statistical packages. Alternatively, you could surf the net and within a few hours download all manner of "free" neural network programs for PC and Unix workstations, you could join various lists and obtain via f.t.p. an amazing number of electronic papers if you wish. You can easily DIY to increase your skills in this as well as many other areas of AI quite readily but here more than elsewhere it is by far the most abundant. There are tutorial systems you can obtain free or for a small fee and any bookshop will readily testify to a surfeit of books on the subject, many of which include discs for a PC with working software. All you need is (a) a degree of confidence that the technology works and is useful and (b) a belief that it is ultimately not too hard to understand. The answers to both concerns are: yes, it works, and yes, it is not too hard. Hopefully this chapter will provide enough of an introduction to get you started. After that, it is up to you to find other books that will take you forward and perhaps even make you an expert.

There are only really two different neural network "architectures" that matter to beginners: supervised and non-supervised. Both need data, lots of data. Note how immediately the term "architecture" confers a degree of grandiose splendour on a fairly naïve and innocent technology. This is a characteristic feature of neural networks, which are richly littered with terms and misused jargon such as "learning", "memory", "human brains", "neurons", "synaptic this or that", and lots of other words designed to impress but more often than not it merely serves to confuse. Neurobabble is perhaps a good word to describe this. You just have to put up with it and get on with attempting to understand what it does rather than be distracted by the linguistic hype.

6.2 SUPERVISED NEURAL NETWORKS

6.2.1 The black box

Probably the most instantly useful neural network is the supervised net. Supervised nets have the capability of learning how to map a set of one or more

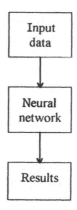

Figure 6.1   A neural network modelling paradigm

inputs on to one or more outputs. That is all they do. It is up to you to try and ensure that they learn something useful. Also what they learn is dependent on the data you use to train them. Confused? Then (re) read Chapter 5.

Here is the ultimate in data-driven empiricism and no doubt this technology does not appeal much to some people who may prefer a more knowledge-based approach. However, where that knowledge base is either deficient or missing then supervised neural networks offer a useful way forward. Furthermore, even when the available knowledge is regarded as sufficient to employ a conventional modelling or statistical approach, neural networks may still be useful because of their freedom from assumptions, their inherent nonlinearity, and their ability to handle noisy data in difficult non-ideal contexts such as those typically found in geography and many social sciences.

Figure 6.1 provides an overview of the neural network approach to building a model. It is quite simple really. Suppose you have three variables X_1, X_2, X_3 and wish to predict the values of a fourth variable Y. You have 1000 observations for all four variables and your objective is to find a way of predicting values of Y given these values of X_1, X_2 and X_3. Now you could do this using a linear regression model that is based on the hypothesis that values of variable Y are a linear function of X_1, X_2 and X_3, viz.

$$Y = b_0 + b_1 X_1 + b_2 X_2 + b_3 X_3 + \text{error term}$$

where b_0, b_1, b_2 and b_3 are parameters that have to be estimated so that the predicted Y values closely match the observed values. The aim is as much to test this hypothesis as it is to fit the data. If the fit is declared adequate and the parameter values for b_0, b_1, b_2, b_3 are "significantly" different from zero, then the model might be declared valid and an attempt made to invent a plausible tale about its meaning.

But what happens if the relationship is nonlinear or the assumptions inherent in the statistical model are not met or the model is declared valid but does not work particularly well? Suppose the unknown relationship between the values of Y and X is a curve of some kind, then fitting a straight line will not give a good representation of it. Suppose the data observations or the errors are non-independent due to spatial autocorrelation or map pattern effects. Again, the assumptions implicit in the linear regression model break down and the statistical estimates for the parameters b_0, b_1, b_2, b_3 cannot be trusted. These and similar problems are common with conventional statistical models. Now suppose you have some theory that allows you to specify a mathematical model that will predict the value of Y given variables X_1 and X_2, for example

$$Y = (e^{-b_1 X_1})/X_2$$

Sadly the same problems occur as befell the statistical model except the specification (viz. the model equation) is now assumed to be correct because it is based on some theory rather than a hypothesis. But what happens if it is not? Is the theoretical basis for the model likely to yield a very good result regardless of the data? Does it apply everywhere or is the model merely a test of the theory? If it fits the data then the theory works, but if it does not fit well, is the theory to be rejected? If the theory is rejected (because of a poor fit) then where does that leave your attempt to model the data? Additionally there is the problem of "calibrating" the model by finding a value for b_1, so some statistical process is involved and in a geographical context questions can again be asked about map pattern effects, problems of data noise, measurement error, etc. Is the model reliable, can the parameters be trusted, does it provide a good enough fit to the data, can it be safely used to predict or forecast values of Y for new values of X? Modelling is not an easy process. Now add in some doubts about the accuracy of the model's specification, its robustness to data errors, and you will soon appreciate the problems. There must be a smarter way! There is, it is called a neural network.

The neural network uses the observed data for X_1, X_2, X_3 and Y to "learn" how to relate these inputs (X_1, X_2, X_3) to the output Y. It does so without being restricted by linearity assumptions or hindered by knowledge of theory that may be wrong, biased or partial. It makes no assumptions about the statistical properties of the data or even about the units of measurements that are used. It is merely seeking a mathematical mapping of the inputs on to the output in what is termed a model-free way. The only restrictions relate to the representativeness of the data and the design of the network. If you want the network to handle spatial autocorrelation then give it spatially autocorrelated inputs if there are grounds for believing that this is necessary for modelling purposes rather than merely due to fears about biased parameter estimates, because the latter are no longer relevant. Spatial autocorrelation or neighbourhood effects can be easily handled by computing additional values for each variable; for example, the average value of X_1 for the first-order contiguous zones, likewise for second- and third-order contiguities. Does it matter? Well you will still need to experiment to find out. Neural networks are a black box technology but they are not automatic or magic. If you put garbage into a neural net then you will get garbage out. You will still need to specify what you (or theory or prior knowledge) consider to be the most appropriate variables to use. You have to experiment with them, testing the effects of changes in design and selection of inputs. However, you can now do this without having to worry about the statistical or mathematical structure of the model. The neural network will do the best it can to model your data given what you provide it with.

Maybe you still prefer a more traditional approach. That is perfectly all right if there is a real alternative. Clearly for linear regression models there is a statistical technology that can be used, but what if X_2 is categorical, X_3 is a zero/one variable and X_1 is continuous. That is still all right, but if Y is categorical as well then you have problems. What if there are two different Y variables (i.e. two outputs and three inputs)? You are beyond what statistical methods can currently deliver! Now let us also make the model nonlinear and you are far beyond the scope of conventional methods, especially if you cannot specify the precise nature of the nonlinear relationship. To a neural network it is all the same, just a set of inputs to be associated with some outputs, somehow! Our brains do this arbitrary "mapping process" quite well and so do neural networks given a reasonable chance and sufficient data from which it can learn the necessary relationships.

6.2.2 How does it work?

The basic process can be broken down into a number of steps.

Step 1   Obtain data relevant to the modelling or relationship prediction task

Divide the data into two (or more) subsets: one for training purposes, one (or more) for model validation. You need a reasonable amount of data, depending on the complexity of your neural network. If you have a very large database then either use it all or select a good representative sample at random or stratify the sample to reflect the cases that matter most. Using it all might be expensive and unwarranted unless the application is really important! There is an approximate rule of thumb which suggests that the number of observations in the training data set should be between 5 and 10 times the number of weights in the neural network. However, this is just a crude rule of thumb. Representativeness is probably more important.

Step 2   Transform or scale the data values to be in the range 0.0 to 1.0

The neural network's output will then need to be transformed back to represent the full range of the Y values. Some argue that it is useful to scale the inputs to between 0.1 and 0.9 to avoid the special cases of zero and one which can slow down training.

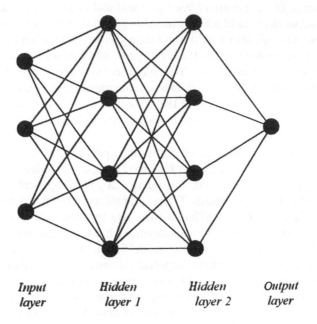

| *Input* | *Hidden* | *Hidden* | *Output* |
| *layer* | *layer 1* | *layer 2* | *layer* |

Figure 6.2   Basic structure of a multi-layer feed-forward neural network

Step 3   Decide on the "architecture" of your network

This involves the following decisions:

1. the number of input variables,
2. the number of hidden layers,
3. the number of neurons in each layer, and
4. the type of network to be used.

A bit of jargon is unavoidable here. Figure 6.2 outlines the principal structure of a multi-layer feed-forward network. The input layer has a neuron for each input variable. In the regression example there are the X_1, X_2, X_3 variables. The output layer has a neuron for each output but with only Y to predict then there is only the one as is shown in Figure 6.2. In-between the input layer and output layer there are one or two (or more) so-called hidden layers, each with a variable number of neurons. Usually you will need two hidden layers. It is the second layer that adds power to the network and permits more complex nonlinear functions to be handled. A third hidden layer may sometimes be useful if the function being modelled is extremely complex, noisy or discontinuous (see Lippmann, 1987). Determining the optimal number of layers is usually a matter for experimentation. This is important and does influence the results (see, for instance, Huang and

Lippmann, 1987; Gorman and Sejnowski, 1988; Wang et al, 1992; Lapedes and Faber, 1988; Flood and Kartam, 1993). You could start with one and then add a second if levels of performance are not too good.

The number of neurons in the hidden layer is sometimes critical but determining the optimum number is a black art. In general it has been shown that the number of neurons in each hidden layer should be related to the complexities of the data (Wang et al, 1994). Some people argue that the number of neurons in the second hidden layer should be at least three times that of the first hidden layer (Lippmann, 1987) but this may well be problem dependent. Again you have to experiment. You do it by trial and error or else use a neural network that grows or shrinks the dimensions of the network for you. Usually too few neurons affects the performance more than too many, but it is not really that simple because the number of neurons interacts with the training process and this reflects the nature of the data and the number of observations being used.

Note also that in Figure 6.2 each of the neurons is fully connected to each neuron in the next layer, but the neurons in hidden layer 1 do not directly connect with the output neuron but go via hidden layer 2. The neurons form a network, hence the name neural network. The interconnections can be structured to be recurrent but that is for advanced networkers. Here things are deliberately kept simple.

Step 4 Training the network

This is potentially the hardest part and the most computer intensive. The basic idea is very simple. Each of the lines connecting the neurons in Figure 6.2 has a weight or value (i.e. a number) attached to them that has to be estimated during training. In addition you now need to understand what a neuron does. The biological inspiration here is particularly strong. A neuron is a summation device, it sums up the inputs it receives and creates an output.

Allegedly our brain's neurons work in an analogous fashion. The McCulloch and Pitts (1943) neuron had a threshold value applied to the sum of the inputs and an output was only produced if the sum exceeded this threshold. A more sophisticated way of doing this is to use a sigmoidal (i.e. S-shaped) squashing transfer function that squashes the sum of all the weights (inputs) received by a neuron on to the range 0.0 to 1.0 or -1.0 to $+1.0$. The gain (or bias or shape) of this function is another parameter that is estimated during training. Figure 6.3 gives an illustration of a neuron in the second hidden layer of Figure 6.2.

The output from each neuron is now a smooth nonlinear function of its weighted inputs. This is again biologically inspired and it is very important because it greatly increases the representational powers of the net. The choice of transfer function is subjective and the sigmoidal function might be regarded as being popular because of its mathematical tractability (e.g. it is easy to differentiate). Each neuron in the net performs the processing outlined in Figure 6.3. The data and order of processing in Figure 6.2 are from left to right. The input

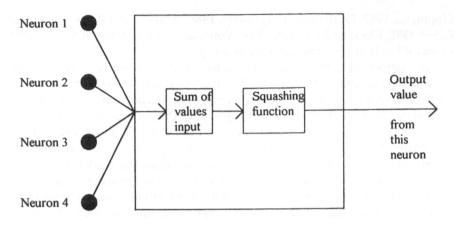

Figure 6.3   Neuron information processing

layer merely transmits the inputs to the neurons in the first hidden layer. The neurons in each layer operate in parallel. This left to right feeding forward of the data from one layer of neurons to another explains why this particular architecture is called a feed-forward multi-layer network.

The power of this neural network comes from its ability to map (in a mathematical sense) virtually any set of inputs on to virtually any set of outputs, given a sufficient supply of training data. The tremendous potential of this methodology comes from the ability of the neural network to identify mappings for virtually anything! If there is a linkage that is recurrent in the data then it will probably find and represent it no matter how complex it might be, provided there are sufficient neurons, hidden layers and adequate training data so that it can represent (or memorise) the relationships. It should be noted that the mappings can extend far beyond those which conventional statistical techniques can cope with, for example, a nonlinear categorical regression model with two outputs; a mapping of a digital representation of free format text describing an occupation on to an arbitrary numeric code; or a regression model that relates continuous real inputs on to a set of neurons that represents the bit pattern of an unsigned integer count of limited precision. However, the neural network is more than merely a memory device. Certainly the weights provide a form of associative computer memory but they have an inherent generalisation and interpolation capability. They can estimate or guess outputs for sets of inputs they have never encountered before provided they are not too atypical of the training data.

If these examples appear a little bizarre or esoteric it is only because they are designed to illustrate the potential representational power of an artificial neural network. To claim they can represent anything may be somewhat of an exaggeration, but they can probably handle most things that are related in some way no matter how obscure or complicated the relationship may be, provided there is a relationship. It is useful then to note that whilst training a neural network may take a long time, once it is trained outputs can be computed very quickly indeed. An obvious application is to train neural networks to replicate the functioning of highly complex mathematical models that are extremely computationally intensive.

The final part of understanding how a neural net works is to discover how actually to train a feed-forward multi-layer network. This is where the back-propagation procedure appears on the scene. The basic idea is easy enough. You have to estimate the weights used by a network. Refer back to Figure 6.2. Each interconnection has a weight that now needs to be estimated. These weights represent the strength of each interconnection. They also act as a type of memory that contains patterns stored by the net during its training phase. The distributed nature of these weights (or memory) makes the net fairly damage resistant; destroy a few neurons and it may still function, albeit at an impaired level (cf. human beings with brain damage). This also gives the net a degree of immunity to data noise and very good representational powers even when not optimally configured. Imagine now that the three variables (X_1, X_2, X_3) for a case in the training data set are input into Figure 6.2 and an output value obtained. This can be compared with the known observed value for Y and a measure of error defined. This information is then used to "correct" those neurons that contributed most to the error. However, given the nature of the network in Figure 6.2 it will not be immediately evident which neurons and what weights are most to blame. So the errors are back-propagated from the output neuron at the right hand side of the net backwards, i.e. reversing the previous feed-forward process so it becomes a feed-backwards one. The weights are then adjusted. This procedure is repeated many times. Gradually the weights stabilise and training ceases. The network can then be used to predict values for other sets of inputs for which the results are known (the validation data) and a measure of performance obtained.

To summarise, the following process would usually be followed:

Step 1   Define the dimension of the net; the number of neurons and the number of hidden layers.
Step 2   Initialise the weights.
Step 3   Select a data case (or batch of cases or complete data set).
Step 4   Apply to net.
Step 5   Back-propagate the errors adjusting the weights, using a "training" method.
Step 6   Repeat steps 3–5 a large number of times.

A key decision is when to stop training. If training proceeds for too long and/or there are many weights compared with training data, the network may overtrain and reproduce the random noise present in the data as well as the relationship of interest with a corresponding loss of generalisation capability. One way of deciding when to stop training is to monitor the network's error levels on a sample of data not used in the training process. Once this starts to increase then training needs to stop.

This training process can also be performed in a number of different ways. Indeed the difficulty of training a multi-layer neural network had originally held up their development. The back-propagation solution to the training problem was not common knowledge until 1986 (Rumelhart et al, 1986). The answer was really not that novel and could have been performed (but only just) 20 years earlier. The real problem was that the experts in Perceptrons were not experts in nonlinear optimisation. If they had been then training would have been viewed purely as a computational problem, viz. find the minimum value of an unconstrained nonlinear least squares function for which partial derivatives of the function can be computed; see for example Fletcher (1971). Instead the classical neural network training method via a steepest descent form of optimisation is really poor at handling nonlinear parameter estimation problems of sum of squares functions. A more efficient (from a numerical optimisation point of view) is a conjugate gradient method that can handle optimisation problems with many thousands of variables, and more recently genetic algorithms have also been used (see Chapter 7). Indeed, a seriously minded neural network modeller would today want to develop some variant of the Adeli and Hung (1995) method, whereby a genetic algorithm is used to find a good starting set of values for a more conventional approach.

Step 5   Test the model and decide whether to change the step 1 decisions and repeat the process

Once the network's weights have been estimated then the performance of the network needs to be investigated using the validation data that were withheld from the training process. These data should be a 20–50% sample of the data. There are several possible things that can go wrong:

1. Overtraining resulting in the net modelling the noise in the data and not just the relationships, resulting in a loss of generalisation capabilities;
2. Too few training cases; there are a large number of weights that are estimated and ideally you will need 5–10 times as many training cases as there are unknownweights (Fitzgerald and Lees, 1994; Haykin, 1994), or else considerable care is needed to avoid problem (1);
3. Poor performance due to too few neurons (or too many), "wrong" variables, and poor selection of training cases; and
4. Inadequate training resulting in poor performance due to the use of suboptimal parameter (weight) values.

If performance is still judged to be inadequate then maybe some of the following suggestions may help:

1. Try reducing the number of neurons, it may be a learning problem;
2. Check that you have preprocessed your data onto a 0.0–1.0 range properly, maybe 0.1–0.9 might be best in order to avoid the top of the sigmoidal curve;
3. Try increasing the number of neurons and/or the number of hidden layers;
4. Investigate whether fewer variables might be useful (you could reduce them using principal component analysis);
5. Try coding your variables differently; for example, put in some transformed values of a key variable as the network may well find it hard to approximate these functions resulting in lengthy training times; and
6. Consider extending the training process; maybe the network has become stuck at a suboptimal set of weights so try some random perturbations before restarting it.

The next step is to establish some degree of confidence that the neural network is working well. You need to compare its performance with any conventional models or techniques that can provide benchmarks (if there are any). Neural modelling can be a brittle technology. It often works extremely well but it may sometimes fail completely, whereas more conventional methods might well be observed to be robust but uniformly poor performers (Openshaw, 1992a). The onus is on you to prove it works well enough to be used in the context in which it is to be applied.

Step 6   Probing the network

The back-propagation trained multi-layer feed-forward perception is a black box. Either you believe it works or you do not; but either way it tells you nothing about the nature of the model it has "found" or built for you. Additionally, you may well wish to apply some statistical methods to the trained net so as to estimate confidence intervals, etc.

The simplest way of probing the network is to pick two of the inputs (holding the remainder constant) and compute a three-dimensional response surface. This offers a visual representation of what the neural network is doing with the two "free" input variables. Other experiments include: reduce the inputs and see if the network will work as well (or even better if training is now more successful), add noise to the data and identify at which point it fails completely, and bootstrap the outputs. The latter is fairly straightforward. You randomly select (with replacement) N from N cases the validation data sets and store the outputs. Repeat this 200 (or so) times and compute upper and lower 95 percentiles of the results. This would constitute approximate 95% confidence limits; see Efron and Tibshirani (1993) for further details.

Numerical experimentation with the neural network will soon convert the black box into, at least, a grey box, and even help improve understanding of the phenomenon being studied. Once you have a computer model that works then use it to explore, probe and otherwise experiment with the model; otherwise what is the point of building it in the first place?

6.2.3 Pros and cons

The neural network has several properties that need to be emphasised because of their uniqueness, they include:

- ability to handle nonlinear functions
- ability to perform model-free function estimation
- ability to learn from data relationships that are not otherwise known
- they can adapt to changing environments
- they can handle noisy and fuzzy data
- they can generalise to unseen situations and
- they are extremely computationally efficient once trained

The disadvantages can be listed as:

- they offer limited understanding of the process or phenomenon being modelled
- subjective design
- the training process is *ad hoc*
- testing and validation are often inadequate from a statistical perspective and
- a restricted dimensional modelling capability

They are good but not necessarily the best or always brilliant.

6.2.4 Spatial interaction modelling using a neural net

Spatial interaction models are widely used to model flows of people, money, traffic, etc. Most of the conventional models were derived by entropy maximising methods in the late 1960s (Wilson, 1970). A simple version of this model can be written as

$$T_{ij} = O_i D_j B_j \exp(-\hat{b} C_{ij})$$

where T_{ij} is the "flow" between origin i and destination j, O_i the size of origin i, D_j the size of destination j, C_{ij} the distance (or cost of travelling from i to j, $\hat{b}$ is a parameter that has to be estimated so that the predicted flow values (T_{ij}) match as closely as possible the observed values, and B_j is a balancing factor computed as

$$B_j = 1/\sum_i O_i \exp(-\hat{b} C_{ij})$$

which is a constraint mechanism to ensure that the constraints

Table 6.1 Example of unrolled trip matrix

Row	T_{ij}	O_i	D_j	C_{ij}	Intrazonal flag
1	T_{11}	O_1	D_1	C_{11}	1
2	T_{21}	O_2	D_1	C_{21}	0
3	T_{31}	O_3	D_1	C_{31}	0
4	T_{41}	O_4	D_1	C_{41}	0
5	T_{12}	O_1	D_2	C_{12}	0
6	T_{22}	O_2	D_2	C_{22}	1
7	T_{32}	O_3	D_2	C_{32}	0
8	T_{42}	O_4	D_2	C_{42}	0
9	T_{13}	O_1	D_3	C_{13}	0
10	T_{23}	O_2	D_3	C_{23}	0
11	T_{33}	O_3	D_3	C_{33}	1
12	T_{43}	O_4	D_3	C_{43}	0
13	T_{14}	O_1	D_4	C_{14}	0
14	T_{24}	O_2	D_4	C_{24}	0
15	T_{34}	O_3	D_4	C_{34}	0
16	T_{44}	O_4	D_4	C_{44}	1

Table 6.2 Performance of various neural network spatial interaction models

Network configurations	Number of parameters	Goodness-of-fit	Standard deviation of errors
4:4:4:1	45	0.811e-1	13.2
4:8:8:1	121	0.764e-1	12.8
4:8:16:1	201	0.983e-1	14.5
4:16:8:1	225	0.983e-1	14.5
4:16:16:1	369	0.104e-1	15.0
4:4:2:1	33	0.894e-1	13.9
4:8:2:1	61	0.894e-1	12.6
Singly constrained conventional model			18.2
Doubly constrained conventional model			13.5

$$\sum_i T_{if} = D_j$$

are always satisfied. In this model it merely ensures that the columns of the predicted trip matrix match the correct totals.

This model is nonlinear and basically states that the flow between any two places (i and j) depends on their sizes and the distance they are apart. The question now is whether or not a feed-forward neural network is able to provide an equivalently good, or better, model.

The first step is to unroll the trip matrix. For example, if there are 4 origins and 4 destinations this can be unrolled to give a data matrix of 16 rows and 5 columns

Table 6.3   Performance of various network models trained on all trips in predicting car
only trips for five years later

Network configuration	Standard deviation of errors
4:4:4:1	4.4
4:8:8:1	5.9
4:8:16:1	4.0
4:16:8:1	4.1
4:16:16:1	4.0
4:4:2:1	5.0
4:8:2:1	4.4
Singly constrained conventional model	3.5 (calibration)
Doubly constrained conventional model	2.4 (calibration)

as shown in Table 6.1. Note that an extra variable has been added to indicate intrazonal trips. Furthermore, the B_j term has been ignored so that the neural network model is effectively unconstrained. However, any constraints can be added as a subsequent step.

The modelling now proceeds as described in section 6.2.2. The algebraic symbols in Table 6.1 would be replaced by items of data. Openshaw (1993a) provides an example of this approach being applied to a 73 by 73 zone journey-to-work data set. The results are shown in Table 6.2 for a variety of neural network configurations. The explanation of these configurations is as follows:

⟨number of input variables⟩⟨number of neurons in first and second hidden layer⟩⟨number of neurons in output layer⟩

All the nets produced levels of performance better than the conventional singly constrained entropy maximising model and many are better than the doubly constrained variant. Remember that the model is unconstrained and that the inclusion of origin and/or destination constraints greatly boosts the performance of the standard interaction models. Clearly the nets work extremely well. The only drawback is the amount of computing time involved. In the runs used for Table 6.2, each net was run for a few hours on a PC, compared with a few seconds for the conventional models. Whether the training process could have been either stopped earlier or else speeded up by changing either the optimisation routine used or the form of the sigmoidal function are matters for further research.

A further test was to investigate whether the interaction pattern captured by the nets in Table 6.2 might be entirely data specific or contained some generally relevant spatial interaction structure. Table 6.3 shows what happens when these nets trained on all trips are applied to car only data. In general, these results are surprisingly good and compare reasonably favourably with the levels of performance that can be achieved on the same data by a standard model.

Table 6.4 Performance of various neural network models of telecommunication flows

Network configurations	Number of parameters	Goodness of fit R^2
3: 5:1	26	0.7071
3:10:1	51	0.7686
3:15:1	76	0.7666
3:20:1	101	0.7773
3:25:1	126	0.7747
3:30:1	151	0.7780
3:35:1	176	0.7667
3:40:1	201	0.7772
3:45:1	226	0.6270
3:50:1	251	0.6400
Conventional model	3	0.6768

6.2.5 Neural net modelling of telecommunication flows

Fischer and Gopal (1994) apply a similar neural net architecture (a multi-layered feed-forward neural net) to model interregional telecommunication flows for Austria. They use a neural network but with only one hidden layer. There are some theoretical results to suggest that a network of this type with one hidden layer of neurons can approximate any continuous function to any desired degree of accuracy. It also permits the neural net to be written out as an equation. However, there is some debate about this justification and there may well be some advantage in considering two hidden layers to provide an additional degree of representational power. Fischer and Gopal (1994) also preprocessed the inputs using a logarithmic transformation scaled into (0,1), partly because this appeared to ease the training of their network. Their neural net only had three inputs (origin and destination sizes together with a distance variable). They compared performances with a conventional log-linear gravity regression model and their results are summarised in Table 6.4. All the neural net models were better in terms of R-squared than the conventional regression model. The predictive performance of one of these models (3: 30: 1) was also superior to the regression model although it seems that the pattern of residuals was broadly similar, viz. they both underpredicted the larger flows and overpredicted smaller flows. The average error was 20.5% for the neural net and 24.5% for the regression model. Maybe they would have achieved a higher level of network performance if they had considered two hidden layers and/or an additional variable or two. They conclude that "The primary advantage of the general neural network model set out in this paper over the classical regression approach to spatial interaction modelling lies in the fact that it has a more general functional form than the gravity model can effectively deal with" (Fischer and Gopal, 1994: 523). They also identified a number of practical problems partly due to the small size of their data (a 32 by 32 matrix of flows) given the number of parameters in their model. These problems include: (1) the issue of overfitting needs further research especially where small data sets are used; and (2) they argue that the validation data set approach may be inadequate and that some other form of model validation should be considered. Despite these caveats they remain enthusiastic about the prospects for neural computing in geography and regional science. They conclude that neural networks "can principally be used to cope with problems such as very large volumes of spatial data, missing data, noisy data and fuzzy information for which conventional statistical techniques may be inappropriate or cumbersome to use" (Fischer and Gopal, 1994: 524).

6.2.6 Try it out!

The spatial interaction modelling system (SIMS) of Openshaw and Glover (1997) contains a wide range of spatial interaction models including a neural network option. Readers interested in experiments with this approach can easily do so using SIMS. Alternatively, there are many sources of "free" neural network software; see, for example, Masters (1995a, b), Muller and Rheinhardt (1991) and Korn (1995).

6.2.7 Some neural benefits

The neural net modelling of spatial interaction data offers the modeller a greatly increased freedom to worry more about the application of the model and much less about its specification. The new flexibility might also be used to experiment with different model designs. For instance, interaction data exist as integer counts yet all the conventional models produce real numbers. The journey to work trips between the zones may be predicted to 14.6! This may not always matter (e.g. if the flow is a real number and not an integer) but sometimes it does. One possibility is to build a neural net that has 16 output neurons, which can be decoded as a 16-bit integer. This is left for the reader to experiment with, the principal problem being the need for a much larger data set.

From a spatial interaction modellers point of view there are a number of possible benefits to be gained:

- better performing models
- greater representational flexibility and freedom from current model design constraints
- an opportunity to handle explicitly noisy data and
- incorporation of spatial dependency in the net representation, which is currently ignored

It also raises a number of interesting questions concerning the generality of the spatial interaction process and the possible viability of seeking an associative memory based approach. The latter type of net might well provide the basis for a universally applicable, precalibrated, spatial interaction modelling net. There is some prospect here of an entirely new approach to modelling spatial interaction based on the recognition that there are only so many different patterns of spatial interaction that can exist. These might be identified, stored in a neural network containing memory, and then used as the basis for intelligent modelling of the world's spatial interaction patterns. The powerful representational properties of neural networks also offer some prospect that zoning system scale and aggregation effects might be taken into explicit consideration, together with time, provided adequate and broadly representative sets of spatial interaction data sets are available for training. Indeed, this highlights a major problem in the "libraries" of training data which by and large do not exist and that generations of quantitative geographers generally have been very careless with their data. If the full potential of exploiting neural networks that can "learn" or be taught spatial patterns is to be realised, then some systematic attempt needs to be made to store and catalogue spatial data sets as training examples.

6.3 UNSUPERVISED NEURAL NETWORKS

6.3.1 Unsupervised training

A key characteristic of the supervised neural network is that it "learns" to associate a set of inputs with a set of outputs using a training data set for which both the inputs and outputs are known. However, it is quite obvious that there is no biological process like back-propagation going on in brains, otherwise we would never learn to walk or speak because it would take too long to learn any of these skills. Whilst some skills are indeed learnt, others seem to have been acquired almost unconsciously without any obvious explicit training or learning process, e.g. many of the senses. The question is whether it is possible to build artificial neural networks that self-organise so that they require no explicit training with a known set of results. This is important because suppose we merely wish that the neural network will find some results for us. Suppose we want the neural network to analyse the data and tell us what structure exists all by itself because we no longer know what to expect and have no training data. It may appear that this is similar to asking for a minor miracle but really it is much less than that, we merely want the neural network to teach itself, and in the process tell us what patterns exist in the data it is has been given.

These unsupervised neural networks are essentially data classifiers. However, data classification is really a partitioning of the input data space into "territories" that have something in common. In a classification context these territories are "clusters" or groups of "similar" cases. In a broader neural network context these territories define spaces that share a common value of some kind. The classification analogy is useful, at least at present, so let us continue using it. You input a multivariate data set (i.e. one with N cases each with M variables measuring different aspects) and you get a classification of the N cases into K clusters or groups. In essence this is exactly what numerical taxonometric methods also do and have done for a long time (for example Openshaw,1983). However, most of these methods are "old" and often their algorithms date from 20 years or more ago. Openshaw (1993b) argues that most of the available census classification tools represent 1960s technology clothed in 1990s computer software. All that has changed is the ease of use, access to the technology, and size of the largest application.

However, it should now be possible to do much better, at least in theory. Computers are about 1 million times faster than 20 years ago and are set to become another 10 000 times faster again by the late 1990s. Sustained teraflop computer speeds on highly parallel processors are confidently expected by the late 1990s. At the same time most data sets for most countries are reaching asymptotic limits in their maximum size; for example, in Britain the largest ever possible people database is about 55 million. In the late 1960s, geographers had large data set size values of two digits, by the late 1970s it had reached 130 000, and it will asymptote at about 55 million and cannot get much bigger. The challenge is no longer just to survive with gigabyte databases by applying the simplest of methods at the cost of quality, but of devising the best possible methods for use with gigabyte databases on teraflop hardware. It can be argued that non-neural methods are not really adequate for making the most of the new data-rich environments of the mid 1990s and beyond. It is not the function that has become obsolete, rather it is the technology used to perform it that has dated. Maybe a neural networks approach might be better.

First let us reconsider the problem. In an increasingly data-abundant era newer and better tools are needed that can help people cope with it. Data reduction via simple descriptive summaries, characteristic profiles or idealised typologies is suddenly in great demand as researchers ask fairly simple but also very vague questions, such as "What patterns exist?"or "Where are the anomalies?" or "What on earth is happening?" People cannot "see" multivariate patterns in massive spatial databases. Without new tools they will find it increasingly hard to cope with the new geocyberspaces within which they increasingly have to operate. Clearly then classification methods are a type of useful data coping and visualising tools that are able to answer at least some of these broad questions. In some areas, such as census analysis, geodemographic classifications attempt to provide this overview and have been very successful as an applied tool (Openshaw et al, 1995).

The basic rule of computational geography is simply stated. If you can now solve problems better than you could previously by throwing computer power at them, then you should do so. Trade off computer power for efficiency and flexibility but only if it is possible to become clever by first becoming dumber and less sophisticated in what we seek to do, so that massive computation becomes feasible. Neurocomputing is a classic example of this philosophy, although many of its advocates might well not consider what they propose as being dumber than conventional practice.

The fundamental attraction of what is termed here neuroclassification is that it seeks to offer a new approach to the classification of explicitly spatial data based on developments in neurocomputing. Notwithstanding all that has been written so far, the first question that should be asked is "why?" Unless you can convincingly answer this question in an honest fashion then you should not proceed to experiment with any of the methods described here. Indeed you should seek counselling because you are probably a victim of the highly infectious neural net virus. It is a very dangerous condition because of the trance-like tunnel vision it can engender in susceptibles. Possible answers to the "why" question are as follows: (1) it is fashionable; (2) it is different; (3) it is flexible; (4) it is better; (5) it is automatic; and (6) it is smart technology. Let us be quite clear here. There is no real point in struggling to master possibly unfamiliar literature coded in yet more strange jargon with a mix of the electrical engineer, the neurocognitive scientist and the biologist, just because it is fashionable to work in the neural networks area. Personal curiosity and research training are certainly worthy objectives. However, there are limits to both, and the latter tends almost by definition to be restricted to established technology. One of the key characteristics of neuroclassification is the belief, or feeling, that it might well yield better classifications that are "smarter" by being more context sensitive to the nature of the data and the peculiarities of its application.

6.3.2 Review of potential neuroclassifier architectures

The single most abiding feature shared by all neuroclassifiers (viz. unsupervised neural networks) is their inherent simplicity. Stripped of all brain biology jargon the technology is wonderfully straightforward. Indeed it has to be, because it is widely recognised that the complexity of the brain is due to the density and interconnectedness of the vast number of neurons, and is not due to the complexity of the individual neurons themselves.

In a general way classification of objects is one of the most fundamental tasks for the human brain. People possess an amazing ability to recognise objects, to extract features of interest from a highly complicated scene and to summarise high dimensional complex sensory data simply and abstractly. It is not surprising, therefore, to find many references to classification and neurobiological terms that also imply classification or something closely related to it in the literature on artificial neural nets. Simpson (1990) identifies 17 different unsupervised learning paradigms; he calls them paradigms because there are multiple variants of each of them. Unsupervised learning is a process of self-organisation whereby the neural network discovers the natural structure of data by itself, using only samples of data and internal control mechanisms. The net trains itself to learn or uncover the principal features present in the data presented to it. This is clearly a classification function but how many numerical taxonomists would have considered what they have traditionally done as an unsupervised training process; or that the classification of a new case is a form of associative recall operation from a fuzzy memory; or that the classification task is simultaneously also a data compression, data mapping and data encoding function? For instance, if you reduce a data set of 500 000 zones and 100 variables to 50 clusters of 100 variables, then you have in effect achieved a data compression factor of 10 000 times. It is true that some information has been lost, but it is also obvious that with a reduction in data volume of 10 000 times you are bound to lose something! The real question is whether or not what is left has any value.

A recurrent key theme in unsupervised nets is that of self-organisation. If the net is to identify common features in its inputs, it must somehow be able to determine what these features are for itself. The concept of self-organisation is biologically motivated, in that there is evidence that parts of the brain seem to operate in that way. Perhaps the principal mechanism whereby the brain self-organises is via competitive and co-operative process. These are not new ideas. Competitive learning was introduced by Grossberg (1972) and Malsburg (1973), amongst others, and has been developed in various ways. Attention here is focused on four particular types of unsupervised learning architecture that may be of greatest relevance to neurospatial classification; the reader interested in a broader typology is referred to Simpson (1990: Chapter 5).

3.2.1 Competitive learning networks

The simplest architecture is the competitive net described so well by Rumelhart and Zipster (1985). See also Grossberg (1976) and Kohonen (1984). In its simplest form a set of processing neurons fight it out to represent data using a measure of dissimilarity. The single winner updates its weights. Over a period of time the weight attached to each process element will provide a summary of any structure or regularities existing in the data on which it was trained. This is clearly very similar to cluster analysis and does little more than identify similarity classes. However, the user has much more control over the training process and can deliberately interfere with the equiprobable distribution of weight, in order to handle better the nature of spatial data. How this is achieved is discussed later.

Rumelhart and Zipster (1985) have extended this basic model to include multiple layers of processing elements and within each layer there can be different groups of processing elements (exclusive or non-exclusive). The hope is that the different layers will identify different forms of structure, applying varying degrees of generalisation and simplification. This is somewhat fanciful and network design is highly subjective, but the underlying objectives are seemingly extremely worthwhile; see Openshaw and Wymer (1991).

3.2.2 Self-organising map

A second major type of architecture is that based on the self-organising map (SOM) of Kohonen (1984). The processing elements have a spatial structure to them, typically they are arranged on a two-dimensional grid. Once a winner is found then updating takes place of the winning processing element but also of those within a certain critical neighbourhood of it, whilst those further away are inhibited. This critical neighbourhood region where the updating occurs is gradually reduced during training. Once convergence is complete, the weights associated with each processing element define an efficient partitioning of the multidimensional data (viz. a Voronoi tessellation). This SOM provides in effect a non-parametric pattern classification. It is widely regarded as one of the most useful of unsupervised neural nets and its use as a neuroclassifier is the subject of much of the remainder of the chapter.

3.2.3 Adaptive resonance theory related developments

A third category of potentially useful neuroclassifiers is the adaptive resonance theory (ART 1, 2) variants developed by Carpenter and Grossberg (1987a, b). They are essentially nearest neighbour classifiers but modelled on the functioning of the brain. The patterns they store are regarded as exemplars and when a "new" pattern is found, then a new exemplar (i.e. group) is created for it. These methods are potentially extremely interesting and there is no reason at all why they would not also perform well with spatial data. They can learn fast (suitable for on-line use) or slowly and can dynamically adapt to the structure found in the data via a vigilance process. The latter is extremely important from a theoretical point of view. Most neural networks (e.g. the back-propagation net) cannot learn new information incrementally, unless it is retrained with the old information alongside the new. Most neural networks have no built-in mechanism for recognising the novelty of the input. How can the network remain adaptive or plastic in response to new inputs and yet remain stable in response to noisy versions of data it has already seen? This is called the stability–plasticity dilemma, indeed as Freeman (1994: 210) points out, "One of the nice features of human memory is its ability to learn many new things without necessarily forgetting things learnt in the past." It would be nice if our artificial neural networks could also do this.

A subsequent variant, ARTMAP (Carpenter et al, 1991), seems to be an even better prospect for further development. The principal problem for the geographer (and many others) is simply that of understanding the neurobiological technical language sufficiently well to understand precisely what is going on. Maybe an example will illustrate this point. Carpenter and Grossberg (1987) write "when a mismatch attenuates STM activity across F1, the total size of the inhibitory signal from F1 to A is also attenuated. If the attenuation is sufficiently great, inhibition from F1 to A can no longer prevent the arousal source A from firing." How this is relevant to an *artificial* neural network remains a mystery to us.

3.2.4 Associative memory nets

A fourth category of unsupervised nets are mainly associative memory devices. That is they store patterns in such a way that they can be retrieved using patterns, parts of patterns, or noisy parts of patterns as retrieval keys; examples are Hopfield nets (Hopfield, 1982, 1984), bidirectional associative memory (BAM) (Kosko, 1988), temporal associative memory (TAM) (Amari, 1972), linear associative memory (LAM) (Kohonen, 1977) and sparse distributed memory (SDM) (Kanerva, 1988). These methods provide a different route to spatial classification, which, if it could be operationalised, would involve building libraries of spatial pattern types and their extensions. It might well become possible one day to think in this way, i.e. of encoding concepts as spatial pattern exemplars (and vice versa), but sadly not at present. These sophisticated pattern-matching methods are likely to become much more important later on than at present. Meanwhile it is a timely thought that neural networks function because they are essentially memory devices. A set of inputs is used to index or address a memory from which something is retrieved (or reconstituted from the bits that are stored) and then output. Maybe what we are witnessing is a hundred different ways of associative memory recall.

6.3.3 Comparisons with conventional classifiers

Finally it is noted that there are some strong similarities between neuroclassifiers and conventional taxonomic methods. Any superficial comparison would immediately suggest that the neurons in a competitive net are fighting to represent data cases in a manner similar to the cluster centroids in the conventional iterative relocation procedure; indeed, they may share the same dissimilarity criteria. Again it can be argued that a K-means algorithm is similar to Grossbergs ART-2 system. Doubtlessly several other superficial similarities might be found. However, there is a very important point here. In nearly all cases neuroclassifiers are functionally quite different; they are not computationally identical, indeed far from it. The neural network learning mechanisms have no conventional taxonomic equivalent. The lateral inhibition characteristics of a Kohonen SOM has no conventional taxonomic equivalent (and one could not be manufactured). Additionally, neuroclassifiers escape many of the problems that afflict conventional methods. For instance, a standard single-move heuristic classifier based on principal component scores has the following problems: it is old technology and might get stuck in a local suboptimum, the data are assumed to be normally distributed and free from outliers (e.g. census data are usually J-shaped), relationships that matter are linear (else the principal component transformation filters them out), each case has the same weight, the data have a uniform level of accuracy and reliability, spatial autocorrelation does not exist (else the principal component scores will be biased), and the cluster morphology is multivariate spherical and minimum variance in an Euclidean distance norm.

None of this need be applicable to a neuroclassifier applied appropriately. However, despite problems, it is clear that conventional classifiers do work. Maybe the users compensate for the failures inherent in the technology; maybe success is more apparent than real because of an absence of benchmarked results; or maybe in many applications the conventional methods still work well enough.

6.3.4 Kohonen's self-organising maps as the basis for a spatial data classifier

Kohonen's SOM is one of the most interesting of all the competitive neural nets. Its fascinating results form the realisation that self-organisation is a very powerful neural process and that parts of the brain certainly seem to operate in a similar fashion. Ritter et al (1992) point out that Kohonen maps demonstrate how a multitude of data processing problems can be solved by means of a small number of powerful basic principles. On this occasion the abstraction from biological detail seems to have been most beneficial. To the geographer the main attraction is initially spurious, i.e. the word "map", but subsequently the spatial concepts involved in SOMs are extremely interesting for a variety of applications. As a neurospatial classifier, the SOM offers a number of attractions: (1) simplicity in algorithmic design; (2) ability to handle immense complexity; (3) nice mathematical properties; (4) user-induced flexibility; and (5) a plausible degree of biological inspiration. All are important. Compared with conventional classifiers it is very simple. At the same time, its self-organising nature offers immense benefits of local adaptiveness and emergent behaviour. The nice mathematical properties mainly relate to the topological preserving nature of the results. Finally, user-induced flexibility reflects the lack of any statistical over-sophistication that might induce delusions of grandeur and statistical rigour. The user is free to experiment and include whatever is considered important without too many constraints on avenues of possible actions, although the onus is firmly with the researcher to demonstrate the validity of the results.

The basic algorithm is really very simple (Beale and Jackson, 1990; Caudill and Butler, 1992; Freeman and Skapura, 1991 and many others provide introductory descriptions; see also Openshaw, 1994a and Openshaw and Wymer, 1995). However, it is important to remember that there are many possible variations and that in any particular application some experimentation will be worthwhile.

A basic Kohonen network algorithm can be described as follows.

Step 1 Initialisation. Define geometry, dimensionality and size of neuron array

This defines the geometry of the map. Usually this will be two-dimensional with the maximum number of "clusters" equal to the maximum number of neurons, although in practice not every neuron need be assigned data, so the actual number can be less. This is a very useful feature in classification in that there is no longer a one-to-one relationship between the number of neurons suggested by the user (usually in ignorance) and the best number of clusters or groups needed for the classification (usually unknown). For example, a 10 by 10 neuron array would contain 100 neurons around which clusters could develop. Each has a set of m data values (one for each variable of interest). So if the classification involves 20 variables and a 10 by 10 array of neurons is being used, then data storage is 10 by 10 by 20 numbers. The one-dimensional neuron map array may also be of interest in that this forces a linear ordering on the data, so that position in the array will also reflect similarity to some degree. This might be useful. It would also be possible to imagine a continuous map that has no edges. Whether this offers any real benefits is uncertain. Finally, it seems to matter little as to whether the neurons are arranged on a grid or have a hexagonal geometry. The advantages of the latter mainly concern a better coverage of the two-dimensional space.

The neurons are simple summation devices that measure the similarity between themselves and a set of values input to the net:

$$c_j = \sum_k^m (A_{jk} - x_k)^2$$

Here c_j is the value for the jth neuron, A_{jk} the value of variable k on neuron j and the input x_k is the value of the kth variable of m. Variables represent one set of inputs to the network. This is a much simpler architecture than encountered with the feed-forward back-propagation network.

Step 2 Each neuron has a vector of M weights (one for each variable). Set these weights to some initial value, usually random values

This merely describes how to start the process off. It might be best to use random realistically scaled values, or even base the initial weights on randomly selected data values, or on random perturbations of variable means. It is probably not too critical provided they are not too extreme.

Step 3 Select a data case that also has variable values and apply any relevant measurement noise to the data

This is the first of the really useful features of SOMs. In a conventional cluster analysis algorithm, the data would be presented in sequential order, each case having, implicitly, the same weighting. Here, however, it is much more useful to sample some data cases much more often, for example to reflect size of area or assumptions about the reliability of the data. This is extremely useful in a spatial data analysis context because small areas with small denominators often possess the most extreme data values. It is much easier to obtain 100% unemployment in a small rural zone with 20 households than in the worst urban black spot with 200 households. The result of this variability in data precision can be catastrophic.

The conventional classifier treats all areas the same and thus tends to form cluster centroids based on the more extreme values (which are least reliable and meaningful) whilst regarding those areas with more reliable data values, to some extent, as outliers. This is the opposite of what you really want to happen. However, if you select cases randomly with probabilities depending on size then the impact of small number problems may now be greatly diminished and, hopefully, the quality of the final classification suitably enhanced.

This is a useful place to add any relevant measurement noise to the data. Quite often in geography the variable being classified will possess different levels of measurement error. For example, in UK census analyses some variables are 100% coded, others are 10% coded. Other databases have missing values for some variables. It would be extremely useful to be able to take into account the varying reliability and accuracy of the data when classifying them. One simple way of achieving this goal is to randomise the values of the M data variables by different amounts to reflect variable and even record specific levels of data noise. This is important with spatial data because noise, error and spatially varying levels of reliability are all important attributes that need to be considered, rather than simply ignored. Neuroclassifiers offer considerable promise in this respect.

A key point to note is that the results reflect the probability density distribution from which the training cases were selected. This is very important because the key advantage offered here is that the user can use whatever probability density function is considered most appropriate and this need not be that defined in a completely arbitrary fashion by the available database. Biasing the training to give greater weight to the most reliable data values would seem to be extremely useful given the nature of spatial information.

Step 4   Find whichever neuron is "nearest" to the data case under consideration

Step 4 is fairly simple. It determines which neurons "win" the competition to represent the data case. There are various ways of measuring "nearness" and "similarity" and, depending on the form of data measurement, different measures might be appropriate.

Step 5   "Update" the M weights for all the neurons in the topological neighbourhood of the winning neuron, otherwise leave alone

This applies updating to neuron weights in the "neighbourhood" of the winning neuron. The clever and adaptive behaviour of the SOM results from this part of the algorithm. The network is gradually "tuned" to different inputs in an orderly fashion, almost as if a continuous mapping of the input space was formed over the network. The ordering and smoothing process is extremely subtle. The outcome is that different parts of the network become selectively sensitised to different input patterns. The size of the "neighbourhood" of the winning neuron is usually a function of time, that is, it decreases slowly as the training process proceeds.

The simplest updating algorithm is to define a block partly based on distance from the winning neuron, so that all neurons within this critical distance update their weights. Kohonen (1984, 1989) defines this as:

$$m_i(t+1) = m_i(t) + \alpha(t)[x - m_i(t)] \quad \text{for } i \in N_c(t) \qquad (6.1a)$$

else

$$m_i(t+1) = m_i(t) \qquad (6.1b)$$

where $m_i(t)$ is the weight vector for any neuron i which lies within the neighbourhood $N_c(t)$ of the best matching (winning) neuron c at iteration t; $m_i(t+1)$ is the updated weight for this neuron i; x is the vector of values for the data case; $N_c(t)$ is the neighbourhood around winning neuron c at time t; and $\alpha(t)$ is a "training" constant, typically $0 \leqslant \alpha(t) \leqslant 1$. It is interesting that training methods similar to this are used in supervised neural networks.

Step 6   Reduce learning parameter and neighbourhood weights by a very, very small amount

The training parameters are slowly reduced so that stability is achieved. It is important to note that the size of the neighbourhood set $N_c(t)$ and the training constant $\alpha(t)$ both reduce slowly as a function of time (really the number of training iterations). Kohonen (1984) suggests that a proper choice for these parameters can best be determined by experience and that certain "rules of thumb" can be invented. He adds, "it may be useful to notice that there are two phases in the formation of maps that have a slightly different nature, viz. initial formation of the correct order, and final convergence of the map into asymptotic form. For good results, the latter phase may take 10 to 100 times as many steps as the former whereby a low value of $\alpha(t)$ is used" (p. 133). Usually, the critical parameters are linearly decreasing functions of t. Kohonen (1989) uses the following scheme for two time periods (t_1 and t_2); for t_1 (the initial coarse structuring period):

$$\alpha(t) = k_1(1 - t/t_1) \quad \text{for } 0 \leqslant t \leqslant t_1 \qquad (6.3)$$

and for t_2 (the fine structuring phase):

$$\alpha(t) = k_2(1 - t/t_2) \quad \text{for } t_1 \leqslant t \leqslant t_2 \qquad (6.4)$$

where t_1 and t_2 depend on the dimensions of the neuron array and not on the number of variables, in Kohonen (1989):

$$k_1 = 0.1$$
$$k_2 = 0.008$$
$$t_1 = 10\,000$$
$$t_2 = 90\,000$$

and N_c decreased linearly from 12 to 1 during $0 \leqslant t \leqslant t_1$ and then remained constant. In essence this gradual reduction in parameters is similar in principle to a cooling schedule in simulated annealing. The structure gradually emerges and crystallises.

Step 7 Repeat steps 3 to 6 until convergence, typically a large number of times; viz. 100 000 or a million or more

The process needs to be repeated a fairly large number of times. Critical factors here are the number of neurons and possibly the size of training data set. It is probable that the best results will only emerge after several million training passes, particularly if noise in the data is also to be represented. Unfortunately, this outer loop is not easily parallelised because of the large number of dependencies involved inside it. Openshaw and Turton (1996) have developed a way out of this problem.

Step 8 Label the neurons and examine the self-organised map

It is often helpful to "map" the weights associated with particular variables, look at the density of data cases by neuron, and watch what happens as particular cases are input into the map. The relative locations of neurons have a spatial structure that may well relate to the characteristics of their neighbours. Do not throw the information away, use it!

6.3.5 Kohonen's self-organising map as a modeller

Kohonen's SOM also serves another function other than feature extraction or classification. Inputs are mapped on to a neuron map in a way that preserves as much of the neighbourhood (topology) of the original data. This process can be readily extended to handle a modelling function so that the inputs are mapped on to a response in an optimal way. A supervised form of the Kohonen net is easily produced. Add an extra variable to represent the output from the net. This variable takes no part in the competition to determine the winning neuron (Step 4) but its weight is updated (in Step 5) as before. Gradually the net learns how to map the inputs on to the observed output. The net is being used as an optimised multivariate look-up table that relates input values to an output. This simple extension has been found to be an extremely effective means of solving certain types of robotic control problem (Ritter et al, 1992).

If no correct result is known then an unsupervised learning variant would involve rewarding the classifier in some way, via a reward function. One way of doing this is to compute (via some optimisation process) a locally optimal value of the output from the net. Updating of the net's input weights only occurs if the winning neurons performance is an improvement, otherwise no updating occurs. There are many possible variations of this unsupervised learning approach to building what are in effect nonlinear regression models. There is an opportunity for you to try this approach out in a spatial interaction modelling context by using SIMS (Openshaw and Glover, 1997).

6.3.6 Some empirical evaluations and case studies

The strongest justification for using a neuroclassifier is that it delivers "better" results than conventional methods. "Better" in a classification context is partly a matter of taxonometric performance, which can be measured by a statistic of some kind, partly a matter of assessing the theoretical attractiveness of a more data-sensitive and flexible technology, and partly the "qualitative feel" that the user has about the classification results; for instance, are they easier to interpret, do they provide a "clear" description of the data? An appreciation of these subjective criteria require double-blind testing and this is left as an interesting area for further research. Attention here is restricted to numeric summary measures.

Openshaw and Wymer (1991) reported the results of empirical tests performed on a small census data set of 120 areas and 45 variables. They compared the total percentage within cluster sums of squares for a variety of neuroclassifiers. The benchmark was a set of classifications produced by what is considered to be the best readily available conventional method (a K-means procedure, see Openshaw, 1983). In all cases the results of the Kohonen SOM-based classifier was an improvement, albeit seemingly not a vast improvement. However, it should be noted that although similar cluster descriptions were obtained, the classifications were not the same, and even for this small data set there was subjective preference for the SOM results.

A second test was based on the same 45 variables but for 9278 census wards in England and Wales (Table 6.5). These results are quite remarkable in that large improvements in performance are obtained. It should be noted that previous attempts to obtain improvements in the performance of these classifications by using simulated anealing failed. Clearly this neural net method is an extremely powerful classifier despite its apparent simplistic nature.

Furthermore, the results suggest that the geometry of the SOM is not too critical in terms of its impact on the results, once more than a relatively small number of clusters are considered. A wider comparison with other types of neuroclassifier is contained in Openshaw and Wymer (1991, 1995). The latter suggest that the SOM is the best classifier. However, the importance of proving "good performance" on your applications cannot be underestimated. It is

Table 6.5 Comparison of neural net results with a conventional classifier

Method used	Number of clusters	% within cluster sum of squares
Conventional	10	40.15
K	10	32.66
$K:3*3$	9	32.03
$K:10*1$	10	30.29
Conventional	20	34.21
K	20	26.82
$K:5*4$	20	24.93
$K:20*1$	20	25.14
Conventional	30	31.16
K	30	23.12
$K:10*3$	30	21.76
$K:30*1$	30	22.00
Conventional	40	27.84
K	40	21.35
$K:8*5$	40	20.23
$K:40*1$	40	20.08

Notes:
The conventional classification was based on a standard k-means procedure (see Openshaw, 1983).
K is a simple competitive net.
$K:a*b$ is a SOM with a by b neurons in it.
(From Openshaw, 1994a)

important to discover when and when not to use neuroclassifiers else it reduces to a matter of having faith that the neurotechnology is always going to be an improvement over legacy methods. Do not be too cautious! The freedom from assumptions and inherent greater flexibility should not be undervalued even if the numeric benefits are harder to assess.

Subsequently the method has been applied to 1991 census enumeration district data for Britain and used to create the GB Profiles research geodemographic system (Openshaw et al, 1995). Interested UK-based researchers can gain access to GB Profiles from the MIDAS system at Manchester. If you are interested in the FORTRAN code for this method then see Openshaw (1994a), particularly the Appendix.

Table 6.6 summarises some of the perceived benefits and problems. However, probably the greatest single attraction of this technology is its flexibility. The SOM concept can be used as the basis for many new and innovative approaches. For example, a modelling situation you could use a SOM to classify the inputs into clusters within which a particular relationship or model or supervised neural network applies. The self-organisation could even incorporate some notion of "goodness-of-fit" from these models. The SOM also provides another way of creating membership functions for a fuzzy logic model, see Chapter 9. In both cases the basic technology is extremely flexible and is under the user's control. On

Table 6.6   Some benefits and problems with a neuroclassifier

Benefits
- Extremely flexible
- Insensitive to non-normality
- No need to impose a linear correlation and principal components filter
- No prior assumption about the morphology of the clusters
- Easy to incorporate data uncertainty
- Spatial autocorrelation effects can be built in during training
- Retains the fuzziness involved in classification
- No need for all neurons to be used
- It is an emergent and bottom-up approach
- Lack of assumptions that matter
- Extreme ease and simplicity
- Evidence of good results
- Results often have a natural feel to them

Problems
- The user needs to demonstrate or prove the results are good, as it cannot be assumed
- Lack of any sound theory to support it
- Areas of considerable subjectivity
- Many different architectures to choose from
- Training and network size parameters are subjective
- It takes a few orders of magnitude more computer time to run than a conventional classifier

offer is a flexible tool for tackling a whole range of geographical problems, if you are willing to spend time experimenting and perhaps indulgent of a degree of innovation. All the indications are favourable and the possible benefits would certainly appear to make the risks worth while.

6.4 CONCLUSIONS

In the light of the last two chapters on neural networks it is amazing that much greater use is not being made of the technology; see, for example, Openshaw (1993c). It is here, it works, it is not difficult to use, but hardly any geographers are using it! It does what conventional methods can do, at least as well; and more significantly, it also does what conventional methods cannot yet do and may never be able to do. There are a plethora of software systems around and perhaps the real question is what can they do for you? Maybe you should try them out. There are certainly many suitable applications, more or less wherever you choose to look; see, for example, Openshaw (1992b, 1994b, c, 1995) and Brunsdon and Openshaw (1993, 1994). Whilst neural networks are not a universal panacea for any or all research problems they do have enormous potential for dealing well with at least some of the systems modelling and spatial analysis problems of geography and social science. The introduction to neural networks is now complete. You should now know enough and have sufficient confidence to start your own experimentation. Good luck!

6.5 QUESTIONS AND ANSWERS

Q   Why are neural nets called artificial neural nets?

A   That is because they are artificial crude emulations of what are thought to be some of the brain's most remarkable properties. They are artificial because they are simplified and not real.

Q   Is the neural net to be viewed as evil technology because of its military history?

A   No, we should not be ridiculous or so sensitive. Any military origins are not visible and do nothing to harm subsequent applications. Whether a technology is judged evil depends on whether it is used for good or bad purposes and this is not a new problem at all. Indeed you could say the same about a lot of things, e.g. life-saving drugs in the wrong hands.

Q   Will neural nets always outperform a more conventional alternative?

A   No.

Q   Do neural networks deskill many analysis and modelling tasks?

A   Yes, but they still need to be applied in an expert and skilful manner. However, maybe these skills are more easily and much more quickly gained than more traditional statistical and mathematical knowledge.

Q   Do neural nets really provide a one-stop shop for all manner of analysis and modelling tasks?

A   Yes, they can be viewed as such but maybe they will be most effectively applied to those problems for which there are few or no conventional alternatives.

Q   Do neural nets usually contain fewer assumptions than conventional methods?

A   Yes, but they are still not totally assumption free or completely automatic.

Q   Are neural nets subjective?

A   Yes.

Q   Are some applications more suited to neural nets than others?

A   Yes, but predicting which might be difficult as well as data and application dependent.

Q   What types of geographical analysis applications are most suitable?

A   Any type of classification, discrimination and regression situation that involves finding a means of mapping (in a mathematical sense) a set of inputs on to a set of outputs under complex, nonlinear, noisy or dynamically changing circumstances.

Q   If it takes 48 hours to train a large neural net, what good is that?

A   Remember that once trained it might only take a few seconds to run. Also 48 hours is not long. Most PCs and workstations spend most of their lives doing nothing. So why not give them something to do! Moreover, what takes 48 hours to run in 1996 would probably have required 480 hours to run in 1986, and 48 000 hours in 1976, and maybe less than 5 seconds by 2006!

Q   Hold on there, is 48 hours of CPU time not worth a lot of money?

A   Oh dear! You are still in the mainframe era. The real cost of 48 hours on a Unix workstation is probably £48/(24 × 365 × 5) × 10 000, plus 20p for electricity, this assumes £10 000 capital cost, five-year life. The answer is £12.12. The cost of the machine doing nothing is only 20p less!

Q   What does fault tolerance mean when applied to a neural net?

A   There is a certain indifference to damage or loss to the weights, perhaps because of data or programming error. This makes the technology attractive to engineers as it will tend to fail or degrade gracefully rather than sudden fail totally. However, this can also make software debugging unusually hard. Genetic algorithms tend to have this property too. Usually though you would not expect your neural network to be damaged in a geographical context, so perhaps this isn't too relevant a feature.

Q   What does the following bit of neural net jargon really mean? Lateral inhibition function, synaptic activity, neuronal arousal, firing.

A   I don't have a clue, nor will many other neural net advocates, so you are in good company.

Q   Hold on there, isn't this a worry?

A   Why should it be? It is merely descriptive neural network details expressed in a particular language that reflects a specific disciplinary orientation. Geographers are almost as good as neurophysiologists at terminological linguistic mystification via jargonisation that, whilst designed to clarify, merely serves to obscure!

Q   Is it possible that during training a back-propagation network quite different sets of weights may produce the same results and/or level of performance?

A   Yes, but it may not matter much or at all because if the "results" are the same or the level of performance is similar then the networks can be regarded as equivalent.

Q   OK, but doesn't this mean it is not possible to completely trust the results?

A   No. The network is being used to represent a model and you are not going to interpret or explain or usually even look at all the individual weights. Individually they have no meaning. It is only when they are interconnected via the network that they have any practical significance.

Q   What happens if the system being modelled suddenly changes. Will the net still provide a good level of performance?

A   It may be able to handle changes because well-trained networks have a capability to generalise. But if the new situation is quite different from anything the network has seen before it may no longer work. The same is true of a conventional model. With a neural network you can incorporate in it a system that monitors its performance and restarts training once the errors become too large, or else in a real-time application, training continues as more data are received. With a conventional model it is back to the drawing board and you will have to start again the entire modelling process and this could take many months of hard labour.

Q   How do you know if a network has hit a local suboptimum during training?

A   You may not! It could simply appear that the level of performance was not particularly good. You could try a different training method, e.g. a genetic algorithm based or a hybrid genetic–conventional approach, or else restart training after a small random kick.

Q   How might a neural net be encoded for a genetic algorithm?

A   Well read Chapter 7 first. You would use a bit string to either represent the weights and/or the interconnections between the neurons. This provides an to alternative training via back-propagation. In this case the network is only used to predict the effects of a given set of weights. The problem is that the bit strings needed could become very long and this might require a large amount of computer time. However, the genetic algorithm is readily parallelised and its robustness to local suboptima suggests that it could well produce superior results, if you can afford the computer time.

Q   Is a neural network merely a special type of associative (computer) memory?

A   Yes. This seems to be a good and easy way of visualising what a neural network does. However, it need not (depending on the type of the network) be purely a look-up function (a Kohonen SOM can function as a multidimensional table look-up function), as the back-propagation net performs an interpolation (or generalisation) as well. But in general the network stores input–output relationships, so that when given a set of unseen inputs it finds the most appropriate output from its memory stored in the network of weights. In this sense it can certainly be regarded as some form of associative memory-based process whereby the inputs act as partial clues to retrieval of associated outputs or response from a memory.

Q   If the artificial neural network (ANN) solves the travelling salesman problem should I get excited?

A   The travelling salesman problem involves finding an optimal route that links N cities. The problem is that virtually every AI method described in this book claims to solve at least some variants of this problem. Maybe some will work better than others. Maybe it might even be interesting to find out, but it is a bit irrelevant too. The success or failure of AI in geography will not be decided here!

Q   What is a fuzzy neural net?

A   The simplest answer is to argue that this is a network that has been trained on data that have been fuzzified in some way, presumably because the data are considered as being best represented in this way. It is also possible to have the neurons function in a fuzzy way. Finally, it has been demonstrated that a neural network can represent a fuzzy logic model. Whilst a fuzzy net might be fashionable it is also an extra level of complexity which is imposed on the data. Don't do it unless it is both necessary and you know what you are doing. It could make matters much worse.

Q   I've programmed my net in C++. Is that OK?

A   Show off! In practice choice of programming language does not usually matter because it does not affect the quality of the results although it may influence ease of programming, software development, maintainability and reusability. We prefer FORTRAN but would normally expect to get the same, or similar, results to a C, C++ or QUICK-BASIC program.

Q   My database contains 250 000 records, is it sensible to train my net on a 1% random sample?

A   Maybe. It depends on the importance of your application, the nature of your hardware, the nature of the data, and your patience! The random sample may need to be stratified to ensure a reasonable coverage of the response variables, particularly if the data are highly skewed. It is particularly important that the net is trained on data representative of the range of numeric conditions characteristic of its application context.

Q   How would you develop an adaptive neural net?

A   That is easy, you keep it training on a database that is subject to constant but progressive change in a dynamic environment. Such neural nets have demonstrated very useful ability as controllers of constantly changing chemical processes.

Q   How do neural nets handle noisy data?

A   They learn that the mappings are noisy. You achieve this by randomising the training data to reflect noisy data.

Q   Does it matter that our artificial neural networks (ANNs) are implemented differently from biological systems?

A   No. Consider this useful quote. Kohonen notes that "It may not be possible to achieve the complexity, flexible learning ability, and high level abstraction capability characteristic of biological organisms. On the other hand, the stability and accuracy of the artificial components can be orders of magnitude higher than those of biological ones. In some tasks it can be a significant advantage that artificial neural networks do not exhibit fatigue, and are not panicked in alarming situations. It is plausible that in the future the computing capacity of artificial neural networks can be increased far beyond that of biological systems. All this gives us promises of developments that we may not yet fully foresee" (foreword to Ritter et al, 1992).

     The secret is to imitate and then improve on nature. There is nothing magic about biological systems. Once the principles are understood, it becomes mainly a matter of engineering to optimise performance. The hard bit at present is merely to catch up with biology and this process may well take a few more decades of hard work.

Q   Is it true that a modern PC works faster than a biological neuron?

A   Yes. The brain consists of many slow processors yet it is an immensely powerful computer because it is able to employ billions of slow processing units on any one problem. It is estimated that it will be another 20 or so years before computers can catch up in terms of raw speed and even this does not mean that they will become instantly intelligent. There is much more to intelligence than sheer computer speed but it helps!

Q   What is parallel processing and how does it compare with serial processing? Imagine the task of digging a 1 km long ditch. If one worker can dig 10 m of ditch per day, then a 1 km stretch would take 100 days. Imagine now there are 10 workers each able to work at 10 m of ditch per day. Provided they organise themselves in an optimal manner, then 1 km of ditch will now take 10 days or 1 day if there were 100 workers. In practice there will be various organisational problems that will result in some of this parallelism being lost; for example, if not all ditch diggers have the same length of ditch to dig or if they operate at different speeds. Towards the end of the dig there will be a delay due to these synchronisation effects whilst waiting for the last diggers to complete. Note that the total person/days expended has not reduced; it will either be the same irrespective of how many workers are digging or may even increase a little due to parallelisation inefficiencies. What has changed is the total elapsed clock time which has reduced from 100 days for 1 worker to 1 day for 100. This dramatic speed-up is possible because ditch digging can be viewed as a series of tasks that be performed concurrently. Likewise in computing, if a particular task can be broken down into a set of sub-tasks that are independent of each other then each could be farmed out to a different CPU and performed at the same time as many other identical tasks. For example, consider forming a dot product based on 10 000 pairs of values:

$$S = \sum_{i=1}^{10\,000} x_i y_i$$

If you have 10 CPUs available then CPU no. 1 can be allocated the first 1000 values

$$S_1 = \sum_{i=1}^{1000} x_i y_i$$

and CPU 2 the next 1000

$$S_2 = \sum_{i=1001}^{2000}$$

etc. Finally

$$S = S_1 + S_2 + S_{10}$$

produces the global result.

This fine-grained example can be extended so that each CPU is executing many hundreds of lines of code. The hard part is, naturally, identifying the parallel activities of your code. Usually, you will need to redesign and rethink your algorithm to tease out the parallelism and then "fiddle with it" to try and increase the amount of time spent in the parallel regions upwards to over 99%. Ideally also total computer times should reduce as a linear function of the number of processors employed, if the method is scalable. Please note that the theory of parallel programming as expressed here appears much easier than its practice. However, it is getting more straightforward as software improves. As the future of large-scale computation is probably massively parallel, then the investment of time and effort will almost certainly be more than justified.

Q   How would you parallelise a neural net?

A   Most artificial neural networks have been developed using serial computers (those with one CPU). You don't have to exploit the parallelism present in a neural network but you could if you wished. How you do this depends on the architecture of the network. In general neural nets can be parallelised at the individual neuron level, sharing the neurons out amongst the available processors as in the brain, but as parallel hardware becomes faster it might instead be better to share the training data between the processors, otherwise inter-processor communication delays would slow down and ultimately dominate the computer times. Sharing out the data so that each processor has a batch of its own to work on would allow much larger training data sets to be used.

Q   Do I need special neural chip hardware for neurocomputing?
A   No. It is true that neural computers could be built with VSLI (very large-scale integration) technology. Indeed such chips already exist but this is only really justified if (1) there is a need for a very fast controller of some kind that has to be embedded in hardware or (2) there is need for a vast neural network. Right now neural network simulators (i.e. a neural network run on a PC or workstation or supercomputer) are sufficient for most, if not all, geographical tasks. However, the possibility of building large-scale dedicated neurocomputer hardware is increasingly real and evokes more than just a little excitement at the prospect of having special purpose neural networks performing specific tasks on specially dedicated hardware.

REFERENCES

Adeli, H., Hung, S.L., 1995, *Machine Learning*. Wiley, New York.

Amari, S.I., 1972, "Learning patterns and pattern sequences by self-organizing nets of threshold elements", *IEEE Transactions on Computers*, **21**, 1197–1206.

Beale, R., Jackson, T., 1990, *Neural Computing: an introduction*. Adam Hilger, Bristol.

Brunsdon, C., Openshaw, S., 1993, "Simulating the effects of error in GIS", in P.M. Mather (ed.), *Geographical Information Handling—Research and Applications*. Wiley, London, pp. 47–61.

Brunsdon, C., Openshaw, S., 1994, "Error simulation in vector GIS using neural computing methods", in M.F. Worboys (ed.), *Innovations in GIS*. Taylor & Francis, London. pp. 177–200.

Carpenter G., Grossberg, S., 1987a, "Invariant pattern recognition and recall by an attentive self-organizing ART architecture in a non-stationary world", *Proceedings of IEEE First Int. Conference on Neural Networks*, Vol. II, IEEE, San Diego, pp. 737–746.

Carpenter, G., Grossberg, S., 1987b, "ART2: self-organization of stable category recognition codes for analog input patterns" *Applied Optics*, **26**, 4919–4930.

Carpenter, G.A., Grossberg, S., Reynolds, J.H., 1991, "A self-organising ARTMAP neural architecture of supervised learning and pattern recognition", in R.J. Mammone, Y. Zeevi (eds), *Neural Networks, Theory and Applications*. Academic Press, Boston, pp. 43–80.

Caudill, M., Butler, C., 1992, *Understanding Neural Networks:* Vol. 1 and 2. MIT Press, Bradford.

Efron, B., Tibshirani, R.J., 1993, *An Introduction to the Bootstrap*. Chapman and Hall, London.

Fischer, M.M., Gopal, S., 1994, "Artificial neural networks: a new approach to modelling interregional telecommunication flows", *Journal of Regional Science*, **34**, 503–527.

Fitzgerald, R.W., Lees, B.G., 1994, "Spatial context and scale relationships in raster data for thematic mapping in natural systems", *Proceedings of the 6th International Symposium on Spatial Data Handling*, Edinburgh, Vol. 1, pp. 462–475.

Fletcher, R., 1971, *A Modified Marquardt Subroutine for Non-linear Least Squares*. AERE Report R-6799. HMSO, London.

Flood, I., Kartam, N., 1993, "Neural networks in civil engineering. 1: Principles and understanding", *Journal of Computing in Civil Engineering*, **8**, 131–148.

Freeman, T.A., 1994, *Simulating Neural Networks with Mathematics*. Addison-Wesley, Reading, Mass.

Freeman, T.A., Skapura, D.M., 1991, *Neural Networks: algorithms, applications and programming techniques*. Addison-Wesley, Reading, Mass.

Gorman, R., Sejnowski, T., 1988, "Analysis of hidden layer units in a layered network trained to classify sonar targets", *Neural Networks*, **1**, 75–89.

Grossberg, S., 1972, "Neural expectation: cerebellar and retinal analogues of cells fired by unlearnable and learnable pattern classes", *Kybernetik*, **10**, 49–57.

Grossberg, S., 1976, "Adaptive pattern classification and universal recoding II: Feedback, oscillation, olfaction and illusions", *Biological Cybernetics*, **23**, 187–207.

Grossberg, S., 1988, *Neural networks and natural intelligence*. MIT Press, Cambridge, MA.

Haykin, S., 1994, *Neural Networks: a comprehensive foundation*. Maxmillan College Publishing Company, New York.

Hopfield, J.J., 1982, "Neural networks and physical systems with emergent collective computational abilities", *Proceedings of National Academy of Science*, **79**, 2554–2558.

Hopfield, J.J., 1984, "Neurons with graded response have collective computational properties like those of two-state neurons", *Proceedings of the National Academy of Science*, **81**, 3088–3092.

Huang, W., Lippmann, R., 1987, "Comparisons between neural net and conventional classifiers", *Proceedings IEEE First International Conference on Neural Networks*, Vol. IV, San Diego, California, 21–24 June, pp. 485–493.

James, M., 1990, "Neuron your own", *Computer Shopper*, March, 155–161.

Kanerva, P., 1988, *Sparse Distributed Memory*. MIT Press, Cambridge, Mass.

Kohonen, T., 1977, *Associative memory – a system theoretical approach*. Springer, New York.

Kohonen, T., 1984, *Self-Organisation and Associative Memory*. Springer-Verlag, Berlin.

Kohonen, T., 1989, "Speech recognition based on topology preserving neural maps", in I. Aleksander (ed.), *Neural Computing Architectures*. Chapman and Hall, Andover 26–40.

Korn, G.A., 1995, *Neural Networks and Fuzzy Logic Control on Personal Computers and Workstations*. MIT Press, Cambridge, Mass.

Kosko, B., 1988, "Bidirectional associative memories", *IEEE Transactions of Systems, Man, and Cybernetics*, **18**, 42–60.

Lapedes, A., Faber, R., 1988, "How neural networks work", *Neural Information Processing Systems*, American Institute of Physics, 442–456.

Lippmann, R.L., 1987, "An introduction to computing with neural nets", *IEEE ASSP Magazine*, **4**, 4–22.

McCulloch, W.S., Pitts, W., 1943, "A logical calculus of the ideas immanent in nervous activity", *Bulletin of Mathematical Biophysics*, **5**, 115–133.

Malsburg, C., 1973, "Self-organisation of orientation sensitive cells in the striate cortex!", *Kybernetik*, **14**, 85–100.

Masters, T., 1995a, *Neural, Novel and Hybrid Algorithms for Time Series Prediction*. Wiley, New York.

Masters, T., 1995b, *Advanced Algorithms for Neural Networks: a C + + sourcebook*. Wiley, New York.

Muller, B., Reinhardt, T., 1991, *Neural Networks*. Springer-Verlag, Berlin.

Openshaw, S., 1983, "Multivariate analysis of census data: the classification of areas", in D. Rhind (ed.), *A Census User's Handbook*. Methuen, London, pp. 243–264.

Openshaw, S., 1992a, "A review of the opportunities and problems in applying neurocomputing methods to marketing applications", *Journal of Targeting, Measurement and Analysis for Marketing*, **1**, 170–186.

Openshaw, S., 1992b, "Some suggestions concerning the development of artificial intelligence tools for spatial modelling and analysis in GIS", *Annals of Regional Science*, **26**, 35–51.

Openshaw, S., 1993a, "Modelling spatial interaction using a neural net", in M.M Fischer,

P. Nijkamp (eds), *GIS, Spatial Modelling and Policy*. Springer-Verlag, Berlin, pp. 147–164.

Openshaw, S., 1993b, "Special classification", in B. Leventhal, C. Moy, J. Griffin (eds), *An Introductory Guide to the 1991 Census*. NTC Publications, Henley, pp. 69–82.

Openshaw, S., 1993c, "Over twenty years of data handling and computing in environment and planning", *Environment and Planning A*, Anniversary Issue, 69–78.

Openshaw, S., 1994a, "Neuroclassification of spatial data", in B.C, Hewitson, R.G. Crane (eds), *Neural Nets: applications in geography*. Kluwer Academic Publishers, Boston, pp. 53–70.

Openshaw, S., 1994b, "Developing smart and intelligent target marketing systems: Part 1", *J. of Targeting, Measurement and Analysis for Marketing*, 2, 289–301.

Openshaw, S., 1994c, "Developing smart and intelligent marketing systems: Part II", *Journal of Targeting, Measurement and Analysis for Marketing*, 3, 31–38.

Openshaw, S., 1995, "Marketing spatial analysis: a review of prospects and technologies relevant to marketing", in P. Longley, G. Clarke (eds), *GIS for Business and Service Planning*. GeoInformation International, Cambridge, pp. 150–166.

Openshaw, S., Blake, M., Wymer, C., 1995, "Using neurocomputing methods to classify Britains residential areas", in P. Fisher (ed.), *Innovations in GIS2*. Taylor and Francis, London, pp. 97–112.

Openshaw, S., Glover, T., Clarke, G., 1997, *Spatial Interaction Modelling System*. GeoInformation International, Cambridge (forthcoming on CD ROM).

Openshaw, S., Wymer, C., 1991, "A neural net classifier system for handling census data", in F. Murtagh (ed.), *Neural Networks for Statistical and Economic Data*. Munotec, Dublin, pp. 73–86.

Openshaw, S., Wymer, C., 1995, "Classifying and regionalising census data", in S. Openshaw (ed.), *Census Users Handbook*, Geoinformation International, Cambridge, pp. 353–361.

Ritter, H., Martinez, T., Schulten, K., 1992, *Neural Computation and Self-Organizing Maps*. Addison-Wesley, Reading, Mass.

Rumelhart, D.E., Hinton, G.E., Williams, R.J., 1986, "Learning internal representation, by error propagation", in D.E. Rumelhart, J.L. McClelland (eds), *Parallel Distributed Processing: explorations in the microstructure of cognition*, Vol. 1. MIT Press, Cambridge, Mass., 318–362.

Rumelhart, D.E., Zipster, D., 1985, "Feature discovery by competitive learning", *Cognitive Science*, 9, 75–112.

Simpson, P.K., 1990, *Artificial Neural Networks*. Pergamon Press, New York.

Wang, Z., Massimo, C.D., Tham, M.T., Morris, A.J., 1994, "A procedure for determining the topology of multilayer feedforward neural networks", *Neural Networks*, 7, 291–300.

Wang, Z., Tham, M.T., Morris, A.J., 1992, "Multilayer feedforward neural networks: a canonical form approximation of nonlinearity", *International Journal of Control*, 56, 655–672.

Wilson, A.G., 1970, *Entropy in Urban and Regional Modelling*. Pion, London.

CHAPTER 7

Evolutionary Computation, Genetic Algorithms, Evolution Strategies and Genetic Programming

In many different problem areas there is a rapidly growing interest in using evolution as a means of solving problems. The idea of "breeding" solutions to computational problems is extremely appealing. It offers a means of creating adaptive programs that continue to perform well even if their environments change, a way of creating new solutions and of scientific discovery, and more generally to create smart systems via a bottom-up paradigm. The basic technology is essentially an extremely powerful general purpose, assumption free search method. What it is used for is really up to you as it is potentially applicable in many different areas of geography.

7.1 INTRODUCTION

Over the last 30 years there has been a growing interest in problem solving based on copying the principles of evolution as found in the biological systems of nature. Various evolutionary algorithms attempt to mimic, in an imperfect and highly simplified way, some aspects of the natural process of genetic inheritance and Darwinian evolution that biological systems use in their continuous fight for survival. Indeed this field, variously known as evolutionary computing (EC), evolutionary programming (EP), genetic algorithms (GAs), evolutionary strategies (ESs), and more recently, genetic programming (GP) (see Fogel et al, 1966; Rechenberg, 1965, 1973; Schwefel, 1981; Holland, 1975; Koza, 1992), is simultaneously one of the most exciting and inspiring areas of AI, as well as one of the simplest. The underlying ideas are extremely straightforward and yet are capable of solving some of the most complicated search and optimisation problems that exist, in an extremely wide range of different applications. As a result GAs are now an extremely rapidly growing field with applications being reported in a very large number of different disciplines. Interested readers should examine the WWW as this subject has generated a considerable volume of submissions.

One of the authors would claim to have accidentally stumbled across the GA more or less by accident in the early 1980s whilst on a forage for something else in the local university's computer science library. By chance he stumbled across an unpublished working paper by de Jong (1975) which described an implementation of a basic GA for a theoretical parallel computer. De Jong happened to be one of Holland's Ph.D. students and was responsible for some of the early research on GAs that converted Holland's theoretical principles into practical methods long before it became a popular technology. However, the method seemed so simple that extreme doubts were expressed as to whether it could possibly work. After all, it contained no sophisticated algorithmic, statistical or mathematical technology. A quickly written BASIC program soon dispelled this fear and started the beginning of a lifelong infatuation with the technology. The technology worked not in spite of its simplicity but because of it. The key attractions then as now are the outstanding ability of the GA to behave in an intelligent way, to adapt to the external environment, to learn from experience without being told or trained in advance, and generally to behave in a smart rather than in a preprogrammed or deterministic fashion. Here is a simple and readily understandable extremely flexible technology which can be used as the basis for building all manner of smart systems. This ability to adapt and learn without being told what to do is fundamental to intelligent behaviour.

Several different types of evolutionary program are now known. Yet they are all based on a common theme, that of simulating genetic processes as observed in natural systems, or are inspired by such observation. Evolutionary algorithms work broadly as follows: create a population of individuals, evaluate their performance in solving some task, generate a new population for the next generation by applying genetic operations to the current generation that use this performance information, and repeat this process a large number of times. The different methods use different genetic operators and the nature of the individuals that comprise the population also differ; they could be a bit string, numeric or computer code of arbitrary complexity. There are different ways of performing evolutionary computation. Perhaps the easiest way is to start with the GA as most of the others can be viewed as variations of it. Be aware though that whilst GAs are simple to describe and program, their behaviour is extremely complex and the underlying mechanisms are still not fully understood.

7.2 GENETIC ALGORITHMS

7.2.1 What is a genetic algorithm?

Genetic algorithms are search procedures based on attempts at emulating the mechanisms of natural selection and genetics. They are biologically inspired. The basic technology has been developed by several people who investigated the use of mechanisms of evolution as a basis for an optimal search strategy when there are vast search spaces. Mitchell (1996: 4–5) writes, "Evolution is, in effect, a method of searching among an enormous number of possibilities for solutions." The beginning of the technology can be traced to the early 1950s when biologists first started using computers to simulate biological systems. However, the current GAs owe much to the work of Holland (1975). The basic idea behind GAs is to do what nature does. Michalewicz (1992) provides the following explanation based on a population of rabbits. Suppose some of the rabbits are faster and smarter and are, therefore, less likely to be eaten by foxes. As a result more of them survive and breed. Of course some of the slower dumber rabbits will also survive because they are lucky. The breeding produces a mix of rabbit genetic material. Some slow rabbits breed with fast rabbits, some fast with other fast rabbits, and some smart rabbits with dumb rabbits, etc. Every now and again some of the rabbits' genetic material will be mutated and a new even faster and smarter super-rabbit appears. Over time the entire population of rabbits becomes faster and smarter because there is a benefit in being faster and smarter in terms of survival. If the nature of the external environment changed to favour a fat, slow but smart rabbit, then the genetic structure of the rabbit population would change to optimise survival. It is a continuous and never-ending process because, of course, faster and smarter rabbits merely encourage the appearance of faster and smarter foxes, because they too have biological systems that adapt and evolve to their environment and needs for food. The GA is a simple method that extends the story of the rabbits to artificial systems that live in a computer.

So a GA seeks to mimic the processes of natural evolution. Many aspects of the biology of the evolution of the species are known. In particular:

1. Evolution is a process that operates on chromosomes;
2. A living creature is created through a process of decoding chromosomes;
3. Natural selection is a link between the chromosomes and the performance of their decoded structures in the context of a particular environment;
4. The process of reproduction is the point at which evolution takes place; and
5. Biological evolution has no memory other than that contained in the gene pool.

These features intrigued Holland in the early 1970s and he set about encoding the principles in computer systems. Quite naturally, because he was a computer scientist, his work focused on algorithms that manipulated strings of binary digits, 1s and 0s, which he called chromosomes. His algorithms sought to simulate the evolutionary process on a population of artificial chromosomes. Like nature, these methods solved the problem of finding good chromosomes blindly. The only information they were given was that performance biases the selection of chromosomes, with the result that the best creations tended to reproduce more often than the worst ones. Over a period of time, the poorest performers become extinct, whilst those best able to survive and perform gradually come to dominate the gene pool. This evolutionary process has parallels in Darwin's theory about the evolution of species. It is a surprisingly simple approach, yet even crude encodings and reproduction mechanisms display highly complex behaviour and can solve some extremely difficult

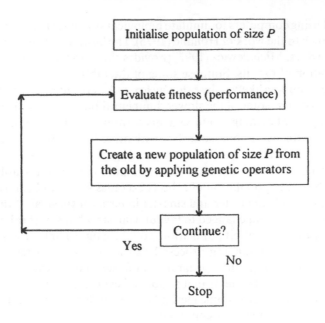

Figure 7.1   A basic genetic algorithm

problems. As in nature, they do so without any explicit knowledge of the decoded world, since they are only manipulators of simple chromosomes. Holland termed this field "genetic algorithms" because their origin lay in the study of genetics. The principal attraction of GAs is their amazing ability easily to solve many previously insoluble problems. It is astonishing, given their simplicity! If you have any doubts then try it out for yourself. You will be surprised at how well they perform. The very worst you can do is fail to improve on what you already have, often you can do much better.

7.2.2 A basic genetic algorithm

Genetic algorithms are essentially a search method, so let us examine how to build a GA for solving a simple search problem that may appeal to the mathematically faint-hearted. Suppose the aim is to find a real number that lies somewhere between 10^{-70} and 10^{+70}. A friend writes down this number and challenges you to write a computer program that can find this number by itself and without being given any explicit algorithm for doing it; such as the binary search discussed in Chapter 3. The outline of a basic GA is given in Figure 7.1 (see also the excellent introductory accounts given in Goldberg, 1989, Davis, 1991 and particularly Mitchell, 1996).

The structure of the basic GA can be described in more detail as follows.

Step 1

Parameterise your problem by deciding how to represent it as a fixed length bit string. This is not too difficult because a single precision real number can be held as a 32-bit binary string in the computer. You merely need to discover how to code any real number as a bit string and vice versa. More advanced readers might then wish to invent their own representation of numbers using fewer bits, for instance to make it into a fixed decimal number of reduced precision. So the real number 47.6 would be stored on a Sun UNIX workstation as

$$
\boxed{01100110011001100111110001000010}
$$

It is this bit string representation that is used in the GA.

Step 2

Decide on the genetic plan to be used. This sounds very grand but in practice it merely involves selecting a population size (P); the probability of applying the three basic genetic operators; a crossover probability (p_c), a mutation probability (p_m) and an inversion probability (p_i); and the number of generations (g). A simple GA might use $P = 32, p_c = 1.0, p_m = 0.01, p_i = 0.01, g = 50$. More about different genetic plans later on.

Step 3

Randomly generate an initial population of P sets of 32 bits, each representing a real randomly generated number.

Step 4

Decode each bit string (viz. convert the 32 bits into a real number) and compute its performance. The GA needs to know when it is doing well, and when it is not. So you need to define a simple function (F) to measure this. Here we use the absolute value of the difference between the decoded number and the target defined as $F = \text{abs}(x - target)$ where x is the real number generated from one of the bit strings and *target* is the value being searched for provided by your friend.

Step 5

Create a new population of P members by applying genetic operators to pairs of parent strings selected with a probability related to their performance. Replace each member of the old population by a newly bred individual.

The basic genetic operators need some elaboration. Crossover is the principal operation and much of the power of the method seems to result from this procedure. Single-point crossover works as follows:

1. Select two parents of strings with a probability that reflects their performance or fitness to breed. The value for F is a measure of performance. Smaller is better so these performance values are transformed (viz. subtract them from the largest value) and then a pair of points randomly selected with a probability dependent on their performance. Strings that perform well are more likely to be selected than poor ones. Suppose we select parents 17 and 24 which have the following bit strings:

   parent 17: **01010110110111110111101111000010** which is decoded as 445.964
   parent 24: **11111100001000011101101101000010** which is 109.758

2. Randomly select a crossover point (k), k is an integer between 1 and 32; e.g. suppose $k = 21$.
3. Create a new bit string by taking bits 1 to 21 from parent 17 and 22 to 32 from parent 24 to create a new string:

   new individual: **01010101101101111101111**101111000010 which is decoded as 445.964

4. Mutation is a random change to the bit string, whereby a 1 changes to a 0 and a 0 to a 1. This is equivalent to a random search so p_m is usually set small. So for each bit generate a random number between 0 and 1.0 and if this is less than p_m then change the bit. Mutation is useful as a means of reintroducing genetic diversity and thus helping prevent premature convergence. It is equivalent to a local random search. For example, changing bit 32 from 0 to 1 changes the offspring value to 0.039311.
5. Inversion involves selecting two cut points at random, k_1 and k_2. With the probability p_i, select k_1 and k_2 at random and create a new string consisting of $1 - k_{1-1}, k_2 - k_1$ reversed, $k_2 + 1$, 32. Inversion is another low-probability event that is designed to prevent premature convergence.

Step 6

Make a note of the best value of the error F so far found.

Step 7

Repeat steps 4–6 G times.

You program your PC and set it going. It will start off badly and rapidly improve. Table 7.1 lists the results you may get with the GA compared with a good heuristic search method from Chapter 3.

Table 7.1   Simple GA experiments with a number search problem

Search method	No. of x's	No. of x values examined
Focused Monte Carlo	1	3–5 million
Genetic algorithm		5000
Focused Monte Carlo	2	Not found after 2000 million attempts
Genetic algorithm		$\cong 18\,000$
Focused Monte Carlo	3	Not much point even trying!
Genetic algorithm		$\cong 18\,000$

Notes: the number of values examined depends on the size of *G*, quite often the best result is found long before *G* is reached except that you have no good way of stopping the search other than arbitrary pragmatism.

The GA will find the exact number your friend chose after about 5000 attempts, whereas the focused Monte Carlo search required between 3 and 5 million depending on the number! Now let us search for two and three numbers. The GA still works but the other method fails after many billion attempts. This simple example illustrates the power of the GA.

7.2.3 So how does the genetic algorithm work?

It is probable that current levels of understanding are somewhat less than perfect. The theoretical foundations of a GA depends on its use of binary bit strings. It is commonly thought that the GA is implicitly searching a space of patterns formed of hyperplanes in $\{0,1\}^L$ where *L* is the length of bit string. These hyperplanes are represented by schematas which are defined using the alphabet $\{0,1,*\}$ where * means either 0 or 1. For example, *1 defines the pattern 01 and 11. The fitness (or performance) of any bit string in the population also simultaneously provides an estimate of the fitness of 2^L different schematas of which it is an instance. This implies that an evaluation of *n* bit strings is also an implicit (or free) evaluation of a much, usually very much, larger number of schematas that they represent. The GA is a search for schematas of higher than average fitness by biasing the sampling individuals towards above average fitness schematas. Holland's (1975) schemata theorem suggests that under certain conditions above average fitness schematas will receive an exponentially increasing number of samples. Holland (1975) also suggests a "building blocks hypothesis" in which new schematas are discovered via crossover, so that partial solutions or building blocks are efficiently combined into higher-order schematas. What this means in practice is that in the previous problem when $P = 50$ and the length of bit string (*m*) set at 32 bits, there are between 2^m and 2^{50} schemata. Holland (1975) suggests that at least 50^3 of them are processed via implicit parallelism, that is, without any need to do explicit computation. As the population size increases so the number of schemata being implicitly represented increases exponentially. As Michalewizc (1992: 52) and others have noted, "This constitutes possibly the only known example of a combinatorial explosion working to our advantage instead of our disadvantage." However, as Mitchell (1996) note, how this discovery process actually works is not known and there is as yet no theoretical basis for the "GA folk theorem" that a GA will outperform other forms of search because crossover allows the powerful combination of partial solutions. In fact the situation is not simple and there are many factors that make a problem easy or difficult for a GA. It is clearly a very powerful tool but it needs to be applied in a careful and intelligent manner. In particular, considerable thought needs to be given to the problem of determining the most appropriate form of problem representation. Problem representation is the way in which a problem is coded as a fixed length binary bit string. There is a danger that this coded representation represents a different problem from that desired to be solved or that an inefficient or inappropriate coding results in poor GA performance. This is very much a trial and error process guided by experience and, in practice, large amounts of empirical experimentation.

7.2.4 Genetic algorithm problems and advantages

Unfortunately GAs can fail by premature convergence. The principal difficulties are:
- The assumption of infinite population sizes;
- The assumption of an infinite number of iterations;
- Coding the problem as a bit string often changes the nature of the problem being investigated and can significantly influence levels of performance that are obtained;
- Fault tolerance makes programming validation difficult since it may still work even if the software contains accidental errors;
- No obvious way of stopping a run;
- Perceptions of algorithmic inefficiency in that performance, whilst often tantalisingly good, is sometimes regarded as not quite as good as the user might have expected, although this may be an unreasonable expectation based on intuition or greed;
- A wide range of different versions of algorithms the performances of which interact with the nature of application and can encourage the enthusiastic user to experiment, and thus expend large amounts of time and energy exploring alternatives of their own making without any significant benefit being obtained (see Table 7.2 for some of the variants);
- Design of GAs is subjective and needs to reflect the nature of the application in some way but the rules for doing this are currently undefined;
- Large amounts of computer time may be required;
- The choice of best algorithm and an optimal parameterisation of it is still a matter of luck; this may not matter but it sometimes does or you may be unaware of the problem;
- It is very easy to become side-tracked by the biological principles, adopt an

Table 7.2   Some different GA variants

- Basic
- Elitist strategy
- Crowding
- Crowding plus elitist
- Stochastic remainder version
- Various crossover methods
- Performance scaling
- Non-uniform mutation
- Asynchronous

overly biological nomenclature and thus cloud the basic principles in a fake biological veneer that is essentially spurious with lavish use of terms such as genotypes, alleles, haploid and diploid chromosomes; in practice most current GAs are single chromosome;

- The GA is a global optimiser and may not therefore be so useful if the aim is to identify multiple optima or multiple slightly suboptimal solutions although it could be rerun to find them;
- Handling of constraints is sometimes a problem especially if they cannot be imposed on the coding of the problem, as not all constraints can be handled via penalty functions;
- Natural evolution is a massively parallel search process; rather than working on a single species at a time, evolution constantly tests and changes millions of species in parallel (Mitchell, 1996: 5) and this aspect is missing from our artificial GAs;
- The ideas of solving problems by breeding or evolving solutions implies a degree of implicit validity that may not be deserved; and
- The measure of fitness is externally imposed on the problem rather than one that can itself either emerge or change over time; indeed evolution in nature not only changes the fitness of organisms but it has mechanisms for changing how fitness is measured.

Despite the length of this list few of these problems are of a substantial practical importance. They are listed here to try and balance enthusiasm for GAs with a touch of reality.

The principal benefits are sometimes overwhelming and are easily overstated. However, they include:

- An extremely powerful, widely applicable search technique that provides a global search for problems with many local suboptima because it performs a multi-directional search that combines local with global searching;
- The search is highly efficient because implicit parallelism is an inherent feature of the method;
- The algorithm is also well suited for highly parallel hardware since the P individuals can be evaluated concurrently and asynchronous versions of GAs

developed to provide excellent load balancing if need be;

- Ease of programming and understanding;
- Offers extremely robust performance in that the results are insensitive to starting positions and can handle (very easily) arithmetic problems (viz. over- and underflows, NaNs, etc.) that would instantly defeat more conventional methods;
- Can be used as a general purpose function optimiser able to deal with a wide range of linear as well as nonlinear problems reasonably efficiently, including those with discrete and continuously scaled variables, and mixtures of them;
- The basic ideas can, and have been, developed further (see later sections for details);
- It inspires new approaches to problem solving based on simulated evolution as a more general paradigm;
- Intelligent search is a very important AI function and a GA is one of the best of the currently available tools; and
- Flexibility and generality of applicability.

Genetic algorithms are far from being a perfected technology but there is much work in progress and many potentially useful ways by which they can be extended further. If asked to summarise their principal virtue, then the short answer would be that they work, often surprisingly well, although occasionally it is surprising that they do not work even better. A very useful and inspirational reference source is Holland (1995).

7.3 OTHER TYPES OF EVOLUTION PROGRAMMING

7.3.1 Non-binary genetic algorithms

The restriction of classical GAs to a binary bit string representation causes some problems, particularly in the area of optimisation (i.e. a one bit change can have a drastic effect on the resulting number) or if the problem being coded requires variable length bit strings! However, the schemata theorem does not depend on the use of bit strings and this has resulted in experiments with larger alphabets and different types of genetic operator (Goldberg, 1990). In practice this involves developing genetic operators equivalent to crossover and mutation that work with real numbers. There are various ways of doing this that you can experiment with.

7.3.2 Evolution strategies

Unlike GAs, evolution strategies (ESs) are designed to solve parameter optimisation problems. They were developed in Germany in the 1960s seemingly independently of Holland's GA work; see Schwefel (1995). They imitate the principles of natural evolution but use a floating point number representation directly, thereby avoiding the coding problem with GAs and the inherent risk that the problem the GA is solving has been accidentally changed because of the bit string coding. Unlike a GA, an ES only uses a mutation operator and the simplest method only uses a two-membered evolutionary strategy. It is even simpler than a GA to program.

The ES algorithm works as follows:

Step 1   Define the number of unknown variables, the function to be optimised, and initial parameter standard deviations.
Step 2   Generate a new parameter value x for an offspring as follows:

$$x(\text{offspring}) = x(\text{parent}) + N(0,\sigma)$$

where $N(0,\sigma)$ is a normally distributed random number with mean of 0 and standard deviation σ. This is based on the biological observation that small changes occur more frequently than larger ones.
Step 3   If the function for the offspring parameters is better than that for the parent, then replace the parent.
Step 4   After a certain number of mutations, the mutation parameter(s) σ is adjusted so that the ratio of successful mutations to all mutations is approximately 1 in 5; so if this success rate is less than 1 in 5 then increase σ a little, else reduce it; a suitable change rate is 0.82 or 1.22. The idea is that this mutation rate needs to be responsive to the performance of the search.
Step 5   Repeat steps 2 and 4 either until a maximum number of generations have been considered or until the size of σ is so small that it has no further effect.

Later versions of ESs have been developed that are a multi-membered ES in which the mutation variance self-adapts rather than changes in a more deterministic way. Also the use of a population of individual sets of parameters provides a better way of handling problems in which the optimum moves over time or where there are considerable levels of noise. Schwefel (1995) provides FORTRAN code for various versions. Experiments suggest that the simplest version works best. Indeed it probably comes as a considerable surprise that such a simple approach (involving a subroutine of about 200 lines of FORTRAN) is able to solve a wide range of constrained and unconstrained nonlinear optimisation problems with great ease and better result performance than many conventional, highly complex, nonlinear optimisation methods. Schwefel (1995) provides a whole series of comparisons. Apart from its simplicity, these ES optimisers have the outstanding advantage that they no longer assume a globally continuously differentiable and globally convex function. The cost is an increase in the number of function evaluations of between one and two orders of magnitude but this is a small price to pay, particularly in today's high performance computing environments. The very worst outcome is a result indistinguishable from that obtainable by more conventional methods.

7.3.3 An empirical comparison of evolutionary strategies with genetic algorithms

The principal difference is the ES algorithm's use of a mutation-only strategy (in the case of the two-membered ES) and, more especially, the lack of need to represent the problem in a coded form. It is purely a numerical optimisation procedure whereas the GA is capable of much more general application. **Which one works best is probably application dependent.** Diplock and Openshaw (1996) describe the results of applying both GA and ES methods to estimate the parameters in a spatial interaction model. They expressed a strong preference for the latter method and also surprise at the lack of robustness of the conventional alternatives.

They examined the performance of both GA and ES parameter estimation methods for three different types of spatial interaction model. First, a conventional Wilson (1971) origin-constrained entropy-maximising model is used:

$$T_{ij} = A_i O_i W_j \exp(-\beta C_{ij}) \qquad (7.1)$$

where

$$A_i = \left[\sum_{j=1}^{n_j} W_j \exp(-\beta C_{ij}) \right]^{-1} \qquad (7.2)$$

where T_{ij} is the predicted number of trips from origin zone i to destination zone j, O_i the number of trips originating from origin i, W_j the attractiveness of destination j and C_{ij} the "cost" of travelling from origin zone i to destination zone j. This model is generally regarded as being well behaved although the exponential deterrence function has some potential for numerical instability if the product of βC_{ij} becomes either too large or too small. Second, a Gonçalves and Ulysséa-Neto (1993) hybrid gravity–intervening opportunity model is considered. This model can be written as

$$T_{ij} = A_i O_i W_j \exp(-\lambda Z_{ij} - \beta C_{ij}) \qquad (7.3)$$

where

$$A_i = \left[\sum_{j=1}^{n_j} W_j \exp(-\lambda Z_{ij} - \beta C_{ij}) \right]^{-1} \qquad (7.4)$$

where Z_{ij} is the number of opportunities intervening between origin zone i and destination zone j when destinations are ranked by distance from zone i. In this model the gravity and intervening opportunities factors are combined to yield a hybrid deterrence function. Finally, a different set of models based on Fotheringham's (1983, 1986) competing destinations model are examined. The model is expressed as

$$T_{ij} = A_i O_i W_j Q_j^\delta \exp(-\beta C_{ij}) \tag{7.5}$$

where

$$A_i = \left[\sum_{j=1}^{nj} W_j Q_j^\delta \exp(-\beta C_{ij}) \right]^{-1} \tag{7.6}$$

Q_{ij} represents the accessibility of destination j to all other destinations available to origin i as perceived by the residents of that origin (Fotheringham, 1983). It can take numerous forms and in this case the term is represented by a common function of attractiveness and distance. This is defined in Fotheringham (1983, 1984, 1985) as

$$Q_{ij} = \sum_{\substack{k=1 \\ k \neq i \\ k \neq j}}^{nj} W_k \exp(\sigma C_{jk}) \tag{7.7}$$

This model can also be extended from this three-parameter (β, δ and σ) version to a five-parameter production-constrained model, which is written as follows;

$$T_{ij} = A_i O_i W_j^\alpha Q_j^\delta \exp(-\beta C_{ij}) \tag{7.8}$$

where

$$A_i = \left[\sum_{j=1}^{nj} W_j^\alpha Q_j^\delta \exp(-\beta C_{ij}) \right]^{-1} \tag{7.9}$$

and

$$Q_{0j} = \sum_{\substack{k=1 \\ k \neq i \\ k \neq j}}^{nj} W_k^\gamma \exp(\sigma C_{jk}) \tag{7.10}$$

Again the "hardness" of calibrating this model results from the complex exponential form of the deterrence function. The exponential function has considerable potential for floating point arithmetic problems once the function's arguments fall outside a fairly narrowly defined range of values. These numeric problems may, if they occur, rapidly propagate through the model via the accounting constraints and, whereas the program may not "fail", the concern here is that this may adversely affect the performance of the nonlinear optimiser resulting in poor parameter estimates. Current practice attempts to avoid these problems by scaling the data to try and avoid arithmetic exceptions; indeed the

Table 7.3   Optimal error values for GA and ES calibrations of a spatial interaction model

Model	NAG	GA	ES
Wilson	16.148	16.148	16.148
Hybrid gravity–intervening opportunity model	16.139	16.145	16.142
Three-parameter competing destination model	15.931	15.930	15.635
Five-parameter competing destination model	16.222	15.856	15.973

Source: Diplock and Openshaw (1996).

single-parameter negative exponential model is well suited to this strategy. Unfortunately, the more sophisticated the model, the more difficult and arbitrary this task becomes and the greater the risk that it will result in a suboptimal set of parameter estimates.

For comparison purposes, results for the conventional NAG (1991) one-parameter optimisation routine "e04abf" and the multi-parameter optimisation routine "e04jaf" are given. Model performance is measured by computing the residual standard deviation.

The results are summarised in Table 7.3. In the case of the conventional model, it can be seen that the GA and ES algorithms find the same function values as the NAG routine but the GA takes much longer to execute, primarily because the run times are determined by the population sizes and the number of generations used in the GA. Also the GA has no simple means of knowing when to stop with the result that what takes the NAG routine 2 seconds requires about 50–100 times longer with the GA. The ES algorithm does much better mainly because it incorporates convergence criteria and typically takes only about two to three times as long as the NAG routine.

The similarity of the results for the conventional model is not too surprising as a plot of the error function for a range of parameter (β) values shows a smooth function with a clearly defined optimum in the central range of values around zero. However, the plot also shows some quite unexpected features. First, this convex region is very narrow in width, ranging from approximately $\beta = -1.5$ to $\beta = +1.2$. For values of β less than -1.5 the function is flat at a constant value. Similarly, for β greater than 1.2 it is also flat for a while but at a much higher value. Then, once β exceeds 6.9 the function appears to drop to zero! The cause of this behaviour is the standard IEEE arithmetic model. Most workstation hardware now conforms to the IEEE Standard 754 arithmetic model (ANSI/IEEE, 1985). This specifies how floating point numbers are to be handled and more importantly here, how various floating point exceptions are dealt with. In particular, underflows (numbers too small to be accurately stored) are handled via a gradual rounding-off process that leads to zero, overflows (numbers too large to be stored) are set to infinity, and invalid operations set the result to a not a number (NaN) flag. These arithmetic problems interact with whatever optimisation procedure is being used to identify parameter values for spatial interaction

Table 7.4   Optimal parameter values for model calibrations

Model	NAG	GA	ES
Wilson β	− 0.2211	− 0.2211	− 0.2211
Hybrid gravity–intervening opportunity model			
β	− 0.2206	− 0.2208	− 0.2253
λ	− 0.0008	− 0.0011	− 0.0013
Three-parameter competing destination model			
β	− 0.2250	− 0.2139	− 0.2944
δ	− 3.4802	− 1.9906	1.8947
σ	1.2669	0.2027	− 0.5169
Five parameter competing destination model			
α	1.1121	0.7985	1.0158
β	4.3319	− 0.2238	− 0.2605
γ	1.3411	0.6657	1.0932
δ	0.5963	− 0.3635	− 1.4454
σ	− 0.4996	0.4296	− 0.0551

models. The GA and ES can handle it whereas the conventional methods become totally confused and can easily produce inefficient parameter estimates.

The parameter values produced by the optimisation methods are also of interest. Table 7.4 (in conjunction with the values of Table 7.3) shows that with the exception of the conventional model, there are differences in parameter values even when overall levels of performance are the same, or very similar. For the intervening opportunity model markedly different λ values with similar β values were found to yield similar error function values even though the signs of the critical parameters accord with expectations. This feature is also characteristic of the three-parameter competing destination model, with the β values being similar whilst the other parameters are very dissimilar. The five-parameter version exhibited large differences in all the optimal parameter values, perhaps due to the model's complexity and the lack of independence between the parameters. The conventional method's estimates for β are distinctly odd, having the wrong sign. This looks very much as if the optimiser has become stuck in the wrong part of the response surface. Inspection of these plots showed many narrow valleys leading to different results particularly as the IEEE arithmetic model interacts with the optimisation process. The GA and ES optimisers perform global searches over this landscape and can be readily made NaN resistant, whilst the NAG routine only goes downhill from the starting values produced by the user and a single NaN produced anywhere will prevent any sensible values ever being produced again by the optimiser. This is a serious defect in a spatial interaction modelling context that may well extend to many other kinds of statistical model in which exponential functions are used, particularly log-linear modelling.

The results demonstrate that even basic GA and ES methods can provide very good solutions for spatial interaction model calibration, albeit with extended computing times. The benefits are most obvious for the more complicated multi-parameter model specifications or when the initial starting values are poorly defined. The results are both reassuring (the conventional optimiser works well) and worrying (similar levels of performance can be produced by different parameter values, and the function landscapes even for the simplest of models contain evidence of arithmetic problems and have only a fairly small area of safe computation). As computer hardware becomes faster so the attractions of simple, relatively assumption-free and highly robust approaches to global parameter estimation can only but grow and allow the geographical model builder to focus more on the task of model design, and worry less about the problems of parameter estimation.

7.4 BUILDING MODEL BREEDING MACHINES

7.4.1 Background

So much for the theory, now let us put it to further geographical use. Openshaw (1988) provides an illustration of how to try and build mathematical models using a GA. This has subsequently led to a commercial product (OMEGA), see Barrow (1993). The justification for this approach is interesting because of what it tells us about why AI is potentially so important and how, with a degree of creative imagination, it can be used in a large number of different ways.

Building good mathematical models of urban and regional systems has always been difficult to achieve for two reasons: the necessary theory of how these systems work is too vague and poorly developed to provide a good model specification, and the observed behaviour of real-world systems is noisy, nonlinear and extremely complex. As a result, over the last 50 years there have been very few genuinely new mathematical models of geographical processes. The only new development of any note was Wilson (1970, 1974) who developed an entropy-maximising model builders' toolkit. If you switch to a statistical route then the mathematics becomes easier but the problem of obtaining or designing good model specification remains unresolved. Essentially, once you leave the world of simple additive linear relationships the infinity of alternative possible nonlinear forms for any model conspires to hinder and ultimately defeat even the most ardent model builders. The traditional way of dealing with such complexity is to reduce the data down to a few variables and then either use linear models or else guess the shapes of the functions via eyeballing scatter plots or perhaps by examining alternatives using a battery of diagnostic checks. It is no surprise therefore that little progress has been made, that few new models have ever been produced, or that indeed few good models exist. In the spatial interaction modelling world, there has been little noteworthy progress over the last 25 years. Given these circumstances the attractions of a model breeding machine are undeniable, if it can be made to work and if the results are understandable, sensible and generalisable.

The objective is simple. The aim might be to develop an automatic equation generator. Openshaw (1983: 1011) explains it as follows "The dream is of some kind of model crunching machine which could be persuaded to search for interesting model specifications in the universe of all possible models relevant to a particular purpose." Using one (or more) data sets, why not search the universe of possible alternative models (i.e. equations) that could be built from the available pieces (viz. equations, rules, unary and binary operators, mathematical functions, observed variables and unknown parameters) to find models that perform well. It is argued that this approach is sensible because in many model-building situations there could well be 10^{50} or more possible alternatives to consider. Clearly many of these models will be complete rubbish but some, perhaps only a few, may well perform brilliantly and if generally applicable to more than one data set they may even constitute a scientific discovery able to suggest new theory created from the data. This ability to create new models and perhaps also new knowledge from data is clearly an important AI goal. It is also extremely relevant to geography as geographers struggle to make use of the information riches that the GIS revolution is creating for them as this approach provides a means of converting raw spatial information into knowledge and useful recurrent general-isations, and perhaps also new concepts and theories.

7.4.2 Model breeding: modelling census relationships

Imagine a simple statistical modelling problem involving some census variables. Suppose that the aim is to predict unemployment given 10 predictor variables that you believe might be related in some way to unemployment. The conventional statistical modelling route would be to use a stepwise regression model in a standard statistical package. It is interesting to note that here the stepwise regression procedure is actually searching a universe of 2^{m-1} alternative models, or in this case 1024 models, using a search heuristic that avoids examining them all. This stepwise modelling task can easily be represented as a model breeding problem as follows:

Step 1   Parameterise the model design process, which in this case only involves the selection of variables.
Step 2   Represent these parameters as a bit string.
Step 3   Decide on a measure of performance.
Step 4   Apply a GA to optimise performance.
Step 5   Keep best model.

With 10 variables available for selection, it is unlikely that you would want more than 5 to be chosen. So the bit string could consist of 5 substrings each of 4 bits which is then concatenated or joined together to yield a single bit string with 20 zero–one numbers in it. Note that 4 bits are sufficient to store in binary an integer between 0 and 15 (viz. $2^4 - 1$). However, as there are only 10 variables that can be indexed by integers between 1 and 10 to select from, there is a fair amount of redundancy here. The simplest encoding would be to use bit strings representing integers between 1 and 10 as defining predictors and the remainder as defining a null variable. If a bit string was decoded (i.e. each 4 bits was converted to an integer) then a bit string might yield (in ascending order) the values 1, 7, 8, 11 and 14. This results in the following linear regression model

$$y = b_0 + b_1 x_1 + b_2 x_7 + b_3 x_8$$

the values of 11 and 14 simply being ignored.

The hardest part of applying a GA is this problem representation process. The simpler it is, the better the results are likely to be. Redundancy is best avoided because it may reduce the efficiency of the GA and extend run times. The shorter the bit string, the better. So an alternative zero redundancy representation is simply to allocate each of the 10 variables available for selecting a single bit; a 1 implies selection, 0 means it is not selected. This of course could result in all 10 variables being used. There are various other possible solutions that you could invent; for example:

1. Ignore it and use a measure of model performance that takes into account the degrees of freedom; for example sum of the absolute errors divided by $(N - M)$, where N is the number of observations and M the number of predictors;
2. Reject models that have more than five predictors in them; or even
3. Add a penalty function to bias performance against models with more than 5 variables, for example, multiply the model's performance by the number of predictors in excess of 5.

Which one works best? Well, you will have to experiment to find out.

How well this genetic stepwise regression procedure works is left as an exercise for the reader. It should not take you more than a morning's work, if you can program. However, you are probably wondering what is the point of using a GA-based stepwise regression procedure when the standard stepwise procedure that exists in all statistical packages is at least 1000 times faster! However, speed need not be everything, especially if the modelling problem is made harder. So let us change the modelling task to allow simple nonlinear models to be created. So instead of a linear model which essentially consists of a parameter multiplied by the value of a variable plus another parameter multiplied by another variable, why not allow the possibility that the connecting addition or subtraction can be a multiplication or a divide? That is, the standard linear regression model

$$y = b_0 + b_1 x_1 + b_2 x_2 + b_3 x_3$$

can be replaced by a multiplicity of nonlinear versions that stepwise regression can no longer handle, for example

$$y = b_0 \: / \: b_1 x_1 \times b_2 x_2 + b_3 x_3$$

Note that the divides and multiplies are performed before the addition and that this model would be evaluated from left to right.

However, this problem can still be easily and simply represented for the GA. One coding scheme is as follows:

1 bit for the b_0 coefficient (1 = present, 0 = missing)

and then repeat this section a small number of times

2 bits for a binary operator (i.e. $+$, $-$, $\times$,$/$)
4 bits for predictor variable index number

The principal additional complication is that the embedded ordinary least squares parameter estimation procedure now has to become a nonlinear least squares optimisation routine based on numerical derivatives because the model may no longer be linear. However, code for these methods is widely available in standard libraries such as NAG. Alternatively, you could add extra sets of 32 bits to the bit string so that the GA would also simultaneously estimate optimal model parameters. The result is a very simple but nonlinear model breeder. The very least it would do would be to reproduce the results of a stepwise regression model. Additionally, it is very easy to make the modeller able to examine an even wider range of models by adding a standard list of mathematical functions that can be applied to each variable, for example log, tan, cos, sin, sqrt, reciprocal, null, cotan. Note, though, that some of the functions and the binary operators need to be "protected" so that division by zeros and other arithmetic problems are avoided.

It is obvious that the model forms that can be created are still limited. This simple model breeder has not the flexibility to explore the full universe of models that can be generated from the available pieces (that is, up to 10 variables, up to 11 parameters, 8 functions and 4 binary operators). One way is to add more and more options to the model description string; see, for example, Openshaw (1988). How this can be done is left to your imagination. There is, however, a trade-off between flexibility in model design, time taken by the GA to produce a good result, the best level of performance achieved, and the complexity of interpretation. Maybe you can get to 80% of the best result very quickly, but attaining even 10% of the remaining 20% might take a very long time and consume many hours of experimentation that could make it questionable as to whether it is worth the effort.

7.4.3 Model breeding: building spatial interaction models

The SIMS software of Openshaw and Glover (1997) allows the user to use this GA approach to breed spatial interaction models without having to program anything. This model breeder works in a similar manner as the previous example.

It is noted that spatial interaction models are still widely used to describe and predict flows of people, money, goods, migrants, etc. from a set of geographically distributed origins to a set of destinations (Birkin et al, 1996). Yet the modern form of these mathematical models was created by Wilson (1970) over 25 years ago and, from a broader historical perspective, their structure has not much changed since their invention 150 years ago. The task of creating genuinely new and totally different models of spatial interaction has proven to be hard and there has been little significant progress since the 1970s. Traditionally, mathematical models are specified on the basis of good or strong theoretical knowledge but in many social sciences the available theories are suspect and at best poor. Additionally, the geographical systems of interest that are now observable via GIS databases are usually neither fully nor properly understood due to the immense complexity of the human systems that are involved. Finally, there is often a mismatch between the available data riches and those required to test or evaluate existing models and theories.

Other factors relate to: the belief that current legacy models work well enough; it is always easier to "borrow" and extend models that exist than it is to develop new models from scratch; model building is no longer a fashionable research activity in geography and today not many geographers possess the heavy duty mathematical modelling skills needed to develop new models via a mathematical route; and geographical model construction is hard. The mathematical and statistical aspects are complex, relevant theoretical foundations are at best weak and often missing, and until fairly recently there was hardly any data on which to calibrate and evaluate them. The GIS era has breathed fresh life into this area by providing an increasingly spatial data-rich environment within which to build models and what is now needed are the tools to develop the new models. Maybe this explains at least some of the attractions of model breeding machines.

In SIMS the model descriptor bit string (dare we call it a gene string?) is made up as follows:

1 bit flag that switches on or off the rest of the substring
3 bits to indicate one of 8 variables (C_{ij}, W_j, O_i, constant 1.0, intrazonal dummy variable, two intervening opportunity variables X_{ij} and Y_{ij} (see Table 7.6), and a competing destination term (Q_j) that the subsequent operations are to be applied to
2 bits to indicate type of parameterisation used, the alternatives are: none, *b, **b, and $+b$ where b is a parameter estimated to minimise the sum of squared errors
3 bits to indicate function to apply, they are: none, exp, log, reciprocal, sin, tan, and two logical variables above and below a parameter value.

Table 7.5   Simple model breeding using SIMS

Model equation	Number of model genes	Goodness of fit
$T_{ij} = A_i W_j^{-1.07} \exp(2.162 C_{ij})$	2	16.2
$T_{ij} = A_i \tan W_j^{1.62}/\exp(0.88 C_{ij})/(1/Y_{ij}^{0.945}))$	3	14.3
$T_{ij} = A_i \, 1.039 W_j \exp(-1.43 C_{ij}) \exp(0.907 \text{Intra})$	4	14.5
$T_{ij} = A_i/Q_j^{2.24} \tan(W_j^{1.73})/Y_{ij}^{1.71}$	5	13.0
Conventional models	n.a.	See Table 7.7

The user specifies how many of these substrings are going to be used. For instance, a set of three would allow the conventional origin-constrained entropy-maximising spatial interaction model to be bred. Note that each model description string contains an embedded nonlinear least squares parameter estimation task. Some of the results for breeding origin-constrained models to fit the data in Openshaw (1976) are given in Table 7.5. The levels of performance are considerably better than the conventional model and many of the models are (because of the model description scheme used here) fairly easy to interpret and appear to be quite sensible spatial interaction models; well, that is if you are interested in the subject.

7.4.4 Model breeding problems

Model breeding raises a number of problems, in particular:
- What do the models mean?
- How robust are they?
- Do they represent generalisable knowledge, or merely highly specific representations?
- Are they sensible?
- Has the GA found nearly optimal results or has the nature of the problem representation hindered the search process resulting in poor results?

The question of robustness can be dealt with by using computational statistical devices such as the bootstrap. Whether the models generalise can be tackled by using multiple data sets and averaging performance. However, deciding what the models mean is much harder because this involves both the need to simplify the mathematical structure of the model and to interpret it. It is clearly not a black box in the same way the neural network is, but equally ability to write down a possibly horrible nonlinear equation might not be of much help. For example, Openshaw (1988) found some very interesting spatial interaction models that performed well but they had no simple interpretation. The obvious solution is to attempt to simplify the maths using an algebraic maths package such as Reduce 2 or Maple, followed by attempts to visualise the constituent subfunctions. Maybe geographers have false expectations and expect to find overly simple, good performance models of highly complex spatial relationships. In any case, at the end of the day the availability of high-performance models, however complex they may appear, is clearly better than having no good models at all. To the non-mathematician, it is all impenetrable gobbledegook anyway!

More serious problems concern the quality of the results, in particular whether or not nearly optimal results are being obtained. One way of providing a degree of insurance is to compare new models with old ones; unless there is a substantial improvement in performance (fit or quality of fit or robustness) then maybe the added complexity is not worthwhile. On the other hand, it is also useful to know that a conventional model cannot easily be improved upon, if indeed this is the case. So on both grounds, model breeding machines would seem to be worthwhile technology for the future.

7.5 GENETIC PROGRAMMING AND EVOLVING COMPUTER PROGRAMS

7.5.1 A basic algorithm for genetic programming

A major problem with GAs that the model breeding experiments highlight concerns the interaction between the problem representation that is used (viz. the binary bit string coding of the problem) and the GA itself. It is apparent that this can be a source of considerable inefficiency. For the special case of optimisation, the ES approach avoids this issue by dealing with the numbers directly. Another way of looking at the problem is that what we really want to evolve is not just a bit string representation of some problem but the computer code that solves the problem. This would offer a far more general solution procedure. Indeed this idea of automatic programming (i.e. have computer programs automatically write computer programs) has a long history in AI. Mitchell (1996) notes that some of the earliest applications of evolutionary computation techniques were aimed at automatic programming, particularly Fogel et al (1966), Cramer (1987) and Fujiki and Dickinson (1987). More recently Koza's work in evolving LISP programs via "genetic programming" has greatly stimulated interest in this area (Koza, 1992). In general genetic programming (GP) provides a far more general, neater, better and highly attractive approach to this problem.

Genetic programming is a recent development of the GA that dramatically increases its applicability as a general and robust method of evolving computer programs to solve problems. As Koza (1992: 695) puts it, "genetic programming can search the space of possible computer programs for an individual computer program that is highly fit in solving (or approximately solving) the problem at hand". Genetic programming may be more powerful than neural networks and other machine learning procedures, and looks like being a major advance. The basic paradigm is both easy and widely applicable. Moreover it appears to work extremely well. Genetic programming changes the nature of the problem representation. You are no longer breeding bit strings that decode as solutions but complete computer programs that themselves represent solutions to a problem. So GP extends the GA approach to offer a means of searching the universe of possible computer programs for an individual program that best solves a particular problem. It neatly avoids the representation problems in GAs and, in terms of the previous example, provides the basis for a really useful model breeding machine. Representation is the key problem in a GA, because GAs operate on coded representations of the problem. A poor representation may well limit the power of genetic search and reduce its efficiency. The conventional GA operates on fixed length encoding, for example the bit string representation of a symbolic census regression model discussed previously. A fixed length representation makes it difficult to represent hierarchical structures and, as the example illustrated, it precluded a fully flexible equation generator. It seems that many problems are best represented as a hierarchical computer program of dynamically varying size, shape and complexity. As a result a fixed length coding is very artificial and restrictive with no dynamic variability in length, often causing considerable redundancy, and an inability to handle complex forms or conditional statements, or iteration or recursion.

In GP the GA is applied to the "program" that directly represents the problem to be solved. The "program" in the Koza (1992) version of GP is a LISP S-expression which in terms of LISP is a computer program of arbitrary complexity. A LISP expression is a hierarchical composition of functions and variables. The whole idea is to apply genetic operators to these LISP S-expressions directly; you can then manipulate symbolic code that represents a LISP program and thus open up a much wider range of problem representations to the GA.

There are a number of steps in Koza's GP paradigm (Koza, 1992: 121). They are:

Step 1 Define the set of variables, parameters and constants to use;

Step 2 Select the set of functions as $+, -, \times, /$, mathematical functions, boolean operators, conditional operators, function causing iteration, functions causing recursion;

Step 3 Design an appropriate fitness measure that is used to evaluate and thus drive the search process;

Step 4 Decide on the parameters and variables for controlling the run, such as population, number of generations, genetic operator probabilities much as in a GA and set the criterion for termination;

Step 5 Generate an initial population of random programs using the set of possible pieces; each must be a valid LISP program;

Step 6 Calculate the fitness of each program in the population;

Step 7 Apply selection, crossover and mutation to the population to form a new population. In Koza's method 10% of the programs (selected randomly in proportion to their fitness) are copied into the new population, the remaining 90% are formed by crossover;

Step 8   Repeat steps 6 and 7 for a number of generations.

Mitchell (1996: 40) writes, "It may seem difficult to believe that this procedure would ever result in a correct program—the famous example of a monkey randomly hitting the keys on a typewriter and producing the works of Shakespeare comes to mind. But, surprising as it might seem, the GP technique has succeeded in evolving correct programs to solve a large number of simple (and some not-so-simple) problems." Indeed Koza (1992, 1994) presents many examples of successful application on a very broad range of problems.

7.5.2 An example of genetic programming

Maybe one example will suffice to illustrate some of the potential. Koza (1992) uses a symbolic regression example to demonstrate the potential of GP. The aim is to discover a program that matches the function

$$y = 2.7183x^2 + 3.1416x$$

for a sample of 20 random values of x in the range -1 to $+1$. The input variable is x and an ephemeral random constant is available. The following functions: $+, -, \times, \%$ (divide that avoids dividing by zero), sin, cos, exp, rlog (protected to avoid negative or zero arguments) are used by the GP. The fitness function was the sum of the absolute errors. He used a population of 500 and a maximum of 51 generations. The best equation emerged at generation 41 and was equivalent to

$$y = 2.76x^2 + 3.15x$$

The slight error here was due to the use of only 20 observations. When 1000 randomly chosen values are used the correct equation was reproduced. Koza (1992) then goes on to demonstrate the use of GP to model econometric data, to rediscover Kepler's third law of planetary motion, to perform symbolic integration, etc.; see also Koza (1994). It is clearly a very flexible and powerful technology that could be widely applied to most, if not all, the problems of computer modelling in geography. This is possibly the greatest step forward in computer programming since the invention of interactive debuggers. So maybe it is worth investigating how it works in greater detail.

7.5.3 More algorithmic details

In the GP algorithm steps 1 and 2 specify the pieces from which the computer programs can be built. It should be noted that most computer programs are constructed from relatively few pieces and that they are all available to GP. Note that in GP there is no concept of a parameter that can be optimised, instead any constants or parameters that appear are generated by the GP process. There is, however, the possibility of specifying what is termed "the ephemeral random constant" which is a randomly generated number. These are created at the beginning of the process and then held constant.

There is no reason to restrict GP to LISP expressions as it can be applied more generally (see Turton and Openshaw, 1994). Consider the following two regression models:

$$y = b_0 + b_1 x_1 + b_2 x_2$$
$$y = b_3 + b_4 x_7 + b_5 x_8$$

These can be "crossovered" in the usual genetic manner at a variety of locations to "breed" a new equation; if the crossover occurs after b_1 in the first equation and after b_3 in the second, this results in a model

$$y = b_0 + b_1(b_4 x_7 + b_5 x_8)x_1 + b_2 x_2$$

A mutation operator can likewise be devised to change any, or all, of these components. Provided a reasonable amount of care is taken during the breeding process, symbolic equations will always yield new, valid, symbolic equations of arbitrary complexity, zero redundancy and of variable length. Clearly then GP is a much neater approach to many problems that find it unnatural to be represented as fixed length bit strings.

7.5.4 Goods and bads

Genetic programming offers therefore a number of important advantages:

1. A much more realistic and much more powerful problem representation using relevant high-level building blocks which significantly extends the applicability of GAs;
2. There is no restriction on the limit of complexity that can be handled since the constructs are of variable, rather than fixed lengths, and their size and complexity can change during evolution;
3. The generated constructs are always legitimate, removing waste and redundancy;
4. There is evidence that it works well in a large number of different application areas (Koza, 1994);
5. An extremely widely applicable technology with many exciting potential applications; and
6. It is a highly parallel algorithm.

Some of the problems include:

1. Will the technique scale up to more complex problems which need larger programs and/or handle equally well problems with many more model pieces than Koza (1992, 1994) used?
2. It has no efficient way of handling parameter estimation within the context of more complicated equations except by embedding a local optimiser;
3. Much of the original work used LISP S-expressions and this wrongly gives the impression that you could not use FORTRAN or C;
4. Extensive computer run times may be required;
5. There are unanswered questions about the genetic design parameters, particularly population sizes;
6. There is uncertainty as to whether Holland's schemata theorem (or something equivalent) still applies although, of course, this may not matter much or at all;
7. How well do the evolved programs generalise to unseen validation data and to what extent do the programs generalise after seeing only a small training data set?

From a model breeding or symbolic regression perspective, a weakness is the requirement that the GP can simultaneously specify a model that performs well *and* discover optimal parameter values. The ephemeral random constant may be able to find good parameter values eventually, but it may well require very large population sizes and large numbers of generations. A simpler solution is to embed within the GP a nonlinear parameter estimation procedure. This can be readily done if the GP is expressed in FORTRAN. Indeed, Turton et al (1997) use a hybrid ES–conventional nonlinear optimiser to avoid problems due to non-convexities in the parameter space. The hope is that this "speeds up" the GP when applied to complex model breeding problems. It certainly avoids the GP fitness function rejecting good models purely because the parameter values are hopelessly inadequate. Other issues in a symbolic model breeding context involve the need to build in robustness. The use of multiple training data sets that all contribute to the fitness function and use of computational statistical procedures such as the bootstrap, if sufficient computer time is available, are both useful devices. However to make much progress the GP code has to be parallelised and recoded for messages passing (MPI) using asynchronous GAs in order to handle efficiently the load-balancing problems that embedded parameter estimation causes; viz. each program requires different amounts of computer time; and then the whole system run on an extremely fast parallel supercomputer. Experiments on 512 processor Cray T3D suggest that the full benefits of GP in a large data geographical GIS context may well require the next generation of parallel supercomputer; and it is possible that this statement will still be true in a decade's time but much less so! On the other hand, suitably sized and simpler modelling problems can often be successfully tackled now, sometimes even on a PC. Genetic programming does not have to be regarded only as a high-performance computing technology, many problems can be easily handled now!

7.6. A GENETIC PROGRAMMING APPROACH TO BUILDING NEW SPATIAL INTERACTION MODELS

Consider again the spatial interaction model. Turton et al (1997) and Diplock (1996) argue that a GP approach using a parallel supercomputer provides probably the ultimate long-term answer to this problem of creating a new species of high-performance spatial interaction model. Again a particularly attractive feature is that the models appear in equation form instead of black box neural nets.

Perhaps unusually, their GP algorithm is programmed in FORTRAN 77 since this allowed implementation on various types of high-performance computer hardware. A FORTRAN implementation may seem a little unusual but it is very straightforward. The LISP S expressions are handled as character strings which can only be combined at certain positions which generate well-formed substrings, thereby completely emulating the LISP tree syntax structure. The equations contained in these character strings are then "compiled" into an efficient form for ease of implementation. In this case the model is decomposed into a serial set of vector operations designed to maximise number-crunching performance on high-performance computing hardware. This is very important because the success of this GP approach, crudely put, depends on how many million models can be evaluated per hour! The code was initially run on a Cray Y-MP and a Fujitsu VPX 1200 vector supercomputer but whilst good levels of vector performance were obtained, it was quite clear that far more computer power was needed. It was subsequently ported on to the Cray T3D 512 node parallel supercomputer at Edinburgh University.

The GP algorithm is naturally parallel because each member of the population of equations can be evaluated concurrently. However, this requires that the population size is some integer multiple of the number of available processors. The initial code was parallelised in a data parallel form. However, it soon became obvious that a different form of parallel GP was needed if further progress was to be made. Subsequently, a parallel GP was developed using a task farm form of parallel programming. The original serial code was rewritten for MPI and an asynchronous GA developed. This asynchronous approach offers almost perfect load balancing on parallel hardware as well as being scalable due to the coarsely grained nature of the parallel computation. It was well suited to the 512 processor Cray T3D.

The GP experiments used the set of model pieces shown in Table 7.6. These reflect the variables commonly used in spatial interaction models of journey-to-work data so that the GP could "rediscover" the conventional model if it wished. Note the addition of three extra variables; a competing destination variable and two intervening opportunity terms. This is to permit various hybrid models to be developed if there is some benefit to be gained. Note also that the origin size is also used as a destination attraction variable, likewise the destination size is also used as origin zone attraction. There are also two logical functions; these functions, < (less than) and > (greater than), are logical operators that permit conditional

Table 7.6   Spatial interaction model pieces

Model pieces
O_i Origin size
W_j Destination size
O_j Corresponding destination size
W_i Corresponding origin size
C_{ij} Travel cost
V_{ij} Intervening opportunities term up to but not including j
X_{ij} Intervening opportunities term that includes destination j
Q_j Competing destinations term
Mathematical operators
      $+, -, *, /, \hat{\ }$
Mathematical functions
      sqrt, log, exp, $<$, $>$

---

statements (i.e. IF statements) to be included in the model. Finally, both the bred and the conventional models are origin-constrained. These constraints are imposed on the GP-predicted trips prior to the calculation of the goodness-of-fit statistic.

The model performance results are shown in Table 7.7 and indicate that the GP bred models offer a significant improvement over the conventional model benchmarks. The gain over the simpler GA-bred models is, however, not as great as might have been expected. Nevertheless, one of these GP models is almost twice as good as the old conventional specification. This is very encouraging. However, the mathematical structure of some (but not all) of these models is quite complex even after attempts have been made to simplify the mathematics by removing redundant bits of arithmetic. Yet despite this mathematical complexity, the structure of some of the models is quite sensible; for instance, distance is often inversely related to interaction volume and destination attractions appear as an important variable. It is also apparent that if superior GP-bred spatial interaction models are to have any major theoretical impact then it will be necessary to extend the model search over several data sets. This would allow model forms to appear that would be generally applicable rather than data set specific. Nevertheless, these early results are extremely good and should stimulate further research into GP applications as a model design tool.

It is possible that the increased awareness of the potential benefits that GP offers could mark the beginnings of a new modelling revolution in geography and GIS. For the first time in the history of quantitative geography there are signs of emergent new types of modelling tools that are sufficiently powerful to deal with the problems and complexity of human systems modelling in the world of GIS. It appears to provide the practical basis for a very powerful model discovery technology The limitations that remain are partly self-imposed (i.e. a lack of faith in scientific modelling and confidence that much further progress can be made) and partly the lack of sufficient computing power needed to sustain these new

Table 7.7   GP generated spatial interaction models

Conventional models	Model error
$T_{ij} = O_i W_j C_{ij}{}^{\beta}$	20.5
$T_{ij} = O_i W_j \exp(\beta C_{ij})$	16.1
$T_{ij} = O_i W_j \exp(\beta \sqrt{C_{ij}})$	15.9
$T_{ij} = O_i W_i \exp(\beta \log(C_{ij}))$	20.5
$T_{ij} = O_i W_j \exp(\lambda X_{ij} + \beta C_{ij})$	16.1
$T_{ij} = O_i W_j Q_j{}^{\delta} \exp(\beta C_{ij})$	16.1

GP models	Model error

$$T_{ij} = \left[2V_{ij}\left(12.0V_{ij}W_jX_{ij}{}^{1.82}W_i{}^{1.82} + 3.34 + 2.0V_{ij} - O_iC_{ij}{}^{-1.82} + O_iW_i{}^{1.82} + \frac{X_{ij}C_{ij}{}^{-1.82}}{W_j} \right) \right]^{-C_{ij}}$$

$$\times \left[\left(W_j + X_{ij} + 3.34 + \frac{X_{ij}C_{ij}{}^{-1.82}}{2V_{ij}} \right) \right]^{-C_{ij}} \times W_j \log(1.67 + X_{ij}{}^{1.67} - 3.0X_{ij}{}^{1.82})$$

$$\times [X_{ij}{}^{1.67} - 2.0X_{ij} + O_i\log(W_i{}^{1.82}C_{ij}{}^{-1.39}) + O_iC_{ij}{}^{-1.82} + W_j]$$

$$\times \left(W_j + \frac{W_j}{2.0W_j{}^{C_{ij}}} \right) \qquad\qquad 11.6$$

$$T_{ij} = W_j \exp[-0.16C_{ij} + 27.9(-0.5\exp(W_j) + W_i) + V_{ij} - 4.1] \qquad 12.2$$

$$T_{ij} = \exp\left(\frac{C_{ij} - 0.17}{W_i{}^{W_j} - 0.16} \right) \times \exp(W_j(C_{ij} - 0.13) + V_{ij}) \qquad 12.3$$

$$T_{ij} = \exp\left(\frac{C_{ij}}{-0.17} \right) \times \left(\frac{W_j}{X_{ij}{}^{-0.47}} + X_{ij} \right) \times \left(\frac{W_j}{W_i{}^{-0.43}} \right) \qquad 13.7$$

$$T_{ij} = \frac{W_iC_{ij}{}^{-0.02}}{W_j} \times (V_{ij} + 0.78) \qquad 13.7$$

$$T_{ij} = 2.0W_jX_{ij}{}^{-1.20} \exp(-0.06C_{ij}) \qquad 14.3$$

developments. It is noted that the latter problem is disappearing fast but that the former is much more problematic.

7.7 CONCLUSIONS

It is quite clear that evolutionary computing is a key AI technology with an amazingly broad spectrum of applications. Viewed from a nonlinear optimisation perspective it provides a more robust and reliable technology for solving nonlinear optimisation problems, handling well optimisation problems, and many other classes of problem that previously could not be solved at all. There are already significant geographical applications (Openshaw, 1988; Diplock and

Openshaw, 1996); no doubt before long there will be many more. However, the technology is equally applicable on a much broader scale. It can be used to create new types of machine learning systems; for example, to evolve rule sets that explain complex behaviour viz. classifier systems. It can be used to perform intelligent exploratory searches of GIS databases (Openshaw, 1994; Openshaw, 1995; Openshaw and Perrée, 1996); it can also be used to breed entire new model forms (Openshaw, 1988; Turton and Openshaw, 1994). In many ways large-scale geographical applications of the principles contained in evolutionary programming are still awaited, but probably not for long. Genetic algorithms and genetic programming are two of the most compelling and hypnotic of all AI technologies. Perhaps it is a pity that they often promise better performances than they deliver in real-world applications. Perhaps there are still a few evolutionary secrets that have not yet been adequately emulated. Nevertheless, they work well enough for many geographical purposes. The technology is sufficiently simple and attractive that it is destined to become the basis for all manner of smart geographical systems in the future.

7.8 QUESTIONS AND ANSWERS

q   I am a beginner in AI in geography. Is this a good place to start and how long before I can reach a research frontier?

A   Yes, we can only think of one better AI paradigm (Alife). You can reach the geographical research frontier very speedily, but maybe you will never reach the non-geographical ones. However does that matter? As a geographer you should be more interested in using the methods that exist and work wonderfully well, is not that more than enough of a challenge?

Q   Who was the "father" of the GA?

A   There are a few contenders here. Rechenberg (1965), Fogel et al (1966), Holland (1975) all more or less devised different technology based on the same source of biological inspiration. Holland (1975) was the only one to employ the full range of genetic operators, particularly crossover. Clearly all were inspired by the same biological idea but responded differently.

Q   Why is the genetic algorithm called genetic?

A   It reflects its origins as an attempt to simulate Darwinian evolution in computer systems. The basic mechanisms of genetics are used to allow one generation to pass genetic information to another. Increasingly people use the term evolutionary computing as a more accurate substitute but maybe genetic algorithms (GAs) will stick.

Q   What is the principal weaknesses of the GA?

A   There are several possible problem areas that are discussed in section 7.2.4. Probably the most significant problem is sometimes there is an intuitive gut feeling that it could do better although usually when you test it on problems with known solutions it works well enough. Maybe this is due to unreasonable user expectations. The second most serious difficulty is a tendency for the user to spend three or more years experimenting with this or that *ad hoc* modification or good idea—it certainly lends itself to use experimentation— whilst getting nowhere. Finally much depends on the careful formulation of the fitness function which is the *only* means by which the GA senses, measures and evaluates performance. It is very good at spotting "holes" in the fitness function that produce unexpectedly good but otherwise totally useless results.

Q   Why does the GA attract so much attention?

A   There are several reasons:

1. It works as an extremely powerful assumption free optimiser that performs well on problems where there are few, if any, alternatives;
2. It is an extremely appealing idea;
3. It is an extremely easy technology to use once the initial unfamiliarity phase is overcome;
4. It has some extremely attractive theoretical properties, particularly that of implicit parallelism whereby each solution considered represents many more that are not explicitly present but are nevertheless implicitly searched—at least, that is our understanding of Holland's schemata theorem;
5. It is adaptive and you can watch the method improve over time, this provides a basis for smart dynamic systems;
6. It is responsive to the environment in which it is located and is thus constantly trying to improve itself;
7. It is inherently suitable for parallel hardware;
8. It is fault tolerant; and
9. It is an excellent way of keeping your machine busy at times when it might otherwise not be used, for example at night; now you can merely leave a GA or GP application permanently running, constantly seeking better models whilst you sleep or do other things.

Q   Is a GA a better nonlinear optimiser than a conventional method?

A   In terms of computer times, no. In terms of the quality of the answer and robustness to multi-local suboptima, discontinuities and noise, it is a resounding yes! It offers some assurance of a more robust solution. Experiments suggest that if the functions are at all complicated or include exponential functions then it is probably very unsafe to continue with non-GA methods.

Q   Is a hybrid GA with conventional optimiser as a fine tuner likely to be useful?

A   Yes. Maybe you can use a GA or ES to discover a region near the global best from which a more conventional method will speedily triumph. Experiment!

Q   Why would someone estimate parameters in a regression model using a GA?

A   There are several excuses, some better than others:

1. The parameter estimation function is non-convex, discontinuous or difficult to handle;
2. The problem contains a mix of integer and continuous predictor variables;
3. To prove the GA works as well as any other function optimiser when there are alternatives;
4. It is easier than coding up a conventional nonlinear optimiser; and
5. There are arithmetic instabilities which would totally upset a conventional optimiser, for example over- and underflows and mathematical library problems; anything using exponential functions is prone to arithmetic problems.

Q How efficient is a GA compared with (a) a linear estimation method; and (b) a conventional nonlinear optimisation method for a well-behaved problem?

A It is not. Maybe it will take 10 to 1000 times as long to find the solution, partly because there are no convergence criteria that can be applied to all problems. So do not do it unless you need to.

Q I've programmed my GA in C++.

A Congratulations. We have used BASIC and FORTRAN and the results are no better or worse than yours would be for the same problem.

Q Where is the parallel computing part of a GA?

A It is mainly in evaluating the fitness function for a population of genes. For example, if you have a population size of 512 and 256 processors available then each can be given two to evaluate concurrently. Once an initial population is established you can keep virtually any number of processors working flat out, with optimal load balancing, simply by breeding a new gene string every time there is a free processor. This is an asynchronous GA.

Q I cannot afford a parallel processor, will it run on a single CPU PC?

A Yes, of course. Indeed virtually all of the GAs in the world are probably still run on single processor hardware so you are not alone.

Q Is two-point crossover better than one point?

A Try it and see. Much of GAs is rule of thumb based.

Q Is mutation needed?

A Mutation is equivalent to a random search. Maybe you could do without it although it is sometimes useful in fine tuning a solution and in avoiding loss of genetic diversity.

Q Is Schwefel's (1995) EVOL algorithm very similar to a focused Monte Carlo search?

A Yes, it is. The principal difference is the use of a normal distribution to define the area of search around current local best. The origins of both methods are, however, completely different.

Q Do GAs only work on bit strings?

A No. You can invent your own set of genetic operations that can work on anything from a number to a more complex entity such as a zoning system. However, Holland's (1975) schematic theorem has only been proven for bit strings, but does this really matter?

Q What are genotypes, chromosomes, alleles and genes and do I need to know a lot of biology before I can use a GA?

A No, you do not need to know any biology or genetics; it is just that this area has tended to use a vocabulary borrowed from genetics. Knowing what these technical terms mean in a biological sense seldom helps much, or at all, in using a GA in a geographical setting. However, Mitchell (1996: 5–6) gives some good definitions.

Q How close should we seek to follow the biological analogy?

A It clearly works but we cannot reproduce it exactly and there may be other more efficient versions of it that are more suitable for the computational experiments. After all in nature the genes lead to a creature as a biological entity, in A-life of the sort relevant to geography we do not want to build anything. We can choose our own selection mechanisms.

Q Is Darwinian evolution the only basis for evolutionary algorithms?

A   No. There is no reason why in the artificial, unreal, synthetic world of AI that other unnatural forms of evolution cannot be considered. In particular there seems to be some benefits in adopting a Lamarckian approach. Here the genes (or bit string) may be modified by a local optimiser so that the modified genes are passed back to undergo the usual genetic operations. According to Ackley and Littman (1994) this may speed up the convergence rate of the evolutionary algorithm by allowing much more rapid changes to occur, although there may be an increased risk of becoming stuck at an inferior local minimum. This may require a more sophisticated algorithm that uses co-evolution.

Q   What is the attraction of GP?

A   Oh . . . it is a generic, highly flexible, widely applicable technology that can be used to tackle virtually any problem that can be regarded as solvable by a computer program. It is, in a way, a means of breeding or creating computer code that is optimised to solve a particular task and then adapt as its environment changes in ways that the original programmer could never have imagined. Now isn't that neat?

Q   How would I use a GA or GP to build a continuously adaptive self-improving system?

A   That is easy. You leave it running. As the data it is running on change so it will automatically try and improve its performance. If the data do not change, then who knows, after six months of continuous running it might suddenly find an entirely new and surprising set of solutions. Usually you will gain a high degree of improvement quite early on, followed by a long wait for further improvements.

Q   I have a network of workstations; can I use them to solve a large GP problem?

A   Yes. Use MPI or some other message passing system to farm out the work. You may, however, need to redesign the GA to allow non-synchronous updating of the population.

Q   What type of geographical problem would a GA and GP find hard to handle?

A   A genetic algorithm finds zone design quite hard because of the problem of representing a zoning system of N original zones as M regions, because of the implicit contiguity constraints. Maybe GP will handle it better, any ideas how?

Q   What types of geographical problems would a GA find easy?

A   Parameter estimation and complex nonlinear optimisation problems (see Birkin et al, 1995), also location–allocation problems should not present too much of a difficulty.

Q   How long will it take to write (a) a GA, and (b) a GP?

A   (a) Less than one hour for a simple one-off version, followed by six months to one year as you experiment and "tidy" it up; (b) a few weeks if in FORTRAN or C, a few hours if in LISP.

Q   Why not use LISP for GP?

A   A matter of (a) preference, (b) addiction to other languages, and (c) FORTRAN or C tends to run much more efficiently on supercomputers. Anyway, we like FORTRAN! Is that a problem for you?

REFERENCES

Ackley, D.H., Littman, M.L., 1994, "A case for Lamarckian evolution", in C.G. Langton (ed.), *Artificial Life III*. Addison-Wesley, Reading, Mass., pp. 3–10.

ANSI/IEEE, 1985, IEEE Standard for binary-floating point arithmetic, *ANSI/IEEE Standard 754* Washington DC, USA.

Barrow, D., 1993, "The use and application of genetic algorithms", *Journal of Targeting, Measurement and Analyses for Marketing*, **2**, 30–41.

Birkin, M., Clarke, M., George, F., 1995, "The use of parallel computers to solve nonlinear spatial optimization problems", *Environment and Planning A*, **27**, 1049–1068.

Birkin, M., Clarke, G., Clarke, M., Wilson, A., 1996, *Intelligent GIS*. GeoInformation International, London.

Cramer, N.L., 1987, "A representation for the adaptive generation of simple sequential programs", in J.J. Grefenstette (ed.), *Proceedings of the First International Conference on Genetic Algorithms and their Applications*. Erlbaum.

Davis, L., 1991, *Handbook of Genetic Algorithms*. Van Nostrand Reinhold, New York.

De Jong, K.A., 1975, "An analysis of the behaviour of a class of genetic adaptive systems", Doctoral Dissertation, University of Michigan.

Diplock, G., Openshaw, S., 1996, "Using simple genetic algorithms to calibrate spatial interaction models", *Geographical Analysis* (forthcoming).

Fogel, L.J., Owens, A.J., Walsh, M.J., 1966, *Artificial Intelligence through Simulated Evolution*. Wiley, New York.

Fotheringham, A.S., 1983, "A new set of spatial interaction models; the theory of competing destinations", *Environment and Planning A*, **15**, 15–36.

Fotheringham, A.S. 1984, "Spatial flows and spatial patterns", *Environment and Planning A*, **16**, 529–543.

Fotheringham, A.S., 1985, "Spatial competition and agglomeration in urban modelling", *Environment and Planning A*, **17**, 213–230.

Fotheringham, A.S., 1986, "Modelling hierarchical destination choice", *Environment and Planning A*, **18**, 401–418.

Fujiki, C., Dickinson, J., 1987, "Using the genetic algorithm to generate Lisp source code to solve the Prisoner's dilemma", in J.J. Grefenstette (ed.), *Proceedings of the First International Conference on Genetic Algorithms and their Applications*. Erlbaum.

Goldberg, D.E., 1989, *Genetic Algorithms in Search, Optimisation and Machine Learning*. Addison-Wesley, Reading, Mass.

Goldberg, D.E., 1990, *Real-coded Genetic Algorithms, Virtual Alphabets and Blocking*. Technical Report 90001, University of Illinois.

Gonçalves, M.B., Ulysséa-Neto, I., 1993, "The development of a new gravity-opportunity model for trip distribution", *Environment and Planning A*, **25**, 817–826.

Holland, J.H., 1975, *Adaptation in Natural and Artificial Systems*. University of Michigan Press, Ann Arbor.

Holland, J.H., 1995, *Hidden Order: how adaptation builds complexity*. Addison-Wesley, Reading, Mass.

Koza, J.R., 1992, *Genetic Programming*. MIT Press, Cambridge, Mass.

Koza, J.R., 1994, *Genetic Programming II: automatic discovery of re-usable programs*. MIT Press, Cambridge, Mass.

Michalewicz, Z., 1992, *Genetic Algorithms and Data Structures = Evolution Programs*. Springer-Verlag, Berlin.

Mitchell, M., 1996, *An Introduction to Genetic Algorithms*. MIT Press, Cambridge, Mass.

NAG, 1991, *The NAG Fortran Library Manual; Mark 15*. The Numerical Algorithms Group Limited, Oxford.

Openshaw, S., 1976, "An empirical study of some spatial interaction models", *Environment and Planning A*, **8**, 23–41.

Openshaw, S., 1983, "From data crunching to model crunching: the dawn of a new era", *Environment and Planning A*, **15**, 1011–1013.

Openshaw, S., 1988, "Building an automated modelling system to explore a universe of spatial interaction models", *Geographical Analysis*, **20**, 31–46.

Openshaw, S., 1994, "Two exploratory space-time attribute pattern analysis relevant to GIS", in S. Fotheringham and P. Rogerson (ed.) *GIS and Spatial Analysis*. Taylor and Francis, London, 83–104.

Openshaw, S. 1995, "Developing automated and smart spatial pattern exploration tools for GIS", *The Statistician*, **44**, 3–16.

Openshaw, S., Perree, T., 1996, "User centred intelligent spatial analysis of point data", in D. Parker (ed.) *Innovations in GIS 3*. Taylor and Francis, London, 119–134.

Openshaw, S., Glover, T. Clarke, G., 1997, *Spatial Interaction Modelling System*, GeoInformation International (forthcoming on CD-ROM).

Rechenberg, I., 1965, *Cybernetic Solution Path of an Experimental Problem*. Ministry of Aviation, Royal Aircraft Establishment, UK.

Rechenberg, I., 1973, *Evolution Strategies: Optimierung Technischer Systeme nach Prinzipien der Biologischen Evolution*, Frommann-Holzboog Verlag, Stuttgart.

Schwefel, H.P., 1981, *Numerical Optimisation of Computer Models*. Wiley, Chichester.

Schwefel, H.P., 1995, *Evolution and Optimum Seeking*. Wiley, New York.

Turton, I., Openshaw, S., Diplock, G., 1997, "A genetic programming approach to building new spatial models relevant to GIS", in Z. Kemp (ed.), *Innovations in GIS 4*. Taylor and Francis, London, 89–102.

Wilson, A.G., 1970, *Entiopy in urban regional modelling*. Pion, London.

Wilson, A.G., 1974, *Urban and Regional Models in Geography and Planning*. Wiley, London.

CHAPTER 8

Artificial Life

According to Prata (1993) artificial life (AL) may well prove to be one of the most significant developments of the twentieth century. He argues: "That's a pretty strong claim in a century whose achievements include space flight, atomic power, computers, lasers, the electronic revolution, relativity, quantum physics, molecular genetics, and mocha chip ice cream" (Prata, 1993: 1). Maybe AL is just the most hyped up of all AI technologies but maybe also there is something very fascinating and special about AL that gives it a degree of importance all of its own. Certainly AL has its own unique, special, self-sustaining form of what can only be described as virulent enthusiasm. It is also of considerable geographical relevancy as the basis for creating smart search tools and as a basic model building tool. It is one area of AI where considerable progress and application are to be expected in the immediate future.

8.1 INTRODUCTION

There is a strong fascination with the idea that "life" can be built into computer software. The realisation that this task is actually quite easy in a trivial way has resulted in the surge of interest in AL (or A-Life as it is often abbreviated) since the late 1980s although the idea dates from the 1940s. Conventionally AL is regarded as having started when von Neumann succeeded in inventing a self-reproducing structure (von Neumann, 1966). It took off when researchers started creating self-reproducing virtual organisms or creatures on their computers that exhibited behaviours that were not explicitly programmed but which evolved out of complex interactions amongst many fairly primitive mechanisms. This came as a surprise because it almost seemed as if something supernatural had taken control of software that should have been totally deterministic in what it did. As Levy (1992: 93) puts it, "If indeed John Von Neumann was to be known as the father of this field, artificial life, Chris Langton was to be its midwife." Indeed the proceedings of the three AL workshops edited by Langton (Langton, 1989, 1992; Langton et al, 1994) did much to establish this area in AI and computer science (as well as biology) and to interest and stimulate many researchers (including the authors) on a global scale. The ideas so clearly expressed in *Artificial Life I* (Langton, 1989) were almost instantly applicable to geographical applications

(Openshaw and Cross, 1991; Openshaw, 1994) and have remained a major source of inspiration ever since.

Artificial life reflects the view that the core or essence of intelligence is the same as the capacity for living. Cohen (1994) observes that it is the pattern of life which makes something alive. Therefore, AL is all about the creation, use and application of **living** computer programs. The idea that a computer program can be "alive" might come as a shock to most people. Cohen (1994: 1) writes: "After all, they don't breath, they don't die, they don't have children, they don't evolve, they don't get old and wither, they don't move about, they don't grow, they don't have metabolisms, and they don't produce waste ... do they?" The correct answer is that "*Yes, they do!*" or could do all these things that wet or natural living systems do. Levy (1992: 3) writes: "The creatures cruise silently, skimming the surface of their world.... They move at varying speeds.... Their bodies ... betray their needs. Green ones are hungry. Blue ones seek mates. Red ones want to fight. They see. A so-called neural network bestows on them vision.... They know something of their own internal states and can sense fatigue. They learn.... They reproduce.... They die.... The name of this ecosystem is Poly World." Of course most computer programs do not do any of these things, but there is a new breed of computer programs out there that do and it is these which constitute AL and make it into one of the most fascinating of all areas of AI. This is very important because it is becoming abundantly clear that the highest levels of machine intelligence are most likely to be gained by building computer systems that are artificially alive, autonomous entities, with an ability to learn for themselves by interacting with the environments in which they are located. If we are not sufficiently clever as to be able to program into them the necessary general purpose intelligence then, maybe, all we have to do is to program computer systems that, in effect, can learn to program themselves. In a way this is what living biological systems do.

The key point to note here is that "life" need not be purely a biological phenomenon involving a carbon-based creation that breathes with a beating heart but can be treated more generally as a living "entity" that shares many or all of the key characteristics also found in biological phenomena. Thus AL took off when it was realised that life-like behaviour can be easily created in computer systems, in software. It is scary technology with a high sci-fi feel about it, but it is also well on the way towards revolutionising thinking about control theory and robotics, so why not also areas of geography? It is certainly based on principles which are widely applicable.

8.2 WHAT IS ARTIFICIAL LIFE?

The classic AL definition is by Langton (1989). He defines AL as "the study of man-made systems that exhibit behaviours characteristic of natural living systems. It complements the traditional biological sciences concerned with the analysis of living organisms by attempting to synthesise life-like behaviours

within computers and other artificial media. By extending the empirical foundation upon which biology is based beyond the carbon-chain life that has evolved
on Earth, Artificial Life can contribute to theoretical biology by locating
life-as-we-know-it within the larger picture of *life-as-it-could be*" (Langton, 1989:
1). Another way of expressing what AL is all about is to regard it as "a field of
study devoted to understanding life by attempting to abstract the fundamental
dynamical principles underlying biological phenomena, and recreating these
dynamics in other physical media—such as computers—making them accessible
to experimental manipulation and testing" (Langton et al, 1992: xiv). The essence
of intelligence in biological systems is a focus on understanding more of the
mechanisms of living autonomy so that it is possible to synthesise lifelike
behaviours within computers and in the process develop more intelligent
problem-solving technology. A key concept is that of emergent behaviour instead
of global control. Langton (1989: 2–3) writes: "Natural life emerges out of the
organised interactions of a great number of nonliving molecules, with no global
controller responsible for the behaviour of every part. Rather, every part is a
behaviour itself, and life is the behaviour that emerges out of all the local
interactions among individual behaviours. It is this bottom-up, distributed, local
determination of behaviour that AL employs in its primary methodological
approach to the generation of life-like behaviours." It is the essence of this
emergent behaviour that is the secret of AL and also of how to use it in
geographical contexts.

Much of AL is also concerned with developing a better understanding of
biological systems. The purpose of this synthetic biology is to re-create biological
phenomena designed to live in alternative, unnatural media, so that it might be
possible to gain a better understanding of more fundamental biological principles. This biological perspective is interesting but of no great geographic value;
here the need is for tools for modelling and analysing geographical systems, not a
better understanding of the biology of life. However, it is still fascinating to
speculate that once it is possible to "play God" in domains that are relevant to
geography, there may be few limits to the possibilities of creating our own types of
AL optimised for solving some of the problems of geography. Thus AL is an
explicitly bottom-up approach to intelligence. It is an attempt to put together
computer-based systems that behave like living organisms by seeking to replicate
in computers the behaviour of life which emerges out of the organised interactions of many different living molecules with no global controller or master
blueprint or universal program that is responsible for the behaviour of every part.
It is inspired by nature because somehow living systems self-organise and
discover how to run themselves within quite broadly defined constraints. No one
tells them what to do. Clearly the need to survive is important and merely by
changing the definition of survival to something that is relevant to problem
solving, maybe we can provide a whole new intelligent approach to many
problems.

Rucker (1993: 5) offers a definition of AL that focuses more on these broader computer aspects; he writes, "Artificial Life is the study of how to create man-made systems that behave as if they are alive." Similarly Prata (1993: 1) writes, "we can describe artificial life as the study of artificially created systems that embody at least some of the behaviours characteristic of 'real' life". To this may be added the authors fondest hope that these artificial systems might be able to avoid replicating human stupidity by artificial means. Bourgine and Vasela (1992: xi) also develop a more applied definition of AL; they write: "we think artificial life can be better defined as a research programme concerned with autonomous systems, their characterisation and specific modes of viability". They argue that the real need is to focus on synthesising the dynamical processes that create, manage and operate the key features of autonomy found in living biological systems. Experiments in creating artificial cockroaches or ants so that we may obtain an improved understanding of how they operate is not of any great geographic interest in itself, other than to suggest that AL concepts able to model the behaviour of ants on a two-dimensional plane might well be able to solve equivalently complex geographic analysis problems. Certainly you need to apply a bit of imagination here! But in principle it should be possible to create various types of artificial creatures relevant to the problems of geography and which learn how to live and then thrive in the spatial data and problem domains into which they are put. The genetic algorithm (GA) provides one means of allowing these creatures to live and survive via interactions with their "local environment". Neural nets would be another basis for building elemental control systems that can be trained to handle particular environments and cope well with the unexpected. No doubt there are many other possibilities, such as fuzzy logic and other types of rules-based approaches.

In all cases the broad objective is similar. The aim is to solve problems of practical importance by creating or synthesising artificial creatures or intelligent agents that discover how to do it for us, else they die! Nature it seems operates like this in a biological domain. It is very cruel; on the other hand it works else we would not be here today. So why not do it ourselves by "playing God"? Does it matter that we subsequently kill the slave creatures that we create? Maybe not at present, but one day maybe it might be deemed otherwise. Meanwhile let us see what AL can do for us. However, beware of the critical social theorist! Already there is more than enough in this introduction for them to declare that AL is a totally evil, amoral and socially irresponsible technology, but is this because such critics would have difficulties understanding that (a) AL comes with its own social context, (b) that it is ungendered, and (c) there is no relevancy whatsoever in using AL as a geographic tool. Much of the historic value systems is subverted by AI, and AL is perhaps the clearest example. Think and worry about the broader implications by all means, but do not let these theoretical and philosophical concerns stop you from trying it out on any problems.

8.3 WHY IS ARTIFICIAL LIFE AN IMPORTANT TECHNOLOGY?

The importance of AL is that it epitomises a very different approach to building AI systems. Much of AI is based on a view of intelligence as a process of manipulating symbolic representations of the world that seek to capture the pure essence of intelligence via some kind of disembodied representational system, that somehow incorporates knowledge and experience. It is this that the Turing test (see Chapter 1) attempts to measure. However, this is a very dull and dumb form of AI. The mechanisms and processes of intelligence are largely algorithmic; they contain no real knowledge or understanding and are imposed in a globally structured top-down manner that makes their performance critically dependent on the skills of the programmer. The AL approach is fundamentally different. The aim here is to build robots or creatures that contain their own nervous systems that allow them to be reactive and exhibit adaptive behaviour to the dynamic environments in which they are located. The intelligence and learning necessary for this function are to be acquired and not given or programmed into them. It is intended to be a bottom-up and emergent form of intelligence. In theory this could well permit the creation of complex types of highly intelligent AL forms much better equipped to perform specific tasks than their creators ever were. Here is a promise of possibly unlimited degrees of AI and possibly where the greatest potential for AI rests. It is here also where it is very easy to become over-enthusiastic and end up exaggerating the potential possibilities to be attained at some unspecified future time whilst neglecting the problems of now. However, why not speculate for a while as to what AL may one day be able to deliver.

Prata (1993) summarises the significance of AL as going beyond that of an interesting new technology because:

1. It may lead to a better understanding of nature's self-organising laws and the nature of life with enormous philosophical and practical consequences;
2. It may lead to self-replicating factories;
3. It may carry life, with no distinction between AL and biological life, to the next level of evolution which would put AL in the once every billion year category of importance;
4. It is a rich source of inspiration for new avenues of research on AI and elsewhere; and
5. Creations of AL may themselves be useful in their own right.

It is too early to know whether these expectations are reasonable, but some undoubtedly are, particularly points 4 and 5.

There are seemingly three key characteristics of life as we know it that might be worth building into our computer systems:

1. Evolution and self-reproduction,
2. Information, and
3. Self-organisation.

Today the surprise impact of realising that AL exists is far less than it was in the mid 1980s. It is interesting, therefore, to see how you would build some simple forms of AL.

8.4 PRIMITIVE ARTIFICIAL LIFE

8.4.1 Cellular automaton

The first computational approach to the generation of life-like behaviour was that of von Neumann's experiment. He imagined a self-reproducing machine, a universal constructor that given a description of itself would construct a copy of itself! This may seem a trifle bizarre but it constitutes a form of AL capable of genuine self-reproduction and it is interesting to note that this idea has been around for as long as there have been computers, viz. since the late 1940s. Von Neumann was worried, however, that his model did not distinguish the *logic* of the process from the *material* of the process. Ulam (1962) suggested an appropriate formalism that has become known as cellular automata (CA), one form of which was widely popularised on early PCs as the Game of Life (Berlekamp et al, 1982); see also Poundstone (1985) and Gardner (1971). This is a very simple demonstration of a form of AL that emerges by a process of self-organisation out of random chaos and yet it is simultaneously a universal computer and a very powerful modelling and systems simulation tool with a breathtakingly wide range of applications from physics to engineering to biological molecules. As Levy (1992: 63–64) points out, there is a view that the basis of life is digital and that our known universe is itself a cellular automaton. He quotes an interview with Fredkin: "Living things may be soft and squishy but the basis of life is clearly digital." We don't know how it works exactly, but instead of computer bits, there is a four-state code [the four base chemicals that make up DNA and whose sequencing forms the genetic code]. And there's some kind of process that interprets it. It's obviously some sort of program, running on a digital computer, it's just that the messages don't come in from a model, they come from chemicals.... The information is overwhelmingly that it is a digital information process, and that life can be mimicked in its entirety by such a process.... If a computer can't do it, nature can't." Well not many people agreed with this statement but viewed in a suitably abstract way it makes considerable sense, although it may not be the only explanation of life, the universe, and everything in it.

Cellular automata have now become a major area of experimental mathematics. Their fascination is that as Wuensche and Lesser (1992: xv) note, "CA

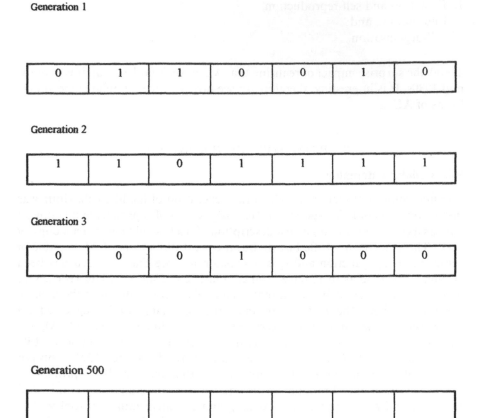

Generation 1

0	1	1	0	0	1	0

Generation 2

1	1	0	1	1	1	1

Generation 3

0	0	0	1	0	0	0

Generation 500

Figure 8.1   One-dimensional cellular automaton

provides a mathematically rigorous framework for a class of discrete dynamical systems that allow complex, unpredictable behaviour to emerge from the deterministic local interactions of many simple components acting in parallel. Such emergent behaviour in complex systems, relying on distributed rather than centralised control, has become the accepted paradigm in the attempt to understand biology in terms of the physics (and vice versa?)." They should have added that CA systems are very simple to build.

4.2 A one-dimensional or linear cellular automaton

This is the simplest form of CA. Imagine a table with seven columns and only one row; see Figure 8.1. Each cell in the table has two possible values; a value of 1 means it is alive and a value of 0 that it is dead. Imagine that there is a generation number associated with each row of the table, i.e. let us call row 1 generation 1. It is also necessary to wrap the row around so that the right-hand neighbour of the last column (in Figure 8.1 this is column 7) is the first column on the same row and similarly the left-hand neighbour of cell 1 is cell 7. Let us set this row of cells to a random pattern of 1s and 0s. Now we need to invent some rules that will determine what happens to these values at the end of generation 2. In a CA what happens to any particular cell depends on the values in the neighbouring cells and its current value. As each cell has only two states and there are three adjacent cells to consider (left, centre, right) then there are a maximum of eight rules that specify how a pattern of values of any three cells at generation 1 will determine the results at generation 2. A complete set of rules has to handle all these possibilities, else the cell will not know what to do. There are 256 different sets of eight rules that could be applied to this one-dimensional CA so even here there is considerable scope for experimentation. Each set of eight rules will probably produce a different result as will different sets of starting values. Herein lies some of the fascination of CA. Even this simple one-dimensional version is capable of generating considerable complexity from very simple rules. Prata (1993) provides some easy to use PC software with which you can experiment, although even a novice programmer should have little difficulty in programming a CA.

Returning to Figure 8.1, let us invent some rules:

Rule 1   If a cell is dead and it is surrounded by other dead cells, it remains dead;

Rule 2   If both a cell's neighbours are alive then it dies or remains dead;

Rule 3   If a cell is dead and either its left or right neighbour is alive then it becomes alive;

Rule 4   If a cell is alive and its left neighbour is alive then it dies;

Rule 5   If a cell is alive and its right neighbour is alive then it survives;

Rule 6   If a cell is alive and its neighbours are dead then it remains alive.

Note that rules 2 and 3 fit two different patterns making a total of eight rules. So start to apply the rules to Figure 8.1 working from left to right. If each generation is stored on a separate line then a simple picture could reveal its history in a visual form as a space-time display. Patterns of immense beauty and complexity can now be produced resembling, for example, the patterning on a mollusc shell (Wolfram, 1983a, 1984).

Packard (1985) and Wolfram (1983b) describe a CA program for modelling the structure of snowflakes. The purpose was to demonstrate that simple rules could duplicate the behaviour of complex living and non-living systems found in nature. Another impressive demonstration was the replication of the motion of flocking birds using a simple net of CA-like rules (Reynolds, 1987).

Reynolds (1987) was able to simulate the flocking behaviour of birds by programming in software a flock of boids that interact with each other whilst obeying three rules: fly in the same direction as other boids, try to match the speed of neighbouring boids, and avoid bumping into them. The tendency of birds to flock is called emergent behaviour. The flock turns and swarms in a way that is not programmed but emerges as the boids interact with each other. The feeling is that this technology might be extremely useful in handling many geographical problems. The problem is how to convert this "feeling" into something useful.

Nevertheless, this one-dimensional CA can be used to demonstrate emergent behaviour. The results depend on both the rules you specify and the initial starting values, just as living creatures depend on heredity and environment. Indeed the eight rules can be regarded as equivalent to a chromosome with eight genes that control the behaviour of the cell, but in common with real wet life the results are unpredictable because they depend on the patterns of interaction with neighbouring cells. Some rules lead to boring behaviour, others do not. Wolfram (1983b) investigated all possible one-dimensional CA and identified four different patterns: dull universes of all dead or living cells, stable configurations that do not change, chaotic patterns of disorganised behaviour, and complex organised patterns that repeat or oscillate over long time periods. The interested reader might like to refer to Wuensche and Lesser (1992) who provide an atlas of one-dimensional CA and some useful software.

So what of the implications for geography? Well it is quite obvious really. *The question is to what extent do simple rules underlie the apparent highly complex behaviour of many human systems?* Reynolds boid example showed that highly complex behaviour (birds flocking) can be created by simple agents interacting with each other under the control of very simple rules. Maybe geographical systems only behave in very complex, nonlinear and sometimes chaotic ways because the underlying simple rules (rather than complex process models) are neither known nor understood. The problems are threefold: (1) being able to deduce (or uncover) the rules, (2) having an imagination sufficiently strong to believe that reality might just be that simple, and (3) finding geographical problems that can be expressed as a CA.

8.4.3 Two-dimensional cellular automaton

The one-row table of Figure 8.1 can be made instantly more complex by making it into a two-dimensional table with n rows and m columns; see Figure 8.2 which shows a 7 by 7 table. Note that in this two-dimensional world (of the map) each cell can have eight neighbours. Figure 8.3 shows the neighbours for any cell in the table, row i and column j. Note that the two-dimensional table would also wrap around to avoid edge effects and create a continuous space. Again if each cell can only have two values (1, 0) there are now 512 rules that can be formulated to handle all the possible transitions and an incredible 1.3×10^{154} different sets of rules that you could formulate. If you relax the restrictions on the cell values then this massive number becomes even more massive!

Building a two-dimensional CA is again easy. You decide on the size of the two-dimensional table (or universe) and initialise it with 0 and 1 values; these

	Column						
Row	1	2	3	4	5	6	7
1							
2							
3							
4							
5							
6							
7							

Figure 8.2   A two-dimensional cellular automaton

	$i-1, j-1$	$i-1, j$	$i-1, j+1$
$i-1$			
i	$i, j-1$	i, j	$i, j+1$
$i+1$	$i+1, j-1$	$i+1, j$	$i+1, j+1$

$j-1$ j $j+1$

Figure 8.3   Neighbourhood for a cell i, j

could be randomly generated or carefully selected to represent something of
interest. Each generation of the table can be regarded as an image in a computer
movie that can be animated simply by incrementing the generation counter. The
interesting but hard part is inventing the rules you wish to apply. The Game of
Life is based on one particular set of rules that a vast amount of manual
experimentation demonstrated produced interesting results (Gardener, 1970). It
was an attempt to devise the simplest imaginable model that could illustrate
something of the infinite power of the universal computer that von Neumann
originally had in mind; this had 200 000 cells with 29 different states for each cell.
Even this was a massive simplification of what was itself a massive simplification!
Conway hoped that the Game of Life would nevertheless display evidence of a
weak form of a living self-reproducing animal (see Levy, 1992: 51).

The Game of Life rules are as follows (Gardner, 1970):

Rule 1 If the sum of the 8 neighbouring cells is less than or equal to 1 then the centre cell is set to 0 and the cell is said to have died from loneliness;

Rule 2 If the sum of the 8 neighbouring cells is equal to 3 then the cell is set to 1 and it becomes alive (i.e. born) if previously it was dead;

Rule 3 If the sum is greater than or equal to 4 then the value is set to zero and this might be regarded as a death due to overcrowding.

There are only three rules (instead of 512) because each represents multiple different rules. As before, the application of these rules creates a new generation. This process is repeated for as long as you wish. The visualisation may be improved by using colour so that static live cells appear blue, static dead cells black, deaths become red and births green, so that the display contains some history from the previous generation.

Once the live CA is set going then various results are obtained depending on the initial configuration of 0 and 1 values. Various shapes of live cells appear, move and then disappear. Some have been given names such as longboats, beehives, ponds, blinkers and traffic lights. Others are much more complex, the classic example being the R Pentomino (a contiguous set of live cells shaped like the letter R). Others called gliders move steadily and more purposefully. Later it was discovered how to create glider guns, puffer trains, shuttling bees, tumbling creatures and various other patterns! Prata (1993) provides some interesting software with which you can experiment. There are also many different WWW sources for PC and Unix software that are free over the internet. However, try not to become too distracted. Toffoli and Margolus (1987: 1) write, "As inexperienced creators, we are not likely to get a very interesting universe on our first try ... once we've been shown a cellular-automaton universe we'll want to make one ourselves; once we've made one, we will want to try another one. After having made a few, we'll be able to custom-tailor one for a particular purpose with a certain confidence. A cellular automata machine is a universe synthesiser." To speed up their work they actually built a special co-processor board for their PC so that they might explore many different universes. As Rietman (1993: 184) observes, "You can easily simulate a different cellular automata universe every few seconds." No doubt this can now be readily replicated on conventional PC or workstation hardware. The problem is that even a simple Game of Life has over 4 billion different universes that you can visit and you could easily spend the rest of your life exploring them.

The Game of Life is really only a demonstration of CA. To be useful you need to change or extend the rules to reflect practical problems that are of interest. Rietman (1994) gives some simple examples of how this can be achieved. If you wish to create fractal flakes resembling the growth of salt crystals then change the CA rules so that a cell becomes alive only if there is exactly one live cell amongst its eight neighbours else it is dead or dies. Start with one central seed cell and it grows to become a big fractal. Start with 0.1% of cells turned on and the screen becomes filled with beautiful fractal flakes (see Rietman, 1994: 181–182). Perhaps one of the most practical outcomes of experiments with CA is to reinforce the importance of bottom-up emergent behaviour as a means of solving problems. Why not let evolution do all the hard work and create situations whereby a pool of possible solutions can interact, evolve and fight it out for the privilege of solving what it is they were created to do?

8.4.4 Cellular automata as a modelling tool

Cellular automata are not just a computer game. Indeed one of the principal attractions is that they are a source of useful models for many investigations in natural science, combinatorial mathematics and computer science; see Couclelis (1985) and Toffoli and Margolus (1987). They appear to be particularly well suited to modelling complex dynamical systems composed of large numbers of individual elements linked by nonlinear couplings. It seems that in many areas of science physics of a statistical mechanics form can be handled in this way (Wolfram, 1983b). In particular CA can be used to solve differential equations and because of their ability to act as a universal computer, they can in theory represent any system no matter how complex if the rules can be defined and there is sufficient computational power available to make it a practical proposition. A CA has the tremendous advantage that it assumes that the complexity of the real world results from the application of simple rules that are local (what will happen depends only on the state of nearby cells) and uniform (the same rules apply everywhere); time occurs in discrete steps, and space is represented by a uniform grid, occupied by cells that have limited memory. The challenge is to discover how to re-express geographical problems to meet these requirements.

It is important not to underestimate the theoretical potential of the technology. For instance, Banks (1971) showed how it is possible to design a universal computing and constructing robot that lives inside a CA. Von Neumann's version involved cells that could have 29 states, 5 neighbours and several hundred thousand cells (von Neumann, 1966). Codd (1968) reduced this to an 8-state CA. Banks (1971) managed an even simpler solution with 2 states and 3 rules that is none the less able to build computing circuitry of arbitrary complexity. Langton (1984) succeeded in creating a CA that self-reproduced with behaviour akin to a real creature. His creatures reproduced, formed a colony and died much like a coral reef. It seemed that the forces of biology could be produced in a computer. Langton (1986) later describes how CA could be used to create "virtual ants". Again it seems that life emerges bottom-up or as Levy (1992: 105) puts it, "The concept described the collective power of small actions rippling upward, combining with other small actions, often recursively so that action would beget reaction—until a recognisable pattern of global behaviour emerged."

In short there is no global blueprint but one emerges bottom-up. This it seems is nature's way of exploiting complex phenomena, it is also how a CA works!

The basic principles of CA are directly applicable to many problems in geography, it is just that they have not been developed as yet beyond a broad and abstract theoretical appreciation; see Couclelis (1985). An important challenge must be to go further than this and develop CA that reflect the processes of geography. In many ways this cannot be too difficult and the two-dimensional, map-like nature should readily suggest many suitable applications if only we looked; for example, evolution of settlement patterns, hill slope evolution, retail structures (Batty and Longley, 1994). There is a rich technology here that has been grossly neglected. Maybe you could seek to redress this neglect?

8.4.5 Building artificial bugs

The interest in CA lies in their ability to show that the repetitive application of seemingly simple rules can lead to complex overall behaviour. This can also be seen in fractals and chaos as well as in CA, in dynamical systems, and is widely evident in nature. The critical question is how to define the rules that either produce complex behaviour similar to that observed in nature or which satisfy some purpose. In both respects CA are possibly an interesting blind alley. The CA become alive but in a highly abstract way. The question now is whether or not there may be many more direct paths to building life-like digital creatures that are simpler and more easily deployed on problems of geographical interest. The answer is, looking back, quite obvious, with a little imagination. Many geographical problems involve questions of spatial search (see Chapter 3) and these search problems have direct parallels in AL that have concerned the development of artificial bugs. Rucker (1993: 54) writes: "Computer A-Life simulations work by building a virtual world in which little computer programs can move about, compete, evolve." In the case of a computer virus these worlds are computer memory and computer code but much of computer AL has used two- dimensional maps termed bug worlds! This should make potential geographical applications somewhat obvious!

So why not seek to construct intelligent and autonomous digital creatures able to perform search functions over maps? This desire readily comes from an understanding of GAs in which the process of natural evolution is simulated inside computers using biological terms such as genes, DNA, etc. (see Chapter 7). It requires no great mental agility to realise that perhaps GAs can be used to breed artificial creatures which are designed to serve a useful purpose. Additionally there are several other ways of achieving this result, so let us examine a few of them.

A very simple bug might be built as follows. You start by creating a world in which it can live, breed, feed and die. A two-dimensional table with N rows and M columns will suffice. A bug has to have some rules that will determine its behaviour; for example, an ability to "see" its neighbourhood, some rules to convert what it senses into movement, and some means of measuring its performance (in terms of food, survival, mating, etc.). Rucker (1993) presents some interesting PC demonstration software called Boppers. Purposefulness or explicit goals are an important aspect of life so this needs to be incorporated into artificial creatures. Bugs need food to survive and they need sufficient intelligence to find enough food to offset their energy needs else they die. This is true of an ant as well as of an exploratory search of a database for patterns (e.g. food). The two-dimensional bug worlds of AL can be readily swapped for the more complex M-dimensional geocyberspaces of GIS. Much of the technology scales! So by understanding how to build artificial cockroaches, ants and other bugs it simultaneously becomes possible to imagine geographical equivalents of these creatures crawling around spatial databases, hopefully doing something more useful than emulate rather poorly the lifestyles of their biological namesakes.

Much of the AL work has involved artificial ants searching for food. Jefferson et al (1992) describe a 32 by 32 toroidal grid where some of the cells have been designated as a discontinuous trail that an ant has to follow; the so-called John Muir trail and the more complex Santa Fe trail. An artificial ant can only sense the cell ahead of itself and then must take one of four actions: move forward one step, turn right (without moving), turn left (without moving), or do nothing. The aim is to devise a means of controlling the ant's movement so that it follows the trail. Success is measured by how many different trail cells it encounters in 200 time steps. Jefferson et al (1992) use a finite state automaton (FSA) representation and a recurrent neural network. This is rather complicated although Koza (1992) provides a very good description.

Even more interesting is the genetic programming (GP) solution that Koza (1992) obtains for the Santa Fe trail. The "ant" was able to follow the trail completely despite its complexity, with single and multiple gaps and gaps at corners. The optimal genetically bred program can be interpreted as follows:

if food ahead then move forward
else
   turn left
   if food ahead then move forward
     else turn right
   turn right
   turn left
   turn right
   if food ahead move forward
     else turn left
   move forward
Go back to beginning (see Koza, 1992: 154–155)

Maybe this helps demonstrate the power of GP. The population size used here was 500 with 51 generations.

A simple neural network to guide an artificial ant could be specified as follows: there is an input neuron with values of 0 or 1 depending whether the cell ahead is on the trail or not; a number of hidden layers; and an output layer with four neurons (each representing one of the four possible moves). The network would be trained by randomly sampling the trail to obtain inputs and outputs. Clearly it can be made more sophisticated by giving it some memory of current and previous locations, viz. have different input neurons to represent the state of the current cell and the previous location. A neat demonstration of a bug controlled by a neural network (neural Ned) is provided by Smiczek (1993). The neural network provides a means by which the bug can avoid obstacles and gain food when wandering through a random world. Flexible rules are needed because every situation cannot be planned far ahead of time. The neural network allows the bug to behave reasonably well and deal with situations it has not seen. The aim is to keep Ned alive as long as possible by gathering food and avoiding barriers. In neural Ned there are four inputs: nothing, food, wall and scent of food. There are three outputs: straight ahead, spin left and spin right. With Ned the user can do the training or it can be done automatically; the latter is usually best. You can get a copy of neural Ned from the WWW.

There are, of course, other ways of building intelligent behaviour into artificial creatures. Prata (1993) provides a program called MicroAnt which uses genes optimised by a GA to sense its environment, forage for food, detect poison and control its social interactions with other ants. Each ant has five genes that map on to a bit string as follows (Prata, 1993: 164):

4 bits that determine how far an ant can see
2 bits to determine movement behaviour (viz. do not move until it sees food, move left, move right, move randomly)
1 bit specifies whether ant avoids poison
1 bit specifies food levels before mating can occur
2 bits to control food saving

Now create a population of ants and apply some rules; e.g. food adds 10 to its food levels, a food level of 0 causes death, poison blocks the ant's view of food, mating occurs when two ants occupy the same location and reduce food levels by 500, etc. The behaviour of the MicroAnts demonstrate a GA. The less successful ants never mate or die due to poisoning, the most successful ones live longer and have more offspring. Again the question geographers should be asking is what can the same or similar search process used by MicroAnts be used for in order to locate localised patterns in a spatial database or breed models of geographical systems that perform well? Can the equivalent of MicroAnts be bred to enable them to hunt for disease clustering or "patterns" that repeat, or well performing statistical models, or indeed emulate in an AL way much of conventional statistical analysis technology? (Openshaw, 1995). Is the emergent bottom-up approach sufficiently powerful to handle some, many or all of the problems that geographers have in their exploration of GIS databases if only we are clever enough to formulate and represent them in the most appropriate way? Or are these conjecture, outrageously unreasonable and totally invalid? The only way to resolve the questions is to try and do it! Are you the person to do it?

8.5 SOME EXAMPLES OF ARTIFICIAL LIFE IN GEOGRAPHICAL INFORMATION SYSTEMS

8.5.1 MAPEX

Openshaw and Perrée (1995, 1996) describe the development of what is termed a user-centred intelligent spatial point data pattern hunting creature. Maybe the best starting place is Chapter 3 in which the development of a geographical analysis machine (GAM) was briefly described. To recap, the GAM consisted of a dense grid of overlapping circles of various sizes. For each of several million circles, spatial data are retrieved and if the incidence of a particular variable (e.g. cancer rate) seemed unusually high then the circle was mapped. The GAM performed a brute force search of the entire map space because there was no other basis for being more focused due to a lack of any trustworthy spatial hypotheses and due to a desire to explore the entire map for patterns without bias or prejudice due to either ignorance or prior knowledge. In the GAM the pattern detector was a circle which can be represented by three parameters (a pair of x, y coordinates and a radius). In an AL approach, the circle becomes a "creature" which can move around the map hunting for extreme cancer rates. The objective might be simply to find a maximum cancer rate location, or to minimise a type I error probability that the observed rate is due to chance. This can be used to measure the performance of any circle at location x, y and any radius r. Clearly if the study region is large and the parameters x, y, r are measured in terms of metres then the number of possible x, y, r values is too big for a brute-force comprehensive search of all possible solutions. The original GAM handled this aspect by using a fairly crude level of geographic resolution and various simplifying assumptions.

The real need underlying GAM is for an intelligent spatial query generator that will suggest to the investigator one or more spatial queries for a GIS that will result in potentially interesting database anomalies being detected. Clearly this is only of interest if the investigator has no good ideas as to where in terms of the x, y and r parameters to look for patterns. The argument is that in a GIS data-rich era this form of ignorance is extremely widespread and unavoidable so that automated, efficient and reliable spatial database exploration tools are urgently needed.

One basic AL approach would be as follows:

Step 1   Code a circle as a bit string. If you want 100 m resolution and a minimal amount of redundancy then maybe you can manage with two 12-bit integers to represent location (x, y) and 12 bits for its radius r. A 15-bit binary integer is sufficient to give less than 40 m resolution for any search in the UK as follows:

   (i)   convert bit strings to unsigned floating point number x, y
      in the range 2^{15-1} or (0 to 32 767);
  (ii) then easting $= (x/32\,767) \times 650\,000$
 (iii) northing $= (y/32\,767) \times 1\,200\,000$

where 650 000 and 1 200 000 are maximum easting and northing 1 m coordinates for the UK. If more resolution is required then assign more bits to the bit string.

Step 2   Decide upon the design of the genetic algorithm and population size (n);
Step 3   Generate n circles using random values for x, y, r;
Step 4   Evaluate their performance;
Step 5   Apply genetic operators with parent selection based on the inverse of the probabilities that the results are random, for example 1.0 − Poisson probability can be used as a measure of fitness. Note that the Poisson probability is computed from data via a spatial query to generate counts of incidence and population at risk for given x, y and r values. Also the Poisson probability is being used here not as a statistical hypothesis test but as a measure of search performance for the decoded bit string. A number of other statistics could be used depending on the nature of the problem. Fisher's exact test might be more appropriate than a Poisson probability if the incidence of the point data is not rare. Or you could invent your own test and evaluate its significance (i.e. a type I error probability) using a Monte Carlo method if sufficient computing power is available.
Step 6   Continue until further search is not considered worthwhile.

The AL component is the circle which can move around under its own control and vary its size. Be careful though to avoid bogus solutions, situations of infinite fitness but of only trivial or no interest; for example, a divide by zero or circles that produce extreme results due to small number problems. Note also that the GA might perform better if Gray coding is used instead of binary coding and even more so by careful scaling of the circle coordinates to produce circles that nearly always lie within the study region and thus attract data thereby reducing the potential for wasted computation. Likewise care is needed to ensure that the bits representing the two-dimensional map coordinates are interleaved else the genetic crossover operator would nearly always result in a move in only a east–west or north–south direction.

    Remember also that the purpose of the analysis is to suggest possible locations to the analyst where further investigation of the data might well be worth while. That is all! The aim is to suggest, not validate, hypotheses. In the GIS-based spatial analysis context this amounts to little more than providing spatial queries that the analyst can use to further explore the database for corroborative evidence. It is possible that a high proportion of such results may well turn out to be spurious, either due to database errors or have no obvious plausible explanation. The point to note here is not the failures but that even a small

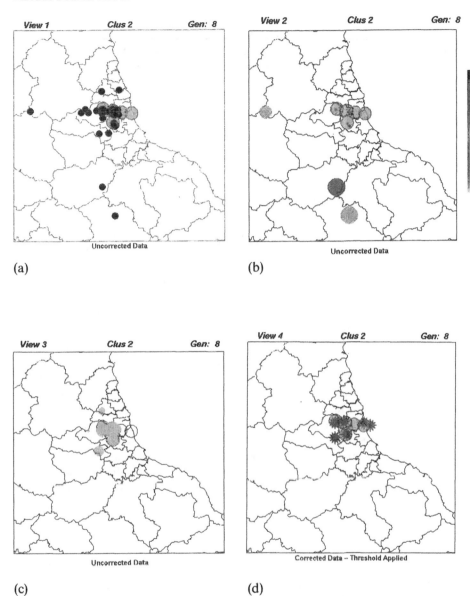

(a)

(b)

(c)

(d)

Figure 8.4   Typical MAPEX movie frames showing different views of the same data

Table 8.1   MAPEX results

Level of clustering	Number of clusters	Results of analysis
20%	One	Found
10%	Three	Found
5%	Five	Some found
Random	None	None found

Source: Openshaw and Perrée (1996).

percentage of successes will make the effort worth while in many exploratory analysis applications.

Openshaw and Perrée (1995, 1996) have developed this approach further by using computer animation to make the GA-based search process visible to the user as well as building in multiple testing and bootstrapping to improve result reliability. In this MAPEX (MAPable data EXplorer) the conjecture is that non-statistically minded users will be able to discover for themselves the nature of any spatial patterns that might be present. They write: "The hypothesis is that the viewer may gain more understanding of the structure within the spatial data set by visualising the progress of the whole search process, than by only visualising the final set of results" (Openshaw and Perrée, 1996: 123). The aim is not merely to show the workings of a GA but to allow the user to watch and thus see the otherwise invisible interactions between data pattern, search process and some statistic of interest. The hope is that this will be sufficient to allow an intuitive, creative and insightful understanding to be gained. They offer MPEG movies showing four standard views of the analysis process (the location of search, the geographical sizes and locations of the search circles, the locations of the more interesting circles, and an iconic representation that shows only the "significant" results after corrections for multiple testing). Figure 8.4 shows some typical movie frames.

Openshaw and Perrée (1996) describe a series of experiments involving synthetic leukaemia data in which realistic patterns were generated exhibiting different levels of clustering. Table 8.1 shows the results that were obtained. In general the method worked very well. The hope is that data containing different types and levels of spatial point patterning will produce computer movies that appear quite differently. The user can then calibrate his or her understanding of the results by reference to various libraries for known patterns. The process is triply intelligent because the search is performed in an AL, bottom-up, emergent way, it incorporates statistical safeguards to reduce the risks of spurious results, and it seeks to present the user with results that can be almost instantly understood. Now is that not being intelligent? Finally, there are numerous ways whereby the basic technology can be improved further, in particular by introducing more sophisticated AL concepts; for example, the search circles could communicate with each other, they could perform local random searches, some could be driven by other search principles, and you could use the ES algorithm of Chapter 7 to give each circle a life of its own. Which one works best? Well, why not try and find out?

8.5.2 More sophisticated geographic information system trispace explorers

Version 1 of MAPEX is restricted to a two-dimensional world. However, there is no reason why the search cannot be performed in much more complex multidimensional universes, with the geographical map being used to present a purely geographical interpretation of these higher-dimensional results transformed into map patterns. Indeed the space–time–attribute creature (STAC) that preceded MAPEX attempted to perform this much more complex search (Openshaw and Cross, 1991; Openshaw, 1994, 1995). The search now needs to occur in three different data domains: geography space, time, and a multivariate attribute space. It is noted that most statistical and geographical analysis tools only operate in one of these spaces; point pattern analysis, time series analysis and classification are all regarded as separate activities. Why not combine them? If we do not, then the risk is that the subsequent simplification of the data by ignoring or removing or simplifying one or more of these data domains destroys some of the patterns that exist, creates false patterns that do not really exist, and in general greatly complicates the pattern detection task. Somehow the data are expected to speak for themselves after they have been strangled by the imposition of multiple protocols, coding conventions and other simplifications imposed purely so that they may be studied by methods that could not otherwise cope with their full complexity. Indeed, a number of key operational decisions can be identified that may well critically affect the results of any analysis. They include:

1. Choice of study region;
2. Selection of data to study, for example choice of disease and other forms of data disaggregation;
3. Choice of covariates that are to be controlled for;
4. Selection of scale, aggregation and choice of areal units;
5. Choice of time period or periods for analysis; and
6. If relevant the choice of hypotheses to test.

Some of these decisions will be informed by purpose. Whilst most are essentially arbitrary, they need not be neutral in relation to their impact on the results of the analysis. For example, a time-varying process may well be extremely sensitive to the choice of time periods for analysis whilst the definition of spatial clustering reflects the choice of variables and time period.

Quite often these data selection decisions reflect the pragmatic desire to manipulate the data into a form suitable for analysis, and the analyst seldom seems to worry unduly about the impact of such decisions on the end results. At the very least some sensitivity analysis should be performed but this is seldom, if ever, done in practice. In a GIS context the analyst is forced to make many selections prior to starting spatial analysis; for example, in spatial epidemiology, the choice of disease types (and thus cases) to study, the selection of one or more time periods, the choice of population-at-risk data, and selection of study region. Additionally, it appears that probably the only patterns that can be found at present are those that exist in a purely spatial domain. Yet even these results are conditioned by all those user decisions that have themselves been superimposed on top of many others that were involved in the creation of the database in the first place. No wonder that critics of GIS emphasise the importance of understanding the contextualisation of the data and that objectivity in spatial analysis is an illusion.

A desirable goal should be to develop methods of analysis that impose as few as possible additional, artificial and arbitrary selections on the data. In short the data should be analysed at the finest resolution at which they are available, in their entirety, and this principle should be applied to all aspects of the database and all forms of exploratory analysis. Computers are now sufficiently fast that there is no longer any requirement for the analyst to impose a large number of artificial and arbitrary data selection and data coarsening decisions purely so that the analysis task remains tractable. It should be an important function of the analysis technology (and not solely that of the analyst) to discover how best to subset the data. Or at the very least, the analyst should have the option not to make possibly "key" choices if he or she does not wish to. It follows then that analysis technology is needed to search for patterns by operating simultaneously in all the relevant data spaces found in a typical GIS database. Table 8.2 illustrates the principal types of data domain interactions that need to be handled.

Openshaw (1994, 1995) describes one way of meeting this goal. Instead of two-dimensional circles in a geography space why not define hypercircles in all three data domains: in map space the circle defines the geographical search region; in time space a rectangle defines start and end periods; in the attribute space hyper-rectangles are used in which each variable has upper and lower values. All these circles/hyper-rectangles can be parameterised (their centre, and widths) and used in a GA to search for localised patterns. It is little more than a generalised version of the MAPEX algorithm presented earlier. The geographer's primary interest is in spatial patterns so why not see the x, y, r circles that result from this multiple data domain and multivariate search as a spatial visualisation of this much more complex and invisible data universe? Instead of trying to visualise directly the geocyberspace formed by the data, with all its complexity and high dimensionality, it is much easier and simpler to visualise it indirectly by watching the geographical behaviour in map space of pattern-hunting creatures as they forage around in these much more complex data domains.

Table 8.2   Different data space interactions

1. Geographic space only
2. Geographic space–time space
3. Geographic space–attribute space
4. Geographic space–attribute space–time space
5. Time space only
6. Time space–attribute space
7. Attribute space

Note: the ordering is irrelevant.

The idea then is to create an AL form that searches for pattern. In essence, a space–time–attribute creature (STAC) that adapts to the database environment via a GA. The resulting "creature" is essentially a flexible shape that can move in space and time. The STAC has the following parameters:

1. Easting and northing coordinates defining its geographic location;
2. A temporal coordinate defining its position in time;
3. A vector of attributes defining its characteristics; and
4. Boundary information which specify limits for all three data spaces.

This hypersphere wanders around the database under the control of a GA which seeks to minimise, for instance, a Monte Carlo test probability that the number of data records captured by any specific hypersphere is due to chance alone.

The basic algorithm is as follows.

Step 1   Define the GA parameters, number of iterations, generation size and number of generations. Decide how to map the parameters that define the STAC on to a bit string for the genetic algorithm;
Step 2   Select initial starting locations at random;
Step 3   Evaluate their performance using a sequential Monte Carlo significance test;
Step 4   The best performers reproduce by applying genetic operators to pairs of bit strings to create a new generation of STACs;
Step 5   Repeat steps 3 and 4 until the maximum number of generations are exceeded;
Step 6   Report the parameters of the best performing STAC and remove the associated data records from the database;
Step 7   Repeat steps 2–6 a set number of times.

The STACs hunt for minimum probability results that are due to chance. The only difficult part is the Monte Carlo significance test. The current algorithm works as follows. Assume that a hypercircle has been identified by the GA. It consists of a set of centre values with a maximum distance (i.e. boundary value) for each. A database of N points has been examined and K points found to lie within the hypercircle so defined. The question now is to assess how unusual it might be to find K from N points in this particular hypercircle. This evaluation can proceed as follows:

(a) count the number of points that lie within the geographic circle regardless of other considerations (call it M);
(b) randomly select M points from N and, ignoring geographical space, count how many lie within the specified time and attribute hypercircles;
(c) repeat (b) a number of times to provide a Monte Carlo significance test for finding K or more points within the specified hypersphere (much computational time can be saved if a sequential Monte Carlo test is used).

This procedure is a generalisation of a Monte Carlo Knox space–time statistic. The difficulty is knowing which of the trispaces to hold constant. Here the geographical aspects of clustering are deemed most important, but the time or attribute spaces might also have been used. It is even possible to evaluate all three and to obtain some average or minimax measure of hypersphere performance. The aim then is to find hyperspheres that capture an unusual number of point instances. An examination of the characteristics of the most unusual hypercircles provides evidence of pattern. Finally, the search process can be made iterative in that, once a good set of points has been identified, the points are removed from the database and the search process restarted.

Human knowledge and insights are still important but it is now applied to a different and later stage in the analysis process. The human must define the broad areas of search. These can be very general (i.e. all the database) or restrictive (i.e. just some subsets). Equally, the results must make sense. Validation is not purely a statistical matter. Patterns that appear very strong in terms of the Monte Carlo significance test may be meaningless (i.e. data error) or of no interest in terms of the application. The end-users should use their skills to decide. This cannot be automated because of the current absence of systematic knowledge in most GIS application areas of what constitutes an interesting and relevant pattern. It is here, once the search domains have been narrowed down, that other manual and interactive linked chart–plot–map graphic displays may be of considerable value. The role of the STAC is mainly to reduce the dimensions and complexity of the search problem to a manageable level. It offers the basis for building an intelligent partner and not much else. This is of course what spatial statistics also offers but there are important differences here, mainly with respect to the high level of automation and the data-richness-related complexity of exploratory analysis in the GIS world.

The general advantages claimed for the STAC approach to exploratory spatial data analysis are as follows:

(a) the search space metric is highly elastic and by changing the locational coding can be made as precise as necessary; this flexibility is important because it allows the technique to define the spatial resolution and scale that are most relevant to the problem under study;

(b) it makes minimal assumptions about the nature of any pattern; the latter is self-evident, later, from the configurational properties of the STAC;

(c) the search process is highly efficient, intrinsically parallel and capable of also using parallel hardware;

(d) the multiple-testing problem is largely avoided by using significance only as a descriptive measure of pattern with no critical cut-off point;

(e) the method is designed to use whatever data exist; and

(f) the paradigm is capable of being generalised and used as the basis for a whole family of spatial data explorers.

The hypercircles can be thought of as AL. The GA gives them behavioural features that are normally found in living organisms. They breed, they die, they survive, they flourish and they can move about in any of the dimensions of the GIS trispace in which they live under their own control. There is no imposed search plan. They are free to respond in whatever fashion they wish in response to the local pattern environments that they alone can sense and experience. So what started out as purely a problem in exploratory data analysis has become an application of AL. It is used here to extend our understanding of the patterns in databases. The objective is to discover or create new insights of patterns and knowledge by studying the behaviour and configuration of these hyperspherical creatures as they attempt to colonise a GIS database. If this AL technology can be perfected then it will provide the basis for an entirely different and more intelligent approach to exploratory spatial data analysis in data-rich but theory-poor situations.

The example here relates to the crime pattern analysis task. It is assumed that crime data might contain useful insights about the existence of spatial and temporal patterns, if they can be identified quickly enough and in a sufficiently flexible manner. This might be regarded as a generic real-time analysis problem involving data from the three principal data spaces likely to be found in a GIS. Indeed, the database used came from an experimental GIS operated by Northumbria Police in one of their divisions for one year. Table 8.3 lists the data that are used. There is no data selection and all the available data are input, although to simplify matters the attribute data were recoded as 0/1s. A crime pattern of interest would be an unusual concentration of events which are "fairly" close in space, "fairly" close in time and "fairly" similar in terms of their data characteristics. It is noted that the definition of "fairly close" and the locations in both geography and time, plus the crime profile of the cases, are left to the STAC procedures to define.

The STAC was run on the entire database. A run to find the first 10 patterns takes less than two hours on a workstation, with most of the time being for the first run. In fact the search usually identifies multiple optima and each run could be used to define several different locations at a time. Table 8.4 summarises the

Table 8.3 Crime data

Variable	Number of variables	Type
Easting and northing	2	Integer
Day number*	2	Integer
Weekend flags*	2	0/1
Modus operandi	12	0/1
Crime type	11	0/1
Day of week*	14	0/1
Time of day*	6	0/1

* Two values are needed because crimes are reported as occurring between two periods of time.

Table 8.4 Typical STAC results

Run number	Best p	Number of points	Easting (km)	Northing (km)	Time (day)	Time interval	Circle radius (m)	Dissimilarity radius
1	0.001	45	727	788	423	16	990	8
2	0.001	8	584	407	227	16	1020	5
3	0.001	9	588	476	432	11	1230	6
4	0.001	7	566	988	235	18	5360	3
5	0.006	147	594	461	197	20	2150	9
6	0.001	6	646	527	409	25	1450	3
7	0.001	19	764	511	453	16	1810	6
8	0.001	7	672	182	251	10	2490	6
9	0.001	40	592	465	403	9	5350	6
10	0.001	7	604	339	427	16	1370	6

Source: Openshaw (1995).

results obtained. The smallest probability values are limited by the maximum number of Monte Carlo simulations which is currently set at 1000. The STAC is highly efficient in that it obtains the best possible results (i.e. $p = 0.001$) very quickly indeed, usually after about 100 evaluations. Clearly it is not difficult to find potential patterns although whether they make any sense is a matter for subsequent review. One problem in a crime pattern analysis context is that there are few known examples of patterns being found due to the difficulties of the task. In other words there are no benchmarked results available. All that is known here is that the database was seeded with some fuzzy pattern and the STAC found it very easily. Some clues as to the nature of the patterns are also given in Table 8.4. The search radii describe the nature of the patterns being identified. In a live situation it would probably be necessary to restrict the STACs to data that were recently acquired with less emphasis on the old data values. However, the potential of this technology should be obvious and it can easily be developed further.

8.5.3 Some other possibilities

By now the reader should be able to invent several other potential viable approaches to using AL to handle explorations of GIS databases. For instance, why not use neural networks to control the search process and to discriminate between real and false patterns? Why not re-express the problem for GP? Why not devise a fuzzy logic controller to assist the search? Turing machines and CA principles can also be used. There is a plethora of technology just awaiting the adventurous or the curious. So why not try some of it out; see if it works or see what causes it to fail. Experiment, play and then experiment some more. So what if it needs a supercomputer or high-performance computing platforms. Is it not important to start to analyse many of the data sets that GIS has created and which are currently neglected? Artificial life provides a rich core of useful tools; all they need now is moulding and applying to whatever geographical problems you happen to be interested in.

8.5.4 Distributed artificial intelligence

A final example is largely non-geographical. There is a growing field known, perhaps confusingly, as distributed AI (Sams Publishing, 1994). The idea is not new but is quite interesting. Cohen (1994) describes his early experiments with "living programs" in 1983 and explains the emergence of new life forms that live in computer systems that can grow, reproduce, age and die, and which can create their own ecosystems. They can be dangerous (i.e. viruses) or perform useful system administration tasks. However, the concepts have been developed much further. Why not create hundreds if not thousands of semi-intelligent agents that co-operate to solve problems? Distributed AI (Gilbert and Doran, 1994; O'Hare and Jennings, 1995) is essentially the study of what happens when a set of "intelligent" computational entities are allowed to interact and communicate with each other. It provides a means of studying human systems including social beliefs, cognitive processes and emotions (Gilbert and Conte, 1995). "Distributed AI (DAI) is about building communities and societies of intelligent objects. Some of these societies may be created to emulate the fundamental aspects of human intelligence, and through co-operation, model our own distributed minds. In other cases, they may be societies of intelligent software, brought together in electronic media to compare and contrast their high-level knowledge in strategic planning sessions or to critique a new design and idea" (Sams Publishing, 1994: 369). These distributed agents can be thought of as simplified models of people; they have memories, a nervous system, rules that condition their behaviour, and various sensors that allow them to see their environments and to communicate with each other. They provide a basis for a new approach to building microsimulation models able to construct artificial societies.

A simple example will suffice to explain some of the attractions. Consider the previous MAPEX or STAC creatures. Imagine what would happen if they started

Table 8.5 Some potential benefits of artificial life

- A robust basis for creating intelligent software
- Can be used to build intelligent agents and robots able to solve problems
- A bottom-up approach to intelligent systems
- Emphasis on emergent behaviour and self-organisation
- Prospect of getting much more back than was put in
- Extremely flexible technology
- Distant prospect of hybrid man–machine systems

Table 8.6 Some possible problems

- Hype and exaggeration
- Unrealistic expectations—playing "God" brings out the worst aspects of human nature
- Potentially severe philosophical, ethical and moral objections to playing with life
- Concern about where it may be leading to in 20–50 years' time
- Fright at the prospect of self-replicating *Silico sapiens* inheriting the earth

to communicate rather than at present completely ignore each other. Communication could be handled in various ways. One interesting possibility would be to create a number of different types of agents: some hunt for patterns, and some others would seek out non-patterns and data unreliability effects. Whenever the latter find "good" matches then they could fix themselves as lighthouses or warning beacons that serve to keep other agents away. Another possibility would be to mix different species of agents in the mating population. Some could move under genetic power alone, others could use hill climbing heuristics to perform a local search, yet others a random walk. Alternatively, the genetically bred creatures could perform a local search based on other methods. A final possibility would be to build up a global fitness surface based on all the explorations. This meta knowledge could also be used to either constrain the genetic paring to promising areas or as a basis for a gradient climbing local search.

A very attractive feature of distributed AI is that you have immense flexibility to experiment. So little has been done in geography and the social sciences and the range of possibilities is so immense, that virtually anything you attempt will be novel and there is a good prospect of success as this is another potentially extremely useful technology for geography.

8.6 CONCLUSIONS

It is clear that AL has developed into a valid scientific engineering and philosophical perspective from which to view the phenomenology of life (Langton, 1994: x). However, from a geographical perspective the potential benefits are more modest and are outlined in Table 8.5. In essence the ability to use AL as a basis for creating intelligent problem-solving tools is the short-term hope and is already showing signs of success. The extremely flexible nature of the technology and its emergent self-organisation is what make it so powerful. On the debit side, there are some concerns and these are outlined in Table 8.6. The notion of being a creator of life will inflame many critics who see no need for AI and will use AL as fuel for their anger and concern at yet more attempts to breathe new life into what they regard as a moribund quantitative geography. However, do not be too concerned about this as it has nothing much to do with modern quantitative geography. The few current applications in geography could well expand a thousandfold over the next few decades as the search for intelligent solutions to many different unresolved problems gathers pace. Artificial life, perhaps more so than any other AI technology, has much to offer and, because of its youthfulness, is currently least well developed. Maybe it is here that geographers may wish to concentrate their effort since in principle at least, AL forms could be created to both replicate many existing geographic tools and to handle many of the outstanding problems.

8.7 QUESTIONS AND ANSWERS

Q   What is life?

A   A good question that is hard to answer since our views on the subject are dominated by life as we know it. A biological virus is probably more living than non-living. An autonomous solar-powered LEGO robot is a life form as is a cellular automaton that self-organises. However, we are so biased in our perception of what is living that we would probably not recognise an alien life form if we stepped on it! In essence life is something you can eat as nearly all living forms on this planet are a potential source of food for us! (Rietman, 1994: xv).

Q   How could something inside a computer ever be considered alive? Should not life be restricted to nature's domain? Can non-organic things really be alive?

A   It is hard to answer this question because (believe it or not) there is no reasonable definition of life. Maybe it is only by making life that we will finally know what life is. At present our best efforts are still somewhat primitive. Meanwhile the answer is yes, computer programs can live.

Q   How is it possible that a piece of software can constitute an AL form?

A   Ask any virus! Software creatures with a life of their own can be either helpful or harmful. They live, spread and breed by themselves; maybe it is a good job they exist only in a machine.

Q   Will some geographers find the concept of AL totally untenable on religious, philosophical or moral grounds?

A   Yes, but it is harmless fun really, although there could be more serious implications in the distant future.

Q   Is not killing a living organism a crime?

A   No, not in this context because the living creatures are not life as we know it and, therefore, no moral or ethical or criminal codes are applicable.

Q   But is it cruel, especially if "they" have done us a useful service?

A   No, not really, they are not alive in any biological sense. Also because we are "God", they can be re-created or reborn whenever we want them to be.

Q What is the difference between "top-down" and "bottom-up" approaches to AI?

A Top-down requires that the rules or algorithms defining intelligent behaviour or response are defined in advance. The unexpected or errors in the programming or knowledge base or heuristics cause failure. In bottom-up approaches, intelligence is acquired and learnt by experience. It is adaptive, flexible, error- and shock-tolerant technology. In general, if it can be done well, it is likely to be a much more profitable avenue of research.

Q Is AL the same as GA?

A No, they are similar but different. A GA is a clever search tool, that is all. It uses evolutionary principles to search for a solution but there is no notion that the bit strings have any intrinsic meaning as entities. In AL, GA principles can still be used but the bit strings are now assumed to have a meaning and a significance—GA is used to control the behaviour of the computer entities but they are in charge of themselves. The artificial creatures which the bit strings represent are instrumental to solving the problem. The original notion lying behind the space–time data explorer, i.e. STAC, was that of a ghost-like entity that attempted to encapsulate or capture "patterns" by enveloping them. Then we discovered AL!

Q Why are cellular automata (CA) regarded as a universal computer?

A A universal computer is a machine that given sufficient time could emulate any machine whose behaviour could be explicitly described. The Church–Turing hypothesis goes on to suggest that such a machine could not only duplicate the functions of mathematical machines but also the functions of nature (Levy, 1992: 24). The weakness here is the qualification "given sufficient time", as this conjecture may well only hold at some limit such as infinity! None the less it is an interesting idea. It has been demonstrated that certain CA also have the properties of a universal computer.

Q How is a CA a parallel computer?

A Each generation (or iteration) is a clock cycle. The updating of the cells proceeds concurrently and can be done in parallel. It is a rather abstract computer but it can be used to simulate the logic of a more conventional computer based on AND, OR and NOT gates. In CA the initial condition is the data input, the rules are the program and the final configuration is the computed result. By increasing the size of the CA and the number of states it can be shown that the CA is a universal computer.

Q What is the greatest strength and weakness of a CA?

A Its simplicity and flexibility is a major virtue. Also its properties as a universal computer are useful in a theoretical sense. As is its ability to represent emergent and bottom-up processes. Its weakness is the need to specify rules, their uniformity of application, the locality of their domain, and potentially the need for vast amounts of computation. If you don't know the rules then a CA is not useful.

Q What is worst aspect of AL?

A You get carried away doing endless computer simulations as you attempt to blindly develop either the necessary expertise or an AL formulation that does what you want it to do (and which you know it would do) in a particular application, if only you could get it "right". Artificial life based systems may well display endogenous levels of intelligence but it still has to be put there, humans have to create the basic building blocks. However, it is well worth while because of the nature of the final systems. The trick is to retain some energy and enthusiasm to be able to make good use of it after having built it.

Q   What is a Turing machine?

A   This is an imaginary automaton. It can be visualised as a sophisticated tape player that could play tapes of any length (i.e. a million miles long) for any time period (i.e. centuries) because it was purely a thought experiment, albeit a very important one (Dewdney, 1989). This idealised machine consisted of a tape as a memory plus a means of reading it. It cycled through a cycle of instructions of the form: read, consult program, change its state, write, move tape reader. Its importance is mainly because it is simpler to prove things about Turing machines than more complicated computers but it is possible to show that any computer is also a Turing machine.

Q   Why are Turing machines relevant to AL?

A   Turing machines have been shown to act as universal computers which can emulate the action of any computer program. They are simply describable and can produce extremely complex behaviour as they can emulate any kind of computation. As such they provide a useful model of the nervous system of AL creatures. In fact the Church–Turing hypothesis speculates that a universal computer could in theory from a logical perspective match the mental function of any living creature provided the tape was sufficiently long. The problem is deciding what program to use. Maybe they are a complication that we can manage without in geography.

Q   What is a geocyberspace?

A   A term coined by Openshaw (1994) to describe the totality of geographical information flows in the era of cyberspaces, internet and virtual reality. More explicitly an example would be a database with x, y coordinates, a time coordinate, and k measurements of some kind. Here there are three different data domains: geography space, time space, and attribute space all with potentially different measurement scales. It is impossible to directly visualise this multidimensional world except as two- or three-dimensional slices that grossly distort it. We know it exists but cannot see it in all its complexity. The hope is that AL will provide us with tools that see, sense, move around within the geocyberspace and then come back and tell us what they have found there in a two- (or three) dimensional form that geographers can comprehend.

Q   Is AL mainly of interest as a spatial analysis tool?

A   No. It can be used to model systems, the behaviour of objects, as well as serve an analysis function. The principal attraction is the high level of flexibility on offer and the power of an emergent paradigm. Also the scale of the activity can be varied from few to many. Here is a technology that could be used to model people or even individual grains of sand in a fluvial environment.

Q   What is the principal assumption?

A   That the complex observed behaviour of much of the real world is really a product of self-organising agents that each follow a small number of rules. The apparent complexity results from the dynamics of their interactions.

Q   What other types of AI also self-organise?

A   Neural networks are also a bottom-up paradigm in which the neurons self-organise to learn or perform a specific task. Genetic algorithms and genetic programming also function in a similar manner.

REFERENCES

Banks, R. 1971, *Information Processing and Transmission in Cellular Automata*. Technical Report MAC TR81, MIT.

Batty, M., Longley, P., 1994, *Fractal Cities*. Academic Press, New York.

Berlekamp, E.R., Conway, J.H., Guy, R.K., 1982, *Winning Ways for Your Mathematical Plays*. Vol. 2: *Games in Particular*. Academic Press, New York.

Bourgine, P., Vasela, F.J, 1992, "Towards a practice of autonomous systems", in F.T. Vasela, P. Bourgine (eds), *Towards a Practice of Autonomous Systems*, Proceedings of the First European Conference on Artificial Life. MIT Press, London.

Codd, E.F., 1968, *Cellular Automata*. Academic Press, New York.

Cohen, F.O., 1994, *It's Alive: the new breed of living computer programs*. Wiley, New York.

Couclelis, H., 1985, "Cellular worlds: a framework for modelling micro-macro dynamics", *Environment and Planning A*, **17**, 585–596.

Dewdney, A.K., 1989, *The Turing Omnibus*. Computer Science Press, Rockville.

Gardner, M., 1970, "Mathematical games: the fantastic combinations of John Conway's new solitaire game 'Life'", *Scientific American*, **223**, 120–123.

Gardner, M., 1971, "On cellular automata, self-reproduction, the Garden of Eden and the Game of Life", *Scientific American*, **224**, 112–117.

Gilbert, N., Conte, R. (eds) 1995, *Artificial Societies*. UCL Press, London.

Gilbert, G.N., Doran, J., 1994, *Simulating Societies: the computer simulation of social phenomena*. UCL Press, London.

Jefferson, D., Collins, R., Cooper, C., Dyer, M., Flowers, M., Korf, R., Taylor, C., Wang, A., 1992, "Evolution as a theme in artificial life: the Genesys/Tracker System", in C. Langton, C. Taylor, J.D. Farmer, S. Rasmussen (eds), *Artificial Life II*, Addison-Wesley, Redwood City, Calif., pp. 549–578.

Koza, J.R., 1992, *Genetic Programming*, MIT Press, Cambridge, MA.

Koza, J.R., 1994, *Genetic Programming* II. MIT Press, Cambridge, MA.

Langton, C.G., 1984, "Self-reproduction in cellular automata", *Physica*, **D**, 20 135–144.

Langton, C.G., 1986, "Studying artifical life with cellular automata", *Physica D*, **22**, 120–149.

Langton, C.G., 1989, "Artificial life", in C.G. Langton (ed.), *Artificial Life*. Addison-Wesley, Redwood City, Calif., pp. 1–47.

Langton, C.G., 1994, *Artificial Life III*. Addison-Wesley, Reading, Mass.

Langton, C.G., Taylor, C., Farmer, J.D., Rasmussen, S., 1992, *Artificial Life II*. Addison-Wesley, Reading, Mass.

Levy, S., 1992, *Artificial Life: the quest for a new creation*. Jonathan Cape, London.

Liepins, G.E., Vose, M.D., 1990, "Representational issues in genetic optimisation" *Journal of Experimental and Theoretical Artificial Intelligence*, **2**, 101–115.

Mitchell, M., Forrest, S., Holland, J.H., 1992, "The royal road for genetic algorithms: fitness landscapes and GA performance", in F.T. Vasela, P. Bourgine (eds), *Towards a Practice of Autonomous Systems*. MIT Press, London, pp. 245–254.

Moravec, H., 1988, *Mind Children: the future of robots and human intelligence*. Harvard University Press, Cambridge, Mass.

O'Hare, G., Jennings, N. (eds), 1995, *Foundations of Distributed AI*. Wiley InterScience, New York.

Openshaw, S., 1994, "Two exploratory space-time attribute pattern analysers relevant to GIS", in S. Fotheringham, P. Rogerson (eds), *GIS and Spatial Analysis*. Taylor and Francis, London, pp. 83–104.

Openshaw, S., 1995, "Developing automated and smart spatial pattern exploration tools for GIS applications", *The Statistician*, **44**, 3–16.

Openshaw, S., Cross, A., 1991, "Crime pattern analysis: the development of Arc/Crime", *Proceedings of AGI Annual Conference*, Birmingham.

Openshaw, S., Perrée, T., 1995, "Intelligent spatial analysis of point data", *Proceedings of the 50th Session of the International Statistical Institute*, Beijing, 797–815.

Openshaw, S., Perrée, T., 1996, "User-centred intelligent spatial analysis of point data", in P. Fisher (ed.), *Innovations in GIS3*, Taylor and Francis, London, pp. 113–129.

Packard, N., 1985, "Two-dimensional cellular automata", *Journal of Statistical Physics*, **38**, 901–946.

Poundstone, W., 1985, *The Recursive Universe: cosmic complexity and the limits of scientific knowledge*. Contemporary Books, Chicago.

Prata, S., 1993, *Artificial Life Playhouse: evolution at your fingertips*. Waite Group Press, Corte Madera, Calif.

Reynolds, C., 1987, "Flocks, herds and schools: a distributed behavioural model", *Computer Graphics*, **21**, 25–34.

Rietman, E., 1994, *Genesis Redux: experiments creating artificial life*. Windcrest, McGraw-Hill, New York.

Rucker, R., 1993, *Artificial Life Lab*. Waite Group Press, Corte Madera, Calif.

Sams Publishing, 1994, *Cyberlife*. Sams Publishing, Indianapolis.

Smiczek, D.S., 1993, *Neural Ned in NED's World*. Shareware.

Toffoli, T., Margolus, N., 1987, *Cellular Automata Machines*. MIT Press, Cambridge, Mass.

Ulam S., 1962, "On some mathematical problems connected with patterns of growth of figures", *Proceedings of Symposia of Applied Mathematics*, **14**, 215–224.

Von Neumann, J., 1966, *Theory of Self-reproducing Automata*. University of Illinois Press, Urbana.

Wuensche, A., Lesser, M., 1992, *The Gloal Dynamics of Cellular Automata*. Addison-Wesley, Reading, Mass.

Wolfram, S., 1983a, "Cellular automata", *Los Alamos Science*, **9**, 2–21.

Wolfram, S., 1983b, "Statistical mechanics of cellular automata", *Review of Modern Physics*, **55**, 601–644.

CHAPTER 9

Fuzzy Logic, Fuzzy Systems and Soft Computing

9.1 WHY IS IT IMPORTANT?

There is really no sound reason for leaving such an important AI technology to the end of the book other than the excuse that it is probably one of the newest and, perhaps, more important. It relates to several other AI technologies (neural networks and genetic algorithms) that need to be described in advance. Maybe the reader will think it so hard that last is best! On the contrary, there is an equally good case that could be made to start rather than finish here! Fuzzy systems thinking is at the cutting edge of practical AI technology today. Indeed there is probably no other AI technology that is not more widely used, yet as has been suggested earlier, there are few examples of it being applied in geography except in fairly trivial ways, for example in viewshed analysis (see Fisher, 1994) and in fuzzy decision-making in a spatial decision support context (see Leung and Leung, 1993a, b). These are applications that do not show fuzzy logic off to its best advantage as they are extremely complex and only give the scantiest of hints at its broader relevancy. It is a very strange state of affairs. If you are at all uncertain about fuzzy logic and whether it is worth investigating further, then the GIS based research simply does not help. Probably the best instant justification for believing that fuzzy logic might be useful can be found in the following two quotations. Von Altrock (1995: ix) writes: "In 1994, Japan exported products at a total of $35 billion that use fuzzy logic or Neurofuzzy." McNeill and Thro (1994: 16) continue this theme by pointing out that "Japan is spending $500 million a year on Fuzzy Systems R and D. And it's beginning to catch on in the United States, where it all began."

A more basic but just as tantalising academic reason is that fuzzy logic extends the domain of computers into areas that were previously considered to be exempt from computation. Perhaps the most concise justification for thinking that this is important is provided by Zadeh (1995: ix) when he writes, "If I were asked to describe as succinctly as possible what fuzzy logic offers in the realms of systems analysis and design, I would answer: a methodology for computing with words." The ability to develop soft computing applications that permit computer models to be specified and built from linguistic statements, based on common sense or theory or rules of thumb, is potentially extremely important. It also offers a refreshingly new perspective on how to go about building better models of geographical systems by handling rather than ignoring or artificially removing the fuzziness within them. Fuzzy logic is more than simply an AI tool but it is increasingly being viewed as an alternative paradigm for science, for modelling systems and for going about building more intelligent systems. What started as a very simple idea of seemingly limited interest or applicability is now increasingly being regarded as a really major advance relevant to an extremely large number of applications. A more AI-focused perspective would also emphasise the unique opportunities it provides for the incorporation of knowledge and other intangible human skills and intuition into computer systems to help them behave in more human and in thus more intelligent ways. A further view is that fuzzy logic injects a fresh impetus into expert systems by allowing them to operate and perform tasks in much more human-like ways.

The whole essence of AI is the development of intelligent technologies that represent knowledge in a manner analogous to the human being's style of information processing but putting it into a form suitable for computer processing. Fuzzy logic is an excellent means of accomplishing this task. It provides a means of translating natural language-based expressions of knowledge and common sense into a precise mathematical formalism or putting it another way, fuzzy logic is a revolutionary technology that gives computers the ability to think and make decisions more like human beings (McNeill and Freiberger, 1994). Undoubtedly over the next few years entire books will be dedicated to fuzzy systems modelling in geography. It has perhaps the greatest revolutionary potential since the quantitative revolution to change conventional thinking about the operation of human systems and how best to model them (Openshaw, 1996).

Zadeh argues that power of the human brain results in part from its ability to process very efficiently fuzzy and imprecise information; see Yager et al (1987). If he is right then this implies that faster and bigger computers will not help much because the hardware is simply not designed to handle fuzzy operations efficiently. He writes, "The human brain, in a way that we don't understand too well at present, uses fuzzy logic" (Zadeh, 1987: 21). To approximate the ways that humans can process vast amounts of information and come up with a qualitative conclusion, requires therefore fuzzy logic. That is to say, the key elements in human thinking are not numbers but labels of fuzzy sets that allow the fast and efficient processing of masses of information by associating vaguely similar patterns relevant to the task in hand. If this is indeed true then many of the attempts by the AI community to build thinking machines would seem to be doomed to fail unless they can incorporate and handle efficiently the inherent fuzziness of the task. The argument can be extended to become even more profound in that the more one thinks about imprecision and the need to model and represent it, the more the problems with the current mathematical approach and precise science seem to become apparent. There is seemingly an increasing need to come to terms with the pervasive imprecision of the real world. Slowly, perhaps grudgingly, it seems that thinking of the real world via fuzzy logic will become the dominant paradigm of science; particularly as the technology is developed that supports this way of thinking. What is needed is a significant shift, not just in attitude but in science (Kosko, 1994). Somehow it is important to recognise that being imprecise does not invalidate the science. It is important also to conquer the long standing and deeply rooted traditions that emphasise preciseness even in areas which are naturally imprecise. Such attitudes and beliefs are very profoundly held and will be slow to shift. It is not easy to accept that becoming less precise and less quantitative might actually be an advantage! However, there are several examples in the development of science where this is the case; fuzzy logic may seem to represent a retreat from science with its traditional emphasis on precision but in those areas where it is applicable it might well be the best form of science. Fuzzy sets are unique in that they make it possible to deal scientifically with subjectivity, a topic that science has traditionally attempted to exclude.

9.2 WHAT IS FUZZY LOGIC?

9.2.1 We live in a fuzzy world

In common with much of AI fuzzy logic is not a new idea. The basic concepts are at least 30 years old. The term "fuzzy" was first proposed by Zadeh (1962) when he discussed the need to develop a new paradigm for mathematics for the purpose of dealing with systems which are generally orders of magnitude more complex than man-made systems. He wrote, "we need a radically different kind of mathematics, the mathematics of fuzzy or cloudy quantities which are not describable in terms of probability distributions'. Three years later Zadeh published his new paradigm; see Zadeh (1965). Much of the early work was dominated by attempts to build a basic and rigorously defined theoretical foundation using lots of complex mathematics. However, in parallel the first practical applications were taking place in control engineering. The rationale for much of this work is Zadeh (1971, 1974). One of the first well-publicised applications that demonstrated the practical benefits of fuzzy logic was Mamdani and Assilian (1975). They showed how a small number of fuzzy IF–THEN rules could be used to control a laboratory steam engine, and that this approach actually outperformed more conventional methods. The basic idea was to incorporate the experience of a skilled human steam engine operator into a computer-based control algorithm based on a set of linguistic rules based on various rules of thumb. The great benefits of this method were its simplicity, its use of knowledge and better still there was no need for a model of the process. The first commercial application was a fuzzy controller developed for a cement kiln in 1975 (Holmblad and Ostergaard, 1981, 1982). Again fuzzy logic was critical because it provided a practical way to make a mathematical model of a skilled kiln operator based on a small number of IF–THEN rules.

The principles of the fuzzy logic controller subsequently spread rapidly via widely read books on the subject (Gupta and Sanchez, 1982; Sugeno, 1985; Terano et al, 1989). Other much publicised applications of fuzzy logic control occurred in Japan, one example being in a water treatment plant and particularly in the Sendai subway which opened in 1987 (Yasunobu and Miyamoto, 1985). However, it is really only since the mid 1980s that fuzzy logic linked to computational methods has succeeded in transforming basic mathematical concepts of fuzzy sets and fuzzy inference into a practically useful and widely applicable technology. This transformation was very rapid with over 400 papers being written on fuzzy logic applications by the late 1980s. The principal attraction was the realisation that due to incomplete knowledge and information, precise mathematics are not always sufficient to model adequately the behaviour of complex systems. In a control engineering context it suddenly became possible in the late 1980s to build microcontrollers that incorporated expert knowledge and human intuition. They were also cheaper to implement and more intelligent in their behaviour than more traditional control theory based approaches. There are numerous potential applications in industrial automation, process control and consumer products, particularly as the new technology was simple enough to incorporate into the microprocessor hardware available at that time. Intelligent control systems incorporating fuzzy logic are being embedded in a vast and increasing number of domestic and industrial products. However, the potential applications go far beyond the design of intelligent controllers and are applicable to many data analysis, decision-making and modelling problems relevant to geography.

9.2.2 So what is fuzzy set theory?

Fuzzy in this context has nothing to do with being confused, it is not that kind of fuzziness. It is all about moving beyond and away from crisp logic. Computers are based on crisp binary 0–1 logic. Many cricketers experience fuzziness in umpires' decision-making every time they play. The authors remember a colleague when asked if the batsman was leg before wicket replied, "nearly", which is a fuzzy response to a decision which has to be crisp (viz. either *yes* or *no*). Maybe McNeill and Thro (1994: 3–7) explain it better as follows. Imagine a bowl of fruit that contains either apples or oranges. If it contains 10 apples and 0 oranges and you ask the question "Is it a bowl of oranges?" then the answer is no. If there are 0 apples and 10 oranges then the answer is yes, it is a bowl of oranges. Suppose one orange is replaced by an apple, is it still a bowl of oranges? The answer is yes. Suppose another orange is replaced by an apple, is it still a bowl of oranges? The answer is yes. Suppose the process continues, at what point does the bowl cease to be a bowl of oranges? You cannot dodge the question by asking for more information because it is all there. It is just that there comes a point when the yes or no decision is quite inappropriate and would be far less precise than if you answered along the lines of "partly a bowl of oranges" or "mostly"; all of which

Table 9.1   A fuzzy fruit bowl

		Is it a bowl of oranges?	
Number of oranges	Number of apples	Crisp logic response	Fuzzy logic response
10	0	Yes	Yes
9	1	Yes*	Predominantly
8	2	Yes*	Largely
7	3	Yes*	Mostly
6	4	Yes*	Just about
5	5	Yes and No?	Sort of
4	6	No	Somewhat
3	7	No*	Slightly
2	8	No*	Scarcely
1	9	No*	Hardly
0	10	No	No

* Implies a subjective judgement about what percentage of fruit in a bowl should be oranges before it can be classed as a bowl of oranges.

are fuzzy answers that lie somewhere between the crisp extremes of yes and no. Table 9.1 illustrates this problem. The restrictions of attempting to handle this problem via two-valued logic should be readily apparent. It also creates many paradoxes where the answer to a question can be both true and false; for example, when the bowl of oranges is exactly half full of apples. Another example is in Kosko (1994). He asks "Does the liar from Crete lie when he claims that all Cretans are liars?" Equally, when does a litre glass of beer become empty? Is it full when there is 0.5 litre left? If yes, remove 10 millilitres, is it still full? If yes, continue until it is empty! But at which point did the level of liquid switch from being full to empty? Of course, the transition is gradual yet quite often we are forced to pretend it is not. It is this problem that fuzzy sets and fuzzy logic seek to address.

Other ambiguities are also possible; for instance if an orange was coated in apple candy is it still an orange? The real answer is "maybe"! With fuzzy logic the whole idea is to escape from the artificialness of two-valued crisp logic and to think in terms of outcomes that can range anywhere between 0 (definitely no) to 1 (definitely yes). A key feature is the use of words rather than numbers to describe the intermediate states, as in Table 9.1 with words such as "predominantly" being used to characterise a bowl that is 90% full of oranges. A fuzzy logic approach allows the quantification of concepts that have no clearly defined boundaries. Linguistic statements that express ideas, intuition, knowledge, feelings, rules of thumb and vague theories are often capable of being interpreted differently by different people because they involve fuzzy propositions. Somehow humans can cope and communicate despite the vagueness and imprecision in the language they use. Indeed language is naturally fuzzy because of the regular use of vague and imprecise terms. Fuzzy sets and fuzzy logic at last provide a computer technology that can cope with the imprecision in a manner akin to that of human beings. This change seems trivial and obvious but crisp logic is deeply ingrained in people's belief systems and cultures. What is surprising is that this crisp approach ever came to be so dominant because if you look at how humans make decisions, fuzziness is clearly the norm. Indeed the more speedy acceptance of fuzzy logic in Japan and China compared with most Western cultures has been attributed to the latter's greater sensitivity to vagueness partly as a result of their philosophical traditions and partly because there is no Aristotelian paradigm to overturn (McNeill and Freiberger, 1994: 135). This may well explain how a technology that was invented and developed in the USA was subjected to years of criticism and misunderstanding at the same time as it was being used in the Far East in a bewildering range of consumer products.

Before Zadeh, a number of other thinkers had toyed with the idea of a logic of vagueness. Lukasiewicz in the 1920s developed multi-valued logic with an infinity of values between 0 and 1 (Lukasiewicz, 1970). The next development occurred in 1937 with Black's general theory of vagueness (Black, 1937). However, it was left to Zadeh (1965) to assemble the parts of the puzzle and put it all together on a sound and rigorous mathematical basis. Zadeh successfully combined the concepts of crisp logic and the Lukasiewicz notion of sets by defining grades of membership. This can be clearly seen in Table 9.2 where the fuzzy results of Table 9.1 are re-expressed in terms of grades of membership. A set (the bowl of oranges) can have members who belong to it partly, in varying degrees. As humans we have little apparent difficulty in knowing when a bowl of oranges is a complete or partial bowl of oranges, or is something else. Fuzzy logic provides a means of handling vague concepts defined by language or words in a mathematical manner, and as such it provides a much better basis for building models of complex systems.

Fuzzy set theory was developed to handle problems that have no sharp boundaries or situations in which events are fuzzily defined. For example, the statement "it is a warm day" or "x is about equal to 9" or a colour that may be quite naturally defined as either being red, slightly red or reddish. It is no longer possible to represent this colour by a simple probability of it being red, since there is no longer any clear or well-defined or crisp boundaries that the probability can represent. In classical two-value systems all classes are assumed to have tightly defined boundaries so that an object can be identified as either being a member of a particular class or not. However, most of the classes found in the real world do not have sharp boundaries. For example, consider how you might represent in two-valued or yes–no logic categories such as "beautiful women" or "tall men" or "good value" versus "bad value". It is clear then that simple probability cannot model all the possible problems of incompleteness. One solution is to generalise two-value logic into multi-valued logic, for example, so that grades of member-ship of beauty become a matter of degree. For instance, this person registers 0.75 on the beauty scale on the continuum from 0 to 1.0. However, fuzzy logic goes beyond multi-valued logic. It takes the concept of beauty and breaks it into subsets of ugly, plain, beautiful, etc. Any person can belong simultaneously to one

Table 9.2 Fuzzy fruit bowl grades of membership

Number of		Is it a bowl of oranges?	
Oranges	Apples	Crisp	Fuzzy
10	0	1	1.0
9	1	1	0.9
8	2	1	0.8
7	3	1	0.7
6	4	1	0.6
5	5	1	0.5
4	6	0	0.4
3	7	0	0.3
2	8	0	0.2
1	9	0	0.1
0	10	0	0.0

or more of these fuzzy sets with grades of membership (viz.) probabilities that range from 0 to 1.

Consider another classical example. What is meant by tall men? If Peter is 5 ft 10 in. does he belong to the set labelled tall men? In crisp set theory it is necessary to select an arbitrary cut-off point, at say 6 ft. So everyone over the height of 6 ft is tall. The membership graph for this set is shown in Figure 9.1; there is a sudden jump at the 6 ft boundary. So Peter is not tall. Even Paul at 5 ft 11.999 in. is not tall, but John who is 1/1000th of an inch taller at 6 ft is regarded as tall. Clearly this crisp representation only really works for non-continuous phenomena that are lumpy in a meaningful way. It is both artificial and misleading.

The fuzzy set approach is to regard the membership function of the tall set as being a gradation between definitely not tall to definitely tall. No one would regard Maureen at 4 ft 6 in. as being tall but some might think that anyone taller than this might be considerably a little bit tall whilst anyone 6 ft 6 in. would definitely be very tall. Figure 9.2 shows how this membership function might be characterised. So someone like Peter at 5 ft 10 in. would have a degree of membership of 0.8, whilst John and Paul would be even higher. If a person's height is less than 4 ft 6 in. then the membership is zero, whilst for those above 6 ft 6 in. it is 1.0. Kosko (1994: 146) writes, "Part of the power of the fuzzy curves comes from how silly it makes non fuzzy sets look." Tall men are either tall or not, but tallness is really a matter of degree. Given that the maths involved was not new, it is amazing that it took so long for fuzzy logic to assert itself.

It is very easy to extend the concept of fuzzy sets to all manner of phenomena which are expressed quite naturally in common usage in a vague way; for example, temperatures such as cold, warm and hot can be readily represented as fuzzy sets; see Figure 9.3. Any temperature between 0 and 40 °C can now be given truth values as members of the cold, warm and hot fuzzy sets. These concepts can

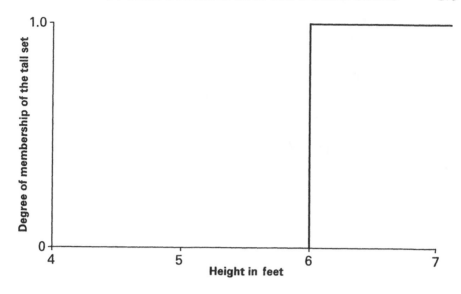

Figure 9.1   Membership of the crisp tall set

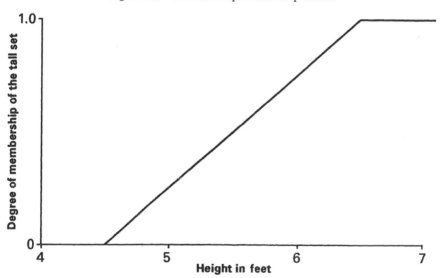

Figure 9.2   Membership of the fuzzy tall set

be readily extended, for example, the statement "the temperature will be around 20 today" can be cast in the same sort of fuzzy set framework; see Figure 9.4. Their membership functions, their shape and domains are, of course, subjective but this is a different operational issue. The more important point is that the linguistic concepts such as tall, hot and around 20 are being cast into a form that can be

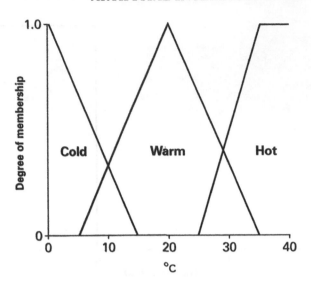

Figure 9.3   Cold, warm and hot as fuzzy sets

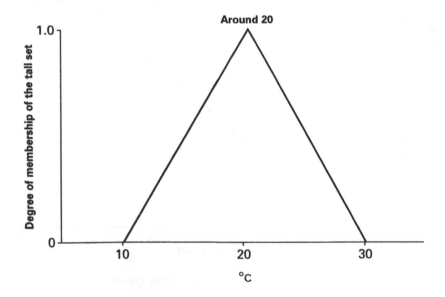

Figure 9.4   The fuzzy set for around 20°C

represented in computer software for which there is also a rigorous mathematical basis for handling the varying degrees of imprecision that is involved.

In short all numbers are potentially fuzzy. A non-fuzzy zero is zero! Its membership function is a spike; see Figure 9.5. A number is either zero or not

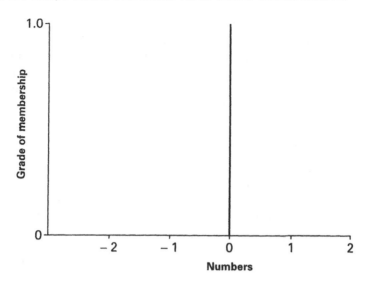

Figure 9.5   A non-fuzzy zero

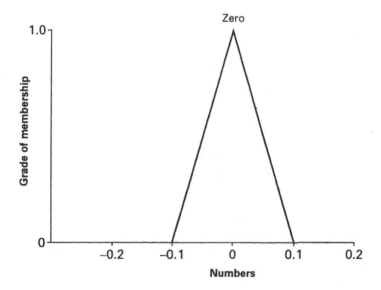

Figure 9.6   A fuzzy zero

zero. But what about numbers close to zero or almost zero or near zero or approximately zero? The number 1 is nearer to zero than 27, 12 is nearer than 6 million so the fuzzy zero might be represented as in Figure 9.6. It could also be represented by a bell-shaped (i.e. normal distribution) curve centred on zero with a specified standard deviation but this is really representing statistical uncertainty which is different (because it is far more precise) from linguistic uncertainty. If the triangle is drawn sufficiently narrow the fuzzy zero becomes a crisp zero. This illustrates another nice property of fuzzy sets. They incorporate crisp logic as special cases where there is no imprecision. As a result it provides an all-embracing framework that keeps what we already have but significantly extends and adds flexibility to it.

9.2.3 Fuzziness versus probability

In essence fuzziness is being presented as an alternative to randomness as a basis for describing uncertainty, but is uncertainty the same as randomness (Kosko, 1990)? Kosko (1992a: 264) writes, "If we are not sure about something, is it only up to chance? Do the notions of likelihood and probability exhaust our notions of uncertainty?" Seemingly many statisticians believe so, particularly the Bayesianists. Others argue that fuzzy logic is really based on very fuzzy thinking and the problems it claims to handle are better solved using more traditional methods of logic and probability. Others are concerned that a focus on fuzziness represents a retreat from a scientific to an essentially non-scientific approach. McNeill and Freiberger (1994: 58) write, "Probability is today the great rival of fuzzy logic, and its champions claim it surpasses fuzzy logic in any task one can devise." The existence of such fairly inflexible and entrenched views partly explains why there has been so much opposition to fuzzy logic, particularly in the USA. However, as von Altrock (1995: 4) notes: "If you have a hammer in your hand, and it's your only tool, then suddenly everything looks like a nail!" The key point here is that randomness (from a probability perspective) and fuzziness are different things both conceptually and theoretically. Fuzzy set theory is not just another form of probability but is really representing a different type of uncertainty. Kosko (1992a: 265) explains it like this: "Fuzziness describes event ambiguity. It measures the degree to which an event occurs, not whether an event occurs. Randomness describes the uncertainty of event occurrence. An event occurs or not, and you can bet on it. The issue concerns the occurring event: Is it uncertain in any way.... Whether an event occurs is 'random'. To what degree it occurs is fuzzy." Fuzziness describes, therefore, the **degree to which an event occurs, not just the probability that it occurs**. Probability deals with yes/no occurrences, it requires ignorance, and is statistical in nature. Fuzziness deals with degrees of occurrence, it does not require ignorance, and is completely non-statistical.

For example, there may be a 20% chance of light rain tomorrow, this is an example of a probability. Whether light rain will occur has a probability of 0.2, but the fuzziness here concerns the ambiguous nature of the expected event, viz. light rain. Whether the event occurs is the domain of probability but the degree to which it occurs is the domain of fuzzy logic. Of course the two can be combined so that there is a 0.2 probability of a fuzzy event labelled light rain occurring. Maybe the statisticians just do not like, or do not see any need for, their probability-based world being embedded in a broader all-containing framework. Unlike fuzziness, probability dissipates with increasing information. So when tomorrow comes it is possible to remove all uncertainty as to whether it rained or not, but the ambiguity about the nature of the event (viz. was it light rain) remains. The fuzziness is still there and has not been removed or diminished by complete information. This may at first appear confusing but the curtains soon lift and the attractions of fuzziness could soon become an obsession. Scientists seem to have overlooked an entire mode of reality.

Consider a final example used by Kosko (1992a). If you ask the question "Is there an apple in the refrigerator?" the answer will be a probability; for example $p = 0.5$, an estimate that can be derived using a frequentist approach or a Bayesian state of knowledge strategy. Now suppose we know that there is a half-eaten apple festering in the fridge. If you ask, "To what degree is there an apple in there?" then this is a fuzzy question, even if on this occasion it is still 0.5. Unlike fuzziness, probability dissipates with increasing information as uncertainty is reduced. Open the fridge door and the probability of there being an apple inside vanishes. It only existed because of ignorance about the contents of the fridge. However, the fuzziness remains; a half-eaten apple is not a complete apple but has a grade of membership of belonging to the set of apples. Fuzziness can coexist with complete information. Uncertainty is not purely due to randomness, or as Kosko (1992a: 267) puts it, "This silent assumption of universal non-ambiguity resembles the pre-realistic assumption of an uncurved universe," although it is doubtful whether many geographers would know what this meant! Nevertheless the point being made here is that fuzziness is a genuine type of uncertainty that deals with event ambiguity. If events are assumed to be unambiguous then there is no fuzziness and only randomness remains, because any event ambiguity (viz. uncertainty as to the nature of the event) has been assumed away. The problem is that the real world is dominated by humans who communicate via an imprecise language and who have created elaborate social and economic systems that operate in an extremely fuzzy way. If AI is to provide tools for modelling these human systems or for mimicking their behaviour or for copying their knowledge bases, then the tools have to be able to cope with the fuzziness that exists everywhere within it.

9.3 BUILDING A FUZZY SYSTEMS MODEL

9.3.1 When might this be useful?

Kosko (1992b) and Buckley and Hayashi (1993) demonstrate that a fuzzy system is in theory able to approximate to any arbitrary level of precision any continuous linear or nonlinear function. This implies that fuzzy systems and neural networks can approximate each other which leads to a symbiotic relationship. Klir and Yuan (1995: 355) write, "fuzzy systems provide a powerful framework for knowledge representation, while neural networks provide learning capabilities and exceptional suitability for computationally efficient hardware implementations". Maybe one interesting prospect is to start by building a fuzzy logic model (for its ease of interpretation and ready incorporation of knowledge) and then implement it as a neural network. The most important point to note here is that a fuzzy logic model has similar capabilities to a neural network in terms of being a universal approximator that can model sampled functions and behaves as an associative memory, viz. these inputs are associated with those outputs. Both technologies are model-free estimators but they differ mainly in how they estimate the sampled functions; the fuzzy systems approach is much simpler, more easily explained and understood. It may appear strange to discuss the use of fuzzy systems as a modelling tool since nearly all applications have been in the area of engineering control; however, it is important to recognise that a fuzzy controller is also a fuzzy systems model (Cox, 1994: 380). Fuzzy systems modelling is, therefore, directly applicable as an alternative modelling paradigm which is valid for urban and regional modelling as well as many other statistical modelling applications in the social sciences. It would appear to be most useful whenever a powerful model-free universal approximator is needed that is capable of a plain English description. Unlike all other statistical and mathematical models, a fuzzy logic model can be given a non-numeric description. In theory this should produce models that are easier to understand once the readers see through the veneer of apparent complexity that disguises the essential simplicity of fuzzy logic. There is also a large fuzzy control literature and set of tools that can be readily imported and used on geographical problems.

In essence a simple fuzzy model is little more than a series of IF–THEN rules that when processed as fuzzy sets connect (or map or transform) a set of inputs to a set of outputs in a nonlinear and non-parametric way. It is a means of giving computers the capability of reasoning with fuzzy numbers in the form of rules of thumb of the type: "if the car goes too fast then apply the brake a little". The knowledge or intelligence comes from associating the two fuzzy events, in this example the speed of the car and the brake pressure. The rules reflect any knowledge you have about the system being modelled. For example, a simple linear relationship between two variables X_1, X_2 and Y can be represented as follows:

Rule 1   If X_1 is **small** and X_2 is **small** then Y is **small**;
Rule 2   If X_1 is **big** and X_2 is **big** then Y is **big**;
Rule 3   If X_1 is **average** and X_2 is **average** then Y is **average**.

Note that these variables have three fuzzy sets that describe their magnitudes. They are given the descriptive but subjective linguistic labels: **small, average** and **big.** They could have quite different numeric value ranges assigned to them. Nevertheless, these three rules constitute a fuzzy model that relates fuzzy values of a variable called X_1 and another called X_2 to a fuzzy output variable called Y. The benefits from this modelling approach depend on the usefulness of rules that are used. Note also that no statistical estimation is involved and that these rules can also be used to represent a non-linear relationship; for example,

Rule 1 If X_1 is **small** and X_2 is **small** then Y is **big**;
Rule 2 If X_1 is **big** and X_2 is **big** then Y is **big**;
Rule 3 If X_1 is **average** and X_2 is **average** then Y is **small**.

This would approximate a U-shaped curve but without having to be precise about the parameters of the parabolic function that a conventional mathematical model would require. So this rule-based fuzzy modelling offers the user considerable flexibility. These fuzzy models behave in a very smooth way; for instance as X_1 increases a little so would Y. It is not lumpy as it would be if the IF rules were Boolean; for instance,

$$\text{if } X_1 = 6.0 \quad \text{then } Y = 4.2$$

is a very crisp and non-fuzzy rule. Fuzzy logic modelling provides a very sophisticated nonlinear modelling capability.

So what types of system may benefit from fuzzy modelling? McNeill and Thro (1994: 15–16) identify five types of systems where adopting a fuzzy approach may be necessary or beneficial:

1. Complex systems that are difficult or impossible to model by any other means especially if they have no firm mathematical basis;
2. Systems controlled by human experts which the computer model is supposed to emulate;
3. Systems with complex and continuous inputs and outputs that behave in a nonlinear way which is not well understood;
4. Systems that have human skills as inputs as the basis for rules, or which seek to use common sense and intuition as the basis for a model; and
5. Systems that are naturally vague, such as those in the behavioural and social sciences, for which the underlying mechanisms are neither known nor static.

To this list can be added:

6. Systems for which there is a wealth of descriptive and theoretical knowledge expressed in a linguistic form from which it is desired to build computer models but without being restricted by the need to provide precise statistical or mathematical model specifications; and
7. Systems for which there is little or no training data on which to estimate anything but there is sufficient knowledge to specify a linguistic model that is to be used to make predictions.

It is argued that one of the outstanding attractions of fuzzy logic modelling is that it provides a means by which soft human geography can be put back on to a more rigorous scientific footing but without having to force it into an inappropriate normal science paradigm (Openshaw, 1996).

Building a fuzzy systems model is in principle straightforward and can be divided into a number of simple steps.

Step 1   Specify the nature of the system to be modelled

This is the hardest part. You need to express in linguistic terms a model specification. This linguistic description of the system of interest encompasses your knowledge, intuition, gut feelings, theory and qualitative understanding about how the system of interest operates.

Consider an example involving a simple one origin distance decay and gravity model. Geographers have for a long time known that in general, as a rule of thumb, few trips (whether for work or pleasure) cover long distances and most only go short distances. In other words, the number of trips diminishes rapidly with distance. This is a linguistic description of a mathematical distance decay model that might be expressed as

$$T_j = b_1 + b_2 \log C_j \tag{9.1}$$

where T_j is the predicted number of trips going to any destination j from a particular origin, c_j the distance travelled and b_1, b_2 are parameters to be estimated such that the predicted T_j values match as best as possible the observed data.

A more sophisticated version of this simple distance decay model seeks to operationalise the notion that the intensity of the distance decay effect can be moderated by the size of the destination zone. Whilst most trips only cover short distances some might involve long distances if the destination zone is large or highly attractive. A statistical modeller could express this notion as an equation that includes a destination zone size term

$$T_j = b_1 + b_2 \log C_j + b_3 D_j \tag{9.2}$$

where T_j is the predicted number of trips ending at destination j, c_j is the distance travelled in order to reach destination j, D_j is the size of destination zone j and b_1, b_2, b_3 are parameters estimated to minimise the errors between the observed and predicted values for T_j.

A mathematically minded modeller might use an entropy-maximisation technique to derive a more theoretically rigorous basis for this model to yield in the following simple model:

$$T_j = D_j \exp(-b_1 C_j) A \tag{9.3}$$

where

$$A = O_1/\sum_j D_j \exp (b_1 C_j) \qquad (9.4)$$

where A is a balancing factor to ensure that all trips leaving the origin zone are accounted for, O_1 is the total number of trips to be allocated by the model and b_i would be estimated to ensure that

$$\sum_j T_j \text{ (observed)} C_j = \sum_j T_j \text{ (predicted)} C_j \qquad (9.5)$$

By contrast, the fuzzy modeller would return to the basic soft ideas that underlie both the distance decay and gravity models. There is no need to be precise about the mathematical specification and this is a tremendous advantage. The distance decay model can be expressed linguistically that most trips involve short distances and the gravity model that most trips involve short distances unless the destination zone is large. So why might a linguistic version of this model be useful? Quite often it is impossible to develop a soundly based mathematical model whilst a linguistic statement of some theory or idea may be available. Furthermore, even when a mathematical model exists it is often a poor representation of the underlying concepts inherent in the linguistic version of the model. So a fuzzy model might still provide a better basis for modelling because it may more faithfully represent the purpose underlying the model, despite its apparent imprecision. Indeed there are many instances in geography where the natural language version of a concept is seemingly much better and sometimes quite different from the much more precise and explicit statistical or mathematical versions that are partial in what they can represent and are assumption dependent. For example, it is one thing to state that trip intensity decays with distance but it is quite another to claim that it follows a negative exponential function of some kind. The fuzzy logic model operationalises the original vaguer and function-free approach and because of this imprecision it may actually be simultaneously more useful and easier to comprehend.

Step 2   Identify and label the set membership functions for each input variable

The input now needs to be given a fuzzy representation with the observed numeric data being represented by membership functions. The only rules here are that the membership functions for the same variable should overlap and it can be observed that many applications have 3, 5, or 7 fuzzy subsets for each variable.

In the distance decay model there is only one input variable (C_j). This is represented as shown in Figure 9.7 by five subsets with the following names, values and shapes: for distances 0–15 the set label is zero (Z) and it is represented

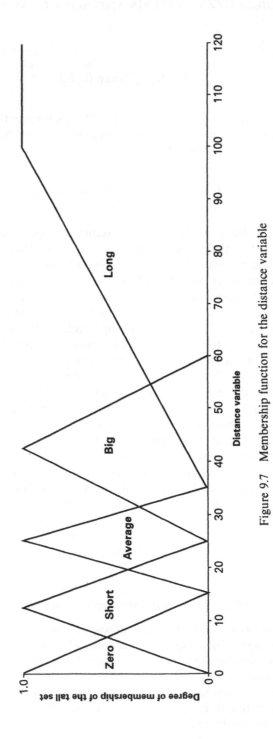

Figure 9.7 Membership function for the distance variable

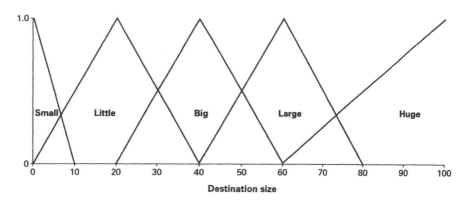

Figure 9.8   Membership function for the destination size

as it is a downward-sloping line, for distances 0–25 it is labelled short (S) and is given a triangular shape, for distances 15–35 it is labelled average (A) and it is also triangular in shape, for distances 25–60 likewise but the label is big (B), and finally for distances 35–100 the label is long (L) and the membership function is an upward-sloping line. In case you are wondering how these particular membership functions were selected, then they are subjective. It was thought useful that they should overlap as it is intended that they capture the imprecision in the definitions of the meaning of the words zero, short, average, big and long. If all this seems highly arbitrary then do not worry, it is meant to be! You are supposed to know on the basis of knowledge, experience, intuition, skills as a geographer, etc. what may be suitable values to either use or start with as a first approximation to be adjusted later. If you do not know then a quick histogram of the values followed by a little common sense may well help. Note also that the labels used do not affect the performance of the model, merely your attempts to understand it later! For example zero could have been relabelled as very short.

For the gravity model it is also necessary to produce membership functions for the D_j variable. Again five membership functions are used with the same shapes as for the C_j variable but different values and labels. They are: 0–10 is small (S), 0–40 is little (L), 20–60 is big (R), 40–80 is large (L), 60–100 is huge (H); see Figure 9.8.

Figure 9.9 shows some of the shapes of membership functions that are sometimes used. In addition to these standard shapes you can estimate their shapes by reference to survey data (if appropriate). Usually a standard shape is used but only because it tends to be convenient. In a modelling context choice of shape for the membership functions is probably less critical than the numeric values used to define the membership functions.

Step 3   Identify and label membership functions for the fuzzy outputs

The output from the fuzzy model is in the form of fuzzy sets which also require membership functions. These need to be realistically scaled.

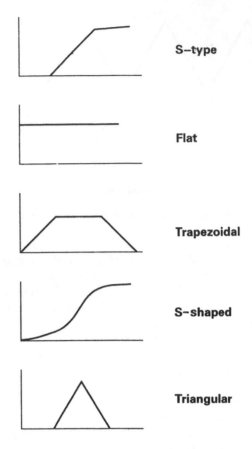

Figure 9.9   Some typical membership functions

Here the model is attempting to predict the magnitude of the trips. Again for simplicity five memberships functions are used with the same shapes as before; well why not! They are shown in Figure 9.10. The labels and ranges are as follows: 0–25 trips are labelled as none (N), 0–10 as some (S), 5–35 as big (B), 20–60 as lots (L) and 35–100 as massive (M).

There could be more or fewer membership functions. In an engineering context the numbers 3, 5, 7, 9 and 11 are often found. It depends on the level of accuracy required. This task is not so easy because the number ranges associated with the membership functions of the output sets determine the numerical outputs generated by the model. Some careful thought is needed here and perhaps some experimentation will help. Alternatively you could revisit these decisions later when evaluating model performance and when wondering what to do to improve it. Experience also seems to suggest that for triangular-shaped sets the overlap should be between 25 and 50% depending on the intrinsic degree of imprecision associated with the two neighbouring states.

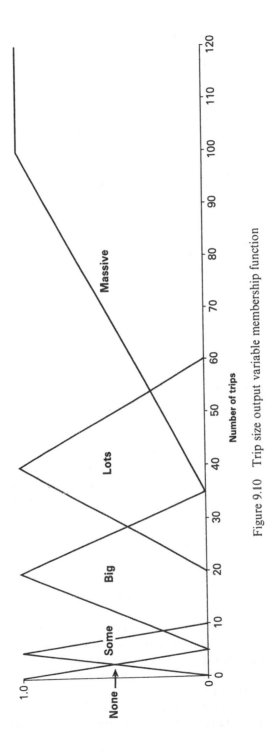

Figure 9.10   Trip size output variable membership function

Table 9.3   A FAM for a pure distance
decay model

Input distance membership set	Output fuzzy trip membership set
Zero (Z)	Massive (M)
Short (S)	Lots (L)
Average (A)	Big (B)
Big (B)	Some (S)
Long (L)	None (N)

Step 4   Creating the rules

The heart of the fuzzy model is a series of IF–THEN rules that connect one or more fuzzy input membership sets to a fuzzy output membership set.

Consider the spatial interaction model example, if a pure distance decay model is desired then the following five rules may suffice:

if distance is **ZERO** then the interaction intensity is **MASSIVE**
if distance is **SHORT** then the interaction intensity is **LOTS**
if distance is **AVERAGE** then the interaction intensity is **BIG**
if distance is **BIG** then the interaction intensity is **SOME**
if distance is **LONG** then the interaction intensity is **NONE**

This can be expressed as a table of fuzzy model rules or perhaps slightly confusingly as a fuzzy associative memory (FAM) (see Table 9.3). A FAM is a transformation that maps fuzzy input sets on to fuzzy output sets. Note that in this distance decay model there is only one input variable and this makes it very simple to grasp what is happening. The term FAM is borrowed from neural networks where an associative memory maps a set of inputs on to outputs. But why is this useful? Why not simply use crisp, numerically precise, IF–THEN conditions? The answer is obvious in that we lack sufficient knowledge to know precisely what numbers to use and if we did then it would merely make the model extremely cumbersome. Additionally, the underlying theory is linguistic and vague, therefore exact numerical definitions for the terms do not exist nor can they. For example, what constitutes a short distance or high interaction intensity is a matter of opinion. If models of this simple linguistic type can be made to work then this significantly extends what can be modelled. At the same time, it greatly eases the modeller's task because no mathematical or statistical knowledge is involved in the modelling process.

A more ambitious gravity model set of IF–THEN rules also needs to take into account the effects of size of destination zone which in a spatial interaction model

Table 9.4 A FAM for the gravity model

Input destination size membership set	Input distance membership set				
	Zero	Short	Average	Big	Long
Small	Some	Some	None	None	None
Little	Big	Some	Some	None	None
Big	Lots	Big	Some	None	None
Large	Massive	Lots	Big	Some	Some
Huge	Massive	Massive	Big	Big	Some

context may moderate the pure distance decay effects somewhat. For example, three of these rules are:

if distance is **SHORT** and destination size is **HUGE** then interaction intensity is **MASSIVE**

if distance is **BIG** and destination size is **HUGE** then interaction intensity is **BIG**

if distance is **LONG** and destination size is **SMALL** then interaction intensity is **NONE**

The underlying assumption here is that large nearby destinations will attract large numbers of trips but smaller ones will still be attractive although much less so. In addition a big long-distance destination may attract lots of trips if the destination size is sufficiently large. This sort of gravity model-type of thinking produces a complete FAM which is shown in Table 9.4. These fuzzy rules determine how the model operates. It may not be necessary to fill all the boxes in the FAM but it usually helps to do so, if only for sake of completeness. The rules are fuzzy because the input variables may each belong to more than one fuzzy membership set and they have degrees of membership associated with them.

Clearly performance of the resulting model depends on both the nature and shape of the membership functions and the content of the FAM. It also requires that the data are suitably scaled given the definition of the membership functions. One very appealing feature of this fuzzy spatial interaction model is that different theories of spatial interaction can be tested by changing the FAM composition. Likewise, it is not difficult to develop FAMs based on more than two input variables, although populating them with rules can rapidly become very tedious. Nevertheless, it is quite clear that FAMs provide a new approach to model representation and one that can be based on soft knowledge rather than solely on mathematical theory and statistical technology. However, if you lack this knowledge then maybe it can be developed for you in **step 9**. The rules can also be deterministic; for example, rule 1 might state that few trips go long distances—other conditional rules then modify this rule. Equally, Boolean rules can be mixed with fuzzy ones although care needs to be taken to ensure that the Boolean rules do not pre-empt all the fuzzy ones; see Cox (1994).

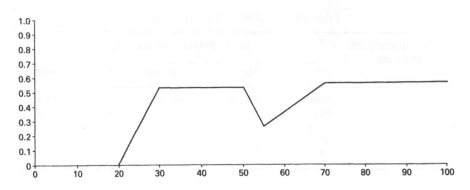

Figure 9.11   Fuzzy output membership function for the distance decay model for a distance value of 7

Step 5   *Apply the model*

The fuzzy rules or FAM define how the input(s) are converted into fuzzy output set membership probabilities. This is achieved by applying a fuzzy logic (or reasoning) process to the fuzzy rules.

In the case of the distance decay model it is very straightforward as the following numerical example shows. For an input distance value of 7 this value lies in the input set ZERO distance set to the degree of 0.53 and also in the SHORT distance category to the degree of 0.56. So two rules in the FAM are applicable to it . This output partly belongs to the MASSIVE trip output set and partly to the LOTS trip set. The corresponding membership functions for these two output sets are truncated at values of 0.53 and 0.56 respectively; see Figure 9.11. This fuzzy output membership set would then be defuzzified in **step 6** to yield a fuzzy model crisp value of 62; or in other words for a distance of 7 units the model predicts 62 trips.

The gravity model is a little more complicated as there are 2 input variables and instead of 5 rules there are now 25 rules to evaluate. Additionally, the fuzzy logic reasoning process needs to take into account the AND part of the rules and infer the output contributed by each rule. The AND part is handled by a conjunction operator which in practice is a MIN–MAX method of fuzzy inference. If a rule fires then the output membership grade is the minimum of the two-input variables membership values. For example, consider the data for the values of distance of 7 destination size of 32.5. According to the FAM in Table 9.4 the following rules apply:

1. Destination size is **LITTLE** and distance is **ZERO** then trips are **BIG** with a membership grade of 0.37;
2. Destination size is **LITTLE** and distance is **SHORT** then trips are **SOME** with a membership grade of 0.37;

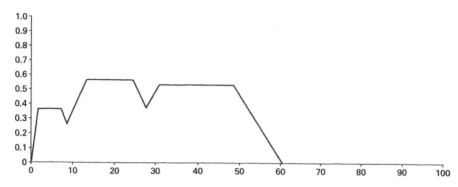

Figure 9.12   Fuzzy output membership function for gravity model when distance is 7 and destination size is 32.5

3. Destination size is **BIG** and distance is **ZERO** then trips are **LOTS** with a membership grade of 0.53; and
4. Destination size is **BIG** and distance is **SHORT** then trips are **BIG** with a membership grade of 0.56.

The resulting fuzzy set membership output function is shown in Figure 9.12. This would then be defuzzified to yield a single crisp model prediction.

Step 6   Defuzzification of the outputs to obtain a crisp number

The result of applying fuzzy inferences is that an output fuzzy set. This is an aggregation of one or more output membership sets that were selected by the FAM rules but then truncated at values determined by the fuzzy inferencing procedure that was used. To be useful this fuzzy output set has to be converted into a crisp number via a defuzzification process so that the model output is a single numeric value that best represents the information contained in the output fuzzy set.

There are various methods of defuzzification. The method used here is the centroid or centre of gravity technique. This is widely used and behaves in a manner akin to Bayesian estimates in that it defines a value that is supported by evidence that has been accumulated from across all the rules. In Figures 9.11 and 9.12 the crisp centroid estimates are respectively 62.7 and 29.2.

Step 7   Model evaluation

Fuzzy models, like more conventional models, need to be validated and their behaviour tested against validation data sets. It is a good idea to copy the neural network practice of keeping some data purely for validation purposes. Moreover, if required, a computer-intensive statistical procedure could also be used to estimate model confidence limits, for example via a bootstrapping process.

Table 9.5   Hypothetical trip data

Destination size	Distance value	Observed trips
27.4	1.0	60.0
56.9	4.0	99.4
32.5	7.0	45.4
5.6	10.0	6.2
74.8	13.0	66.6
41.4	16.0	29.4
57.4	19.0	32.6
5.5	22.0	2.5
88.7	25.0	32.1
30.3	28.0	8.8
44.7	31.0	10.3
75.8	34.0	14.0
20.1	37.0	3.0
3.8	40.0	0.4
10.6	43.0	1.0
85.9	46.0	6.4
13.6	49.0	0.8
1.8	52.0	0.1
93.1	55.0	3.5
77.9	58.0	2.4
10.4	61.0	0.3
44.1	64.0	0.9
45.7	67.0	0.7
60.4	70.0	0.7
67.1	73.0	0.7
83.4	76.0	0.7
73.5	79.0	0.5
10.5	82.0	0.1
57.1	85.0	0.2
52.3	88.0	0.2
12.0	91.0	0.0
76.6	94.0	0.2
77.8	97.0	0.1
23.1	100.0	0.0

Note though that there is no lengthy or complex model parameter calibration process, whether the model works well or poorly is a function of the membership function used and the composition of the FAM. Whether a fuzzy model works well can also be determined by comparing its performance with conventional alternatives. However, it may be worth accepting some loss of performance for a simpler non-mathematical interpretation. Also fuzzy systems modelling is still in its infancy; it may be too much to expect that the very first clumsily built model you hastily fling together late one Friday afternoon should immediately outperform much more mature models on which many thousands of years of person-effort and much research money have been expended. However, despite this caveat, maybe you will be pleasantly surprised at the levels of performance that can actually be achieved with very little effort.

To evaluate the fuzzy models some hypothetical trip data are given in Table 9.5. The data are generated by the following function:

$$T_j = D_j \exp\left(-\,0.075C_j\right) A$$

where

$$D_j = 100 \times R\,(0,1.0)$$
$$C_j = 1, 4, 7, 10, 13, \ldots 100$$
$$A = 430 \,/\, \sum_j D_j \exp\left(-\,0.075C_j\right)$$

$R\,(0, 1.0)$ is a random number generator. The aim was to create hypothetical data with observed trip values in the range 0–100.

The distance decay model produced the results in Table 9.6 with a sum of absolute errors of 224. Given the massive simplicity of the model and the fairly arbitrary nature of its construction it did quite well and successfully represents the distance decay phenomenon. By comparison, a simple log-linear regression distance decay model (eqn 9.1) produced an error of 258. The fuzzy gravity model did a little better with an error of 213; see Table 9.7. For comparison the unconstrained negative exponential gravity model has an error of 186 and the linear regression gravity model (eqn 9.2) an error of 232. Remember that the fuzzy model involves no parameter calibration process and that data were generated by a negative exponential function which gives the negative exponential model a distinctly unfair advantage. Note also that none of these models are constrained. However, there is no reason why an accounting constraint cannot be introduced. This ensures a degree of model consistency (viz. the predicted trips exactly equals the number that left the origin zone) and also removes the need to scale the output set values to reflect the nature of the data.

Step 8   Manually tuning the model's membership functions and FAM

In a knowledge-rich situation defining the membership functions should not be a difficult task. In others, as in much of geography, it is inevitably a matter of at best informed guesswork, at worst an extensive process of trial and error. The input data membership functions critically affect how the data are represented to the model whilst the nature of the output membership sets determines the numerical values generated by the model. Both can be highly data specific. An extensive programme of manually fine tuning of either or both the membership functions and FAM will often be critical. The number and the numeric domains of the membership functions are often more critical than their shape.

Table 9.6   Fuzzy distance decay model results

Distance value	Observed trips	Predicted trips
1.0	60.0	76.4
4.0	99.4	69.2
7.0	45.4	62.7
10.0	6.2	56.5
13.0	66.6	48.6
16.0	29.4	38.0
19.0	32.6	32.7
22.0	2.5	27.6
25.0	32.1	20.0
28.0	8.8	18.9
31.0	10.3	17.0
34.0	14.0	11.6
37.0	3.0	5.0
40.0	0.4	5.0
43.0	1.0	4.9
46.0	6.4	4.9
49.0	0.8	4.8
52.0	0.1	4.7
55.0	3.5	4.5
58.0	2.4	3.7
61.0	0.3	0.7
64.0	0.9	0.7
67.0	0.7	0.7
70.0	0.7	0.7
73.0	0.7	0.6
76.0	0.7	0.6
79.0	0.5	0.6
82.0	0.1	0.6
85.0	0.2	0.6
88.0	0.2	0.6
91.0	0.0	0.6
94.0	0.2	0.6
97.0	0.1	0.5
100.0	0.0	0.5

As an example of what can be done the FAM in Table 9.4 was manually modified to try and improve the performance of the model. The revised FAM is shown in Table 9.8 and the improved results in Table 9.9. The improved model had an error of 92. In a real application the nature of the FAM contains considerable useful information about the nature of the spatial interaction process. A particularly appealing feature is that no mathematical or statistical knowledge is required to interpret it as the fuzzy model rules can be expressed in words; indeed, there is no equation or statistical parameter estimates or error terms to worry about. Additionally, there are no critical assumptions that may dramatically affect the results.

Table 9.7   Fuzzy gravity model results

Destination size	Distance value	Observed trips	Predicted trips
27.4	1.0	60.0	29.4
56.9	4.0	99.4	65.9
32.5	7.0	45.4	29.3
5.6	10.0	6.2	15.6
74.8	13.0	66.6	64.7
41.4	16.0	29.4	22.3
57.4	19.0	32.6	31.7
5.5	22.0	2.5	4.2
88.7	25.0	32.1	20.0
30.3	28.0	8.8	4.9
44.7	31.0	10.3	14.8
75.8	34.0	14.0	18.1
20.1	37.0	3.0	0.6
3.8	40.0	0.4	0.6
10.6	43.0	1.0	0.7
85.9	46.0	6.4	18.8
13.6	49.0	0.8	0.6
1.8	52.0	0.1	0.8
93.1	55.0	3.5	16.6
77.9	58.0	2.4	13.3
10.4	61.0	0.3	0.7
44.1	64.0	0.9	4.0
45.7	67.0	0.7	4.2
60.4	70.0	0.7	5.0
67.1	73.0	0.7	5.0
83.4	76.0	0.7	5.0
73.5	79.0	0.5	5.0
10.5	82.0	0.1	0.7
57.1	85.0	0.2	4.9
52.3	88.0	0.2	4.6
12.0	91.0	0.0	0.6
76.6	94.0	0.2	5.0
77.8	97.0	0.1	5.0
23.1	100.0	0.0	0.6

Step 9   Optimising model performance: adaptive fuzzy systems modelling

The conventional fuzzy model is non-adaptive. Much higher degrees of intelligence may be gained if the system has some means of reorganising itself in a permanent way so that its performance improves or so that it can better respond to new stimuli or different data. A completely adaptive fuzzy model would be able to modify the membership functions, the nature of the FAM, and the weighting associated with the various rules. The basic structure of a fuzzy system is shown in Figure 9.13 and that of an adaptive fuzzy model in Figure 9.14.

Table 9.8   A revised FAM for the gravity model

Input destination size membership sets	Input distance membership sets				
	Zero	Short	Average	Big	Long
Small	Some	None	None	None	None
Little	Some	None	Some	None	None
Big	Massive	Big	Some	None	None
Large	Massive	Lots	Big	None	None
Huge	Massive	Massive	Big	Some	None

Table 9.9   Revised fuzzy gravity model results

Destination	Distance value	Observed trips	Predicted trips
27.4	1.0	60.0	57.9
56.9	4.0	99.4	65.9
32.5	7.0	45.4	53.7
5.6	10.0	6.2	4.3
74.8	13.0	66.6	64.7
41.4	16.0	29.4	22.3
57.4	19.0	32.6	31.7
5.5	22.0	2.5	4.2
88.7	25.0	32.1	20.0
30.3	28.0	8.8	4.9
44.7	31.0	10.3	14.8
75.8	34.0	14.0	12.1
20.1	37.0	3.0	0.6
3.8	40.0	0.4	0.6
10.6	43.0	1.0	0.7
85.9	46.0	6.4	4.9
13.6	49.0	0.8	0.6
1.8	52.0	0.1	0.7
93.1	55.0	3.5	4.9
77.9	58.0	2.4	3.7
10.4	61.0	0.3	0.7
44.1	64.0	0.9	0.7
45.7	67.0	0.7	0.7
60.4	70.0	0.7	0.7
67.1	73.0	0.7	0.6
83.4	76.0	0.7	0.6
73.5	79.0	0.5	0.7
10.5	82.0	0.1	0.7
57.1	85.0	0.2	0.6
52.3	88.0	0.2	0.6
12.0	91.0	0.0	0.6
76.6	94.0	0.2	0.7
77.8	97.0	0.1	0.7
23.1	100.0	0.0	0.6

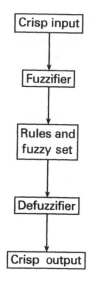

Figure 9.13   A fuzzy system model

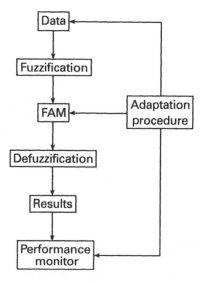

Figure 9.14   Adaptive fuzzy model

The simplest adaptive fuzzy modeller is to associate weights with each entry in the FAM. The weights determine how much each rule affects the final outcome of the model (von Altrock, 1995). These weights can be estimated using a neural net learning method.

Another approach to a fuzzy adaptive system involves changing the membership functions as a means of improving performance or responding to changes in the data. The simplest method is to broaden or narrow the fuzzy sets according to feedback on model performance. For example, if the model overpredicts, then for each fuzzy output set that was accessed, narrow them slightly, that is move the left edge of the domain to the right and the right edge to the left; else broaden them. The problem now is that of overlap. The truth membership of a vertical line constructed through a region of overlap must not exceed 1.0. It is not difficult to devise heuristics to do this fuzzy set adjustment by a trial and error process. However, the ultimate fuzzy modelling system is one that attempts to learn or discover the membership functions and the rules so as to optimise its predictive performance by itself. The integration of fuzzy logic with neural networks and genetic algorithms provides the basis for this type of extremely powerful approach to model-free modelling of complex data. Model-free modelling is a computer model that is not based on any explicit set of equations. Instead a machine learning procedure (i.e. neural network or fuzzy logic modeller) learns or discovers how to map a set of input values on to a set of outputs. It is, if you prefer, a black box model. Ross (1995: xv) argues that "The integration of fuzzy logic with neural networks and genetic algorithms is now making automated cognitive systems a reality in many disciplines. In fact, the reasoning power of fuzzy systems, when integrated with the learning capabilities of artificial neural networks and genetic algorithms, is responsible for new commercial products and processes that are reasonably effective cognitive systems (i.e. systems that can learn and reason)."

A genetic algorithm (GA) provides an obvious way of estimating optimal FAMs and membership functions to yield best performing models (see Chapter 7) (Karr, 1991,1994). Quite simply the FAMs and the membership functions can be coded as bit strings and a measure of fitness devised based on how well the resulting fuzzy model fits the data. Consider first FAM optimisation. The distance decay FAM in Table 9.3 can be optimised using a GA. The FAM entries correspond to integers in the range 1–5. The GA uses a binary representation so 4 bits would allow numbers in the range 1–15 to be used. This can easily be converted into integers between 1 and 5. The optimal FAM for the distance decay model is not much better than previously, reducing model error from 224 to 217 with only one change to the FAM in Table 9.3; the **SOME** category was replaced by **NONE**, reducing slightly the number of long-distance trips and improving the model's performance slightly.

The two-dimensional Table 9.4 FAM for the gravity model presents a much more interesting challenge. The optimal FAM is shown in Table 9.10 and results in a model error of 91; a tremendous improvement, but still yields interpretable results that conform with common sense and intuitive plausibility.

The next step is to optimise both the FAM and the output membership functions. This requires that the membership function can be parameterised and clearly there are several ways of doing this that allow varying levels of flexibility for the GA to optimise. The scheme used here is described in Figure 9.15. The triangular membership functions are represented by a start number and a base

Table 9.10   GA optimised FAM for gravity model

Input destination size membership sets	Input distance membership sets				
	Zero	Short	Average	Big	Long
Small	Some	Some	None	None	None
Little	Some	None	None	None	None
Big	Lots	Big	Some	Big	None
Large	Lots	Big	Some	Some	None
Huge	Lots	Massive	Big	Some	None

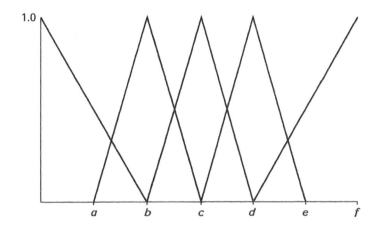

Figure 9.15   Parameterised membership function

length and the entire sequence is scaled to ensure that $a + b + c + d + e + f$ is equal to the range of observed data values (usually termed the universe of discourse). This approach is a little inflexible but has the merit of retaining the same linguistic labels that are originally devised since the logical ordering has not been changed. Altering the membership function is equivalent to a human changing the conditions under which the rules are applied, rather than changing the rules themselves. The model's performance is now 188 for the output membership function shown in Figure 9.16. The optimal FAM is essentially similar as before: **LOTS, BIG, SOME** and **NONE**, but with the removal of the **MASSIVE** category. It seems that the **MASSIVE** category is not needed and the rest have spread themselves out to cover the domain of interest. The only exception is the **NONE** fuzzy set which has narrowed.

Perhaps more interesting is when this strategy is applied to the full gravity model. Everything is now estimated by the GA. The performance of the model reaches a new peak at 61 which is a substantial improvement. The FAM is shown in Table 9.11. Again it makes some sense with a tendency for interaction to diminish with distance but this is moderated by the size of the destination

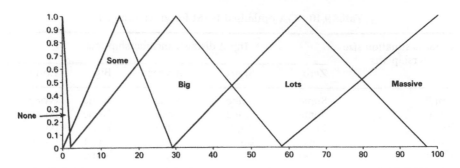

Figure 9.16   Optimal distance decay model output membership function

Table 9.11   FAM for genetically optimised fuzzy gravity model

Input destination size membership sets	Input distance membership sets				
	Zero	Short	Average	Big	Long
Small	Some	None	None	None	None
Little	Lots	Some	Some	Some	None
Big	Massive	Big	Lots	Some	None
Large	Massive	None	None	Some	None
Huge	Massive	Lots	Lots	Lots	Some

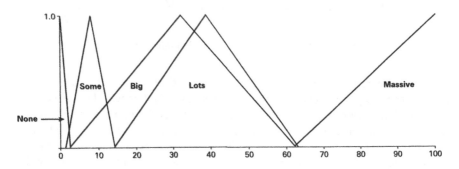

Figure 9.17   Optimal output membership function after genetic optimisation

variable. The genetically engineered optimal membership functions are shown in Figures 9.17–9.19. There are considerable changes and clearly not all these fuzzy sets appear to be needed (particularly for the destination variable) as high levels of overlap suggest that some could be removed.

The main problem with hybrid GA fuzzy models is their need for sufficient data to enable optimal settings to be obtained and, perhaps, a fast workstation. On the other hand, the results have an intuitively obvious interpretation in both the shape of the membership functions, the nature of the FAM, and possibly also the

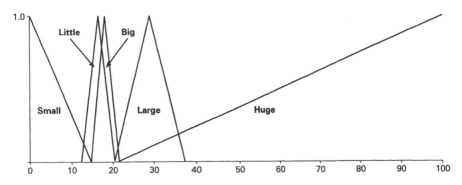

Figure 9.18 Optimal membership function for destination size after genetic optimisation

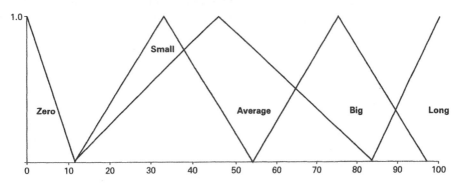

Figure 9.19 Optimal membership function for distance after genetic optimisation

strength associated with the various rules. Clearly this is an extremely powerful modelling technology that has much to commend it in certain circumstances.

9.3.2 Fuzzy spatial interaction modelling

The reader interested in developing their own fuzzy spatial interaction models can do so using the SIMS software (Openshaw and Glover, 1997). This offers the fuzzy modelling functions discussed in this book as well as more advanced alternatives. Yet SIMS is simple enough for a first-year undergraduate geographer with no prior training in mathematics or statistics to use.

9.4 CONCLUSIONS

9.4.1 Fuzzy modelling is in principle simple

Fuzzy systems modelling is not particularly difficult. The overall process is shown in Figure 9.13. The nicest aspect is that the technology is widely applicable to many different situations, both numeric and non-numeric, and that the models can be given an interpretation that is easy to understand.

9.4.2 Some advantages

Fuzzy logic based modelling offers a number of potential benefits:
- It provides a linguistic non-numerical, non-mathematics and non-statistical based approach to modelling complex systems;
- It is a fairly simple approach with few values or rules being required to handle considerable complexity;
- It is inherently a nonlinear analysis and modelling tool;
- It relates inputs to outputs without having to understand the system, resulting in potentially improved levels of performance over more conventional approaches and permits rapid prototyping, since a researcher does not have to know everything about the system before starting work;
- It offers a transparent box approach to modelling that is inherently more understandable than a neural net (because you can readily look inside the box to find out what is going on);
- Ease of design and ease of explanation to others;
- Robustness because of its ability to handle imprecision;
- Makes good use of existing intuition and knowledge, both soft and hard, in a direct manner so that there is no need to pretend that we know nothing about the system of interest even when we do;
- Fuzzy logic models have a high degree of inherent parallelism;
- The technology can be embedded in other methods to create various hybrid modelling systems; for example, neuro fuzzy systems modelling is, believe it or not, a most delightful, natural and easy technology for which there are many working examples in many different areas. If you are at all interested in modelling complex systems then this is good technology for you to explore; and
- It addresses many of the concerns that are often levelled against quantitative geography, since this is a non-positivistic technology that can handle soft concepts and lays bare the areas of ambiguity and subjectiveness that deconstructionists like so much.

If you at all interested in modelling complex systems then this is a good technology for you to explore.

9.4.3 Some disadvantages

There are always problems or drawbacks with a method. Fuzzy logic is no magic panacea, it will not always work or work well! It is much less of a black box approach than neural networks and this may create problems; for example, if FAMs that are difficult to comprehend produce good results. Other possible problems include:

- The psychological and cultural prejudice that many people hold in favour of crisp systems or mathematically precise models may precondition the user to expect failure or to look for unsurpassable problems even if there are none;
- Rule-based modelling is essentially simple and whilst useful is limited to those situations where this approach is possible;
- There is an underlying curse of dimensionality whereby the number of rules is a power function of the number of input variables, which inevitably restricts fuzzy models to systems that can be characterised by few (i.e. less than 10) variables or else requires the use of neural networks to create the membership functions;
- Fine tuning or optimisation of performance is often necessary (because of inadequacies in the knowledge that specified the system) and this is not always easy, although a GA approach is a useful aid here;
- Optimisation using GA may well require high-performance computing or highly parallel hardware if there is a large number of input variables or a large number of cases in the training data set;
- The usual moaning about the lack of a theoretical justification, although the use of knowledge to specify the rule base should usually invalidate this complaint.

9.4.4 So what!

Fuzzy logic is of considerable relevance to AI because it attempts to emulate the way the brain deals with information, in imprecise terms. Fuzzy logic is built around reasoning in degrees of truth rather than in black and white terms; for instance, we can sense that a room is hot or cold without needing to know its precise temperature. It is very attractive in part also because it attempts to emulate how the brain thinks rather than emulate the processes by which it works.

Fuzzy systems have a unique advantage over most other modelling tools. They are easy to set up, computationally efficient once established, and very robust. Clearly fuzzy logic and modelling have had a long gestation period. Maybe its time has come. There is a great potential here but equally there are many avenues that still need to be explored, researched and solutions developed. The incorporation of fuzzy set theory and fuzzy logic into computer models works best in applications where intuition and judgement are important. According to Ross (1995: 5), fuzzy logic works best in two types of situations:

1. Very complex models where understanding is strictly limited or judgemental;
2. When human reasoning, human perception or human decision-making are inextricably involved.

To these may be added two more categories:

3. There is knowledge of how a system works but little or no data to build a conventional model; and
4. When the systems are highly nonlinear and extremely complex.

By contrast, simple linear systems are not much improved by adding fuzzy logic to them. It is not a panacea for all modelling problems. However, under appropriate conditions it can be extremely useful. Our understanding of many processes is largely based on imprecise human reasoning even if the information we can generate is extremely precise. As technology improves so we can become much more precise but quite often the extra precision is not needed or is wasted. In an engineering context more precision means more cost; however, if we can tolerate a lesser degree of precision, then we can reduce costs. Fuzzy logic provides a means of exploiting the tolerance for imprecision. Fuzzy technology is proclaimed in Japan as the "keyword" for the 1990s. Although the technology involved is relatively new it is of such a fundamental nature that it will be a core research tool by the turn of the century. Fuzzy logic is a smart technology because it combines the knowledge you already have with other knowledge that only a machine learning procedure can uncover for you. It is inconceivable that this valuable and useful technology will not also revolutionise many of the existing models in geography as well as offer the basis for several new ones.

9.5 QUESTIONS AND ANSWERS

Q So why leave fuzzy systems until so late in this book if they are so important?
A It really is deserving of a separate text. The justification for dealing with it last is that it builds on earlier chapters concerned with expert systems, neural nets and genetic algorithms. To this extent, its location is quite logical.
Q Fuzzy implies "wish-washy" connotations of vagueness and imprecision. Is this so?
A No. Fuzzy systems are represented by well-defined deterministic functions. The action of a fuzzy system is anything but wishy-washy!
Q Does the term "fuzzy" not carry rather negative connotations?
A Unfortunately yes, particularly in the English-speaking Western culture. In Japanese, for example, the word "fuzzy" does not imply disorganisation and imprecision as it does in English.
Q How can a science that is less than precise be useful?
A Ask a weather forecaster! Well it is all a matter of what levels of precision are appropriate. In many social sciences, the concepts and theories will never be capable of being precise because of the complexity of the human systems that are of interest. Human beings are not strongly controlled by universal laws and thus the potential attractions of a technology for dealing with their complex systems of organised complexity are undeniable. Fuzzy logic offers an almost ideal approach.
Q Where are the mathematics?
A There are 20 years, or more, of hard to understand mathematical proofs and treatises that provide a firm basis for fuzzy set theory. It is only fairly recently

that several reasonably understandable, simple, books have appeared to put it all into context; see for example McNeill and Thro (1995) or von Altrock (1995).

Q   Is the use of the term "fuzzy" unfortunate because it implies vagueness?

A   Indeed the alternative was vague logic! Fuzzy implies a hazy outline, something not seen quite so clearly, or being unclear and ambiguous. Its strength is that it provides a scientific approach based on rigorous mathematics for dealing with concepts and the semantics of natural language in which whilst the meaning is understandable the properties of the objects cannot be determined by simple yes or no evaluation.

Q   How do I discover the best number of input sets to use to represent a particular variable?

A   Most engineers use small odd numbers such as 3, 5, 7 and 9. More gives you greater accuracy than less but maybe you do not want too many.

Q   If I have 20 input variables is there any good way of simplifying it?

A   There are two possibilities; either decide on two or three good ones on the basis of theory, intuition or domain-specific knowledge; or use an unsupervised self-organising neural net to reduce the 20-dimensional space to two (or one or three) dimensions formed by the neuron array you use. The self-organising map Kohonen network can be used to preprocess your data; see Kosko (1994) for details.

Q   If I estimate a value for the variable age as 26.7 years with an accuracy of ±5, is this the same sort of fuzziness that fuzzy set theory deals with?

A   No, it is really quite different. The variable age is not represented as a single number but you would define different subsets of age each with a label; for example, young, middle-aged and old. The imprecision is in knowing what the concept young or old means and has nothing much to do with your estimate that a person is aged 26.7 years ±5. You could use this 26.7 ±5 information in assigning the value of 26.7 to the age subsets; for example by simulating values for it that reflected its uncertainty and then using the average. In practice this is probably not worth while as statistical methods exist for dealing with it, viz. Monte Carlo simulation.

Q   Is there an immediate benefit to replacing the arithmetic in a conventional mathematical model by fuzzy arithmetic?

A   Probably not, unless there are good grounds for believing that the meaning of the terms used in the model are better represented as fuzzy numbers. This may not always be true or apparent in how to devise appropriate or useful membership functions. However sometimes the variables might be imprecise due to sample or measurement error. However, this form of uncertainty is best handled statistically. If in doubt read again the section on fuzziness and probability.

Q   Fuzzy logic is only relevant to control engineers interested in building smart washing machines.

A   Wrong! They also provide a basis for modelling complex nonlinear systems and, moreover, they can handle many of the problems addressed by neural nets.

Q   What benefits does fuzzy logic offer over a neural network approach to modelling?

A   The fuzzy systems approach has a number of special features:

(i) it can use existing knowledge directly rather than having to infer it via a training process;

(ii) it is a "transparent box" in that the results can be more readily understood and provide insight via the FAM entries (or rules) that produces the best results, compared with the black box nature of neural networks;

(iii) it is based on attempts to emulate how the brain thinks rather than how it may work;

(iv) maybe a greater degree of parallelism;

(v) if the data being input into a fuzzy system model are vastly different from that on which it was trained/developed, then this is often immediately obvious or can be readily deduced, whereas the operations of a neural net on such data are much harder to predict or even spot that the problem exists.

Q   If I had to choose between neural networks and fuzzy logic which should I prefer?

A   They are not either/or technologies. If in doubt try them both. Maybe on some applications involving fuzzy genetic modelling the back-propagation network may be trained faster. On problems with many input variables the number of rules in a fuzzy system explodes; it is a power function of the number of input variables. For systems with many variables (5 or 6 or more) then neural networks might well be best. The tremendous strength of fuzzy systems is its simplicity. Swamp it in data and this is soon lost but so too is the analogy with human thinking.

Q   Which of the following models will work best: logistic regression, neural network or fuzzy logic model?

A   Probably an artificial life based equivalent! That apart, it is a matter of horses for courses and there is unlikely to be a globally correct answer applicable to all possible circumstances. On the other hand, both the neural network and the fuzzy logic approaches function as universal approximators so maybe they will tend to provide the best results particularly in noisy and nonlinear situations.

Q   What is a hybrid system?

A   An attempt to combine neural networks with fuzzy sets would be a hybrid system. For example, fuzzy membership functions can be used to normalise input data for a neural net, or a neural net trained to identify fuzzy set membership values as their outputs which are then used in a fuzzy system. You could also combine them both, for example so that the neural network fine tunes a fuzzy system. In general it seems that combining different methods and then either selecting the best in the context of a particular application or combining the results often yields "better" results than those provided by any single method; "better" might well mean possessed of greater robustness.

Q   How on earth do I estimate confidence intervals on the predictions made by a fuzzy model?

A   The same way as you would for a neural net, use bootstrapping and other

computer-intensive statistical methods. The advantage is that these estimates are usually quite robust.

Q   Does a fuzzy model make otherwise idiot modellers into world class experts?

A   No, not really. It is true that a genetically optimised fuzzy model fed with the
"wrong" variables may still "work" but it would probably do so much more
efficiently if an expert had put some thought and intelligence into the process.
It is not a pure black box of the neural network sort, it can use knowledge that
exists and then add to it. Indeed this ability to use existing knowledge, rather
than pretend it does not exist, stands fuzzy logic based models apart from all
others.

Q   In what senses can a fuzzy logic model be considered to be fault tolerant?

A   That is easy. If you delete entries in the FAM at which point does it fail
completely? Kosko (1992a) demonstrates that, rather like a neural network,
performance degrades gracefully and that you have to do massive amounts of
damage before it stopped working in his backing up a truck control problem.
Whether this also applies to fuzzy models in a geographical context has yet to
be discovered and may seem quite irrelevant. On the other hand, if a fuzzy
logic model is very robust and continues to work well despite having many
rules removed, then maybe the converse is also true. That is, in a geographical context the fuzzy model might start out damaged (by lack of knowledge)
and still do something useful!

REFERENCES

Black, M., 1937, "Vagueness: an exercise in logical analysis", *Philosophy of Science*, **4**, 427–455.

Buckley, J.J., Hayashi, Y., 1993, "Fuzzy input–output controllers are universal approximators", *Fuzzy Sets and Systems*, **58**, 273–278.

Cox, E., 1994, *The Fuzzy Systems Handbook*. AP Professional, Boston.

Gupta, M.M., Sanchez, E. (eds), 1982, *Fuzzy Information and Decision Processes*. North-
Holland, Amsterdam.

Fisher, P.F., 1994, "Probable and fuzzy models of the viewshed operation", in M. Worboys
(ed.), *Innovations in GIS 1*. Taylor and Francis, London, pp. 161–175.

Holmblad, L.P., Ostergaard, J.J., 1981, "Fuzzy logic control: operator experience applied
in automatic process control", *ZKG International*, **34**, 127–133.

Holmblad, L.P., Ostergaard, J.J., 1982, "Control of a cement kiln by fuzzy logic", in M.M.
Gupta, E. Sanchez (eds), *Fuzzy Information and Decision Processes*. North-Holland,
Amsterdam, pp. 398–399.

Karr, C.L., 1991, "Genetic algorithms for fuzzy logic controllers", *AI Expert*, **6**, 26–33.

Karr, C., 1994, "Adaptive control with fuzzy logic and genetic algorithms", in R.R. Yager,
L.A. Zadeh (eds), *Fuzzy Sets, Neural Networks, and Soft Computing*. Van Nostrand
Reinhold, New York, pp. 345–367.

Klir, G.J., Yuan, B., 1995, *Fuzzy Sets and Fuzzy Logic: theory and applications*.
Prentice-Hall, New Jersey.

Kosko, B., 1990, "Fuzziness vs. probability", *International Journal of General Systems*, **17**,
211–240.

Kosko, B., 1992, *Neural Networks and Fuzzy Systems*. Prentice-Hall International,
Englewood Cliffs.

Kosko, B., 1992b, "Fuzzy systems as universal approximators", *Proceedings of First IEEE International Conference on Fuzzy Systems*, San Diego, pp. 1153–1162.

Kosko, B., 1994, *Fuzzy Thinking*. HarperCollins, London.

Leung, Y., Leung, K.S., 1993a, "An intelligent expert system shell for knowledge based GIS:1, the tools", *International Journal of GIS*, 7, 189–199.

Leung, Y., Leung, K.S., 1993b, "An intelligent expert system shell for knowledge-based GIS: 2, some applications", *International Journal of GIS*, 7, 201–213.

Lukasiewicz, J., 1970, "In defence of logistic", Works in L. Borkowski (ed.), *Selected Works*. North-Holland, London.

McNeill, F.M., Thro, E., 1994, *Fuzzy Logic: a practical approach*. A P Professional, Boston.

McNeill, D., Freiberger, P., 1994, *Fuzzy Logic*. Simon and Schuster, New York.

Mamdani, E., Assilian, S., 1975, "An experiment in linguistic synthesis with a fuzzy logic controller", *International Journal of Man–Machine Studies*, 7, 1–13.

Openshaw, S., 1996, "Fuzzy logic as a new scientific paradigm for doing geography", *Environment and Planning A*, 28, 761–768.

Openshaw, S., Glover, T., 1997, *Spatial Interaction Modelling System*. GeoInformation International, Cambridge (forthcoming on CD ROM).

Ross, T.J., 1995, *Fuzzy Logic with Engineering Applications*. McGraw-Hill, New York.

Sugeno, M. (ed.), 1985, *Industrial Applications of Fuzzy Control*. North-Holland, Amsterdam.

Terano, T., Asai, K., Sugeno, M., 1989, *Applied Fuzzy Systems*. A P Professional, New York (English translation in 1994).

Von Altrock, C., 1995, *Fuzzy Neural Systems*. Prentice-Hall, Englewood Cliffs, New Jersey.

Yager, R.R., Ovchinnikov, S., Tong, R.M., Nguyen, H.T. (eds), 1987, *Fuzzy Sets and Applications: selected papers by L.A. Zadeh*. Wiley, New York.

Yasunobu, S., Miyamoto, S., 1985, "Automatic train operation system by predictive fuzzy control", in M. Sugeno (ed.), *Industrial Applications of Fuzzy Control*. North-Holland, Amsterdam, pp. 1–18.

Zadeh, L.A., 1962, "From circuit theory to systems theory", *IRE Proceedings*, 50, 856–865.

Zadeh, L.A., 1965, "Fuzzy sets", *Information and Control*, 8, 338–353.

Zadeh, L.A., 1971, "Towards a theory of fuzzy systems", in R.E. Kalman, N. DeClaris (eds), *Aspects of Network and Systems Theory*. Holt Rinehart, Winston.

Zadeh, L.A., 1974, "A rationale for fuzzy control", *Journal of Dynamic Systems, Measurement and Control*, 3–4.

Zadeh, L.A., 1992, "Foreword", in Kosko *Neural Networks and Fuzzy Systems*. Prentice-Hall International, Englewood Cliffs, New Jersey, pp. xvii–xviii.

Zadeh, L.A., 1995, "Foreword", in C. von Altrock, *Fuzzy Logic and Neuro Fuzzy Applications Explained*. Prentice-Hall, Englewood Cliffs, New Jersey, pp. xi–xii.

CHAPTER 10

Conclusions and Epilogue

10.1 AN EMERGING ERA OF THE SMART MACHINE

The last decade has witnessed a dramatic increase of both the interest in and the availability of so-called "intelligent technologies". Some of these developments have been motivated by attempts to emulate aspects of human functionality, others have been inspired by ideas borrowed from biology. However, all have been driven on by a consuming desire and increasing need for smart computing to help in problem solving. Indeed, the future is unavoidably one that will be increasingly populated by intelligent systems and intelligent machines. *The AI revolution is now over.* It is here! From Wall Street to the Pentagon, from commerce to science, more and more new applications and products that use these smart technologies are emerging every day. The current low levels of machine intelligence are set to increase rapidly over the next few decades as computer speeds increase and as we discover how to make better use of the new tools. Artificial intelligence is real. Many of its methods are proven technology. There is not a high degree of risk in using it and it is being used in applications that are being expanded at a phenomenal rate. It allows us to solve problems that cannot be handled by any other means. To survive as a geographer, planner or social scientist, you need to discover how to use, exploit and also further develop the new nascent intelligent technologies. This is as true of geography as it is of many other subjects. However, AI is not just about computer technology, it is simultaneously a set of tools, a way of thinking and a paradigm for doing in the computer and IT age.

Artificial intelligence can be regarded as virtually any kind of computational method that uses knowledge (defined in the broadest possible sense) or computer algorithms or even sheer brute-force computational power designed to add or inject a degree of AI or smartness of a non-deterministic sort into computing applications and problem-solving procedures which previously lacked it. There is nothing to be afraid of—AI can range from the trivial to the mundane, from massive multi-billion pound efforts involving hundreds of highly skilled experts to something you can "knock up" in an afternoon after a visit to the pub! You can write your AI applications in visual BASIC or C + + or whatever, it is not the programming language you use that makes it AI. Whether AI works well or fails is really up to you. Whether you decide to use AI and become an AI expert, using it to do geography in a better or different way is again up to you. Likewise, whether you decide merely to study the spatial diffusion of AI and observe its effects on others, is also your decision. Maybe the latter is easier than the former and also "safer" and a more ready source of instant descriptive publications particularly if you expose the social, economic and political inequalities the AI/no AI dichotomy will undoubtedly create. On the other hand you would be losing out on the excitement of working to develop AI applications in geography that may well determine the future directions of the subject as a whole. The AI yes/no dichotomy applies to individual disciplines as much as it does to the world economy.

Artificial intelligence is future essential because many different people working in many different application areas really do want and need far more intelligent computer systems. Some are simply swamped in data, others need new tools to improve current practices; a few want intelligent, creative partnerships with intelligent machines as the basis for new products; or maybe like ourselves others are tired with having to put up with dumb lumps of plastic wires and silicon that give back nothing more than they were once given and usually much less. The modern world is a terribly complex place and IT is increasing its complexity at a rapid rate. We now need all the help we can acquire, if we are to survive. Virtually everywhere you look organisations, businesses, governments and people are gaining access to more and more data at faster rates and at wider band widths. Many businesses now know that their future is critically dependent on how they exploit the new opportunities created by IT. However, be warned, the same applies to subject disciplines such as geography that are affected by IT developments. The common problem is that the technologies for capturing, managing and manipulating information now far exceed those for its analysis and use, yet to survive we do need to develop the new technologies that can cope with all aspects. Maybe putting our future hopes on AI is not such a daft idea but to be successful it has to be performed in a purposeful and sustained way. In subjects such as geography it may also need a few years of shelter from the bitter criticisms of the misinformed, the ill-informed and the maliciously minded computer Luddites characterised by overactive social consciences, imaginations and deconstructionist tendencies. Given time they will go away and fade into the background. What they are doing is attempting to make being dumb into a virtue whilst "Canute-like" choosing to ignore most of the fundamental IT changes happening all around them. At best it is a delaying tactic that may, in the longer term, ironically be useful to AI by postponing AI uptake until some of the risks have diminished and the hype has been replaced by common sense.

Meanwhile, be aware that AI is universally applicable because smart or artificially intelligent machines will always be useful. Indeed the range of applications is potentially endless; ranging from toasters that brown but do not blacken bread, to windscreen wipers that vary their speed according to the amount of moisture present, to clever washing machines, self-adjusting TV sets, etc. There is virtually no limit to the consumer products and research tools that will not benefit from the presence of some autonomous levels of intelligence. We already have some of these products, perhaps without realising it; for instance ABS, engine management systems, smoke and burglar alarms, lifts, etc. No doubt soon we will have many more. It follows then that the external world is becoming increasingly filled with AI technologies, most of which are unseen and unrecognised as such. However few would at first sight seem to have any direct geographical worth. Even the world's smartest fuzzy logic and multi-micro-processor-controlled washing machine cannot as yet outperform even the poorest of geographical models! But then it was never intended to. The real point is that the same technology that underlies the neurofuzzy intelligent controller technology used in a washing machine can be used as the basis for modelling fuzzy geographical systems in a much more realistic way. All that is needed is for geographers to understand, to transfer and to apply generic AI technology. There is no need for geographers to pioneer or have to invent anything, it already exists; they "only" have to understand and apply it to their problems.

Seemingly, as humans, we have this insatiable desire to amplify and expand our intelligences by artificial means. It started with the calculator, it was continued by the computer, and AI is only the latest part of this trend of intelligence amplification. Historically much of the amplification has been either small, at worst negative, and the levels of AI reached have been low. Building smart machines that can compete with humans in any non purely arithmetic tasks has proved very difficult. Building machines able to outperform humans has proved even harder. Let us be frank. The appearance of really intelligent machines, able to think for themselves with high (or super) levels of intelligence, will probably not happen during our lifetimes. Maybe they are still 100 years away. However, you do not need to wait for such advanced or fantastic or futuristic sci-fi dream technology before AI starts to be useful. There is an almost immediate pay-off available now with the expenditure of only a modest outlay of effort and only a most modest degree of risk.

10.2 GEOGRAPHICAL HOPES

The fundamental belief in seeking to use AI in geography involves the expectation that one or more of the following will happen:

1. A wide range of geographical computer applications will become smarter;
2. A reduction or removal of many of the legacy of constraints, barriers and restrictions on what geographers can do with computers in a wide range of analysis and modelling applications;
3. Improvements in performance and an enhanced flexibility in many computer applications;
4. A broadening of computer applications beyond those traditionally involved in quantitative geography;

5. A joining and sharing of the benefits that various AI tools seem to have brought to several other disciplines; and
6. The emergence of geocomputation as a high-performance computer-fuelled and AI-based paradigm for tackling many of the problems of geography.

There is a strong feeling that over the next 5–20 years the whole technological basis underpinning geography in all its forms will change. The AI revolution in geography is a gradual, almost imperceptible, creeping diffusion of new ideas and new methods. It has been going on at a slow pace for at least a decade. The diffusion will speed up as more and more geographers realise that there are existing and instant uses for much of the technology as plug-in replacements for poorer performing conventional methods, as the basis for better quality results, and as a means of handling previously impossible problems. Artificial intelligence is an immediately applicable technology. It is here now, it is available now; and you can readily show people what it can do. Moreover, there are no obvious limits to its potential growth as it is a technology that has no obvious bounds to its applicability. It is also a technology that can only become better during the twenty-first century. The main constraints are not the lack of need or of potential uses but of users who understand enough of what the different strands of AI can do and promise *in their fields of geography*. Seek more information. Raise your levels of understanding. The more you know about AI the greater the number of potential and successful applications there will be. It is usually possible to use existing AI tools to outperform conventional methods that are both old-fashioned and dumb. This is important, because whilst the ultimate in AI technological development in many areas is still some way off, it is critically important not to underestimate or undervalue that which already exists. A principal objective of this book was to emphasise this point. There are now sufficient applicable AI tools in existence today to dramatically change the way that geographers go about doing their species of geography. It is hard to imagine many, or in time any, areas of the subject escaping unscathed. Some applications are more immediate, almost instant, others require a much greater expenditure of time and effort, and a few may have to await fundamental advances in computer hardware speeds and data availability.

10.3 DOUBTS AND QUESTIONS

The AI revolution has been and gone. Ignore it if you wish. Currently you still have that luxury but for how much longer? The questions you need to ask yourself are:

1. How can I benefit from these developments?
2. What else needs to be done so that I can gain some of the potential benefits of being artificially intelligent?
3. What light, opportunities, potential does it offer that may be relevant to what

you are interested in?
4. What sort of training and reskilling do I now need?
5. What major new research opportunities does AI create for me in the future?

In many ways AI is a personal decision. It has nothing much to do with this or that flavour of geography. It comes with no underlying scientific or philosophical paradigm, nor is it only applicable to only this or that species of geography and thus can be ignored by everyone else. It is just a smarter way of doing geography.

Some will wrongly regard AI as yet another stage in the development of quantitative geography. Others will mistakenly consider it to be an extension of GIS. Yet others will view it incorrectly as being a rebirth of mathematical and scientific geography. **But**, it is really none of these although AI could be all of them. It is also roundly condemnable as technology in search of problems that fit what it can do. The latter is also true. So what of it! Is it really a problem in that there is so little in geography that does not fit into what AI can do?

Some will see AI as yet another (yawn, yawn) rebirth of rampant logical positivism. What a sad comment! Since AI itself is philosophy free, it is only constrained by the philosophical prejudices, biases and intellectual baggage of the users that they impose on it, not that of the developers or the inventors. Oh dear, another heresy! Who cares. But AI is simply too important to the future of geography regardless of type or nature, to allow the "knockers" to get out their knocking tools and to start inventing hosts of social science scare stories before they have understood what AI can do. Of course, AI will be used by the rich and powerful to gain more riches and more power. It could easily be used by governments to develop systems of people control, to predict unacceptable human behaviour in advance of it happening, to violate human rights and civil liberties, to save lives by discovering preventable cancer clusters or cause untold misery by creating "fear" in people who were previously unconcerned, and to affect people's lives and patterns of existence by either denying them products and goods or by changing their accessibility to the facilities and services they use and need; to pick but a few applications at random. There are undoubtedly many many more that the serious critic could highlight! Like GIS, AI can be both a good and a bad technology; it can be used to save lives or kill; and it can be used to control, empower, enslave and liberate. So what of it? The same is true of both the hammer and the sickle! Some seem to think that because "the military" funded some of the work that all of AI is tainted technology. Rubbish! You can rest assured that whatever it was that the military funded that might be regarded as killer technology is (a) unpublished and (b) not available in any AI toolkit you will ever use. But then such people may well regard physics as tainted (because of atomic bombs) and mathematics to be the ultimate evil skill because it is used in everything, and computers to be instruments of war because the military own a few and use them in targeting weapons! If your world is full of such thoughts, get rational, go and take a cold shower!

The tremendous opportunity created by AI is an opportunity to both expand the domain of computing in geography and to change the way we use computers to do geography. Sure there is a great deal of hype. OK there is also a lack of rigour in some areas. And yes, there is a historical legacy of unfulfilled user expectations and of unwarranted claims for what AI claims it can do. But do not forget, there is also plenty of evidence of success that it actually does work in at least some applications that matter and are significant to the world today. Old-timers who remember the first neural net revolution of the 1950s and 1960s are amazed that the second neural net revolution of the mid 1980s and beyond is still (10 years later) going strong. It works, is useful, and it is widely applicable.

10.4 A RESEARCH AGENDA

At this point it might be useful to outline the principal research areas where further research might well be most beneficial. This list is not meant to be complete but one that relates to the content of this book. A number of topic areas are identified and dealt with individually. Note that in nearly all cases the research agenda is focused on applications of AI in geography rather than the development of new AI tools. This reflects the view that the challenge for geography is to make good, appropriate and full use of tools that already exist.

10.4.1 Artificial intelligence in spatial analysis relevant to geographic information systems

There are a number of key needs here that AI can help to meet, particularly:

1. Artificial life based explorers able to search the two-, three- and higher-dimensional data spaces that constitute the geocyberspace for hitherto unknown patterns and relationships. How nice it would be to have access within GIS packages to highly visual intelligent spatial database explorers. This is a generic, widely applicable function that would be tremendously useful if only someone could develop and perfect it.
2. Tools based on AI are needed to complement the existing statistical spatial analysis technologies. It is important that they require fewer assumptions that matter and are better able to handle rather than ignore the special characteristics of spatial data. Neural networks would seem to promise a very useful plug-in replacement for many conventional statistical tools that would be far easier for many geographers to cope with rather than the alternative statistical technology that is highly complex, highly mathematical, highly assumption dependent, often does not work particularly well, and ignores most of the special features of spatial information. Why on earth did geographers ever think many classical statistical methods were useful?
3. Upgrade existing parameter estimation methods to use more robust estimation techniques based on evolutionary computing. It is a matter of concern

that conventional methods are so sensitive to arithmetic problems, non-convexities and discontinuities in the function landscapes they are applied to.
4. Develop a new generation of automated real-time analysis, monitoring and alarm systems. As developments in IT provide increasing amounts of real-time data, so there is a need for smart, autonomous, analysis and pattern detection tools able to operate unattended and in a real-time environment. There are various ways of using AI to meet this need.

10.4.2 Spatial modelling in geographic information systems

There are several almost instantly available applications that need demonstrating, then followed up with diffusion into teaching and research practice:

1. It seems very important to consider re-engineering existing models using neural networks and fuzzy logic based models. Many of the models that exist are nonlinear, old, based on many assumptions of questionable validity and generally ripe for upgrade. The research questions are whether or not the potential benefits offered by AI-based methods translate into practice, whether or not the new methods can emulate the legacy models and whether the new methods offer any additional insight into the underlying processes. Research is urgently needed to find out the answers.
2. The adoption of a hybrid modelling strategy (one that combines a mixture of AI-based models and mathematical models) might well offer performance and reliability gains, particularly if the AI components are used to enhance the parts where the conventional models are most suspect. Suddenly there is a multiplicity of new modelling tools (after years of more of the same). It is important that there is a new burst of enthusiasm for building computer models of geographical systems at a time when computer systems are about 1 million times faster and our modelling tools are at least a million times better!!
3. As over half the world's population now live in urban areas, it is a disgrace that the best urban models date from over 30 years ago. Model building technologies based on AI need to be used to create new generations of models that work.

10.4.3 Applications in human geography

A separate theme involves the use of AI to broaden the domain of computer applications in human geography. This might also be regarded as broadly equivalent of importing some science into those soft areas of geography where science was largely rejected as unworkable because of the complexity of the subject. This presumption against science is challenged by AI and it is very important to consider whether it really does have much or anything to offer. From an AI perspective, the question is how can the knowledge that the soft geographer has built up be used in building computer systems? The use of a fuzzy logic approach is one area of potential importance that needs further consideration. Another is the belief that AI provides the basis for building models of human systems at the individual level. Human systems modelling is an emerging grand challenge area of considerable academic and practical importance. Human geography and social science have an important role to play here. The task is not easy and it may well require a sustained programme of interdisciplinary research spread over several decades. Nevertheless, it is important not to underestimate its tremendous long-term significance. There are also real dangers both to the people being modelled and to the disciplines that the models embrace. If social science prefers not to do it, then no doubt other engineering disciplines will prove to be far less reluctant.

10.4.4 New applications

Artificial intelligence creates the prospect of new approaches to previously impossible problems:

1. Model discovery using genetic algorithms and genetic programming is one area of considerable practical importance in the spatial information rich world created by developments in IT and GIS. The critical questions are: (a) does it work, (b) is it a practicable path towards knowledge discovery, (c) how generalisable are the results, and (d) are the models of any substantive worth? These are significant questions of considerable research and commercial importance.
2. Fuzzy thinking is a revolutionary technology. It has many applications in geography. Of particular importance is their application to create a fully functional fuzzy GIS. Another is their incorporation into spatial decision support systems.
3. The development of parallel algorithms is needed to permit the application of several AI tools to large spatial data sets. This is important if geography as a spatial information science is to be able to effectively exploit the spatial data riches that now exist.

10.4.5 Real-world demonstrators

The uptake of AI is critically dependent on awareness that the technology really does work in a particular subject area. Nothing is better than a wide range of geographical examples of AI at work in a range of geographical settings. Empirical comparisons with legacy technologies are also needed. The critical question here concerns evaluating whether AI is able to make substantial and insightful contributions to knowledge. There is also an opportunity for geographers to use their AI tools in commercial and other applied work. There is strong affinity between many of the analysis problems of the commercial sector and geographical research; only the details of the spatial data and the context are different. There is an opportunity to use AI as a data leverage device able to gain access as a spin off (for research) to databases not hitherto in the academic sector.

10.4.6 Teaching

It is important to introduce AI technologies into the undergraduate teaching curriculum via appropriate computer-aided teaching and user-friendly software packages. Despite an aura of apparent complexity, AI is in fact a simple subject. The essential straightforward nature of most of the methods is disguised and hidden from many potential users by a mix of two cunning devices: a veneer of unneeded and unnecessary mathematics and jargon.

10.4.7 Social consequences

A final research agenda item concerns the need for research into the consequences of having many AI computer systems and an increasing dependence on them. What are the real social impacts of the technology? What hidden power agendas does it contain? How can people be protected from intelligent machine abuse?

10.4.8 Geocomputation

A final thought is that a convergence of IT technologies is under way. If you combine AI with high-performance computing with vast amounts of spatial information then it suggests that there is an emerging new paradigm for doing geography (and several related subjects), that of geocomputation. Maybe we can compute our way out of the problems we face in geography using AI to complement our inadequate concepts, using AI tools to improve our modelling and spatial analysis technologies, and use teraflop computing machines to make it all work. Basic research is needed to investigate how this dream can be moved from small demonstrator projects to become a dominant paradigm for geography.

10.5 CONCLUSIONS

As the world progresses further into the IT era so it will need to develop better, more efficient, and intelligent information-processing technologies. Clearly and indisputably, AI is a key part of this process. You really should seriously consider adding AI to your toolkit, expand your horizons, and let your imagination loose with an AI toolkit at your disposal. High-performance computing, GIS data riches, and AI applicable tools provide the basis for doing geography in the twenty-first century. So are you one of the lucky few who can make a start on it now? Or are you predestined through no fault of your genes to become either a watcher or an admirer or a knocker? Maybe this book might help dispel at least some of the myths and inspire readers to accept the AI challenge and to go on and develop some really useful and important AI in geography applications. Right now virtually anything you do with AI will be (a) publishable and (b) novel because of the very low base of existing AI applications in geography. Perhaps the greatest remaining challenge is the need to demonstrate by as many diverse case studies as possible some of the new and substantive research findings that AI has made possible. This is important in order to dispel fear that AI is not a scholarly activity of much or any great worth and that significant benefits can be gained by using it. The authors have done the best they can in helping to stimulate this debate and fuel your imagination with a broad range of AI technologies. *The rest is up to you*!

10.6 QUESTIONS AND ANSWERS

Q Does AI always outperform older methods?

A Not necessarily. It can fail if insufficient computer power is available or if the problem is too simple; or even too hard. It is not an infallible magic panacea that will always work well. For example, a GA was noted to produce a solution twice as poor as found using a simpler heuristic. The poor performance was due to too small a population size and use of a PC instead of a high-performance computer.

Q Is AI the next grand paradigm for geography?

A No, it is not so much a paradigm as a set of tools and a way of thinking. The principal exception to this view is that of fuzzy logic which provides a different paradigm for doing science as a whole and this would include human as well as physical geography.

Q What is the single greatest achievement offered by AI?

A A capacity to solve problems that are unapproachable by any other route.

Q What AI technologies show most promise in the short term?

A A short list would have to include neurocomputing, fuzzy logic modelling, evolutionary programming and artificial life.

Q I have just read *Ground Truth* (Pickles, 1995). Is any of it relevant here?

A Yes there is a social context to AI as well as GIS.

Q Is AI likely to be more fashionable in 10 years' time when more software is available and the core technologies are better understood?

A Yes, that will be true; but why wait? There is already a surfeit of software and knowledge available now. What is needed are product champions and missionaries. Have you got what it takes to be one of those?

Q Does AI replace conventional methods or complement them?

A It does both. In the short term it extends the available toolkit particularly in areas where they are deficient.

Q How is AI a way of thinking?

A Well it encourages you to think that maybe there are better, smarter, more intelligent ways of doing what you do.

Q I never understood statistics and I do not think GIS is relevant to geography. How should I view AI?

A Anyway you like! Maybe it can help you to introduce a computing (note: not statistical, not mathematical, not GIS) component into your research. Perhaps this might be useful to you. You must decide.

Q My supervisor/guru/religious leader/favourite geographer does not like AI. Should I accept this wisdom?

A   Please yourself. The chances are that they have not the vaguest idea of what
     AI is all about, that they are living in an essentially pre-IT age and are passing
     their prejudices to your generation of geographers. You should make your
     own mind up! The present and the future is IT dominated. If you wish to survive
     and prosper then maybe you need to develop an IT way of thinking—AI is part
     of this process, GIS and quantitative geography may not be!

REFERENCES

Pickles, J., 1995, *Ground Truth*. Guildford Press, London.

Index

Printed and bound by CPI Group (UK) Ltd, Croydon, CR0 4YY

10/07/2024

14526734-0001